WOMEN IN TURKISH SOCIETY

SOCIAL, ECONOMIC AND POLITICAL STUDIES OF THE MIDDLE EAST

ÉTUDES SOCIALES, ÉCONOMIQUES ET POLITIQUES DU MOYEN ORIENT

VOLUME XXX

NERMIN ABADAN-UNAT (ED.)

WOMEN IN TURKISH SOCIETY

TUTA SUB AEGIDE PALLAS · EJB ·

LEIDEN
E. J. BRILL
1981

WOMEN IN TURKISH SOCIETY

EDITED BY

NERMIN ABADAN-UNAT

In Collaboration with

DENIZ KANDIYOTI AND MÜBECCEL B. KIRAY

LEIDEN

E. J. BRILL

1981

Le but de la collection est de faciliter la communication entre le grand public international et les spécialistes des sciences sociales étudiant le Moyen-Orient, et notamment ceux qui y résident. Les ouvrages sélectionnés porteront sur les phénomènes et problèmes contemporains: sociaux, culturels, économiques et administratifs. Leurs principales orientations relèveront de la théorie générale, de problématiques plus précises, et de la politologie: aménagement des institutions et administration des affaires publiques.

The series is designed to serve as a link between the international reading public and social scentists studying the contemporary Middle East, notably those living in the area. Works to be included will be characterized by their relevance to actual phenomena and problems: whether social, cultural, economic, political or administrative. They will be theory-oriented, problem-oriented or policy-oriented.

ISBN 90 04 06346 3

PRINTED IN HUNGARY

We have to believe that everything in
the world is the result, directly or
indirectly, of the work of women.....
A country which seeks development and
modernization must accept the need for
change. The weakness in our society
lies in our indifference toward the
status of women... We must have Turkish
women as partners in everything, to
share our lives with them, and to value
them as friends, helpers, and colleagues
in our scientific, spiritual, social and
economic life......

Mustafa Kemal ATATÜRK

Say Istanbul and a textile factory comes to mind:
High walls, long counters, tall stoves ......

A nineteen-year-old working mother
Is dazzled by the white foamy flow of silk
But printed silk is no good for nappies
Now if she could get a roll of ivory-white calico
She could do so much with it: curtains, sheet, underwear,
The thought of ivory-white calico makes her eyes sparkle.
When she dies giving birth to a third son
She is still longing for a roll of calico.
Young mothers like her are sixpence a dozen
At the factory somebody else takes her place
That's the way it is: if one goes, another comes.
Azrael, may you get your just reward.

Bedri Rahmi Eyüpoğlu
from "The Saga of Istanbul"

Transl. Talât Sait Halman
from Ed. Nermin Menemencioğlu

Turkish Verse, Penguin Book,
London 1978, p. 238

TABLE OF CONTENTS

Part Three
Continuity And Change In Sex Roles

Part Four
Religion and Political Behaviour

FOREWORD

Unlike quite a few recent publications dealing with particular aspects of women's studies—for example, the political participation of women, women in the work force, fertility and sex roles, or the comparative legal status of women—this volume is an attempt to give the reader a multifaceted picture, reflecting the problems and dilemmas encountered by the women in one rapidly changing society. The underlying assumption is that a comprehensive presentation of the socio-economic issues pertaining to *one single* country will afford the reader a better grasp of the relationship between the status and problems of women and such basic issues as underdevelopment, dependency and the struggle for rapid structural changes.

A major impetus for the preparation of this book came from the Population Council. Thanks to the valuable suggestions and help of Dr. Frederic C. Shorter (Cairo) and Miss Judith Bruce (New York), the Turkish Social Science Association, organized a seminar entitled, "Women in Turkish Society". The purpose of the seminar, held in Istanbul from May 16—19, 1978, was to discuss and exchange ideas on topics that now make up the Table of Contents of this book.

In addition to Turkish social scientists, civil servants, planners and writers, a number of representatives of the Third World, such as Vina Mazumdar (New Delhi) and Dr. Fatima Mernissi (Rabat), were invited and generously participated in the discussions. The eminent Danish economist, Ester Boserup, was also invited but, unfortunately, due to illness was unable to attend.

Besides giving an opportunity to probe into a number of hypotheses, the seminar discussions helped correct a number of wrong assumptions and thus, afforded the participants with a more comprehensive view of the situation.

The encouragement to undertake the ambitious project of preparing a book about women in Turkey came first from Professor Dr. C. A. O. van Nieuwenhuijze, the editor of the series, "Social, Economic and Political Studies of the Middle East". His generous support and continued efforts to provide a means of publication for work done by scholars in this area deserve a hearty vote of thanks.

My next bunch of thanks goes to the authors who contributed to this book and without whose specialized knowledge and sensitivity this book wouldn't have been possible.

I am extremely grateful to Professor Mübeccel B. Kıray and Dr. Deniz Kandiyoti for their constant good will, constructive criticisms, and their precious methodological advice. In addition, I am equally grateful to Dr. Fatma Mansur-Coşar whose generous assistance and indispensable comments allowed us to finalize the text.

I would also like to acknowledge the meticulous work of Mrs. Munise Aren, former librarian of the Middle East Technical University in Ankara, who helped edit the comprehensive bibliography in Turkish and other languages. The selected bibliography in this volume was taken from her more detailed one which has been published separately.

Of all my colleagues, friends and authors who so graciously assisted me in the hard, time-consuming process of completing this volume, I am particularly indebted to Mrs. Türköz Erder and Miss Serap Can, Assistant in the Faculty of Political Science, Ankara University. Without the remarkable efforts of these two friends and colleagues, neither the typing nor the solution of the myriad problems concerning the seminar could ever have been realized. My most sincere gratitude also goes to Mrs. Julie Tüzün, who very carefully edited the English text.

My wholehearted thanks also go to Norma Erdem, Oya Aksoy and Nurhan Bengi for typing the final drafts.

Finally my deep gratitude goes to my husband, Professor Dr. Ilhan Unat, who besides providing me with priceless intellectual guidance, contributed daily to the realization of a "de facto" egalitarian family life.

Nermin Abadan-Unat
Şile, August 1978

INTRODUCTION

Turkey is the only Muslim country in the Middle East which, due to progressive political choices (such as the abolition of the Caliphate, the adoption of secularism reinforced by constitutional law and the unification of education), has pursued a systematic policy to separate religion from state. Furthermore, by adopting the Swiss Civil Code in 1926, Turkey became the first Muslim country to eliminate as a whole the rules of the *Sharia*, the Muslim legal code which advocates sex segregation and unequal legal treatment. Such deep and entrenching reforms obviously cleared the path for comprehensive and measurable changes in the status of its womanhood.

Yet, fifty years later, a multitude of problems still affect Turkish women, especially those living in the rural areas. These problems force us to reconsider the merits and efficacy of past policies. They also lead us to ask a series of timely and rather important questions: To what extent can "revolutions of legal systems" change the traditional life style of the majority of women in a given country? Which major economic, social, and/or political factors are directly or indirectly responsible for accelarating or retarding this process? Does a significant intrusion of females into the organized labor force during crisis periods, such as war, encourage a social movement in favour of equality for women? And if so, once the extraordinary conditions pass, will the old patterns return? Does religion, ideologically or value-wise, still maintain its decisive hold on the amount and degree of women's social and political participation? What have been the genuine reasons for granting Turkish women political rights? Is a high degree of electoral mobilization and participation sufficient to eliminate women's marginality in politics?

The purpose of this book is to present a comprehensive analysis of the achievements and problems of Turkish women in the late 70's. In this regard, the pioneering role of Mustafa Kemal Atatürk, founder of the Turkish Republic, is obvious. Nevertheless, it is equally important to understand the reasons for his actions. Women in Turkey have come to some degree of revolutionary consciousness primarily by way of the ideas, the actions and the organizations initiated by Atatürk, his closest friends and colleagues. Yet, these men were the product of a Muslim society. They internalized their basic values in a sex-segregated society. This relevant observation might perhaps give a clue to some of the ambivalence inherent in the results obtained so far and eventually furnish some theoretical explanations with regard to change in sex role distribution and sex segregation.

When we look at various sociological, anthropological or socio-psychological theories (Goode 1963, Bett 1957), all seem to show that shifts in sex roles or changes in the status of women are directly dependent on changes in the economic system. A different approach, however, centered upon social crisis furnishes an additional dimension. According to this approach, rapid modernization and crisis, for example war, often seem to bring women into "male" positions, at least for a time (Boulding, 1966), under the guise of national mobilization of all resources. In other words, during periods of crisis, economic or military demands may, at least temporarily, lead to a breakdown of cultural norms and ideals pertaining to men's and women's tasks. The crisis theory is useful in that it illustrates the importance of the time element necessary for change as well as the possibilities and limitations for change in a society with deeply rooted sex roles. This approach is also quite useful for making a sharp distinction between the effects of unifying nationalistic movements versus ideologically oriented action geared at permanent structural changes.

The Turkish case, which can be evaluated partly with the help of the crisis theory, contains a large variety of factors among which class formation undoubtedly takes first place. Other major factors are: the impact of the national liberation war, the decrease in women's seclusion and exclusion from public life, systematic educational efforts as a part of a comprehensive Western-oriented modernization program, the shift towards a capitalist economic system, the introduction of new technologies leading to a growth in the industrial and service sectors, the elaboration of national development plans, and the persistence of cultural dualism.

The essays in this volume have been divided into four sub-sections. The introductory chapter presents a historical balance sheet of the successes and failures over the past fifty years. This is followed by the first subsection in which the demographic trends of Turkey's social fabric, the health conditions pertaining primarily to women's reproductive functions, fertility behaviour and deficiencies due to inadequate nutrition are discussed in light of regional development levels. A basic question, such as "the value of children", has been examined according to age, income, occupation and class with the help of socio-psychology.

The second subsection deals with all problems related to women's economic participation, the modalities of rural-urban migration, and the upgrading of the labor force during the process of economic development. The commonly held assumption that there is a positive correlation between "education", "women's labor force participation" and "development" is widely discussed. The astonishingly high proportion of Turkish women in all liberal professions as well as their share and role in civil service is also treated.

The third subsection is devoted to changes in sex roles. Gender differentiation is used here to include a division of tasks, which is accompanied by a consistently different personality formation. The underlying assumption is that the extent and mode of sex differentiation are more the results, rather than the determinants, of changes in other social and economic relations. In other words, there is less potential for change in sex differentiation than there is in social class and technology.

The last subsection attemps to measure the influence of religion, the major tradition-fostering element in a Muslim society. It also contains an assesment of the actions of Mustafa Kemal Atatürk who conferred upon Turkish women political rights without setting up a system to ensure that they would be able to make full use of these rights.

It is hoped that, by presenting a comprehensive analysis of a developing, secularized, Muslim country that undertook pioneering political decisions in the field of women's rights and modernization half a century ago, a new source of comparison for social scientists will be realized. The fact that all the contributors to this volume are women social scientists was indeed not the result of a deliberate option, but rather an unavoidable choice. In present day Turkey, almost all researchers in this field are women. This fact might perhaps serve as the best evidence that the improvement of women's legal status in a developing society greatly contributes to the emergence of a vigorous elite of women scholars and intellectuals.

It is the sincere belief of the editor that, with the devotion and growing interest of the new generation of Turkish men and women, many of the urgent problems of the silent majority of Turkey's "second class" rural and urban women will be investigated and that their contributions will lead to a more articulate female population and a more democratic society as a whole.

NERMIN ABADAN-UNAT

SOCIAL CHANGE AND TURKISH WOMEN

To radically change the status of Turkish women and transform them into responsible, self-confident citizens was one of the main aspirations of the founder of the Turkish Republic, Kemal Atatürk. He cherished the ideals of equality between the sexes, equal opportunity for education, and family life not based upon a lifelong tie of one-sided bondage. These ideals led Atatürk to focus his attention mainly on the elimination of polygamy, sex differentiated legislation and traditional Islamic ethical norms. Even though he didn't interfere in the inner sphere of women's private lives, by prohibiting the veil, for example, he devoted most of his time and energy to the introduction of a series of legal and administrative reforms including the right to vote. According to Atatürk, the emancipation of women would come about of itself with the help of egalitarian legislation.

However, a balance sheet of the last fifty years clearly indicates that revolutionary efforts through law have only resulted in partial changes in both the status and role of women in Turkish society. Republican reform has not been able to remove essentially wide national disparities. Visible discrepancies between town and country, class and region persist. Due to traditional socialization patterns, attitudinal changes of women in terms of spouse selection, marriage, and inheritance are slow, resistance is frequently encountered, and, accordingly, a bride price is still demanded in many parts of the country. Yet, a comparison of Turkey with other Middle Eastern countries in terms of women's place in society and their economic and social influence shows that this country no doubt represents a vanguard. The policy to make full use of educational facilities, which has been systematically followed, has led to a sizeable women elite, especially visible in the area of academia, the liberal professions, art and literature as well as in the different echelons of managerial and clerical activities.

The scope of this paper is to briefly assess the major areas of change and resistance over the last fifty years and to point out Turkey's major contemporary problem areas. In order to fully assess the results of the planned as well as the spontaneous changes, a quick historical overview, sketching the various phases of this development, appears timely and necessary.

1. The awakening—Evolution of the status of women in Ottoman society during the XIXth century

Initiatives to promote the emancipation of women began within the Ottoman Empire as far back as the first half of the 19th century. Those in favour of a radical Westernization of Turkish society asked for the introduction of monogamy into the imperial household and the elimination of the Sultan's odalık (concubine); free choice of feminine garments; noninterference of the police in women's private lives; greater consideration toward women in general; freedom of choice in matters of marriage; the suppression of intermediaries in marriage arrangements; the creation of a medical school for girls; the adoption of a European civil code; the abolition of polygamy in general and the outlawing of repudiation, that is arbitrary and summary divorce.[1]

Another group of intellectuals of that period who were deeply imbued with the idea of Turkish nationalism and who categorized the call for European education as nothing but Montmartrian immortality deplored polygamy, repudiation and the veil.

Even the Islamic traditionalists, who advocated segregation, were ready to concede to women the right to dispose of their own property, to walk alone in the streets, to frequent women's organizations and to attend primary and secondary schools.

Although women's life in the Ottoman Empire was hampered by innumerable restrictions, it would be erroneous to assume that they were completely passive sufferers. Initiatives to encourage more and better education for women were carried out vigorously during the last half of the 19th century. For example in 1863[2] Sultan Abdul-Aziz ordered the opening of a teacher's training college for girls. In the beginning, the education given to girls in this and similar institutions to follow consisted solely of the memorization of the Koran, but later the curriculum was

---

[1] Pervin Esenkova, "La Femme Turque Contemporaine, Education et Rôle Social". *IBLA*, Tunis 1951, p. 285.

[2] Tezer Taşkıran, *Cumhuriyetin 50. Yılında Türk Kadın Hakları*, Ankara, Başbakanlık Kültür Müsteşarlığı Yayını, 1973, pp. 27—28. For the curriculum of Girl's Teacher Schools see Faik Resit UNAT, "*Türkiye Eğitim Sisteminin Gelişmesine Tarihi bir Bakiş*", Ankara, Milli Eğitim Basimevi, 1964, pp. 92—105.

changed to be more secular. Abdulhamit, who curiously enough prohibited the wearing of the çarşaf (veil) instead of the ferace (dustcoat), in 1881[3] announced that he was in principle in favour of educating women. He wanted to see women trained in a way that would make them helpful to their husbands.[4] However being hostile to non-Islamic ideas, in a 1901 decree, he forbade the employment of Christian governesses in schools and private households.[5]

A logical consequence of these sporadic innovative actions was that only a small Ottoman bourgeoisie could emerge; thus, these emancipatory movements were strictly class-bound. Only the girls of wealthy families, who were educated privately by European governesses, began to aspire to more freedom as a result of their exposure to French and English literature. Another elite group of young girls from the same stratum were nourished on new ideas and different principles by being permitted to attend foreign schools such as the American College for Girls in İstanbul which was founded in 1875. Only they suffered from the preavailing impact of polygamy, the way Halide Edip, the novelist, described her frustration first vis-à-vis her father and later toward her husband.[6]

Bolder steps became noticeable after the return to constitutional rule in 1908, following the dethronement of Abdulhamit. The first women's club „Red-White" (the color of the Young Turks) was founded in 1908 in Salonika. Several other associations for the promotion of women's education enlarged their activities. The "Association for the Betterment of Women", especially under the presidency of Halide Edip, was involved in various issues and problems. The secretary of the "Ottoman Society of Women", Kadriye İhsan, in 1910 allowed her photograph to be taken for publication.[7] Educated women from the upper-class started to discard their veils or to use very thin ones. In 1912, unveiled Turkish women attended a reception at the American Embassy. Obviously, all these innovations were only practiced by upperclass Ottoman women.

---

[3] Gotthard Jaeschke, "Die Frauenfrage in der Tűrkei", *SAECULUM*, X, Heft 4, p. 361.

[4] Jean Melia, *Mustapha Kemal ou le Renovateur de la Turquie*, Paris, 1929, p. 94.

[5] Charlotte Lorenz, "Die Frauenfrage im Osmanischen Reiche mit besonderer Berűcksichtigung der arbeitenden Klasse", *Die Welt des Islam* (6), 1918, p. 72.

[6] Halide Edip Adıvar, *Mor Salkımlı Ev*, Istanbul, Atlas Kitabevi, 1967, 2nd ed., pp. 22—23.

Halide Edip, *Conflict of East and West in Turkey*, Lahore Jamia Milia Extension Lectures, p. 193.

[7] Tezer Taşkıran, *op. cit.*, pp. 55. Also see Tezer Taşkıran, *Women in Turkey*, Transl. Nida Tektaş, Istanbul, Redhouse Publ. 1976, p. 45.

The most radical women's association was the "Ottoman Association for the Defence of Women's Rights". In 1913 the President of the Association, Nuriye Ulviye Mevlan, started a journal entitled "Women's World" (Kadınlar Dünyası), where, beginning in November, 1913, photos of women were printed. During the Balkan War, the women's branch of the Red Crescent began to train Turkish nurses. The most relevant cultural association of the Young Turks, namely the "Türk Ocağı", started in November, 1913, to organize lectures for women; there, Turkish women, predominantly of Russian origin, made important suggestions and proposals.[8]

2. World War I and the entrance of Turkish urban women into public life

The real impetus for a more comprehensive change came during World War I. Due to the crisis of war, large numbers of veiled and secluded women were catapulted into public life. Suddenly jobs were offered to women in ammunition and food factories thus enlarging the number of working class women. A law was prepared by the Ottoman Ministry of Trade to allow for the creation of a kind of "female labour force". In the stocking factory of Urfa alone 1,000 women were employed. In Izmir, Sivas, Ankara and Konya about 4,780 women were employed in rug production. In Aydın about 11,000 and in Kütahya, Eskişehir and Karahisar about 1,550 were involved in textile manufacture.[9]

Parallel to this growth, banks, postal services, central and municipal administrations, and hospitals opened their doors to women as well. In 1915 Enver Pasha's wife, princess Emine Naciye, created an association to promote the employment of women in various sectors of industry. During the same year an imperial decree (irade) permitted discarding the veil during office hours. However, these changes, accelerated by the demands of the war machine, did not meet general approval. Despite the fact that women had begun to contribute to the functioning of public offices, they were often forced by the police to return home if their skirts were shorter than the officially prescribed length.[10]

---

[8] Muhaddere Taşçıoglu, *Kadının Sosyal Durumu ve Kadın Kıyafetleri.* Ankara, 1958, p. 11. Charlotte Lorenz, *op. cit.*, p. 73.

[9] Muhaddere Taşçioğlu, op. cit., p. 45 Fũsun ve Tunç Tayanç, *Dünyada ve Türkiye'de Tarih Boyunca Kadın*, Ankara, Toplum Yayinevi, 1977, pp. 110—111.

[10] Enise Yener, "Eski Ankara Kıyafetleri ve Giyiniş Tarzları", *Dil, Tarih* ve *Coğrafya F. Dergisi*, XIII, Vol. 3, 1955.

The large scale military involvement of the Ottoman Empire not only introduced women into Turkey's urban public life, but it also contributed to the challenge of the supremacy of the SHARIA. The leader of this fight became Ziya Gökalp, "the father of Turkish nationalism", who was appointed to teach sociology at İstanbul University from 1915 on. In his poems as well as in his essay on the „Foundations of Turkish Nationalism", he openly demands equal rights for women with regard to marriage, divorce and succession. No doubt his ideas, even if not fully, greatly inspired the lawmakers in their draft proposal pertaining to the Family Law of October 25, 1917.[11] While the draft proposal still did not fully repudiate polygamy as such, it included special clauses for a monogamic marriage.

3. Turkish women as militants and soldiers (1918—1923)

Surprisingly, the collapse of the Ottoman Empire and its after effects only slightly slowed down the ongoing struggle for emancipation, Thus on March 19, the Minister of Education, Ali Kemal, opened courses for women at the Faculty of Philosophy in İstanbul. In 1921, coeducational classrooms were created, where girl students were permitted to lift their veil only during the lectures. In 1922, Dr. Safiye Ali, Turkey's first female physician, opened her clinic in İstanbul.[12]

In addition to increased education among upper-class women, other subjects began to attract attention. The landing of Greek soldiers in Izmir on May 15, 1919 and the occupation of İstanbul by British soldiers, followed by similar actions of French and Italian armed troops in the South of Anatolia, aroused violent outrage and protest throughout all strata of the population.[13] These events provoked, among other things, a growing political activism among Turkish women. Not only did large numbers of women participate in open-air meetings in İstanbul where speakers, such as writer Halide Edip, Nakiye Elgün, the Chairman of the Teacher's Association and Münevver Sami, a student representative,

---

[11] Niyazi Berkes, *Turkish Nationalism and Western Civilization*, London, 1959, p. 252, p. 303. Ziya Gőkalp, *Tűrkçűlűğűn Esasları*, 1970.

[12] Naciye Yűcel, "Tıp Alanında Tűrk Kadını" in *Cumhuriyetin 50. Yılında Çalışma Alanlarında Tűrk Kadını*, Istanbul, Sermet Matbaasi, 1974, pp. 64—66.

[13] The newspaper "Tűrkoğlu", published in Bolu, reports in its issues of October 30, 1921 about the military accomplishments of 12 women who fought battles with their own weapons. The same newspaper also reports the promotion of a woman called Fatma from corporal to the rank of sergeant. Tezer Taşkiran, *op. cit.*, p. 81.

addressed huge crowds, but a number of bold young women also joined Mustafa Kemal's forces in Anatolia, where the War of Independence was about to start.[14]

Another interesting change took place during this period. Contrary to the past, women not only mobilized themselves for special warfare purposes, but also attempted to directly influence politics. On September 9, 1919 the newspaper, "İrade-i Milliye", announced the foundation of the "Anatolian Women's Association for Patriotic Defence" in Sivas. This association established branches in Amasya, Kayseri, Niğde, Erzincan, Burdur, Konya, Denizli, Kastamonu and Kangal. The Niğde branch alone reported in 1920 to have 1,090 registered members,[15] the majority of whom were the wives and daughters of civil servants and teachers as well as of local merchants. In a short time they became the female counterpart of the core group of Mustafa Kemal's bureaucrats, soldiers and merchants.[16] The major aim of these associations was to show the European public that the whole Turkish nation was united and determined to fight for its independence.

4. The status of Turkish women as reflected in parliamentary debate

From the beginning of his political struggle, Mustafa Kemal, a fierce opponent of autocratic rule, attached great importance to representative government. This explains why he successfully struggled to re-establish the dissolved Ottoman parliament under a new name, the Turkish Grand National Assembly, during the war of Independence on April 23, 1920. The relatively short and concise constitution of this pre-republican interim period was based on the principle of a union of powers; the country being governed by an assembly government. This assembly was the arena for sharp political fights. Although officially there were no political parties, two competing fractions constantly clashed. These quarrels occurred most often on issues relating to women. Further, once the arguments ended, no more action to modify the exploited status of women was taken. Although Mustafa Kemal publicly acknowledged

---

[14] Afet Inan, *Tarih Boyunca Türk Kadınının Hak ve Görevleri*, Istanbul, Milli Eğitim Basımevi, 1975, pp. 127—128, (Atatürk Serisi, No. 10).

[15] Afet Inan, *op. cit.*, pp. 127—128. Also see Şirin Tekeli, *Kadının Siyasal Hayattaki Yeri Üzerine Karşılaştırmalı Bir Araştırma*, Doçent Thesis, unpublished, Istanbul, 1977, mimeographed, pp. 272—273.

[16] Sirin Tekeli, *op. cit.*, footnote 39, pp. 418—419.

the heroic deeds of Anatolian women in his speech of February 3, 1923 and promised that "Turkish women shall be free, enjoy education and occupy a position equal to that of men as they are entitled to it"[17], the devisive composition of the first Turkish Grand National Assembly obliged him to postpone most of his reformist plans. Society at that point was not ready to look upon its women as equals to men. Speakers for the progressive wing, such as Tunalı Hilmi bey, attempted several times to translate Turkish women's longing for equality into legal measures, but the conservative majority of clerks and small town merchants succeeded in blocking them.

Two parliamentary debates in particular further illustrate this negative attitude. The first, a bill concerning syphilis control (session 122, 1921),[18] and the second, dealing with electoral law,[19] led to violent discussions. Defenders of women's rights (Emin bey and Tunalı Hilmi bey) were not granted the floor, they were grossly insulted and the sessions were suspended. Proposals such as these compelling women to have medical control and including the female population into calculations for the size of voting districts were bluntly refused. The decision of the Ministry of Education to invite the female teacher corps to the National Convention on Education led to a general investigation and finally ended with the resignation of the incumbent Minister.[20]

However, Mustafa Kemal, during his various visits to the countryside, continued to declare himself in favour of egalitarian measures. He argued, for instance, in Konya (March 21, 1923), about six months before the proclamation of the Republic, that "the fact that our women, who are subject to much less encouraging conditions, have been able to march along with men, sometimes even ahead of them, is clearcut proof of their equality and their outstanding ability". Thus, Mustafa Kemal, faithful to his farsighted strategy, kept on preparing public opinion for deep-seated changes, the culmination of which was the adoption of the Swiss Civil Code in 1926.

---

[17] *Atatürk'ün Söylev ve Demeçleri II*, January 21, 1923, pp. 147—148.

[18] Tezer Taşkıran, *op. cit.*, pp. 91—95.

[19] Tezer Taşkıran, *op. cit.*, pp. 96—99. For a more detailed narrative see Afet Inan, *op. cit.*, pp. 134—138. For the full text see *Zabıt Ceridesi*, Devre I, Ictima Senesi, 4. cilt 28, pp. 222—350.

[20] Tezer Taşkıran, *op. cit.*, p. 96.

5. Legal equality for Turkish women

One of the contradictory aspects of Turkey's stand on women rights lies in its ambivalent on the improvement of the status of women. Almost all major progressive measures were given, rather than fought for. For this reason the situation shortly before the adoption of the Swiss Civil Code deserves some attention. During the second term of the Turkish Grand Assembly, an attempt was made to codify the 1917 Family Law. The commission in charge approved of marriages at the age of 9 for girls and 10 for boys and of polygamy. It furthermore gave women the right to divorce their husbands only under certain conditions, but it upheld the right of men to repudiate their wives. The very mild, almost unnoticeable reaction of educated women to such measures became a matter of criticism in the Turkish press—Necmettin Sadak in "Akşam"[21] denounced the passive attitude of women. Even feminists, such as Halide Edip Adıvar expressed their criticism, not from the point of view of women's rights, but rather from the angle of conditions favouring a harmonious married life.

How can such passivity be explained? According to Şirin Tekeli, once the extraordinary conditions of war had passed, a country with almost no industry was unable to develop and sustain jobs for its women outside the household. Thus, the perennial glorification of the ideal women being "good housewives, mothers and companions" was bound to continue.[22]

How then, can we explain the sudden transition to a European Civil Law System?

The reasons should be sought within the general setting of the political forces inside and outside parliament, rather than from within the movement for women's rights, itself.

Atatürk, anxious to present to the world a "modern face", began to encourage significant initiatives to eliminate the obvious inequalities in public life, thereby diminishing the political weight of conservatives. An interesting example of such an action is the decision of the İstanbul police chief to order the removal of a curtain separating men and women

[21] Necmeddin Sadak, "Kadınlarımız ve Aile Hukukuna Ilişkin Kararlar", *Akşam*, January 7, 1924.

[22] Şirin Tekeli, *op. cit.*, pp. 275—276.

passengers in public transportation.[23] This decision became a matter of discussion in parliament, where it was asked whether or not it was contrary to the principles of a "Moslem Republic".

Atatürk, determined to fight against the conservative forces gathered around the Ministry of the SHARIA, succeeded in passing legislation, definitely changing the ideological scope of public life. The first law was the abolition of the Caliphate and the second was the promulgation of the Law for Unification of Instruction, both on the same day, March 3, 1924. The second law brought all religious schools and minority schools under unified control, thus enabling the leaders of the young Republic to extend the right to an education to both sexes.

Determined not to wait for long term evolutionary processes, Atatürk proceeded from there to use codification as an accelerator for social change. On February 17, 1926, a slightly modified version of the Swiss Civil Code, which was found by the commission to be the most suitable to the principle of secularism, was adopted at one session where only speeches in favour were made. For Atatürk and his supporters the granting of equality before law for men and women was the realization of a promise given long before, but even more than that, it was a symbol to the world that the new Turkey was adamant about "reaching a level of contemporary civilization".[24] Arguments in favour of the law also refllected this way of thinking: "The new law incorporates such principles as monogamy and the right to divorce—principles, which are required for a *civilized world*"[25] Thus, all the major rights conferred on Turkish women were much more the result of the unrelenting efforts of a small "revolutionary elite", rather than the product of large scale demands by Turkey's female population.

The Turkish Civil Code, which became effective on October 4, 1926, made polygamy illegal and gave equal rights of divorce, thus formally insuring the freedom and equality of women. Custody of the children, unlike in the past, was given to both parents. (Art. 262). In case of death, custody was entrusted to the remaining spouse. In case of divorce, a judge would decide which parent should have custody (Art. 264).

Equality in inheritance was granted; unlike the old law where women were granted one-half, one-quarter, one-seventh, or even one-eighth

---

[23] According to a regulation issued in 1923, "Husband and wife may sit next to each other provided they are not acting against the law in public transportation vehicles. No police can prevent an honourable woman from sitting next to her husband."

[24] Atatűrk's Speeches, *op. cit.*, Vol. II., pp. 85—87.

[25] T. B. M. M. Tutanakları, (Parliamentary Records), February 17, 1926.

depending on their relation to the deceased (Art. 439). Marriage, in order to be valid, had to take place in the presence of the bride, which meant the abolition of marriage by proxy. Equality with regard to testimony was accepted. In the old court procedure, the testimonies of two women were equal to that of a man. Finally, the new civil code prescribed a minimum age for marriage that was slightly different from that in the Swiss Civil Code. At first, the age limit was 18 for men and 17 for women, but later, in 1938, the legal minimum age limits were reduced to 17 and 15 respectively, while the absolute minimum age in special circumstances was kept at 15 for men, but lowered to 14 for women (Art. 85).

How egalitarian is the Turkish Civil Code? The Swiss Civil Code itself reflects the traditional point of view. For example, it does not contain a principle of absolute equality between husbands and wives. Accordingly, the husband is the head of the family. The wife does not have the prerogative to represent the marital union (Art. 154). She must follow the husband, who alone is entitled to choose a domicile (Art. 152, II). The wife is required to participate in the expenses of the household, be it by contributing in financial matters or by assuming tasks in the household (Art. 190). In case the wife wants to assume a profession or work outside the household, she must obtain the consent of the husband (Art. 159), which may be tacit approval as well. However, the wife may freely dispose of her material goods; the rule in marriage—unlike, for instance, the Napoleonic code— is separation of property and goods; and the wife has an unlimited right of acquisition.

How did such a legal transplantation function? Although Turkey's choice in favour of the adoption of a Western legal code provided a favourable climate for change in the status of women, even without the accompanying major socio-economic structural changes, much of the content of the Civil Code has remained dead letter, especially in rural areas with a strong feudal character. However, the Civil Code takes on a more functional character with the increase in urbanization, migration, and industrialization. It also becomes more functional as education levels rise and as more and more women participate in the industrial and service sectors of the economy.

Among the demands proclaimed by 27 women's associations on the occasion of the Women's Year Ankara Congress (5—8 December, 1975), the following major legal demands were set forth:[26]

[26] Türk Üniversiteli Kadınlar Derneği, Ankara, *Türkiye Kadın Yılı Kongresi, 1975*, Ankara, Ayyıldız Matbaası, 1978.

1. The status of family head should not be confined solely to the husband,
2. The wife should not be obliged to adopt the husband's family name,
3. The prerogative of a husband to forbid his wife the practice of a profession or employment should be abolished,
4. Legal, educational and administrative measures to abolish the "bride price" (Başlık) should be implemented,
5. The prohibition of a religious ceremony before a civil marriage has been registered should be reinforced,
6. In order to equalize tax obligations, individual income tax declarations for husband and wife should be required,
7. The right to join the armed forces should be granted again,
8. Women civil servants and workers should be able to take one paid year leave of absence after childbirth,
9. The agricultural Social Insurance bill should be passed in order to assure peasant women social security rights,
10. The living conditions of prostitutes should be improved so as to discourage traffic of women,
11. Legal provisions should be enacted in order to prevent the exploitation of female children, who have been apparently "adopted", but in fact are employed in domestic service (besleme).

As one can easily detect, most of the demands cited represent imperfections in a functioning legal system, based in principle on the equality of sexes. However, some of these points are of a more serious nature.

There is no doubt that the most critical point lies in the nature of institutionalized prostitution. According to Law No. 1593, the Ministry of Health and Social Welfare and the Ministry of the Interior are jointly responsible for determining the location and the administration of brothels. Art. 129 of this same law mentions a category of women, "who are performing prostitution as a profession and as a means of subsistence". This article is in direct contradiction to Art. 435—36 of the Turkish Penal Code, which strongly forbids activities which encourage prostitution. Prostitution is a social problem deeply related to socio-economic factors. Thus, it is impossible to prevent solely by applying deterrent measures. In the absence of adequate employment opportunities, poor families, sometimes even middle class ones, are compelled to permit prostitution of their women. As rightly pointed out in the Report on the Status of Women in India, if women are to become equals of men in society, society must ensure economic, social and psychological security for them and protect them from this form of exploitation. Yet, in Turkey the fact that the woman in question is a prostitute is still seen as a criteria for attenuating circumstances, leading to a reduction by two-thirds of the sentence in cases of rape and kidnapping (Art. 438). This article has recently been abolished in Italy, the place where Turkish lawmakers received their inspiration for it. Unfortunately however, Turkish public opinion has not yet focused its attention on this topic.

The secularized legal conventions have been adhered to in those places where the economic structure has changed substantially. Legally, religious marriages are not recognized; yet, they in fact exist. They prevail in the present day, small, semi-isolated settlements as the norm, enjoying the consent and tacit approval of the community. Further, they were encouraged both in the 1950's during the Democratic Party government as well as by the Justice Party and the National Salvation party in the 1960's and 1970's, as this was one way of making use of religion for political ends. The prevalence of these unions is confirmed when one takes into consideration the paucity of registered marriages (Table 1) or when one looks at the number of children who, by legal definition, were born out of wedlock. In 1950 alone, 7,724,419 children were registered under various laws to legitimize such births.[27]

The close relationship between registered marriages and divorces and the developmental level of Turkey's regions, as well as their distribution pattern between the urban and rural population, is quite evident. (Tables I and II).

The high number of civil marriages and divorces registered in the major metropolitan areas such as İstanbul, Izmir and Ankara, clearly indicates their higher level of development as opposed to that found in regions with a semi-feudal structure (the southeastern regions), where socio-economic backwardness is additionally accompanied by a distinctly different cultural framework.

Nevertheless, it must be stressed that the idealistic vision of the modernized society envisioned by Atatürk has provided Turkey's increasingly aware womanhood with an excellent point of departure for further emancipation, freedom and social participation. Turkey still represents the only Muslim country in the entire Middle East where, aside from secondary legal problems, the major goals for the enfranchisement of women as individuals and citizens have been realized.

---

[27] Nermin Abadan, *Social Change and Turkish Women*, Ankara, SBF, 1963, p. 23 (SBF Yayin No. 171—153).

Table I

Urban – Marriages in absolute figures in selected provinces, 1950 – 1974

Provinces	*1950*	*1960*	*1974*
Ankara	3.019	5.236	10.461
Istanbul	10.057	12.323	26.445
İzmir	3.599	4.666	10.269
Afyon	746	912	2.056
Aydın	942	1.260	2.451
Burdur	331	398	935
Ağri	42	123	132
Bingöl	35	34	86
Van	96	224	413

Source: For 1950 and 1960, T.C. Evlenme İstatistikleri, 1932 – 1960, Nr. 418. For 1974, T.C. Evlenme İstatistikleri, 1974, Nr. 787.

Ankara, Istanbul and Izmir represent the three metropolitan provinces, Afyon, Aydın and Burdur are provinces located in Çentral Anatolia and the Aegean region.

Ağri, Bingöl Hakkâri and Van are provinces in Eastern Anatolia.

Table II

Urban – Divorces in absolute figures in selected provinces 1950 – 1974

Provinces	*1950*	*1960*	*1974*
Istanbul	929	1.129	1.501
Ankara	—	727	1.057
İzmir	—	806	595
Afyon	208	187	158
Aydın	208	398	410
Burdur		110	139
Ağri		10	10
Bingöl		4	13
Van	5	13	29
Hakkâri		1	3

Source: For 1950 and 1960, T.C. Boşanma İstatistikleri, 1932 – 1960, Nr. 419. For 1974, T.C. Boşanma İstatistikleri, 1974, Nr. 775.

6. Turkish women as voters (1934—)

It is no wonder that, because of valid historical reasons such as their being excluded from active economic participation due to the Ottoman Empire's semi-colonial status in the XIXth century and their exclusion from public life due to Islam's ideological definition of second class subjects, Turkish women have never developed a genuine and effective suffragette movement. Demands to be "permitted" to participate in election activities were first expressed hesitantly, then neglected for sometime, and then finally granted. Relevant sources on this subject furnish opposing explanations. According to Tezer Taşkıran, the driving forces for political rights were the publicly articulated demands of the Women's League in 1927 and growing pressure from public opinion.[28] Afet İnan gives a different explanation. According to İnan, difficulties in teaching democratic rules as a part of civics education, as long as women were deprived of political rights, gave way to serious discussions within Atatürk's inner circle and thereby led to a constitutional amendment.[29]

The hypothesis of Ş. Tekeli, a young political sociologist, is based on an overall evaluation of the Western powers attitude, reflected by their press, toward Atatürk's transitional one party rule. Her hypothesis seems to be correct if one considers that, in spite of repeated demands, Atatürk waited until 1930 then suddenly decided to have a constitutional amendment proposed by Ş. Kaya, which opened the door for political representation and participation of women in municipal elections.[30] According to Tekeli, the real reasons for the 1930 move, and later the one in 1934, lie within the prevailing political forces of the time. In 1930, some European newspapers attempted to draw parallels between the one party systems of the period, especially Mussolini's in Italy. Atatürk, extremely anxious to differ from any kind of fascist movement, gave an interview to the "Vossische Zeitung" in which he stressed "revolution and dictatorship, even if necessary, can only be used for a short time".[31] In order to

---

[28] Tezer Taşkıran, *op. cit.*, pp. 72—73. Afet Inan, *Medeni Bilgiler ve Mustafa Kemal Atatürk'ün El Yazıları*, Ankara, 1969, pp. 3—4.

[29] *Zabit Ceridesi*, Parliamentary Records, Vol. 17, Devre III, Session 3, March 20, 1930.

[30] Cited by Şirin Tekeli, *op. cit.*, pp. 282—284.

[31] Mary R. Beard, *Woman as Force in History*, London, Collier-MacMillan, 1946, pp. 22—23.

prove his genuine belief in a true democratic system—even while continuing to implement a tutelary democracy—Atatürk granted political rights to Turkish women, and in doing so, moved his country ahead of some Western democracies. That same year, an abortive attempt to move over to a multiparty system was carried out in Turkey too.

Thus, Turkish women, who were given political rights in municipal elections in 1931, first used their prerogatives in 1933 and were elected both in İstanbul and elsewhere to municipal and eldermen councils.

During this same year, Hitler's Nazi Party rose to power and confined its womanhood to "Kind, Küche, Kirche". Atatürk, a staunch nationalist but extremely sensitive about not being classified in the same order as Europe's power lusty dictators, realized that democracy was closely related to the active role played by citizens.[32] Thus, on December 5, 1934, the Grand National Assembly adopted a proposal presented by İsmet İnönü and 191 deputies, which conferred on all Turkish citizens having reached the age of 22, the right to vote in national elections. In addition, all citizens 30 years of age, men and women, were given the right to be elected. It is worthwile to note that one of the speakers in favour of this bill, Sadri Maksudi, stated: "Today there are countries which have undemocratic regimes, where women are deprived of political rights. The granting of political rights to Turkish women is a natural consequence of Turkey's evolution toward a true democratic system".[33]

Assuming that Ş. Tekeli's thesis is correct, the electoral results are self-evident. As long as female political representation was regarded for its independent "symbolic value", the number of female representatives was high. It declined after Atatürk's death and the transition to a multiparty system. For example, when first elected to the parliament, 18 seats (4.5%) were held by women; this number fell in 1946 to 9 (2%), in 1950 to 3 (0.6%) and, after 1960, they never again reached the 1965 level of 11 women M. P. (1.8%).[34]

For a number of writers (Afet İnan, 1965; T. Taşkıran, 1976) the entrance of Turkish women into politics completes the necessary framework of their more active participation in society. The underlying assump-

[32] Nermin Abadan, *op. cit.*, p. 9.

[33] Şirin Tekeli, "Siyasal Iktidar Karşısında Kadın", *Toplum ve Bilim*, No. 3, 1977, p. 69.

[34] Deniz Kandiyoti, *Women's Place in Turkish Society, A Comparative Approach, Current Turkish Thought*, New Series, No. 30, Spring 1977. See also Deniz Kandiyoti, "Sex Roles and Social Changes: A Comparative Appraisal of Turkey's Women", *SIGNS*, Journal of Women in Culture and Society, Vol. 3, No. 1, Fall 1977.

tion is that, with increasing educational opportunities and comprehensive social security measures, Turkish women will be able to make full use of their new legal status. This approach, however, has been increasingly challenged. For most of Turkey's post-war social scientists and young writers, the status of women is determined by their role in production and their economic participation. (M. Kıray, 1963, S. Timur, 1972, D. Kandiyoti, 1971). Women's subjugation or dependence is the outcome of their socio-economic position. Accordingly, increased awareness, commitment and involvement in politics and autonomy in political action and behaviour are not instilled by persuasive means; but rather, they emerge from such deep-seated changes in the social structure, as internal and external migration, urbanization and industrialization. Since Turkey's transition to a multiparty system coincides with the end of Turkey's self-imposed economic autarchy, the position of Turkish women should be evaluated in light of these major challenges.[35]

7. *Turkey's changing social structure and its impact on women's status*

Atatürk and İnönü, adopting an elitist approach, firmly believed that the exploitation of women could be remedied by placing great emphasis on all levels of education and that women's new legal status would lead to their increased participation in public life. This attitude was reinforced by the importance attached to the principle of secularism, the separation of religious from state affairs. With the transition to the multiparty system in 1946, and the growing influence of new middle class, the character of Turkey's mixed economy changed greatly. Instead of etatism, private enterprise received manifold support. As a consequence, new technologies were introduced; mechanization of agriculture was followed by fast internal migration, urbanization and unbalanced industrialization. In addition after 1960, government regulated exports of excess labour resulted in a massive exodus to Europe.

All these deep-seated changes in Turkey's social fabric no doubt affected its womanhood too. The least touched group, of course, has been the nomadic group, predominantly located in Eastern Anatolia, who are practically situated outside the economic and political system of the country.

According to D. Kandiyoti, Turkey's newly emerging pattern can be

---

[35] Ismail Beşikçi, *Doğuda Değişim ve Yapısal Sorunlar*, Ankara 1969, p. 187.

divided into six basic types: (a) nomadic, (b) traditional, rural (c) changing rural, (d) small town, (e) newly urbanized-squatter (gecekondu) and (f) urban, middle class, professionally employed or housewife.

(a) *Nomadic women:* In *nomadic* tribes, scattered in Eastern and Southeastern Anatolia, women's contribution to production is very high and their procreative role is much esteemed. However, due to the asymetric division of labour, males dominate all activities having to do with the "public" sphere. Male authority is obvious in all walks of life. Women's authority can only be detected within the family—a natural consequence of the heavy bride price—and even then, only after they have produced sons and acquired a prestigious position within the family. Inheritance rights for girls are not admitted.[36]

(b) *Traditional—rural:* Whereas nomadic tribal life represents a closed world of its own, the rural setting has been subject to significant changes in Turkey. In villages dependent on the cultivation of some form of subsistence crop, the traditional life style of peasant culture is quite conservative, in that women are not admitted into the male world. However, depending on the geographic and economic conditions these *peasant women* are: (1) totally involved in home production, (2) additionally involved in traditional crafts such as carpet-weaving, (3) working full time in the fields, or (4) because of external migration, entirely in charge of agriculture. More often than not, their labour input determines the type and volume of production. Their status in these traditional, closed-up rural communities is defined by a male dominated hierarchy. This constant predominance can be seen in Table III.

In traditional villages, the female status determinants are also constant, namely, child bearing and advancing age. Whatever their place in production may be, their labour goes largely unrecognized, the specialized

Table III

Distribution of Turkey's Population According to Sex and Activity in Agriculture in Percentage

Sex	*1955*	*1960*	*1965*	*1970*
Men	63.1	60.9	58.1	53.1
Women	96.1	94.9	94.1	88.7

Source: DPT, Toplumsal Yapı Araştırması, 1977, pp. 36–37

[36] Deniz Kandiyoti, *op. cit.*, p. 17.

areas and public dealings remaining within the male sphere. Although in 1969, 497 out of 1,000 active persons in agriculture were female, they were economically defined as "unpaid workers of family enterprises".[37]

(c) *Women in changing rural setting:* The big turn in rural areas coincides with the introduction of new technologies, the mechanization of farming and its consequently fast internal migration. The absorbtion of villages into the national market economy, along with the exceedingly high exodus of excess labour to foreign industrial centers, has turned some members of peasant families, at the beginning solely males and later predominantly females, into wage earners. With the changing economic function of fathers and brothers, women's status has been redefined. The ultimate domain of male authority has decreased. Free choice of marriage partners, self-determined consumption patterns and independent investment by younger women have become noticeable. (Abadan-Unat, 1976).[38] Along with these changes a new life style, largely dependent on remittances from abroad has developed. In this setting consumption tends to be conspicuous. These women, having been pushed out of agricultural production and no more preoccupied with home-produced food and clothes, have started to emulate small town ways with increased afternoon visits, use hair-dressers and cosmetics, and generally urban patterns of consumption.

Briefly, rural change has meant a redefinition of male authority relations. This ranges from greater loyalty to the daughter as well as to the female head of the migrant workers' family. There, the wife/mother, living most of the years alone, shapes the life of her dependents almost completely herself.

(d) *Women in small towns:* Although the attitudes toward veiling, segregation and mixing with male visitors are more relaxed, women in small towns, because of the greater emphasis on the public sphere and the absolute disappearance of female labour, are rather confined to their residential neighborhoods. In these settings, as pointed out by P. Benedict, M. Kıray and F. Mansur,[39] female leisure, which is almost non-

---

[37] TIB, *Türkiye'de Kadının Sosyo-Ekonomik Durumu*, Ankara, 1975, p. 65. Füsun ve Tunç Tayanç, *op. cit.*, p. 118

[38] Nermin Abadan-Unat, "Implications of Migration on Emancipation and Pseudo-Emancipation of Turkish Women", *International Migration Review*, Vol. II, No. 1, 1977, pp. 54—55.

[39] P. Benedict, "The "Kabul Günü": Structured Visiting in an Anatolian Provincial Turkish Town", *Anthropological Quarterly*, Washington, D. C. 47 (1), 1974, pp. 28—47 Mübeccel Kıray, *Ereğli: Ağır Sanayiden Evvel Bir Sahil Kasabası*, Ankara, DPT 1964. Fatma Mansur, *Bodrum: A Town in the Aegean*, Leiden, E. J. Brill, 1972.

existent in rural areas, has resulted in larger social networks—which have been facilitated by the institution of "kabul Gün", reception day. In short, the determinants of status among women in the small town are more directly related to their husband's positions.

It might be said that the entrance of new values and life styles into the villages of rapidly economically changing rural settlements, such as in the Marmara and Aegean regions, represent a faster process of change than that in small towns.

(e) *Women in newly urbanized settings (squatters):* Turkey's astonishingly rapid rate of urbanization, which in fact preceded industrialization, ushered in a unique housing phenomenon, the Gecekondu (over night houses); and out of these areas came a quite distinct type of women. In Turkey, as in many developing countries,[40] the transition from traditional agriculture and household industry to modern organized industry and services demands new skills. Women, handicapped by the lack of opportunities to acquire these new skills, find themselves unwanted by the economy. Kemal H. Karpat, in his study on gecekondu life, shows that, while 93% of the newly settled men were employed, only 30% of the women could find employment, out of which 59% were only temporarily employed, their status being predominantly domestic servants.[41] The high degree of mobility, which is inherent in *gecekondu* women, reveals itself in their aspiration: 23% female versus 12% male wanted to have factory work.[42] However, jobs in industry for women are not abundant. The total female population over 12 years of age employed in industrial enterprises in 1943 was 78,767. A quarter century later this figure has only risen to 143,400, while the same figure for men increased fivefold.[43] Nevertheless, it is quite accurate to assume that the workers —men and women—in the projected massive industrialization program for the 1980's will come from these squatter quarters.

Gecekondu women tend to have an astonishingly high degree of self-confidence —69%of the women versus 59% of the men consider themselves to be the most trustworthy and reliable persons.[44] This can be

[40] Indian Council of Social Science Research, *Status of Women, A Synopsis of the Report of the National Committee*, New Delhi, 1975, p. 10.

[41] Kemal H. Karpat, *The Gecekondu, Rural Migration and Urbanization*, Cambridge, Cambridge University, 1976, Table 4. 3, p. 102.

[42] Kemal H. Karpat, *op. cit.*, 116.

[43] The proportion of female labor to the total of labor force declined from 40.76 in 1960 to 36.2 in 1975. Hamide Topçuoglu, "Tűrk Toplumunda Kadının Sosyal Statűsű", *Tűrkiye Kadın Yılı Kongresi*, Ankara, 1978, p. 89, Table: 19.

[44] Kemal H. Karpat, *op. cit.*, Table 6. 11, p. 154.

partially explained by the large percentage of nuclear families in these areas (62.5% in Izmir, 72% in Ankara).[45] In line with their confident way of thinking, gecekondu women insist on having a say in the choice of their future husbands (47%). The people in the gecekondu's aspirations for their children and their desire to become more integrated into city life is indicative of the deep changes which have taken place.

Although gecekondu women certainly encounter major difficulties in integrating themselves in urban life by retaining a number of the elements of village culture, they still represent one of the most dynamic innovators in Turkey's modernization process. Their strong motivation will surely have a decisive impact on the socialization process of generations to come.

(f) *Urban middle class women (housewife/employed)* : Unlike traditional rural women, more than three quarters of the economically active urban women are not gainfully employed; 81% qualify as housewives.[46] Nevertheless, the number of female wage earners is increasing; needless to say, in a way reflective of Turkey's uneven industralization and employment patterns. Certain regions, such as Marmara and the Aegean, as well as the three provinces with metropolitan cities, show the most rapid growth. (Table IV).

Table IV

Female wage earners by year and region in percents

Years	*Central Anatolia*	*Black Sea*	*Aegean and Marmara*	*Mediterranean*	*Eastern Anatolia*	*Three Big Provinces*
1955	1.2	1.2	4.7	4.4	2.0	18.9
1960	4.6	1.4	5.8	3.8	1.4	25.0
1970	6.0	5.3	11.0	10.7	4.0	40.8

Source: Gül Ergil, op. cit. Table 13, p. 47

Indeed, the female working class is growing rather slowly (78,767 in 1943—143,000 in 1968).[47] In this area, the big explosion has taken place outside of Turkey: in W. Germany alone, there were 173 women workers

[45] Emre Kongar, *Survey of Familial Changes in Two Turkish Gecekondu Areas*, Paper submitted to the Social Anthropological Conference, Nicosia, September 1970.
[46] Gũl Ergil, *Toplumsal Yapı Araştırması*, (DPT No. 1607, SPD. 298) Ankara, p. 23.
[47] Hamide Topçuoğlu, *op. cit.*, pp. 92—93.

in 1960 versus 143,611 workers in 1975.[48] There was a marked cyclical variation in the proportion of female departures, which rose sharply during the 1967 slump and declined as the cycle picked up again.

Within Turkey the more impressive growth lies, not in the industrial sector, but rather within the service sector, where the public services have especially attracted a high number of women. While in 1938 there were only 12,716 female civil servants, this figure rose in 1970 to 123,812 (18.9% in this sector). Thus, one can easily state that a visible "bureaucratization" of qualified female manpower has taken place in Turkey.[49] The penetration of women into the civil service is more noticeable in the lower and middle level positions. More precisely, 31.6% are in the fields of education, 26.3% in tourism, 22.2% in health and 19% in labour relations. These areas, generally defined as "service sectors oriented towards social goals", have been slowly abadoned by men. Of course, 'labour relations' is still considered a male domain.

Basically, what motivates women to enter public life? Two empirical studies, conducted over a 20 year period, reveal quite interesting similarities.[50]

For the great majority, economic needs force women to secure for the family a "second source of income", although for many professional women work is a primary tool for self-expression. Thus, whenever a role conflict situation between work and family life arises, retreat from work has been the preference. This is even true for women with higher education belonging to liberal professions (H. Topçuoglu, 1957; O. Çitçi, 1974).

These individual preferences are undoubtedly the by-products of a rather anti-feminist climate that has been reinforced by mass-media campaigns and television programs such as "Five Minutes". Thus, urban women are caught up in two opposing currents of thought. One current continually drives into society's head the idea that woman's primary function is to be a good wife and mother, while the other current argues that women should take advantage of all opportunities that give them a chance for self-expression and more freedom. Perhaps at this point we should ask if Ş. Tekeli's class-oriented conclusion is true that "work is

---

[48] Abadan-Unat, *op. cit.*, 33—34.

[49] Mesut Gűlmez, "Tűrk Kamu Gőrevlilerinin Sayısal Evrimi", *TODAIE Dergisi*, 1972, p. 44.

[50] Hamide Topçuoğlu, *Kadınların Çalışma Saikleri ve Kadın Kazancının Ile Bűtçesindeki Rolű*", Ankara 1957. Oya Çitçi, „Women at Work", *Turkish Public Administration Annual*, 1975.

a necessity for women of the peasant and industrial classes whereas it is denied to the members of the bourgeoisie".[51]

Even given the above conflicts, one important fact should be remembered. Of all the Moslem countries, Turkey has so far produced the highest number of educated women on all levels. In Turkish universities, women's share of the academic personnel, long before the Women's Lib Movements, was far ahead of Europe.[52] This observation is equally true for women occupying high posts in the judiciary.[53]

Nevertheless, all these achievements since 1926 should not result in unjustified euphoria. Because of the deep changes taking place in the socio-economic structure, the great majority of Turkish women, like women in all developing countries, are seriously handicapped. Their handicap does not come from legal restrictions, but rather from structural inequalities. Their access to education depends greatly upon urbanization and the realization that schooling has functional value. Although the composition in urban primary schools is almost fifty/fifty for girls and boys, only one third of these girls enter secondary schools. This rate declines to one fifth in higher educational institutions.

Due to constant and decisive influence of advertising, particularly in the women's pages of the press, women of all classes, especially those living in urban areas, have acquired a growing tendency to spend for the purpose of conspicuous consumption. These women, indeed, display a false consciousness about priorities. These tendencies, instead of moving urban women towards a greater understanding of public issues, are diminishing their interest in politics. Nevertheless, as everywhere, small, articulate groups of women, determined to have their say in politics, are getting stronger. Partly backed by the charismatic personality of political leaders such as B. Ecevit and his party's efforts to involve women in the political process, these small bands have become a strong political force. For the time being it would not be erroneous to say that given the weak class consciousness of employed women, their interest in public issues is of an ambivalent nature. During exceptional periods, such as electoral campaigns, it is high, during normal periods rather low. Again, this is not surprising since their rights were bestowed upon them and not fought for.

[51] Şirin Tekeli, *op. cit.*, p. 299.

[52] Nermin Abadan, *Social Change and Turkish Women*, SBF, Ankara 1963, p. 17.

[53] In 1973 there were 149 women judges in Turkey out of a total of 3,022 (4.8 %: 95.2 %). Again in 1970, out of 10, 670 lawyers, there were 1,952 women lawyers. (10.7 %—89.3 %). Tezer Taşkıran, *op. cit.*, p. 161. Compare with Ayse Őncű's paper "Women in the professions: why so many?" in the same volume.

Even so, the path toward a more free, independent, responsible and politically aware type of women is widening. Turkish women are becoming increasingly aware of their subservient role as an unpaid household labour force. For some, the remedy lies within a general change of the political system; for others, human will power is the answer.

The impact of the changing structure of production and the changing determinants of what women do, how they do it, and how they are recognized or not recognized for it has created a great deal of conflict in women's attitudes and values. The resulting inconsistencies are reflected more and more in contemporary literary works. Recently, women writers, such as Nezihe Meriç, Füruzan, Adalet Ağaoğlu and Sevgi Soysal, have successfully described and analysed the superficial "pseudo modernism" of new urbanities, the clash between traditional/progressive value judgements, and the deliberate adoption of the "feminine mystique" so cleverly disguised behind a systematic campaign for increased mass consumption.

Which of the following factors, urbanization, industrialization, or migration has affected Turkish women most? Does Boserup's observation concerning rural change also apply to Turkey by widening the productive gap and leaving women the performance of simple manual tasks? As D. Kandiyoti rightly indicates, in Turkey, rural change did not intensify the already existing asymmetry between sexes, but rather the social stratification of males. Those who controlled the new agricultural technology and land resources consolidated their economic position; the rest were pushed into a marginal category.[54] In other words, the changes for women merely complemented the changing relationships in the male world. Similarly, urbanization has not unconditionally led all city dwellers to the nuclear family pattern. As S. Timur has shown, high income professionals are adopting an egalitarian, small family pattern, where as poorer families must pool their resources in extended families.[55]

External migration, which covers to some extent the impact of industrialization, if extended for a long period of time, is quite an effective change inducing factor. A number of empirical research studies[56] (A. Kudat 1975; Mübeccel Kiray, 1976) have shown that not only do women

[54] Deniz Kandiyoti, *op. cit.*, p. 64.

[55] Serim Timur, *Türkiye'de Aile Yapısı*, Ankara, 1972, p. 175, (Hacettepe Üniversitesi Yayinlari D-15).

[56] Mübeccel Kıray, "The Family of the Immigrant Worker" in N. Abadan-Unat, Ed. *Turkish Workers in Europe, 1960—1975*, Leiden; E. J. Brill, 1976, pp. 214—216.

migrant workers assume the role of family head, but they also acquire a whole set of new prerogatives, completely absent in their home country. Among these new rights one can list the right to choose the type and place of work as well as the permanent domicile; the right to determine the amount of savings, investment and expenditure; the right to decide upon their children's education; and finally, the right to decide upon family size both in terms of children and adhering other members. Indeed, detailed empirical data indicates that it is the employed female migrant workers who decide which relatives of friends are to be invited for short/long stays abroad. To a great extent, the duration and type of employment abroad seems to determine the degree to which Turkish women adjust to a given society. Transitional employment situations seem to lead solely to the acquisition of new consumption patterns.[57]

As far as education is concerned, functional education programs geared at meeting the specific needs of a given environment introduce women to specialized jobs and professions, especially in large urban centers. These new situations also produce a number of important side effects, such as an awakening political interest, class consciousness, awareness of social and economic rights, and the need for self fullfillment. Instead of blindly adopting the bourgeois components of the passive wife and motherhood ideology, some modern young women in industry and the services sector are striving toward goals such as the acquisition of an independent personality and the ability to make a free choice in terms of husband and number of children.

The difficulty in realizing these goals, when one considers the uninterrupted contradictions between cultural and traditional values, the limitations of legally bestowed rights, and the economic realities, is obvious. These obstacles are further enhanced by the deliberate efforts of a mass consumption oriented market; a sex segregation based bourgeois ideology; and, the intensive efforts of political organizations, anxious to mobilize large groups of women to devote themselves solely to religious practices. As Mernissi reminds us, enouragement of traditional saint's rituals by administrative authorities who oppose any trade unionist or political movements is a well-known tactic in Third World politics.[58]

---

[57] Nermin Abadan-Unat, see footnote 38, p. 54—55.

[58] Fatima Mernissi, "Women, Saints and Sanctuaries", *SIGN*, Journal of Women in Culture and Society, Vol. 3, No. 1, Autumn 1977, p. 112.

8. Major approaches to the problems of social change and women's status

Having briefly sketched the major features of social change as they relate to Turkish women, it now seems necessary to present very briefly the major approaches to this problem as reflected in Turkey's mass media and press.

(a) *The evolutionist, legalistic* approach can be summarized as follows: Women's emancipation and the realization of an egalitarian, civilized, Western type of society can be basically achieved through radical, comprehensive legislative and administrative measures. This idea can be found in "A Vindication of the Rights of Women", published by Mary Wollstonecraft in 1872, in which she states "the faults of women were the natural consequences of their education and station in society... Let women share the rights and they will emulate the virtues of men".[59] Equality before law, equal pay for equal work, together with equal opportunities for education as well as the right to vote, once transformed into legal provisions, will supposedly produce in the long run a new generation of women, eager to become active, participating citizens.

This approach places very little, if any, importance on deep rooted structural changes. The major vehicle for change is considered to be an array of legislative measures, large scale publicity for egalitarian valuc judgments and, more recently, insistence on women's participation in the labour market, and the reduction of family size with the help of family planning. This evolutionary model, reborn under the modern version of feminism, wants to transform woman's world into a unisex male one without questioning the real reasons for this capital delay.

(b) *The radical, class-oriented, structural approach* assumes that a woman's social, economic and cultural problems differ in nature according to the social class to which she is affiliated. These special affiliations determine the range of alternatives open to a person in economic space. In the specific framework of the Third World countries, unless basic changes are made in the economic and social spaces, proposals such as those which encourage women to work, heighten their level of education and the concomitant provision of social services, will not work. Legal reforms solely produce a social system in which women's political role always remains a "symbolic" one. This is mainly due to the fact that their political choices largely depend upon the influence of two major

[59] Mary Wollstonecraft, *A Vindication of the Rights of Woman New York, w. W. Norton, 1967.*

institutions, namely, the "family" and "religion" and the role both of these institutions perform. Adherents of the radical, class-oriented, structural approach blame the capitalist system for this situation and maintain that it is wrong to focus on women's problems. According to them, a new societal order will automatically bring about the desired solution.

Some protagonists of this approach have added an additional dimension to this problem which is connected with the prevailing world economic order and characterized by a hierarchy built around the current international division of labour and class structure. This hierarchy is dominated by the international flow of capital (multinational corporations) in the metropolitan centers. Multinational decisions fundamentally influence the political-economic life of peripheral countries in the "Third" or "developing" world. Women remain almost entirely unrepresented at this level. Thus, the "international class system", the "national class structure" and "household politics" are interrelated.

(c) *The cultural sex-role sterotype approach.* Sigmund Freud's paradigm "Is anatomy destiny", has recently led a great number of social scientists (psychologists, anthropologists, sociologists), to deal with the cultural dimension of women's position in society. According to this approach, the core of the female problem today is a problem of identity. A great number of cultures, especially the Islamic one, do not permit women to accept or gratify their basic needs and to grow and fullfill their potential as human beings. This has led a number of social scientists to deal with cultural sex-role stereotyping, attempting to delineate the major problems in each phase, such as sex-role attribution in the primary and secondary socialization processes, as well as the assessment of occupational segregation as cause and consequence of such a socialization pattern. Experiences, such as government support for changes in traditional sex roles (Sweden); greatly increased participation by women in traditionally masculine occupations (Soviet Union) and, the development of strategies to eliminate sex-role stereotypes from the educational systems, have contributed to the growth of this approach.

Quite a few authors have combined the major ideas of these approaches. Without entering into a detailed discussion of these apparently juxtaposing views, while supporting the major theses of the structural approach, it seems imperative to agree on one important point. Regardless of the social model a society like Turkey adopts, it is of major importance that action be taken to modify and improve the status of its millions of "second class citizens". The realization of an egalitarian, free and democratic society, where men and women may develop their personalities, requires much more reliable, scientific knowledge, data and research. This intensified research will enable politicians, policy makers, legislators, opinion leaders, planners and scholars, to conceive more effective strategies and policies.

Conclusion

Options in the form of placing priorities on total sexual liberty, sex segregation in favour of women, insistence on the decisive importance of the women's rights movement or sentimental attachment to past legal reforms, are certainly not the proper vehicles for an efficacious and comprehensive emancipation of all Turkish women. It is also obvious that no social problem can be isolated and treated by one-sided recommendations, such as family planning, vocational training or rural development projects.

Every society needs for its advancement and for a harmonious balance between industrialization and rural development, intelligent, mature, knowledgeable men and women. The political solution to be adopted will no doubt remain a constant issue of debate and will not disappear from the agenda of public discussions. But during this process of selecting the most efficacious remedies, one point should not be overlooked. The veil cast upon the myriads of problems, consciously or unconsciously perturbing the great majority of Turkish women, has not been lifted. Turkish women deserve to be carefully studied, their problems to be exposed and discussed. More knowledge means more power. Turkish women and men are rich with innate abilities. It is the duty of Turkish researchers to help to detect the manifold obstructions which prevent the emergence of a free and equal young generation of women and men dedicated to the survival of Turkish democracy.

PART ONE

POPULATION, HEALTH, NUTRITION

The Measles Lament

I have seen this village under whose roofs
The children languish with the measles....
Their eyes and chests and faces—oh, that abandoned field
Stares with such innocence from among the red poppies.

They are all unaware of the measles and of death,
Unaware of the death that blooms on their dirty faces....
And, suddenly, they turn into a fallen rose.
Babies are dying all of a sudden, unaware of death.

Ceyhun Atuf KANSU, *Kızamık Ağıdı*
Translation: Talât Sait HALMAN

"I went and planted myself before the Agha. 'Agha', I said, 'my wife is dying. I must take her to the doctor'. The Agha laughed. 'Ismail', he said, 'don't you know our women? They lie and lie in bed, sick beyond hope you would think, but they always get up in the end. They don't need doctors. They're tempered in steel, they are. What are you worrying about? You go on with your work'. 'No' I said, 'Agha, whatever I have let it be yours, yours as your mother's milk. My cotton, my sesame, my wheat, I give it to you freely. Let it be yours......... but get me twenty-five liras'. He yielded finally and gave me the money. I got a cart and took her to the doctor, but he wasn't there, he had gone away on holiday. I searched the town from end to end. Finally I found a health officer, one of those who give quinine injections. He came out and looked at Zala, who seemed to be drawing her last breath.

"He leaned over to my ear. 'But she's done for', he whispered. 'Let her be'. I said, 'It had to happen. You give her an injection'. 'I can't give an injection to one at the point of death', he said. 'What's the use?' I put the money before him. 'Here', I said, 'is your money. Give her the injection. I'm paying you, aren't I? You'd give an injection to this tree, to my horses if I paid you to. What is it to you? Is it your business? Give her this injection, brother', I said, 'so that my conscience be at rest, so that people should not cover me with curses, so that friend and foe should see'. He was a good man and gave her an injection. I made him give another one. 'Give her another one, brother, I owe such a lot to Zala......' He gave it to her. Her skin was stuck to her bones, just skin and bones, Aunt......That's what Zala had become.....You wouldn't believe it. If you'd seen her with your own eyes, you'd have said, 'This isn't Zala'.

"It was midday when I hitched the horses to the cart. The world was crackling in the heat as we started for home. If she's to die, I thought, let it be at the farm. It was so hot, so unbearably hot. The huge plain, the whole world was ablaze. We had hardly traveled halfway home when Zala sat up erect all of a sudden. She was going to say something, but she couldn't say it. Her head fell back. I heard her murmur, 'a chance in a million......My child......' softly, so low I could hardly hear".

YAŞAR KEMAL, "The Baby", Transl. Thilda Gökçeli
Evergreen Review, Vol. 4, No. 14, Sept.—Oct. 1960, 106—107

INTRODUCTION

During recent years a large number of social scientists dealing with the urgent needs of the Third World have been constantly warning politicians and policy makers about the threat the "population explosion" poses in terms of development. These alarming predictions and calculations as well as the preventive measures proposed by international organizations, like the Club of Rome and the UN, have all focussed during recent years the attention on the issues directly related to fertility and family planning. Yet, recent studies of women clearly show that the question of encouraging or preventing population increase cannot be dealt with as an independent variable. This problem is inextricably linked to many socio-economic structural factors, i. e. health, nutrition, migration and employment.

The status of women, and their educational level in particular, whether or not they are gainfully employed, the nature of their employment and their position within the family are all factors that have been found to influence family size. A subsistence economy is a major driving force for high fertility and, unless altered, resists all kinds of family planning schemes. Furthermore, women's right to decide freely and responsibly on the number and spacing of their children is closely interrelated with such demographic variables as age at marriage, age at birth of the first child, quality of pre-natal, delivery and postnatal care and recourse to illegally induced abortions.

It is also essential to examine the socio-economic elements which determine the demographic structure. Migration and unhealthy urbanization lead to sex imbalances, for example, the erosion of the male population in villages due to migration to foreign countries or the strikingly high male population in large cities due to urban migration. These sex imbalances can be detrimental to the stability of urban/rural life and to individual and family welfare. Special development efforts are required to solve such demographic, economic and social problems. More specifically, unless effective, decentralized education and health facilities are organized in the rural areas, it is unrealistic to expect a decrease in the high illiteracy, fertility and mortality rates. Finally, the drastic increase in life expectancy figures for women forces us to reconsider the concept of "Women's dual role" which was presented by Alva Myrdal 20 years ago.

It is in light of these general considerations that the topics in this subsection have been treated. Leila Erder, who wittingly remarked that information concerning women before the Republican period could only be derived from fiscal surveys, indicating once more the decisive role of economic factors, gives an extremely well-balanced and cohesive picture of Turkey's demographic composition over the years.

A few of the important results of her analysis are: a) a continual increase in the proportion of girls at young ages of dependency b) an increase in life expectancy for urban women, indicating the close relationship between developmental level and chances for survival, c) striking regional differences in fertility and mortality rates. The eastern provinces have an exceptionally high fertility rate, but they also have the lowest life expectancy.

Erder's projection for the year 2000 indeed offers the reader a very provocative question. In the year 2000 according to her prediction, some 26.7 million women—Turkey's total population today—will live in urban areas. Will they lead their lives in peripheral activities or become part of the organized labor force?

The essays of the two researchers from the medical profession, Baysal and Tezcan, shed light on a number of health problems, some of which are peculiar to Turkey's female population. Tezcan, with survey data, pinpoints the major reasons for high fertility as well as for abortion despite its illegality. Her findings reinforce the assumption that under certain circumstances newly urbanized women may import their own fertility patterns unless farsighted educational schemes and employment opportunities are provided.

The cultural norms that particularly affect women's health are attitudes towards marriage, age at marriage, fertility rate, sex of the child, type of family (extended/nuclear), the place of women in the family and the expected role of woman as defined by social conventions.

Baysal proves, similarly to Tezcan and in line with numerous studies undertaken in developing countries, that the link between women's reproductive function, sex selective diseases and poor health are inextricable. As was the case in India, the neglect of maternity and child health services in Turkey and the over-concentration of efforts on family planning seem to have defeated the ultimate objective of the family planning program itself.

Kâgıtçıbaşı's paper attempts to investigate the prevailing fertility pattern by using the social psychological criteria of the "value of the child". Within such a framework, the value of children for parents assumes importance in terms of the motivational dynamics underlying fertility behavior. Methodologically, this research represents a new field of application for cost benefit analysis. The dominant sex related attitudes appear once more to be decisive. Reasons for wanting or not wanting a child seem again to be closely related to place of residence and economic factors such as income and occupation. Kâgıtçıbaşı's findings confirm the necessity to adopt an inter-actional approach to women's and men's work, because the social transformations aimed for almost always involve shifts in reciprocal relationships between men and women.

Timur focusses on family structure and formation as an excellent indicator of women's status in society. Her data shows that certain family types influence and to a great degree even determine the intra-family relations and the individual behaviour of family members in certain areas.

LEILA ERDER

THE WOMEN OF TURKEY: A DEMOGRAPHIC OVERVIEW

1. The Statistical Personality of Women

Information on women from census or fiscal surveys before the Republican period in Turkey is virtually non-existent. The Ottoman administrator's zest to enumerate the population was vested in his concern about probable returns to the imperial coffers and his efforts centered on identifying tax-payers. These were traditionally almost always adult males.[1] This is not to say that there was a concerted effort to discount the role of women in production. In the western province when women in fact performed the tax-paying role of the head of household, they were recorded as conscientiously as were the males.[2] However, such cases were rare in this region and even more so in Anatolia.

Universal counts, launched in the second half of the nineteenth century, give us our first comparative figures on women relative to men and on subsections of the population.[3] And immediately a persistent dilemma raises its head. From the outset women are noticeably underestimated, at least in a numerical sense. The respondent to the census taker has traditionally been the head of the household and, since usually a male, our information on women in the household is filtered through his knowledge, estimation and, indirectly the importance he gives to their presence. If our comments repeatedly refer to age misreporting, sex ratios and mortality of women relative to men, we must recall that we are the prisoners of an enumeration system which gives us second-hand information on most women. In other words the person wishing to assess the labour-force is confronted with a classification system which may have little relevance to the actual economic activity of women.

---

[1] L. Erder, "The Measurement of Preindustrial Population Changes: The Ottoman Empire from the 15th to the 17th century". *Middle Eastern Studies*, Vol. 11, No.3 (1975), pp. 248—301.

[2] Halil Inalcık, *Hicri 835 Tarihli Suret-i Defter-i Sancak-i Arvanid*, (Ankara: Türk Tarih Kurumu, 1954).

[3] L. Erder, "Patterns of Population Change in Nineteenth Century Anatolia", Princeton University Conference in the Economic and Social History of the Near East, 1974.

If the first problem is one of census administration i. e. only male respondents, the second falls squarely within the domain of the analyst. The paucity of categories which suit research questions on women directly reflects a lack of concern about pressing more deeply into the demographic characteristics of the second sex. Whether as members of the labour force, rural-urban migrants or workers abroad, it is men rather than women that have drawn the attention of the analyst in Turkey. Women are viewed as an adjunct group. In internal migration, where their numbers are smaller and their patterns of movement presumably predicated on male initiative and previous male moves, studies have either examined only males or the total population.[4] Consequently, we learn remarkably little about women and their demographic characteristics from census materials.

2. The Female Population of Turkey in Historical Perspective

In the sections below we shall summarize the major features of the demographic structure of Turkey's female population. This represents a distillation and synthesis of a large number of studies, referred to in the appropriate sections.

Change over time, whether in terms of mortality, fertility or migration is a central part of the development of Turkey and the state of Turkish women today. Although those past trends are pregnant with implications for the future, few of them are as clear as policymakers and the public would like to think today. Women have at different ages experienced throughout their lifetime exposure to environmental conditions which have welded the present demographic structure and expectations of women in 1975. But policies have responded slowly, if at all, to these cumulative changes. A chronological view, that follows separate cohorts over time offers a perspective which we may overlook with our personal concern for the present and our own age group.

We shall first examine the overall growth of the female population and then turn to the components of this growth: mortality, fertility and migration. Urbanization, the shift in population from rural to urban areas, is a subject in itself and a prominent part of demographic change

[4] Exceptions are: Samira Yener, *1965—1970 Döneminde Iller Arası Göçler ve Göç edenlerin Nitelikleri* (Ankara: Devlet Planlama Teşkilatı, 1977). Nermin Abadan-Unat, et al. *Migration and Development*, Ankara Ajans Türk, 1976.

in Turkey since the early 1950's. To understand these features, we shall review our knowledge of urban-rural differentials and regional disparities in each section as these differentials reveal more about the position of women in countries like Turkey undergoing late and dependent economic growth than do the national figures. They also raise fundamental doubts about images for the future.

Future images are composed for the most part by planners, policymakers and journalists. The last section reviews their expectations about the way women will contribute to future population growth and raises a number of questions about their premises.

3. Sources

Ironically, the availability of data on women in Turkey has not been accompanied by a widespread evaluation of these new sources. For the most part, we are left with cut-and-dried material. To imagine women rejoicing in the birth of a child, dying from self-induced abortion or struggling to move their families from a village house to a city shack is left to the reader.

The Turkish population census, first conducted in 1927 and subsequently repeated thereafter from 1935 onwards, offers the most continuous source of information on the demographic features of Turkish women.[5] To abstract only the female population and review its development devoid of its male counterpart would leave as incomplete a picture as to examine the population as a whole. Women constitute our focal point but men, their inseparable counterpart, are reduced in this paper somewhat artificially to occasional references. They nevertheless constitute a group with which to compare and evaluate the changes in women's mortality, migration and economic characteristics. Only fertility, magnanimously accepted by demographers as the sole province of women, will be left exclusively to their domain. Questions raised about changes in childbearing performance necessarily involve some thought about the association of women with men.

---

[5] L. Erder, "Nüfus Sayımı: Ihmal Edilen bir Kaynak", in S. Karabaş and Y. Yeşilçay, *Türkiye'de Toplumsal Bilim Araştırmalarında Yaklaşımlar ve Yöntemler.* (Ankara: Middle East Technical University, 1977), pp. 99—116.

4. Population Growth and Women: 1935—1975

Turkey's first national population census in 1927 recorded 13.6 million inhabitants. If adjusted for the incorporation of Hatay in 1938, previously a part of Syria, this figure rises by some 90,000 inhabitants. Of 16.2 million inhabitants recorded in 1935, 51% were female. Turkey's population, at the last count in 1975, was 40.3 million and its female proportion was 48.6%. This growth is summarized in Table I below.

Table I

The Female Population of Turkey 1935–1975

Census Year	*Number of Females ('000's)*	*Sex Ratio (Males/Females×100)*
1935	8 221	97
1940	8 922	100
1945	9 344	101
1950	10 420	101
1955	11 831	103
1960	13 591	104
1965	15 441	105
1970	17 598	102
1975	19 603	106

Source: Census of Population adjusted for international migration Adjusted figures to 1960 from P. Demeny and F. C. Shorter, *Türkiye'de Ölüm Seviyesi Doğurganlık ve Yaş Yapısı Tahminleri*, p. 54.

The low sex ratios observed until after World War II reflect the deficit of males from repeated military campaigns during the late years of the nineteenth century and through the Turkish War of Independence. The idolization of the village women's contribution to national liberation and then the responsibility of the educated women to the cause of national development explains the high value attached to women in a society robbed of much of its manpower.

The total growth rates and the female population followed the same general lines. Rates for males for each intercensal period were consistently higher than for the female population as a whole as normal reproduction patterns filled out the base of the pyramid, reducing the effect of deficits among males in the older age groups. (See Table II below).

If the impact of international migration is extracted to give a notion of gains from natural increase, we observe a somewhat different pattern.

Table II

*Total and Female Population Numbers and Intercensal Growth Rates 1935–1975**

Census Year	Total Population ('000')	Total Intercensal Annual Growth Rate (percents)	Female Population ('000')	Female Intercensal Annual Growth Rate (percents)
1935	16 158		8 221	
1940	17 821	1.96	8 922	1.64
1945	18 790	1.06	9 344	.92
1950	20 947	2.17	10 420	2.18
1955	24 065	2.78	11 831	2.54
1960	27 755	2.85	13 591	2.77
1965	31 151	2.31	15 394	2.49
1970	35 321	2.51	17 598	2.67
1975	40 025	2.50	19 603	2.16

Source: Census of Population

* Growth rates calculated by the author, $P_t = P_0 e^{rt}$ where P_0 = Population at the first census, P_t = Population at the second census, (t) years later.

International migration raised the national growth rate in the 1950's as immigrants from former Ottoman lands continued to seek refuge within the borders of the modern Turkish Republic. After 1960, on the other hand, the net effect was negative as departures, then viewed as temporary, for jobs abroad in Europe reduced somewhat the rate of national growth. (See Table III).

Annual intercensal growth rates for the female population lagged slightly behind those for males before World War II, partly due to the filling out of the age pyramid, particularly on the male side where there had already been heavy deficits from war, and partly due to the poor mortality conditions for women during the 1930's. After the Second World War, they followed roughly parallel lines, with women registering slightly higher rates during the most recent decade because of their superior gains in the probability of survival.

In general, the years between 1927 and 1945, were ones of slow growth as mortality remained high. After 1945 rapid expansion from an improvement in mortality conditions raised the growth rate by three quarters to a half of its pre-World War II level.

The sex ratios for the total population, presented in Table I, give a very limited notion of the structure of the female population because

Table III

Annual Intercensal Growth Rates for Males and Females Adjusted for Territorial Change and the Effects of International Migration

(1) Period	(2) Males Annual Period Growth Rate (percent)	(3) Females Annual Period Growth Rate (percent)
1935–1940	1.90	1.25
1940–1945	1.17	.90
1945–1950	2.13	2.15
1950–1955	2.88	2.41
1955–1960	2.83	2.67
1960–1965	2.64	2.55
1965–1970	2.22	2.62
1970–1975	2.45	2.33

Source: Author's calculations based on P. Demeny and F. C. Shorter adjusted populations through 1960. Own estimates thereafter. 1960 population used as reference.

Table IV

Age Distribution of Turkey's Female Population By Age Groups, Percentage

	Selected Census Years		
Age Group	1935*	1950*	1975**
0–4	15.8	14.5	15.0
5–14	22.9	22.3	25.6
15–44	42.4	44.5	42.2
45–64	14.6	14.8	12.4
65	4.3	3.9	4.8
TOTAL	100.0	100.0	100.0

* Population Adjusted for International Migration

** Adjustment For Age Misreporting and International Migration Included

they summarize differences at all ages. When examined by age groups a more revealing pattern emerges.

The distribution shows a young population and, over time, an increase in the proportion of girls at the young ages of dependency, below the age of 15. The high proportion of women in the reproductive ages, 15—44, continues throughout the era as a major characteristics of the female population.

The age distribution in itself suggests the burden born by women in the raising of children. Women in the age groups 20—44 bear, for the most part, the burden of childbearing and child raising. The dependency ratio or burden for women, children 0—9 divided by women in the reproductive ages 20—44, is compared for selected census years in Table V.

Table V
Burden at Selected Dates

	Selected Census Date		
	1935	*1950*	*1975*
(1) Children 0-9 ('000's)	5 266	5 736	11 031
(2) Women 20-44 ('000's)	31 042	3 555.7	12 546
(3) Burden (3) (1)/(2)	1.70	1.61	.879

Source: Author's calculations based on census results adjusted for international migration and age misreporting.

The table shows a decline in the dependency ratio for women, especially after 1950. The reasons for this decline are taken up in the following sections on mortality and fertility.

5. *Mortality Characteristics of Women*

In societies undergoing the demographic transition from high to lower levels of mortality, women usually register greater gains than men in improved survival and exhibit a life expectancy at birth that exceeds that of their male counterparts. Such is the case in Turkey.

Studies based on census materials have shown clear improvements for women since 1935 and, perhaps with the exception of the first decade, women have outdistanced men in their gains.[6] This pattern is true for

[6] The basic source for this historical evaluation of the Turkish population using census materials is Paul Demeny and Frederic C. Shorter, *Estimating Turkish Mortality, Fertility and Age Structure: Application of Some New Techniques*, (Istanbul, Istanbul University, 1968).

the nation as a whole. Regional and urban-rural survey results from the 1960's also suggest that women may have registered similar gains in different regions of Turkey although, as we shall see below, there are substantial urban-rural differentials in mortality conditions.

Preceding World War II, women had a slightly lower life expectancy than men. Taking the life expectancy at age 5 as an index, because of the high level of child relative to adult mortality in Turkey, we find that women who survived the age 5 on the average could expect to live 50 years. This measure assumes that the cohort would experience the mortality conditions experienced by older cohorts as they move through their life cycle. Men on the other hand, had a somewhat higher life expectancy at age 5, 51.5 years. In spite of the fact that Turkey did not enter World War II, these levels dropped during the war years for both men and women, men losing more on the average. National preparedness for war, including mobilization, rationing and general nutrition are likely to have played a role.

This decline proved only temporary and immediately following the war a radical improvement commenced in the mortality conditions of adults. Modern medicine, the eradication of malaria, the campaign against tuberculosis and later antibiotics as well as greatly improved road connections had an impact on raising the probability of survival for women. In the period between 1945 and 1955 the life expectancy at age 5 for women rose to 57.1 years and by 1965 stood at 61.2 years. Current estimates vary but 62.8 years for women and 58.3 years for men may be noted as one index of the expectation of life at birth for the period between 1975 and 1980.[7] Women have thus continued to register greater gains in their probability for survival than men. In this respect they are not the "second" sex.

When differentials between urban and rural areas are examined, however, clear gaps in this transition process emerge. These differentials reflect a much earlier process of social change which, if figures were available, could be traced most likely to the early part of the nineteenth century. Port cities, especially Turkey's two real metropolitan areas of İstanbul and Izmir, were absorbed into the western Mediterranean world in the nineteenth century not only in their trading connections

[7] Sosyal Planlama Dairesi, "Dördüncü Beş Yıllık Kalkınma Planı Nüfus Tahminleri", State Planning Organization, (limited circulation report), 1977.

but in the provision of urban infrastructure and modern health facilities.[8] Conditions in the Anatolian hinterland remained much as they had been for centuries and in fact may have worsened as repeated mobilization for a series of wars drew off rural males and commanded more and more of the meagre agricultural surplus.[9] This surplus was siphoned off not only to feed troops but for export through the growing demand of European trade. It also went to the Ottoman Debt Administration which had been forced by European banks and their governments to collect each year a portion of the Empire's production as payment on the Ottoman Government's unpaid debts. Where port cities in the sixteenth century were once the demographic sinkhole of the Empire, maintaining their numbers more from an influx from the hinterland than from natural increase,[10] they now became the points of growth from natural increase as much as from (urban) migration.[11]

Mortality differentials today reflect the difference between the western and coastal areas of Turkey and the central plateau and eastern provinces. No reliable indices on these differentials are obtainable before the 1960's when a series of national sample surveys were launched. Results from the Turkish Demographic Survey, centered on 1967, show the central and eastern provinces to have the lowest life expectancy at age 5 for both males and females, 60.3 years for females.[12] The index for provinces rimming the Black Sea and Mediterranean Coast and especially for the Aegean provinces in the West, many of them with no coastal connection but long traditions of coastal-oriented commercial agriculture and trade, was over three years longer.

Even greater, however, was the differential between the metropolitan areas of Ankara, İstanbul and Izmir and the rest of the country. The same

---

[8] Ilhan Tekeli, "Evolution of the Spatial Organization in the Ottoman Empire and Turkish Republic", in *Regional Policy: Readings in Theory and Application.* ed. J. Friedmann and W. Alonso. (Cambridge: MIT Press, 1975), pp. 655—679 and Ilber Ortaylı, *Tanzimattan Sonra Mahalli Idareler 1840—1878*, (Ankara: TODAIE, 1974).

[9] L. Erder, "The Making of Industrial Bursa: Population and Economic Activity in a Turkish City 1835—1975", diss. Princeton University, 1976.

[10] L. Erder and S. Faroqhi, "The Development of the Anatolian Urban Network in the Sixteenth Century", *Journal of the Economic and Social History of the Orient*, to appear.
Compare with E. A. Wrigley, "A Simple Model of London's Importance in Changing English Society and Economy 1650—1750", *Past and Present*, 37 (1967).

[11] L. Erder, "The Making of Industrial Bursa", Chapter II.

[12] Turkish Demographic Survey, *Hayati Istatistikler* (Ankara: Sağlık Bakanlığı). 2 Vols., 1967 and 1970.

index was nearly 65 years for these centers. The survey also registered high survival probabilities for women in urban areas, defined as communities with 2,000 or more inhabitants. While women in rural areas as a whole showed life expectancy at the age of 5 of 61.6 years, women in cities could on the average expect to live 3.2 years longer. As with mortality improvement in general, women showed greater gains in the cities in comparison to rural areas than did men.

One of the distinct features of mortality for Turkey, as gains have been registered in survival, is the sharp difference between child and adult mortality.[13] In the absence of historical information, it has been hypothesized that the rapid gains in improved life expectancy have accrued more to adults than to children, perhaps because the response to illness among infants requires greater speed in sensing that onset of illness and in seeking modern medicines and treatment. Feeding customs may also be another factor. Nevertheless, the fact remains that infant mortality in general and mortality among female infants especially in the eastern provinces remains exceptionally high.

The national life table constructed from the Turkish Demographic Survey for 1967 showed that 20% of Turkish children died during the first five years of life. A high percentage of total deaths in the population are found among children, partly because the population as a whole is a very young one, with a high proportion in the young ages. Nevertheless, over half of all deaths registered in a year are among children under five years of age. The infant death rate, the yearly number of infant deaths (between exact ages 0 and 1) divided by the number of births in a year showed a variation between 170 and nearly 250 per thousand in the early 1960's. Estimates from the 1975 census give an infant mortality rate of 133 per thousand.[14] Even the lower figure, probably a more reliable estimate and indicative of improvement, is high. When looking at the childbearing performance of women in the next section, this attrition of children must be kept in mind as one of the determinants that may serve to maintain high fertility.

---

[13] P. Demeny and F. C. Shorter, *Estimating Turkish Mortality, Fertility and Age Structure*, pp. 12ffl20.

[14] F. Özbay, S. Yener and F. C. Shorter, "Accounting for the Trends of Fertility in Turkey", UN/UNFPA Expert Group Meeting on Demographic Transition and Economic Development, Istanbul, 27 April—4 May 1977, p. 3.

6. *Childbearing of Women*

Various measures are useful in distinguishing the reproductive performance of women, their fertility. International comparisons are more easily made with the crude birth rate, the birth stream divided by the population. This, however, is heavily influenced, by the age distribution of the population. Other criteria, such as the proportion of young children, give an approximate idea of the birth rate, but serious problems are encountered when there are doubts about the reliability of enumeration for children under 5. This is the case in Turkey.

Total fertility measures the number of children that a woman would have on the average if she lived through her reproductive years, age 15 to 45 or 50, and as exposed to the prevailing risk of childbearing. The gross reproduction rate is a handy indicator of generational change because it singles out female children among the total number of children expected to be born by a woman given the measure of total fertility. This indicates the potential number of new mothers in the next generation per married woman who lives through the childbearing years.

Survey results from the early 1960's showed a high level of total fertility, close to 6.5 for the nation as a whole. That is, an average woman living through the reproductive years subject to the fertility schedule observed for different cohorts of women, would have born seven children by the time she completed her childbearing years. This yields a gross reproduction rate of 3.17, assuming a sex ratio at birth (male births divided by female birts) of 1.05. The high contribution of fertility to the rate of population growth, especially in view of falling mortality discussed in the preceding section, is self-evident. If this estimate places Turkey among those countries with exceptionally high fertility rates, it conceals a more important aspect of childbearing in Turkey: the sharp contrast between urban and rural areas and different regions of the country.

Estimates for the rural areas of the country yield total fertility considerably higher than the national average, in excess of 7. Metropolitan areas, however, yielded estimates of total fertility that were nearly half the national average. These sweeping metropolitan-rural differences echo those observed for mortality. While we have no historical information for comparison, hypotheses about the socio-economic variables to explain these differentials need to incorporate not only differences in economic structure, the contribution and burden of children in farming systems versus the cities but also the mores of Turkey's old port cities. Their trading and social ties with European cities in the 19th century may have made it more socially acceptable for families to delay the marriage of their daughters beyond the age of puberty. Marital fertility, too, is an important feature. Considerable control of childbearing within marriage appears to be an old and widespread phenomenon in these cities.

Smaller cities and towns are closer to the national average than to the metropolitan areas, with a total fertility slightly above 5 and a gross reproduction rate of 2.44. Regional differences are just as striking with fertility, as with mortality, and there is evidence that these also long antedated the period of modern surveys. The eastern regions show exceptionally high fertility, both in the northeastern and southeastern provinces. The likelihood of the southeast claiming the highest fertility rate in Turkey, over 8, has recently been bolstered by independent Syrian estimates for areas in the north of Syria directly adjacent to the Turkish border.

Demeny and Shorter have applied an estimation procedure to find birth rates involving a set of calculations that take age misreporting of children (the proportion of children under 10) and mortality into account from census figures.[15] These estimates of crude birth rates are useful for regional and international comparisons. Their crude birth rate estimates ranged from 23 per 1000 for metropolitan areas to 50 per 1000 for the rural population in the mid-1960's. In the more developed Aegean and Marmara regions, the rates were about 40, while in the east they were as high as 60 per 1000.

Studies, since the early 1960's have indicated that there is an incipient decline in fertility, and these results have had considerable influence on expectations for the future. The 1970 Population Census indicated that national fertility had fallen, perhaps, to 5.2[16] The Turkish Demographic Survey had earlier shown total fertility for İstanbul, Turkey's lowest, as 2.65. When preparing the Third Five-Year National Development Plan, a major assumption in the population projections was that fertility in general would continue to decline so that by the year 1995 women in the nation as a whole would be bearing children at İstanbul's current pattern. However, until there is firm evidence that rural-urban migration

[15] P. Demeny and F. C. Shorter, *Estimating Turkish Mortality, Fertility and Age Structure*, pp. 34—42.

[16] S. Yener, *III. Beş Yıllık Planda Nüfus Projeksiyonları için Kullanılan Yöntem*, (Ankara: State Planning Organization, 1973), p. 10.

leads to a decline in fertility among new urban women and until the socio-economic determinants of these fertility patterns are explored more thoroughly, such expectations seem to be based on tenuous assumptions.

7. Women on the Move: International Migration

Men, not women, have dominated studies of internal migration in Turkey. The cause for this bias is all too obvious. Urban growth from migration has attracted the attention of policymakers and scholars, all of them city people, and it is the influx of young males, not females, that characterized the shift from villages to cities until the mid 1960's. There has also been a metropolitan bias on the part of young males. In the most recent period for which we have data, 1965—1970, the three metropolises of Ankara, İstanbul and Izmir registered the largest gains from rural-urban migration. Of the rural-urban migrants to these three metropolises, 50% went to İstanbul, 33% to Ankara and 11% to Izmir.

This male and metropolitan bias has obscured a variety of changes which can now be observed through the studies of Tekçe, Gedik and Yener.[17] First, in the most recent years, rural-urban migration has concentrated more on provincial centers outside the hegemony of the older metropolitan areas. These growth centers show a sex ratio of migrants that suggests families are now moving as a unit, or establishing a new residence together in a relatively short period of time.

Secondly, the early wave of male migrants has now produced a wave of female migrants which has evened out the sex ratio of large urban areas, elevated earlier by heavy male immigration during the 1950's. Thirdly, the role of women in the economy of rural areas during this transition period and thus their expectations from city life may well have changed radically. Left in charge of managing the family farm for considerable periods of time, their changing place in the rural economy needs careful scrutiny.[18]

[17] A. Gedik, "A Causal Analysis of the Destination Choice of Village-to-Province Center Migrants in Turkey, 1965—1970", diss. University of Washington, 1977. Belgin Tekçe, *Türkiye'de Şehirlere Göçler; 1955—1960 ve 1960—1965 Dönemlerine Ait Tahminler*, (Ankara: Devlet Istatistik Enstitüsü, 1976). S. Yener, *1965—1970 Döneminde Illerarası Göçler ve Göç edenlerin Nitelikleri.*

[18] See L. Yenisey, "The Social Effects of Migrant Labour on the District Left Behind: Observations in Two Villages of Bogazlıyan", in *Migration and Development*, ed. Nermin Abadan-Unat, *et al.*, pp. 327—370.

Voluntary migration represents an economic investment entered into not only by the migrant himself but by the family as a whole. It is commonly suggested that the level of modernization determines the percentage of females who participate in migration.[19] But the term modernization, as in so many cases, is a vague concept. To some it presents the unwarranted dangers of white lights and free women, but to a great many others it implies risks for family income, and difficulties in getting a foothold in a totally different job market.

Women's place recently in internal migration shows a distinctly different pattern from the earlier male concentration at the young active ages between 20 and 30. While their numbers are still lower than males, their distribution by age is spread out more evenly. One suspects that those at the younger ages are moving more as family units and those over thirty are joining spouses who gradually established permanent bases in the cities during the late 1950's and early 1960's.[20]

Selectivity is prominent among female as well as male migrants. They show a higher average level of literacy than their counterparts in their provinces of origin. Female migration is distinguished by shorter distance moves. In 1970 new growth poles such as Kayseri, Konya, Edirne, Erzurum and Elaziğ, headed the list of gains from migration among the female population. Among the eastern provinces selectivity in terms of women with high educational levels in comparison to the rest of the provinces has been prominent in recent years.

Women migrants as participants in the labour force show low percentages in comparison to their male counterparts. Male migrants as participants in the labour force in 1970 on the average ranged between 65 and 85% while female percentages ranged between 10 and 15%.

8. Perspectives on the Demographic Future of Women in Turkey

To speak today of the year 2000 is not futurology. It is barely a generation away. Girls born now will have entered or be candidates for the

[19] William L. Parish, "International Migration and Modernization: The European Case", *Economic Development and Cultural Change*, Vol. 21, No. 4, (July, 1973).

[20] On the investigation of this process for a squatter-housing district of Istanbul see: Tansı Şenyapılı, "Integration through Mobility", *METU Journal of the Faculty of Architecture*, Vol. 3, No. 2, (1977), pp. 237—252.

[21] For a detailed analysis see: S. Yener, *1965—1970 Döneminde Illerarası Göçler ve Göç edenlerin Nitelikleri.*

labour force in the year 2000; they will be marrying and beginning their reproductive lives then. New wives of today will only just be completing their childbearing years. There is already built into today's demographic structure a dynamism which will produce staggering changes not just in the numbers but in the structure of the female population.

The 1975 census, after adjustments for international migration, reported a female population of 19.8 million. A conservative projection, assuming substantial gains in the life expectancy and a considerable decline in total fertility, yields a female population of 35.6 million in the year 2000, nearly double the present number of women.[22] If fertility declines more slowly than expected this figure could be a good deal higher.

If we assume, however, that women in Turkey will experience a fertility decline that nearly halves their present level of total fertility, bringing it to the pattern currently observed for İstanbul, there will be nearly 16 million more women, practically as many as live in Turkey today.

The changes this would produce in the age structure have implications for women's demands for jobs, child care and health services. Table VI summarizes the change in the proportional share of different age groups of women in the female population.

Table VI

Comparative Age Structure of Women 1975–2000

Age Group	*1975*		*2000*	
	Nos. ('000's)	%	*Nos. ('000's)*	%
0–14	7 889	40.4	11 467	32.2
15–64	10 832	54.8	20 585.2	57.8
65	960	4.8	3 562.4	10.0
TOTAL	19 780.5	100.0	35 614.6	100.0
*20–44	6 118	30.9	13 248.6	37.2

The salient changes in age structure are the decline in the proportion of girls under 15, the increase in women in the working ages and the rise in the proportion of women over 65 years of age. If women in the reproductive ages, 20—44, are singled out, the increase in the potential labour force is even more striking. Much of the gain registered by women

[22] S. Yener, *III. Beş Yıllık Planda Nüfus Projeksiyonları için Kullanılan Yöntem*, Appendix 2, "Alternative C".

in the working ages is produced by the rise in the number of women in the reproductive ages. This group is shown separately at the bottom of the table. Their numbers wil be more than doubled. Not only will they have fewer children to care for but there will be many more of them demanding new services and conditions. The fertility decline hypothesized in this projection incorporates both a fall in the total number of children they will bear in their life time and the completion of childbearing at younger ages. With a drop in the mean age of childbearing, women will be ready to enter the labour force on a full-time basis earlier and to stay in it longer.

Behind this projection rests the assumption that urbanization will continue in Turkey and bring with it socio-economic changes in the roles of women that will influence their reproductive behaviour as well as enable them to benefit from the better health services and conditions witnessed today in Turkey's larger cities. The latter is expected to reduce both their own mortality and the mortality of the children they bear. There is reason to look at the expected trends in the urban and rural distribution of the population which form the underpinnings of this perspective.

In 1935, 16.5% of Turkey's national population, or some 2.7 million inhabitants, lived in cities with 10,000 or more inhabitants. The total number of city-dwellers in the whole country was no more than the population of a metropolitan center. By 1970 the proportion of the population in cities had risen to 35.8 percent. With high rates of natural increase, the total number of rural inhabitants continued to rise in spite of internal migration from villages to cities, which shifted large numbers from the rural into the urban category.

The State Planning Organization in the Third Five-Year Development Plan expects the recently observed high rates of urbanization to continue, and the decline in the absolute number of villagers to commence only after 1985.[23] It assumes that 75% of the total population will be living in cities of 10,000 or more inhabitants in 1995, implying an urban population of 48.6 million. The rural population, on the other hand, will have declined to 16.3 million inhabitants, for some magic reason, thus equalling the total population of Turkey in 1935.

---

[23] "Urbanization Trends and Forecasts for Turkey, 1970—1995", *III. Five-Year Development Plan*, (Ankara: State Planning Organization), see also
Samira Yener, "Population Projections" in *The Population of Turkey*, ed. F. Karadayı, S. Timur, M. Mancura *et al.*, (Ankara: Hacettepe, The Institute of Population Studies, 1974), p. 133.

What does this imply for women? If such rates of urbanization in fact materialize and women close the gap, between the number of male and female migrants, thus evening out the sex-ratio between villages and cities, some 26.7 million women will be living in cities. This is as many women as Turkey's total rural population today. It is in these farming areas where women's participation in the labour force is highest. The six largest cities today show low labour force participation rates for women.

Large numbers of these women, most probably a higher proportion than observed in the national projection, will be in the prime years of their childbearing and working lives. Their place in a new urban world, whether they live out their lives in peripheral activities and marginal sector jobs or become part of the organized labour force, or whether they live in residential areas with tolerable environmental conditions or in squalor and hopelessness, depends both on the national economic policies of today and the move to active city planning. Otherwise, assumptions about falling fertility and major improvements in both child and adult female mortality may well be pipedreams or a placebo.

Such prophecies for the future, even only a generation away, may restrict our vision and critical capacity. Both the theory of demographic transition, and its underlying assumptions of industrialization and urbanization as experienced in the West, may turn attention away from areas where women are most seriously affected.[24] Rather than focusing more on health services in rural areas where infant and female mortality are highest and where work conditions are hardest, they may continue to direct investment disproportionately to cities.

These prophecies can also lead to the comforting feeling that the process of urbanization, in itself, is going to produce socio-economic changes which will require little in the way of active programs to ameliorate or even maintain the current level of environmental and work conditions for women. We have yet to see convincing evidence that urbanization and the demographic transition in Turkey give cause for expecting change similar to that experienced in the industrialized nations.[25]

If work opportunities in the city to replace women's productive roles

[2] For a critical review of the demographic transition theory see: John C. Caldwell, "Toward a Restatement of Demographic Transition Theory", *Population and Development Review*, Vol. 2, Nos. 3 and 4 (1976), pp. 321—366.

[25] On this question in general see:
Janet Abu-Lughod and Richard Hay, Jr., eds. *Third World Urbanization*, (Chicago: Maaroufa Press, 1976) and
Milton Santos, *Les villes du tier monde*, (Paris: Genin, 1971).

in rural areas fail to materialize, tension is bound to mount. As noted earlier, female labour force participation rates today are low. Competition for a slot in organized city jobs will become more intense and the low participation of women in marginal activities today is bound to change.

While outside the purview of this paper, an additional number of questions need to be raised. Rural women may well "import" their own fertility patterns and may not necessarily change them, even in a generation.[26] The response to new health conditions, improved child survival, the cost of children and their contribution to family income requires time.

In family economies, income originates not only from city jobs but from the working of family land in the village. Thus, the division of productive activity among family members in the city and village may also help maintain high fertility, even with rapid urbanization. In addition, the structure of the urban economy and job opportunities for children in street peddling, repair shops and other parts of the marginal sector may encourage high childbearing performance. The economic structure of Turkish cities, women's place in this structure, and their perception of the cost and benefits of urban living require close scrutiny.

---

[26] Gino Germani, "The City as an Integrating Mechanism: The Concept of Social Integration", G. H. Beyer, ed. *The Urban Explosion in Latin America*, (Ithaca: Cornell University Press, 1967).

SERIM TIMUR*

DETERMINANTS OF FAMILY STRUCTURE IN TURKEY

In Turkey, there has been increasing interest over the last ten years in the social demographic factors affecting family size and the composition of families and households. Since three large nation-wide demographic surveys have already been conducted (in 1963, 1968, and 1973, respectively), a very rich source of data exists to investigate the interrelationship between family structure and demographic change.

Based on some of these data, this chapter attempts to analyze some of the processes that underline structural change within the Turkish family, specifically, what factors and forces change family types and how these family types, in turn, affect other areas of individual behavior and social action.

Methodology

The data for this chapter are taken from the "1968 Survey on Family Structure and Population Problems in Turkey", conducted by the staff of Hacettepe Institute of Population Studies. The main objective of this survey was to empirically examine the applicability to Turkey of some of the current theories on family structure and population dynamics. Data were collected on family type, the process of family formation, and marital relations; fertility level; knowledge, attitude, and practice of family planning; and the process of migration. Stress was laid on the socioeconomic and rural-urban correlates of these variables, as well as on regional and rural-urban differentials.

The survey was based on a nationwide multistage probability sample of 4,500 households. Turkey displays large urban-rural and regional differences in several social and economic characteristics. In view of these variations among regions and urban-rural residential units, cross stratification was done by five geographic regions and by community

* This article has been published in its original form in Ed. James Allman *Women's Status and Fertility in the Muslim World*, Praeger New York 1978, pp. 227—242. The editor acknowledges gratefully the courtesy to reprint the article.

size. The five geographic regions and stratified urban-rural communities were:

Geographic Regions	*Size of Communities*
Central Anatolia	Metropolitan centers (Ankara, Istanbul, Izmir)
Black Sea coast	Cities (population, 50,000 and over)
Western Turkey	Cities (population, 15,000 – 50,000)
Mediterranean region	Towns (population, 2,000 – 15,000)
Eastern Turkey	Rural areas (less than 2,000)

Family Types

Almost all the world's population live in family units, but the types and structures vary not only from one society to another but, also, from one class to another within the same society. The simplest type of family is a unit consisting of a married man and woman with their offspring. This unit is referred to as the *conjugal* family, when the accent in on the husband-wife relationship, and the *nuclear* family, when it is viewed as the basic unit of all more complex forms. The head of a nuclear family is independent, neither subject to the authority of any of his relatives nor economically dependent upon them.

Different criteria can be used to distinguish more complex or extended families from simple nuclear families: number of mates (monogamy, polygamy, polyandry); residence after marriage (patrilocal, matrilocal, neolocal); degree of authority (equalitarian, patriarchal, matriarchal); generational prolification (vertical versus horizontal); and so forth.

A crucial factor in the study of family types should be to determine the nature of the immediate family. The relation of the family of procreation (conjugal or nuclear family) to husband's and wife's families of orientation (their parents) is very important. This is clearly seen when we look at the explanations given about the nature of the two polar family types: the patriarchal extended family and the independent nuclear family.

Patriarchal Extended Family

Social scientists have characterized the patriarchal extended family as one in which the nuclear family is controlled by the head of the patrilineal extended family. The father has great power over his sons, and the husband over his wife. Relationships are not egalitarian. Marital choice is determined by the parents, and age at marriage tends to be quite young. To facilitate parental control, the newly married couple usually live with the parents. There are economic exchanges in connection with marriage. Sons generally follow their father's occupation; thus social and geographical mobility is limited. This type of family is seen as being best suited to an agrarian society with little mobility and simple specialization.

Independent Nuclear Family

In an independent nuclear family, neither parents nor the couple have many rights or reciprocal obligations in regard to each other. Parents do not choose the new couple's residence location—it is neolocal. Mate choice is done by the people involved. Age at marriage is determined by the fact that youngsters have to be old enough to provide for themselves. The husband's occupation, rather than that of the patriarchal father, determines the family's status. Occupation is no longer hereditary due to an increase in social and geographical mobility related to industrialization. The independent nuclear family is thus seen as a function of industrialization and urbanization.

Most theoretical explanations of changes in family structure view industrialization and urbanization as the primary determinants. The emergence of the small nuclear family is generally seen in sociological theory as a consequence of the urban-industrial revolution. In fact, the structural-functional approach postulates a functional interdependence and implied causality between the urban-industrial complex and the small nuclear family. Over time and through the processes of social change, industrialization, and urbanization, the extended family will be superseded by the independent nuclear family. Since extended families were thought to be prevalent in rural preindustrial societies, it was assumed that the typical residential family in these societies was the extended family, containing representatives of three or more generations and, perhaps, several collateral relatives. This generalization was sustained by a few superficial observations, such as that extended families were more prevalent in rural than in urban areas, and cross-culturally, that extended families were more prevalent in underdeveloped agricultural societies than in developed industrial societies.

Recently, however, several arguments have challenged those generally accepted ideas. Considerable statistical evidence from underdeveloped countries, as well as historical research dealing with preindustrial societies, show that a large majority of people live, and have lived, in nuclear families. The extended family is not predominant in actual practice, except for the wealthy minority.

On the basis of empirical research, many demographers and family sociologists now agree that the extended or joint family is an ideal, polar type. Bogue observed that while the extended family (where three or four generations live together under one roof or within one compound) is a part of the cultural standard of many countries, it occurs in fact primarily among the upper classes. Thus, the extended family as described and discussed in the literature of family sociology and cultural anthropology appears to be more a sociological tradition than a statistical reality.

The extended family was considered to be the modal form in rural areas of Turkey until quite recently. It was commonly believed that change toward the nuclear family would occur with industrialization, urbanization, and modernization. Based on the data from the 1968 nationwide survey, let us look specifically at the socioeconomic factors associated with Turkish family types.

Family Types in Turkey

The term *family*, as used in this study, refers to the domestic family; the definitions of family types given below refer to a set of related persons who share a dwelling unit.* In any society, a detailed classification of who lives with whom would require a rather long list of definitions. Here, we will classify family types that differ structurally and systematically ignoring random variations.

Four basic types emerge when members of the household are classified according to their status with respect to the household head: (1) a nuclear family, composed of husband, wife, and their unmarried children; (2) a patriarchal (lineal) extended family, composed of a man and his wife and their married sons and wives with their children; (3) a transient extended family, in which the male, who is the head of the household, his wife, and his unmarried children live together with either the man's or his wife's widowed parents and/or with their unmarried siblings; and

* In other contexts, the term *family* is sometimes used in a wider sense to include persons tied to each other by kinship but residing in different households. This study adopts the UN definition, stating that "a family cannot comprise more than one household" (United Nations, "Principles and Recommendations for the 1970 Population Censuses", 1969).

(4) a dissolved family or nonfamily household, in which one spouse is missing due to separation, divorce, death, and so forth.

This classification was not done mechanically, according to the number of generations or number of married couples and so forth, but was based on who was the head of the household. Although both patriarchal extended and transient families are three generation families, in distinguishing these two types of families, the emphasis was placed on who was the head of the family, the father or the son. We classified a family as being a patriarchal extended one when the patriarch owned the property and controlled the labor of all under his roof, whereas in the transient extended family, the son was the household head and chief breadwinner.

It was observed that 60 percent of all families lived in nuclear households, 19 percent were patriarchal extended, 13 percent transient extended, and 8 percent were either dissolved families or nonfamily households. As expected, the proportion of nuclear families decreased from 68 percent in the metropolitan areas to 55 percent in the villages. In spite of this pattern, however, patriarchal extended households were clearly the minority in rural areas, comprising one-fifth on the households in small towns and only one fourth in villages with less than 2,000 population. The national estimate of transient extended families (13 percent) did not vary by community size, this family type comprised virtually the same proportion in both urban and rural areas (see Table I). Let us now turn to the factors that produce and maintain certain family types.

Socioeconomic Correlates of Family Types

Our survey data yield results similar to studies carried out in other countries, showing that the extended household can stay together only so long as its land or other wealth can support it and it can offer adequate opportunities to the younger generation. Evidence of the relationship between amount of property and type of family is provided by data on occupation and family type.

Classification of families by male occupation shows, surprisingly, that the highest and lowest proportions of nuclear families are found in rural areas. In rural areas, the farmers—especially those who own the most land—generally live in extended families, whereas the landless farm workers have the largest proportion of nuclear families. The proportion of nuclear families is less than half (44 percent) among farmers, rises to

Table I

Family Types, by Place of Residence, in Turkey, 1968 (percent)

Family Type	Place of Residence: Metropolitan	Large City	City	Town	Village	Turkey
Nuclear	67.9	65.8	63.3	61.5	55.4	59.7
Patriarchal extended:	4.6	9.7	9.5	20.0	25.4	19.0
Household head plus married sons	0.5	1.6	0.5	4.0	5.6	3.9
Household head plus married son and unmarried children	2.2	4.0	3.6	8.6	10.5	7.9
Household head plus one married son	1.0	2.5	3.9	5.1	6.7	5.0
Joint (household head plus married brother)	0.1	0.1	0.7	1.2	1.9	1.3
Household head plus married daughter	0.8	1.5	0.8	1.1	0.7	0.9
Transient extended:	12.4	11.6	15.0	12.7	13.3	13.1
Household head's mother	3.8	4.4	6.3	5.4	6.5	5.7
Household head's father	0.0	0.5	0.7	0.4	0.9	0.7
Household head's unmarried siblings	1.4	1.1	0.9	0.6	0.9	1.0
Household head's mother and/or father, and/or unmarried sibling, and/or other relatives	2.8	3.9	4.8	4.0	4.1	3.9
Household head's wife's relatives	4.4	1.7	2.4	2.2	0.9	1.3
Dissolved or nonfamily household:	15.0	12.9	11.9	5.7	5.9	8.3
One parent, children	8.9	7.8	7.7	3.3	3.8	5.1
Unrelated household	6.1	5.1	4.2	2.4	2.1	3.2
Total:						
Percent	100.0	100.0	100.0	100.0	100.0	100.0
Number	545	1,012	743	461	1,715	4,476

Note: Totals slightly different from 100 due to rounding.

64 percent among share-croppers, and is extremely high among farm workers, rising to 79 percent. In urban areas, the proportion of nuclear families is highest (77 percent) among the professionals. Their economic independence from the parental household gives them freedom to form nuclear families at the time of marriage. The proportion of nuclear families is also high among workers (74 percent), decreasing to 69 percent among artisans and craftsmen. The relationship of property to family type can also be observed among businessmen, who have the highest proportion of extended families in urban areas. Among businessmen and industrial entrepreneurs, who are highly concentrated in the

largest cities, only 64 percent live in nuclear households. There is clearly a tendency for families owning more property to have an extended family system, whether or not industrialization and urbanization are involved. (See Table II.)

Table II

Family Types, by Occupational Groups, in Turkey, 1968 (percent)

Occupation	*Family Type*			*Total*	
	Nuclear	*Transient Extended*	*Patriarchal Extended*	*Percent*	*Number*
Commerce and businessmen	64.1	25.9	10.1	100.0	45
Professionals and administrators	76.9	8.5	14.2	100.0	51
Clerical	73.6	18.8	9.7	100.0	338
Artisans and craftsmen	68.7	17.8	18.6	100.0	630
Workers	72.3	11.0	16.7	100.0	522
Farmers	43.8	16.8	39.4	100.0	903
Sharecroppers	63.6	20.2	16.3	100.0	47
Agricultural workers	79.3	4.4	16.2	100.0	73
Unemployed, other	70.9	9.5	19.7	100.0	49
Total number	1,619	450	589	–	2,658

The survey data also show that extended families entail larger landholdings. The average size of a farm is 30 decares for nuclear families, whereas it rises to 127 decares among patriarchal extended families. Among families owning less than 10 decares of land, 59 percent live in nuclear households and only 22 percent live in patriarchal extended families, whereas among those owning more than 100 decares of land, this relationship is completely reversed, with 58 percent living in patriarchal extended families and 23 percent living in nuclear families. This overall correlation between size of land owned and size of family is also observed within each geographic region. (See Table III.)

Other socioeconomic variables, such as education and income level, do not show any consistent relationship with family type. The proportion of nuclear families is highest among illiterates and the highest educational group, whereas it is lowest among those with a middle-level education. Similarly, per capita family income, considered by itself, does not reveal any association with differences in family type. In towns and cities, no relationship is observed between income level and family types. In rural areas, high per capita family income is associated with the extended family form, whereas in metropolitan areas, families in high

Table III

Family Types, by Amount of Land Owned, in Turkey,[a] *1968 (percent)*

Amount of Land (decares)[b]	*Family Type*			*Total*	
	Nuclear	*Transient Extended*	*Patriarchal Extended*	*Percent*	*Number*
1–10	58.6	18.2	23.3	100.0	250
11–24	45.9	19.6	34.5	100.0	222
25–50	42.0	12.5	45.5	100.0	256
51–100	36.3	12.2	51.3	100.0	128
More than 100	22.6	19.2	58.1	100.0	83

$X^2 = 61$; $df = 15$; $P < .01$.

[a] Landless agricultural families are excluded.

[b] One decare = 1,000 square meters.

income brackets are usually nuclear. Thus, the association between variables, such as education and family income with family type, can only be understood with reference to the occupational groups, with their distinct characteristics of educational attainment and income level. For example, nuclear families predominate among farm workers and small farmers in rural areas and among unskilled laborers in urban areas, all of whom are mostly illiterate. The family type characteristic of professionals and civil servants in urban areas who have university education is also nuclear. On the other hand, extended families are prevalent among large landowners and those who own middle-sized farms in rural areas and among artisans, retailers, and so forth in the urban areas who have medium levels of education.

Most people, especially in rural areas, place a high value on the extended family. A very high proportion of peasants (75 percent), by their own admission, aspire to live in an extended family, which they see as an indication of prosperity and prestige. This apparent social emphasis on large families appears inconsistent with the vast number of nuclear families. But it is not, when we consider that only the wealthy landlords can afford large families; for the poor, lack of land makes the ideal difficult to achieve.

Rules of Residence and Family Cycle

Cross-sectionally, at any given point in time, a majority of Turkish families live in nuclear households. A very large majority live in extended households at the time of their marriage. However, during the lifetime of most couples, they live in different family types. A cross tabulation of current family type by the family type at marriage shows that a high percentage of families were at one time part of an extended family. Sixty-two percent of all families were patriarchal extended, and 14 percent were transient extended, at the time of their marriage; only 24 percent were formed as independent, neolocal nuclear families. Even among families that were nuclear at the time of the survey, only 37 percent were formed as nuclear households when they were first married. Our data show that newly married couples break away from the extended household and become independent nuclear families shortly after marriage. More than half of the families that were patriarchal extended at marriage became nuclear in less than four years; three-fourths did so in less than ten years time. Although demographic factors, such as death (16 percent) and migration (25 percent) are important in dissolution of the extended family, the most important reason given for the breakup was financial difficulties (42 percent) and internal family conflicts (17 percent).

In Turkey, especially in the villages, couples usually experience a cycle of family types. Patrilocality is the rule at marriage, and the young couple is expected to reside in the groom's parental home, thus becoming a part of the patriarchal extended family. Soon after marriage, however, the young man breaks away from his father's household to form his own nuclear family. After separation, when the man's own sons grow up and get married, they also reside at their father's household, for a time, forming a patriarchal extended family. This pattern is very clear and consisttent, especially in rural areas. We observe a cyclic development of the extended family, in which a married man passes through three stages of family life: within his father's household, in his own independent nuclear family, and as the patriarch household head of an extended family.

The major cause for leaving the parental household shortly after marriage appears to be the poverty of the family. If the father is landless or without other productive means, sons leave out of necessity; each son must find means to support his own nuclear family. If the father has a little land, married sons have to work for someone else as hired laborers or sharecroppers in the same village or in surrounding towns. When the family ceases to be the unit of production and when there are other ways to earn an income besides depending on family resources, the patriarchal extended family breaks down. Economic limitations prevent all but the fairly well-to-do from maintaining such extended households. It is not surprising then that extended households, functioning as common production and consumption units, form a small percentage of village households.

One might wonder why more couples do not establish a neolocal nuclear household at marriage rather than beginning as part of a patriarchal extended family and separating shortly thereafter. The answer lies in the traditional marriage customs, requiring expensive wedding ceremonies and the payment of bride-price. Traditional marriage rules and the extended family form are a series of functionally related phenomena. It is the father's duty to arrange the marriage of each of his sons, for it is very rare that the amount of money needed can be secured by the groom without the cooperation of his family. Since the marriage of the son is financed by the family—using the father's property and the labor of the other members of the household—the groom and his wife are obliged to stay and work in the father's house for some time after marriage. The married son is expected to support his father, at least until all his brothers get married.

Economic necessities are reflected in the area of attitudes and norms. A newly married couple is expected to follow the usual patrilocal pattern. Although in actual practice most families live in nuclear households, norms and values seem to idealize extended families. When the respondents were asked if they would like to live with their married sons in the future, 73 percent of men and 79 percent of women said yes. As would be expected, the proportion of affirmative responses varies by place of residence: 90 percent of men in rural areas, 66 percent of those in towns, 53 percent of those in cities, and 31 percent of men residing in the metropolitan areas of Ankara, Istanbul, and Izmir expressed this wish.

Formation of Marriage

Since the family plays an important role in marrying their offspring, it is not surprising that it also exerts a great influence in selecting marriage partners for their children. The extended family is not only the most important social unit but it is also the unit of economic production in agricultural areas. Marriage takes place by parental arrangement, since it involves not only the husband-wife relationship but the integration of the bride into the extended family. Consequently, it is expected that the choice of a spouse for the son or daughter will be made by the head of the family. If marriages are arranged by parents, then we can expect that they will also limit the possibilities for male-female acquaintance and will try to block opportunities for youngsters to meet future spouses.

Parents arrange a large majority of marriages in Turkey. Over two-thirds of the women in our sample in all places of residence and in all types of families said that their marriages had been arranged, with or without their consent (67 percent and 11 percent, respectively). Only 13 percent of the women said that they made their own choice, with their family's consent; 9 percent said that they had to "elope", since they could not convince their parents to agree to their own choice.

When men in the sample were asked about who made the final decision about their marriage, only half of them said that they had decided themselves. We also found that men who were able to open a new independent house at marriage were freer with regard to mate selection and marital decision than men who had to live in their father's house (see Table IV).

Table IV

Final Decision Maker in Choice of Spouse for Men, by Family Type, in Turkey, 1968 (percent)

Decision Maker	*Family Type*				
	Always Nuclear	*Currently Nuclear*	*Transient Extended*	*Patriarchal Extended*	*All Types*
Parents	12.0	37.6	43.2	50.3	38.3
Other relatives	21.8	8.4	5.3	6.6	8.1
Himself	64.3	51.9	49.5	41.4	51.6
Others	2.0	2.1	2.0	1.8	2.0
Total percent	100.0	100.0	100.0	100.0	100.0
Number	542	1,109	461	598	2,709

$X^2 = 113$; degrees of freedom (df) $= 9$; $P < .01$.

Since among extended families marriage is conceived as an alliance between two families and not simply as an agreement between two individuals, two other consequences emerge: economic transactions accompany marriage, and marriage among relatives is encouraged. The customs of bride-price payment and preferential marriage rules among certain relatives are means whereby the heads of families are able to control the marriage of their offspring. As can be seen from Tables V and VI, in half of the marriages, bride-price was paid, and one-third of all couples were relatives. Among the couples who were related, 78 percent were married to first cousins.

Our data reveal that among patriarchal extended families, the payment of bride-price is quite common, and the amount paid is very high. On the

Table V

Proportion of Related Couples, by Family Type and by Place of Residence, in Turkey, 1968 (percent)

Place of Residence	Family Type				
	Always Nuclear	*Currently Nuclear*	*Transient Extended*	*Patriarchal Extended*	*All Types*
Metropolitan	12.5	17.8	24.6	26.0	17.0
City	14.8	21.1	18.2	24.2	19.4
Town	11.4	27.3	22.4	17.6	21.3
Village	27.6	35.0	39.2	38.4	35.7
Turkey	20.2	29.0	31.9	34.3	29.2
Number	118	309	141	260	828

Table VI

Proportion of Women for Whom Bride-Price Was Paid at Marriage, by Family Type and by Place of Residence, in Turkey, 1968 (percent)

Place of Residence	Family Type				
	Always Nuclear	*Currently Nuclear*	*Transient Extended*	*Patriarchal Extended*	*All Types*
Metropolitan	8.5	31.4	28.5	26.0	19.0
City	34.7	45.9	31.9	47.9	40.7
Town	44.6	47.6	45.6	50.1	47.5
Village	58.2	60.4	61.1	68.8	63.3
Turkey	41.4	52.3	50.5	63.8	53.1
Number	279	583	274	503	1,639

other hand, in "always nuclear" families—currently nuclear families that were established neolocally—bride-price is paid only in few instances, and the amount is negligible. Apart from being highly associated with the patriarchal extended family system, bride-price is also found to be substantial where the economic contribution of the bride through labor is quite high.

This finding supports the view that sees bride-price as a compensation for the loss of work represented by the loss of a daughter. The custom of bride-price payment was most widespread in the rural areas of Eastern Turkey, the Black Sea coast, and Central Anatolia, where it is known that the economic contribution of women in agriculture is quite high. The importance of this marriage custom seems to have declined greatly in urban centers, as well as in the rural parts of the Mediterranean region and Western Turkey, where agriculture is highly mechanized. It can be concluded, then, that with urbanization and mechanized farming, bride-price will no longer be functional but will carry a symbolic meaning for some time and will soon disappear.

Household Types and Intrafamily Relations

Family types defined as *always nuclear*, *currently nuclear*, *transient extended*, and *patriarchal extended* not only denote the forms of household but cover the status and roles of the family members. It might be expected, therefore, that these different types of families will also differ significantly in authority pattern and role structure. This is indeed the case. In patriarchal families, inheritance, succession, economic resources, and social status are all concentrated in the hands of male heads of households, who, in turn, have absolute authority over the other members of the family. The responses to the question, "Who has the most say in your family?" well reflects the power structure in the family. Although 95 percent of male respondents in nuclear families stated that they were the chief decision makers in their families, this proportion decreased to 28 percent among patriarchal extended families. (See Table VII)

In an attempt to measure intrafamily relations on three different dimensions of family life, a "family modernity scale" was formed,

Table VII

Who Has the Most "Say" in the Family, by Family Type, in Turkey, 1968 (percent)

Has Most "Say"	*Family Type*				
	Always Nuclear	*Currently Nuclear*	*Transient Extended*	*Patriarchal Extended*	*All Types*
Husband (himself)	94.3	95.2	75.2	28.2	74.2
Wife	1.2	0.8	0.6	0.4	0.7
Husband's father	0.1	2.0	8.6	61.5	18.4
Husband's mother	0.7	0.4	10.1	4.1	2.9
Wife's parents	0.0	0.0	3.1	0.4	0.5
Others in the family	3.6	1.6	2.4	4.4	3.3
Total percent	99.9*	100.0	100.0	99.0*	100.0
Number	518	1,069	441	573	2,601

$X^2 = 1{,}524$; $df = 24$; $P < .01$.

* Columns 1 and 4 differ slightly from 100 due to rounding.

utilizing responses to a series of 16 questions. The three dimensions were classified as follows: (1) the decision-making process, (2) sex role ideologies and the degree of dominance patterns, and (3) husband-wife companionship—joint participation or segregation of conjugal roles. In both urban and rural areas, the patriarchal extended families were the most traditional and nuclear families the least traditional, as measured by this scale. Due to the conventional association between economic resources and authority, power and social status are concentrated in the hands of the male heads of households. In the patriarchal extended family, all members are under the authority of the patriarch. All the monetary and other decisions concerning the family are made by him. (See Table VIII)

Table VIII

Scores of Family Modernity Scale, by Family Type, in Turkey, 1968 (percent)

Scale Score	*Family Type*				
	Always Nuclear	*Currently Nuclear*	*Transient Extended*	*Patriarchal Extended*	*All Types*
Modern (21–34)	28.5	16.9	14.9	3.6	15.1
Transitional (35–42)	28.3	37.8	31.4	16.3	28.7
Traditional (43–64)	43.2	45.2	53.8	80.1	56.2
Total percent	100.0	100.0	100.0	100.0	100.0
Number	680	1,183	554	798	3,215

$X^2 = 382$; $df = 6$; $P < .01$.

In the nuclear family, however, husband-wife relations are relatively more egalitarian, and the wife may participate in decision making. However, the most universal characteristic of all types of Turkish families seem to be the subordination of women. This is especially true for patriarchal extended families in rural areas, where bride-price is paid at marriage and the amount of it is substantial. Despite the substantial economic contribution and hard work of the bride, her status is low, since she had no control over the produce of her labor and receives no retribution.

Even when urban rural residence is held constant, power structure in the family and family modernity are highly associated with family type.

Conclusion

Our data show that the creation and maintenance of certain types of families are usually shaped by the primary property and work relations. When income and occupation come to depend on factors not controlled by the extended family, as when wage labor becomes common, this creates the possibility of change in the extended family. Independent nuclear families become more prevalent, whether or not urbanization, industrialization, or modernization are involved. However, industrialization and urbanization increase the proportion of nuclear families in the sense that these processes necessarily increase the proportion of people who earn their livelihood from wage labor.

Our data also reveal that once certain family types are formed, they, in turn, influence, and to a great degree even determine, the intrafamily relations and individual behavior of family members with respect to marriage patterns, formation of marriage, age at marriage, family authority patterns, and husband-wife relationship.

The connection between family structure and fertility are not very clear. Although it is commonly believed that the extended family, which features large households and encourages high fertility, is the premodern form, while the nuclear form, with small households and low fertility, is the family of modern industrial society, there exists little sociological evidence to support this belief.

In Turkey, fertility is high among the nuclear families of agricultural laborers and unskilled industrial workers, whereas it is much lower among the urban extended families of men in commerce and business. Both the decline in fertility and the existence and prevalence of certain family types are closely related to the overall process of social and economic development. But the interrelationships and the interaction between family structure and demographic changes are not yet well understood. Further research directed toward the mechanisms involved in changes in which the family is thought to be acting as an intermediate agent is needed.

ÇİĞDEM KÂĞITÇIBAŞI

VALUE OF CHILDREN, WOMEN'S ROLE AND FERTILITY IN TURKEY

INTRODUCTION

Women's role in family and society has always been intimately associated with childbearing and fertility. In fact, women's liberation movements in many parts of the world have attempted to undermine this close association and to propose additional non-childbearing-roles for women. Yet, a thorough understanding of the complex interrelationships between women's concepts of and attitudes toward children, and their fertility behavior is largely lacking and is needed for a better assessment of women's roles.

The Turkish Value of Children (VOC) study aims, among other objectives, to throw some light on the relationships between the attitudinal and behavioral correlates of fertility in the context of women's intra- and extra-familial roles. Some of the findings of the study examining these interrelationships will be discussed in this paper.

THE VOC PROJECT

The VOC Project is a nine-country comparative social psychological study which has evolved through three phases. The first phase, initiated by the East-West Center of the University of Hawaii (Fawcett, 1972), was carried out in six countries: The Republic of China, Japan, Korea, the Philippines, Thailand and Hawaii. Small samples of parents were used in this phase (Arnold et al., 1975; Bulatao, 1975; Arnold and Fawcett, 1975; Buripakdi, 1977; Wu, 1977).

In the second phase of the project mostly nationally representative samples of 2000—3000 respondents were used. The countries which participated in this phase are Indonesia, Korea, the Philippines, the Republic of China, Singapore, Thailand, Turkey, Germany and the U. S.

[1] The principal investigators include Russell Darroch and Masri Singarihmbun (Indonesi), Sung Jin Lee (Korea), Rodolfo Bulatao, (Philippines), Tom Sun and Tson-Shien Wu (Republic of China), Betty Chung and Peter Chen (Singapore), Chalio Buri Pakdi and Nibhon Debavalya (Thailand), Çiğdem Kâğıtçıbaşı (Turkey), Lois

The third phase, which is about to start, involves cross-cultural comparisons based on the second phase data.

The Turkish VOC Study is one of the nine comparative country studies comprising the total VOC Project. The Turkish project started in 1974 with an exploratory pilot study, conducted with a selected sample of 189 married respondents. Based on this work, the nationwide study was carried out in 1975.

Conceptual Framework

The concept of the "value of children" has been used in attempts to understand the determinants of fertility. Especially within economic and social psychological approaches the "value" that children have for their parents has been given special attention.

Within the social psychological framework, the value of children for parents assumes importance in terms of the motivational dynamics underlying fertility behavior. As the needs of individuals are emphasized, needs satisfied by children come to the fore. The theoretical framework for the social psychological approach has been provided by Fawcett (1972), Hoffman and Hoffman (1973), Berelson (1973) and Arnold, et al. (1975).

The value of children is conceptualized in functional terms as the sum-total of costs and benefits that parents obtain from having children. These benefits and costs, in turn, are viewed as complex variables, including at least three dimensions, namely, psychological/emotional, social and economic. Thus the VOC concept refers to the perceived difference between these various benefits and costs.

A number of positive and negative values of children have been assessed. These values are conceptualized as intervening between antecedent background and social psychological variables and the consequent fertility-related outcome.

Hoffman (USA) and James T. Fawcett and Fred Arnold, Brian Flay and Esther R. Mechler (Germany).

The Turkish VOC Project has been supported by the International Development Research Centre of Canada.

Method

In the Turkish VOC study interviews were conducted with a nationally representative sample of 2305 married respondents. Of these 1763 (76.5%) were females and 542 (23.5%) were males.

The sampling design utilized was multi-stage stratified random sampling. Stratification was done in terms of levels of development. Three different groups of provinces namely developed, intermediate and less developed, were delineated on the basis of composite socio-economic indices (DPT, 1972, p. 12—15 and 54—59). In addition to these three categories the three metropolitan areas of Istanbul, Ankara and Izmir were each treated as a "self-representative area". Within the three levels of development, the urban populations were further stratified into four strata in terms of their populations, excluding again the three metropolitan areas. Rural areas having a population of less than 2000 comprised the fifth stratum. The second and third stage sampling units were blocks and subblocks drawn systematically from these strata.

From the households selected according to the above procedure married respondents were interviewed. The criteria for eligibility required that the respondent be living together with the spouse for at least six months, and the wife had to be under the age of 40. The average interviewing time was one hour and 15 minutes.

The questionnaire used in the national survey was developed on the basis of the experience with the previous Turkish pilot questionnaire as well as with the questionnaire applications in the other VOC countries. A core questionnaire was thus developed in order to allow for cross-national comparisons.

In final form the questionnaire contained 103 questions. The topics covered were the following: Parity (existing number of children); desired number of children; number and sex preferences; ideas about quality in children; general values; financial expectations from children; birth control (attitudes, knowledge and use); decision contexts (belief in internal vs. external control of reinforcement); sex roles, education and occupation; mobility; mass-media participation; family type; income.

Descriptive Characteristics[2]

Age

The mean age of the respondents was 29 for females and 34 for males. Thus, this was a somewhat young sample as a result of our screening criteria. Almost half (47.7%) of the women respondents had married between the ages of 15—17. 30.5% were between 18 and 20 at first marriage; and 8.6% each married either at less than 15 years of age or between 21 and 23. Marriages at 24—26 were only 3.3% and all those at later ages totaled a mere 1.3%. These figures show the predominantly early marriage age for women in Turkey and have significant implications both for fertility and women's status in the Turkish family. Marriage at such young ages lengthens the childbearing period of the woman, and contributes to her high fertility. Having many children, in turn, keeps the woman tied down and thus unavailable for non-child bearing functions outside the home. Also, the very young age of the child-bride contributes to her low status in her husband's household vis-à-vis her husband and in-laws, thus reinforcing the traditional intra-family status hierarchy.

Education

67.3% of the female respondents (52.8% in the sample) had no formal schooling; 16.3% (23.5% weightless) were primary school graduates and only 8.6% (11.9% weightless) had a high school education or more (the mean was 1.9 (2.7 weightless) years of formal education). The general education level of the males was higher. 52.8% (33.3% weightless) of the males had no schooling; 24.0% (34.4% weightless) graduated from primary school; and 17.7% (13.3% weightless) had high school education or higher. The mean for male education was 3.1 (4.4 weightless) years.

These figures clearly show the prevalent low levels of education and are similar to some other national survey results (e.g. Tuncer, 1976, p. 106). The extremely low female education level is striking, with obvious implications for the status of women in society. Thus, the level of formal

[2] As national representation is sought in the Turkish VOC study, all the figures given in this paper are weighted population figures, unless indicated otherwise.

education among Turkish women does not appear to be much different from that of other Moslem countries in which very low levels of female education are consistently reported (Timur, 1977).

Employment

74.9% of the women were not working at the time of interviewing. Of these, only 20.8% had ever worked since marriage. 36.5% of those who were working were family workers, not earning money but contributing to the family income, or were doing part time work at home. One important reason for the obtained high percentage of non-working woman is the fact that in the rural context most women who are in fact working consider themselves to be "not-working" (Kâğıtçıbaşı, 1977, p. 42).

16.7% of the females and 8.4% of the males were unskilled laborers. This was due mainly to a higher percentage of women who were working as landless agricultural laborers (10.3%) as compared with men (1.4%) who were doing such work. More men, on the other hand, were factory workers. Entrepreneurs such as small store owners were also mainly males. Some professions demanding high academic training, such as university professors were equally distributed among men and women though both rated very low (3%).

Income

Generally low family income was reported by the respondents, the mode being 1000—2500 TL per month (between $ 700 and $1700 per annum in line with $ 940 annual per capita income in Turkey for 1977). Very small percentages were reported above 6.000 TL per month. These low income levels probably reflect only actual cash income and not additional income in goods.

Family Type and Mobility

Three main family type categories were delineated with subcategories within each. These are nuclear, patriarchally extended and transient extended. The main difference between patriarchally extended and transient extended family types is whether the household head is the married son or his father. The latter case is typically a patriarchally extended family, whereas the former is a transient extended family. A transient extended family is on its way to becoming a nuclear family. Patriarchally extended families comprised 19.5% and transient extended 16.6% of all the families.

Over half of the respondents showed no mobility or linear mobility (within similarly populated dwelling areas, such as small town→small town). 24.4% of the total population were villagers who had never lived in an urban area. This constituted 74.4% of all the villagers. 36.6% were residents of small towns and villages, who had no urban living experience. As many as 35.5% of the respondents, on the other hand, had migrated from villages and small towns into the larger cities and the metropolitan areas.

Parity

The number of living children reported ranged from 0 to 13, the mean being 2.8. 76.8% of the respondents had 1 to 4 children while only 15% had more. Those without children comprised 8.2% of the total. 35.6% of the female respondents had children who died after live birth and 37.9% had pregnancies not resulting in live birth.

General Values

Even though most of the questions concerned attitudes and behavior related to children, some more general value questions were also asked of the respondents. Responses to these will be presented here briefly.

Life Values

Of the various values presented, two most important ones were chosen. Table I gives the values chosen as the most or second most important by the respondents.

Clear cut sex differences are seen in some of the values ranked as most or second most important. The most striking difference is seen in "being close to spouse" which, together with "having a happy home", is of the most importance for women, whereas for men it is hardly important. Though "having a happy home" is the most often chosen value for men, also, it is of much less importance for men relative to women. These findings point to the home-bound role of women and their inferior, dependent status vis-à-vis their husbands. Men endorse more frequently values implying social recognition such as "achievement", "to be accepted by others" and, more traditionally, "continuation of family name" and "to be remembered after death". The latter values have implications for fertility especially in terms of boy preference. Finally, "financial security" is of great relevance, being even more important for men, who are considered responsible for the financial well-being of the family.

Table I

*First and Second Most Important Values**

	Men %	*Women %*	*Relative Weight***
To Have a Happy Home	45.1	61.0	53.5
To be Close to Spouse	22.4	61.1	42.9
Financial Security	35.4	26.8	30.8
Carry on Family Name	29.3	13.5	20.9
To Be Remembered After Death	17.9	13.9	15.6
To Achieve Something, To Succeed	20.5	6.2	13.4
To Be Accepted by Others	18.8	6.9	12.4
Not To Be Alone, To Have Friends	5.7	4.7	5.3
To Have Fun and Entertainment	4.0	3.4	3.7

(x^2 significant at beyond the .001 level)

* In this table and the following ones, more than one response was coded for each respondent, thus, percentages add up to more than 100.

** In this table and the following ones relative weight refers to the weight (%) of that category for the total group.

In summary, through 1st and 2nd choices of people among general life values two different patterns emerged characterizing men and women. Their subjective values, in fact, appear to reflect their generally different life styles, outlooks and roles.

Internal vs. External Control

Another significant sex difference appeared in belief in internal versus external control of reinforcement. Belief in internal control of reinforcement, after Rotter (1966), means a tendency to assume full responsibility for one's actions and lot in life contrasted with a tendency to attribute this responsibility to an outside agent, such as God, fate, other people, etc. which indicates belief in external control. Thus, belief in internal control appears to imply an autonomous, self-reliant, active behavioral tendency, whereas belief in external control implies a passive, fatalistic outlook.

On the three items measuring this variable, women consistently demonstrated more belief in external control than men (t-tests significant at beyond the $p < .001$ level for all three items). The implication of this finding for differential individual modernity, varying world views and roles of men and women are obvious. It fits in with a previous finding (Kâğıtçıbaşı, 1973) of greater belief in external control among high school girls than among boys. This obtained sex difference is most probably due to the differential socialization of girls and boys in Turkish society, where more autonomy, responsibility, self-reliance and freedom are expected of the boys than of the girls.

Table II

Intra-Family Decision Making

	1: Mostly the Wife	*2: Tog-gether*	*3: Mostly the Hus-band*	$\bar{X}$ *for women*	*SD for women*	$\bar{X}$ *for men*	*SD for men*	*t*	*p*
	%	%	%						
Who decides about buying something expensive?	8.6	20.5	69.5	2.59	0.72	2.70	0.57	8.45	.001
Who decides about how many children to have?	12.5	38.4	44.6	2.37	0.91	2.55	0.84	11.08	.001
Who decides about using B.C.?	22.6	42.4	33.9	2.03	0.70	2.14	0.50	9.38	.001
When there is a disagreement about an important decision?	4.9	13.2	80.2	2.72	0.60	2.84	0.41	11.80	.001

Family Dynamics

A number of questions inquired into family dynamics and decision processes. Tables II and III give the questions and their relevant statistics.

As can be seen from table II, in answers dealing with decision making within the family there are consistent sex differences in the relatively greater frequency of reporting male decision making by men than by women. This difference may be due to actual differences in the perception of power relations. On the other hand, it may, at least partially, be the result of social desirability or the tendency to appear more powerful than one really is. Regardless of this difference, however, the more important finding appears to be the consistently high frequency with which both men and women report greater male-decision making rather than female decision making in the home. This was expected and fits in with other results reported earlier with similar implications for sex-based status differences in the family.

If different values are attributed to children by men and women, these could throw some light on the different needs of men and women.

Table III

Communication and Role Sharing Between Spouses

	No %	*Yes* %	$\bar{X}$ *for women*	*SD for women*	$\bar{X}$ *for men*	*SD for men*	*t*	*p*
Have you talked with your spouse about how many children he/she wants?	36.2	63.8	1.65	0.48	1.63	0.49	2.10	.05
	Never	Rarely	Sometimes	Regularly				
Does your husband help with the housework?	36.2	17.4	39.7	7.4				
	No	Yes						
Do you do things together with your spouse outside the house?	33.2%	66.8%						

Values Related to Children

Furthermore, if different values are attributed by parents to sons and daughters, knowing these could contribute to a better understanding of the pressures and expectations playing a part in the socialization and eventual status of boys and girls.

Advantages and Disadvantages of Children

Some of the items dealing with the value of children will now be presented with these questions in mind. Table IV presents the spontaneously given advantages and disadvantages of children grouped into a number of main categories.

When asked, people are able to verbalize a great number and variety of advantages and disadvantages of children (50 different codes were needed each for the advantages and disadvantages). The richness of these spontaneous responses alone shows that nothing can replace a child. This is especially noticeable in the perceived advantages of children.

As can be seen from table IV, for both men and women the most frequently mentioned advantage of children is their providing primary group ties and love, which is even more prominent for women. This is followed by the security that children provide for their parents, again being more noticeable for women. The utilitarian value of children (such as their household help) is also more emphasized by women who probably benefit from such help more. On the other hand, expansion of self through children (such as continuation of one's name) and children providing adult status and social acceptance appear to be more salient for men. The stimulation, fun and joy that children provide is also somewhat more salient for men than for women who are rather more burdened by children. This is apparent from the disadvantages of children emphasized much more by women, namely, restrictions on parent's freedom and unpleasant aspects of childrearing. In fact, expect for the economic disadvantages of having children, which is the most salient category for both sexes but is emphasized more sharply by men, all the disadvantages are more salient for women.

The more frequent perception of children's disadvantages by women is also seen in the answers to some other questions and can be considered a general finding of the study. It may be interpreted in terms of women

Table IV

Percentages of Spontaneously given Advantages and Disadvantages of Children by Men and Women

Advantages	*Men* %	*Women* %	*Relative Weight* %	*Disadvantages*	*Men* %	*Women* %	*Relative Weight* %
Primary Group Ties, Affection, Love	41.4	46.0	43.8	*Economic*	58.6	41.8	49.6
love and companionship while young*				Financial cost, general or specific			
Make a family				Cost of education			
Security	26.1	32.0	29.2	*Concern about the Child*	30.3	32.4	31.4
security in old age				Fear of doing a bad job			
(general/financial)				Worry/Responsibility (emotional)			
Stimulation, Novelty, Fun	25.7	22.0	23.7	*Restrictions on Parents' Freedom*	17.9	34.9	27.0
activity, joy pleasure from watching them grow				They are a lot of work			
				Time, attention, inconvenience			
Social Definition and Adult Status	20.8	17.6	19.2	*Unpleasant Aspects of Child Rearing*	10.7	24.2	17.8
Parenthood is socially expected useful activity				I hate disciplining			
				Noise, disorder, fighting			
Utilitarian	15.4	19.0	17.3	*Health*	0.9	6.0	3.6
help in household chores brings income				Being pregnant			
				Having an abnormal child			
Expansion of Self	22.1	11.3	16.4	*Marital Strains*	1.4	1.0	1.2
family continuity				Disagreements over children			
carry on family name				Children make divorce difficult			
Morality	15.7	4.4	9.7	*Social Issues*	0	0.3	0.1
Altruism				Overpopulation			
Religion							
Creativity, Accomplishment, Competence	5.2	3.5	4.3	*Miscellaneous*	2.1	1.6	1.9
various achievement				When they are unloving/absent			
satisfaction from having good job				No desire to have children			
Influence	0.2	1.1	0.6				
To have control over their development							
Social comparison	0	0.3	0.2				
competition							
No Advantages	1.5	3.4	2.6	*No Disadvantages*	18.3	10.5	14.1

(for both advantages and disadvantages are significant at beyond the .001 level)
Typical examples for the category

carrying the burden of childcare in the Turkish society. This appears to be a basic factor underlying the rather sharp sex-role differentiation within the family, as well.

The relatively greater awareness of children's disadvantages on the part of women must underlie the fact that smaller numbers of children are desired by women than by men. For example, the average desired number of children for women is 3.9 whereas it is 4.4 for men, the difference being highly significant ($t = 2.81$, $p < .005$). The same type of difference is also seen in ideal number of children (4.38 for women and 5.7 for men; $t = 3.82$, $p < .001$).

Wanting and Not Wanting Another Child

The two most important reasons for wanting and not wanting another child throw further light on the childrearing role of the woman and her status in the family (Table V). Starting with reasons for *not* wanting another child, we see that women's responses fit in with their above-stated perceptions of the general disadvantages of children. Specifically, another child requiring a lot of work and constricting freedom are reasons given more frequently by mothers than by fathers. For both sexes financial burden of another child is the most relevant reason, being even more pronounced among the mothers.

As for reasons for wanting another child, noticeable differences exist between women and men in three reasons. For men, to carry on the family name is the most important reason for wanting another child. This social-traditional function of the child appears to be a "male" value as is also evident from the general advantages mentioned before. It is inherently related to wanting another child in order to have a son, holding the third place in importance for both men and women. Wanting another child to have a daughter is of noticeably less significance, especially for men. This fits in with 73.7% son preference contrasted by 21% girl preference in the whole group, as assessed by another question. These findings undoubtedly provide clear evidence for the differential value and status of the two sexes in Turkish society.

For women old age security is the most important reason for wanting another child, showing their basic economic insecurity. For men, also, this is the second most important reason. As we will see shortly, this old age security value of children has special implications for son preference, higher status of the male and for fertility, in general.

Table V

Reasons for Wanting and not Wanting Another Child

Reasons for Wanting	*Men* %	*Women* %	*Reasons for not Wanting*	*Men* %	*Women* %
Old Age Security	31	40	Financial Burden	35	44
To Bring Spouses Closer	18	33	Fear of Insufficient Care and Attention	31	28
Carry on Family Name	31	14	Discipline Problems	26	22
To Have a Son	22	23	Worry About Children's Health	20	25
To Enjoy Seeing Children Grow	16	12	Would be a Lot of Work	18	26
Financial Help Now	26	23	Overpopulation	22	8
Fun to Have Children Around	14	12	Difficult for Wife to Work	19	17
To Have Someone to Love	13	11	Wouldn't be As Free	11	14
For Siblings	6	9	Too Old to Have a Child	10	8
To Have a Daughter	7	11	Would Have Less Time for Spouse	6	9
For Help in Household Chores	9	11			
To Induce Men to Work More	7	3			

(x^2 for reasons for both wanting and not wanting are significant at beyond the .001 level)

Of special interest is women's second most important reason for wanting another child (which is almost as high as the first), namely, to bring the spouse closer. The very noticeable sex difference in this variable shows that it is women who feel this need rather than men. In the interviews this need was sometimes reflected in such expressions as to have a child to bring the husband back home. This has implications for the home-bound, dependent and inferior position of the woman, as discussed before in relation to general life values. It also points to a rather important function of childbearing, not usually mentioned in literature, in strengthening the tie between the spouses and raising the value of the wife to the husband.

Sex Preference

Reasons for wanting a son or a daughter point to the sex-specific satisfactions that children provide their parents. The differential values of girls and boys are consequently, implied (Table VI and VII).

As seen in tables VI and VII the distributions of the spontaneously given reasons for wanting a son and a daughter are quite different. Even though many similarly important reasons are given for wanting a son, forming an even distribution, only two prominent reasons are sharply differentiated from the rest for wanting a daughter. One of these two is the girl's personal qualities (such as girls are more understanding, soft, lovable, mother companion etc.) which is very prominent and almost twice as important for the mother as for the father. The other is girls' utilitarian value of household help, being about equally relevant for both parents.

Table VI

Important Reasons for Wanting a Son

	Men %	*Women %*	*Relative Weight*
Financial Help in Future	29.2	31.7	30.6
Carry on Family Name	34.6	18.5	26.0
Personal Qualities	22.9	26.7	24.9
Father Companion			
Maintain ties to the Family			
Financial Help Now	23.2	24.9	24.1
Easier to Raise	18.0	20.9	19.5
Can take care of himself			
Have more opportunities			
Expectations	23.2	12.1	17.4
For the country			
Education			
Boys Preferred by Society			
Traditional Role	9.4	11.5	10.6
Protect Family Psychologically			
Same Sex Identification	0.8	7.4	4.2
For Father			
To have someone like me			
Sex Balance	1.3	3.7	2.5
Miscellaneous			
Positive Feeling for Boys	4.0	4.5	4.2

(x^2 is significant at beyond the .001 level)

Table VII

Important Reasons for Wanting a Daughter

	Men %	*Women %*	*Relative Weight*
Personal Qualities	44.5	80.8	63.8
Mother companion			
Stay closer when older			
More lovable, understanding			
Help in the House	42.1	43.3	42.7
Sex Balance	13.6	3.9	8.4
Traditional Role	7.6	3.3	5.3
See her grow up and have children			
Less financial burden			
Social Returns	5.2	2.4	3.7
Meeting new people through their marriage			
Increase population			
Easier to Raise	2.0	3.5	2.8
More obedient			
Don't have to be educated			
Expectations	2.3	0.4	1.5
See her achieve something			
Economic Benefits	1.4	1.2	1.3
Bride Price			
Miscellaneous	7.0	3.3	5.1
Not very important to have a girl			
I just want a girl			

(x^2 is significant at beyond the .001 level)

Boys, on the other hand, are wanted for the many satisfactions that they provide; in other words, their instrumental value is high. This value is realized in such divergent directions as providing financial help in the future and while they are young, carrying on the family name (especially important for fathers), their personal qualities and their being easier to raise than daughters.

This last point needs some elaboration. Why should it be easier to raise a boy than a girl? The answer most probably lies in the widely held concern with the reputation of a girl, in the value put on her chastity and the need to protect it. This generally felt need to protect the girl has been proposed (e. g. Kâğıtçıbaşı, 1977; Meeker, 1976) to further reinforce the restricted, home-bound role of the woman and her expected dependency on the man. Many responses expressing the belief that men have more opportunities or that life is easier for a man reflect the widespread perception of status differences between the two sexes.

Aspirations and Expectations Related to Children

Ideal images of sons and daughters spontaneously verbalized by parents further add to our understanding of sex-role differences (Table VII). Education, achievement and work are more often aspired for the son than

Table VIII

How Would You Like Your Son/Daughter To Be

Desired Qualities	*Son*			*Daughter*		
	Men %	*Women* %	*Relative Weight*	*Men* %	*Women* %	*Relative Weight*
Morality	78.1	54.9	65.8	56.7	37.4	46.5
Honest, responsible, reliable trustworthy, dependable						
Be useful to society						
Religious						
Educated	34.8	44.5	39.9	24.8	37.1	31.4
Conjugal Family Roles	6.2	10.2	8.4	39.7	41.7	40.8
Be a good spouse, have a happy marriage						
Achievement and Work	31.7	41.8	37.1	17.3	13.1	15.1
Successful (specific career achievement), make something of himself						
Hard working, set goals and accomplish them; pursue what they want; productive						
Extended Family Ties	13.7	14.6	14.2	17.3	13.1	15.1
Be good to parents, respectful, loyal						
Well Mannered, Polite	8.7	12.5	10.8	11.1	13.7	12.5
Modern Personality Traits	7.7	6.0	6.8	5.9	7.8	6.7
Not dependent on others, self reliant, confident, serious, straightforward, realistic, commonsense wise						
Other Personality Traits	7.0	5.9	6.5	5.6	3.9	4.7
Well liked, accepted by others						
Friendly, nice personality, get along with others						
Superficials	0.6	0.6	0.6	0.4	1.8	1.1
Neat, well-groomed						
Handsome, good-looking, pretty						

(x^2 for both sons and daughters are significant at beyond the .001 level)

for the daughter. The conjugal family role (having a happy marriage), on the other hand is distinctly aspired more for the daughter than for the son.

An interesting difference observed between women and men in their aspirations for both their sons and daughters is the relatively greater emphasis women put on education compared with the greater importance men attribute to mortality. It appears that women aspire for their children to acquire the means for status improvement that they, themselves, lack to a great extent. Yet, women's aspirations for achievement/work for their sons is greater than that of their husbands, but not for their daughters. This is evidence that the traditional familial role of the woman is well accepted by women.

Table IX

The Kind of Economic or Practical Help Expected from Children While they are Growing Up or After they are Adults (%)

Type of Help	*Expect from Sons*				*Expect from Daughters*			
	Men		*Women*		*Men*		*Women*	
	Yes	*No*	*Yes*	*No*	*Yes*	*No*	*Yes*	*No*
Give part of their salary to you when they begin working	67	33	77	23	26	74	60	40
Help support their younger brothers and sisters through school	87	13	87	13	67	33	76	24
Contribute money in family emergencies	88	12	95	5	62	38	85	15
Help around the house	80	20	65	35	91	9	94	6
Support you financially when you grow old	88	12	93	7	67	33	80	20

Table X

How much would You Expect to Rely on Your Sons/Daughters for Financial Support when You Grow Old?

	Men		*Women*	
	Sons	*Daughters*	*Sons*	*Daughters*
A great deal	30	16	33	19
Average	17	16	16	12
A little	7	10	14	17
None	21	43	12	27
Depends on children's economic situation	8	6	10	8
Depends on children's willingness	4	2	6	7
Depends on parents situation	4	2	5	4

Ideas about how parents would like their sons/daughters to be when they grow up may be related to their expectations from their children. These expectations have been conceptualized as mainly material/instrumental benefits. As can be seen from tables VIII and IX, material contributions are expected more of the sons than of the daughters. Expectations from daughters pertain mainly to household help and to emergency situations. The *degree* of reliance on sons is also greater than on daughters. These differential expectations from sons and daughters appear to be inherent in the values attributed to them by parents.

INTERRELATIONSHIPS AMONG BACKGROUND VARIABLES, VALUES AND FERTILITY

Many of the perceived advantages and disadvantages of children discussed before appear to have significant relations to some of the background variables. Furthermore, certain values, social psychological and family dynamics variables also relate meaningfully to each other and to fertility outcome. We will deal with these relationships for the whole group.

Considering first the relationship between the level of development of the respondents' dwelling area and the advantages of children cited, we find that "general security in old age" decreases in importance as we proceed from underdeveloped to metropolitan areas. It is mentioned by 23.6% of the respondents from less developed residential areas; by 20% of those who live in intermediately developed areas; by 16.5% of those who live in developed areas and only by 10.7% of those who live in metropolitan centers.

Whether the respondent has been nonmobile in a village or a small town or whether he has shown any rural→urban mobility changes his perceptions of the advantages of children considerably. "Primary group ties, affection and love" is mentioned more and more as we proceed from a village to a metropolitan center (mentioned by 39.5% of nonmobile village residents and 72.3% of nonmobile metropolitan center residents). For the mobile population the more upward they move on the urbanity scale the more their perceptions of the advantages shift from utilitarian to psychological and love oriented ones. Among those who have shown mobility from a village to a metropolitan center "primary group ties, affection and love" is mentioned much more frequently (68.7%) than the village inhabitants (39.5%). The same pattern is seen in small town to metropolitan center and medium size city to metropolitan center migration also. "Security in old age" and "utilitarian values" of children are mentioned by 52.0% and 31.5% of nonmobile village residents respectively and by only 35.1% and 14.7% of those who have migrated to a metropolitan center respectively.

Among women's occupations, for the unskilled agricultural laborers and family workers "security in old age" (mentioned by 41.3% and, 45.1% respectively) is nearly as important as "primary group ties, affection and love" (mentioned by 45.7% and 59.3% respectively). As these are rural occupations, "utilitarian" values of children are also cited frequently by those who fall in these occupation categories (29.5% and 23.3% respectively), while they are not mentioned at all by those in urban occupations, such as professionals or managers in public and private sectors. "Small entrepreneurs" value mostly "security in old age" (52.0%), then "primary group ties, affection and love" (44.2%) and utilitarian values of children (39.7%).

Respondents' income is also related with the advantages cited. As income increases, "expansion of the self", "primary group ties, affection and love" increase in salience, while "security in old age" and "utilitarian advantages of children" are mentioned less. Among the "noncash income" group security in old age is very salient as these respondents live in rural areas where they have no social security (71.1%)

Both wife's and husband's education significantly relate to the advantages cited. "Primary group ties, affection and love", which is the most salient value for all education groups, increases as education increases. On the other hand, the importance of "security in old age" decreases as both wife's and husband's education increase ($r = -.18$).[3] Wife's education also shows a negative relation with numbers of children wanted ($r = -.11$), even when the influence of age, income or family type is controlled. The relationship between numbers of children wanted and the status of wife's occupation becomes significant ($r = -.09$) when the effect of wife's education is controlled. The pattern is the same for the husband. High status of husband's occupation is related to low number preference ($r = -.14$).

Education is also strongly related to parity (number of already existing children) and to desired number of children. When the effect of age is controlled, the correlation between wife's education and parity

[3] All the correlation coefficients (r) reported in this paper are significant at or beyond the .05 level.

increases from −.26 to −.31; that between husband's education and parity increases from −.22 to −.29. Both husband's and wife's education correlate −.12 with number of desired children.

Of the general values assessed, "being close to spouse" is negatively related to parity and family planning and positively to child birth intention. Thus especially women who have few children think that an additional child contributes to the bond between spouses. "Importance of continuing the family name", on the other hand, relates positively to parity and boy preference. "Importance of economic security" relates positively to expectation of financial help from children (r = .15) and to ideal (r = .11) and desired numbers of children (r = .08).

Male decision making in the family relates to other intra family variables such as role differentiation (r = .11) and (lack of) communication between the spouses (r = .14). These social psychological variables relate to fertility behavior and attitudes in a consistent way: male decision making relates to higher parity (r = .10). Communication between spouses on the other hand, relates to lower parity (r = −.08) even when the effect of SES is controlled. Communication between spouses is negatively associated with boy preference (r = −.07) and seems to induce lower ideal and desired numbers of children (r = −.09) and −.10 respectively).

Belief in external control is related to higher parity (r = .17) and to decision making by husband on deciding about the number of children (r = .17). Another traditional variable, namely, boy preference is also greater for those who believe in external control (r = .10) and who depend on sons for old age security (r = .15). Finally, those who believe in external control are much less concerned with overpopulation (r = = −.25). As indicated before, women believe in external control more than men and are also found to be less concerned than men with overpopulation.

Media exposure correlates with communication between spouses (r = .18) (lack of) sex-role differentiation (r = −.16), decision mindedness (r = +.39), and concern with overpopulation (r = .36). Those who experience more media exposure have fewer children (r = −.13), desire less (r = −.10), and tend not to emphasize traditional reasons for wanting another child, such as boy preference (r = −.17). They prefer having no children to many (r = .13) and intend to use family planning sooner. Women have less media exposure than men.

Conclusion

The various findings of the Turkish VOC study reflect the differences between men and women both in their general values and outlooks and also in their values, desires and expectations related to children. These two different sets of values, furthermore, are quite similar and they acquire meaning and function within the context of the traditional family structure and dynamics.

Thus, for example, being close to spouse is a very important value for women, but not for men, this being understandable in the context of status and sex-role differentiation and male decision-making within the family. Accordingly, another child is wanted by women for old-age security and to bring the spouse closer whereas men want it mostly to continue the family name. The desire to have a son, important especially for men but also for women, further reflects the differential status and value put on the sexes in family and society. It is understandable in terms of the instrumental value of the son in providing financial benefits and old age security for both parents and continuation of the family name for the father. Thus, achievement-oriented aspirations are held by both parents for the son but not for the daughter, whose future conjugal role is endorsed widely. The higher educational aspirations of the mothers for their daughters therefore, are not really hopes for a change of life styles for women.

Women who have less education, less media-exposure, less decision-making power within the family and, probably thus, greater belief in external control emerge as more "traditional" than men. Yet men appear to have more "traditional" child-related values in terms of desiring more children emphasizing the importance of family name and showing greater son-preference. Women, in spite of their more constricted general outlook on life, appear to be more conscious of the disadvantages of children, especially the financial burden, restrictions on freedom and work load that children cost them. Thus, they desire fewer children than men.

This sex difference in child-related values and desires has important implications for educational efforts to inculcate non child-bearing roles for women. As women already appear to be aware of the costs of children, these costs could be further emphasized in three directions: a. The costs of children could be clearly associated with large numbers of children; b. Disadvantages of children could be made more salient; and c. such an awareness could be instilled at earlier ages. Thus, educational programs and communications designed to increase women's status by lowering fertility could utilize effectively the knowledge of women's child-related values.

Even if possible, utilization and effective manipulation of general and child-related values is not the whole answer. In order to be of widespread and long lasting effectiveness, education and persuasive communication should take place within the context of substantial socioeconomic structural change and development. This, in turn, benefits from large scale social and economic planning and policy development.

REFERENCES

Arnold, F. et al. *Introduction and Comparative Analysis*. Vol. I, The Value of Children: A cross-national study. Honolulu: East-West Population Institute, 1975.

Arnold, F. and Fawcett, J. *Hawaii*. Vol. 3. The Value of children: A cross-national study. Honolulu: East-West Population Institute, 1975.

Berelson, B. The value of children: a taxonomical essay. In *The Population Council Annual Report 1972*, 17–27. New York: Population Council, 1973.

Bulatao, R. A. *Philippines*. Vol. 2, The value of children: A cross-national study. Honolulu: East-West Population Institute, 1973.

Buripakdi, C. *Thailand*. Vol. 4, The value of children: A cross-national study. Honolulu: East-West Population Institute, 1977.

DPT—Illerin gelismislik düzeylerinin saptanmasinda bir yöntem denemesi (1972) Ankara: DPT Publications No. 1252, SPD 250. (A method for assessing the development levels of provinces.)

Fawcett, J. T. (Ed.) *The satisfactions and costs of children: Theories, concepts and methods*. Honolulu, East-West Center, 1972.

Hoffman, L. and Hoffman, M. The value of children to parents. In Fawcett, J. T. (Ed.) *Psychological perspectives on population*. New York: Basic Books, 1973.

Kağitçibaşi, Ç. Cultural values and population action programs: Turkey. Report prepared for UNESCO, 1977.

Kağitçibaşi, Ç. Psychological aspects of modernization in Turkey. *Journal of Cross Cultural Psychology*, 4, 157–174, 1973.

Meeker, M. E. Meaning and society in the Near East: Examples from the Black Sea Turks and the Levantine Arabs (II). *International Journal of Middle East Studies*, 7, 2, 243–270, 1976.

Rotter, J. B. Generalized expectancies for internal versus external control of reinforcement. *Psychological Monographs*, 80, 1, 1–28, 1966.

Timur, S. Demographic correlates of woman's education: fertility age at marriage and the family. In Proceedings of the IUSSP International Population Conference, Mexico, vol. 3, 463–496, 1977.

Tuncer, B. *Ekonomik gelisme ve nüfus* (Economic development and population). Ankara: Hacettepe University Publications, 1976.

Wu, T. S. *Taiwan*. Vol. 5, The value of children: A cross-national study. Honolulu: East West Population Institute, 1977.

SABAHAT TEZCAN

HEALTH PROBLEMS OF TURKISH WOMEN

Women are an integral part of every society. By their fertility they ensure the continuation of the human race and by their productivity they actively contribute to the wealth of nations. In many parts of the world, and in Turkey particularly, women carry out these functions amid a myriad of health problems, and it is these problems to which this paper addresses itself. Further, we shall mainly concentrate on the fertile period (15—44 years of age) during which time the problems of feminine health differ drastically from those of the male.

To some, the state of being in good health simply means the absence of disease or handicap. If this point of view is taken serious individual and community health problems may be overlooked, for example the problem of high fertility itself and its counterpart, abortion due to high fertility. We shall, therefore, include in our definition the presence of those factors which secure the physical, mental and social wellbeing of the female.

As in other areas of female life, one learns very little about the diseases peculiar to Turkish women, and their frequency, from national statistics. For this we must look to local studies such as the ones conducted in Etimesğut in the 1970's.

Etimesgut is a district northwest of the city of Ankara with approximately 60,000 inhabitants. It has received socialized national health services for more than ten years during which time the Ministry of Health and Social Welfare and Hacettepe University have jointly run the health services and at the same time have conducted a series of field studies.

In a study conducted in the rural Ergazi health center of the Etimesğut District (Akın, 1970) gynecological disorders and their correlates were studied in 379 women over 15 years of age. It was found that pelvic relaxations had occurred in 51% of the women studied, inflammatory diseases of the genital system in 37.5%, varicose veins around the perinea in 20% and tumors of the uterus or ovary in 10.5%. Further, a positive relationship was observed between the number of pregnancies that a woman had had and the presence of gynecological disorders. Of the 379 women studied, 52% of the 106 women who had given birth to less than 4 children suffered from gynecological disease. The remaining 273 women, who had given birth to four or more children, encountered a gynecological disease frequency of 71%. In other words, as the number of births increased so did the proportion of women with genital illnesses.

Other studies were conducted in the semi-urban (Sincan) and rural (Yenikent) health centers of the Etimesğut District (Güven, 1972 and Egemen, 1972), to determine the frequency of physical and gynecological diseases among married women between the ages of 15—44. It was found that the majority of women in both areas suffered from dental problems (tooth decay/Pyorrhea), these being followed by intestinal parasites which were twice as prevalent in the rural area (Table I). While a large

Table I

The most Frequent Diseases among Fertile Women in Sincan and Yenikent, Etimesğut District, 1971

Disease	*Semi-urban (Sincan)* *N = 271* *Dis. Frequency (%)*	*Rural (Yenikent)* *N = 261* *Dis. Frequency (%)*
Tooth decay	64.6	66.3
Pyorrhea	56.8	60.5
Intestinal parasite	22.9	43.9
Anemia	20.7	15.3
Hypertension	8.9	17.2
Mean number of pathology per woman	2.9	3.0

proportion of the women in the semi-urban area suffered from anemia, cases of hypertension were more frequently observed in the rural women. The average number of physical pathologies per woman was about 3.0 for both areas. Further, of the four diseases mentioned, save intestinal parasites, all were found to be positively related to the increasing number of pregnancies.

The most frequent gynecological disorders in both areas, were cervical pathologies. (Table II). These were followed by pelvic relaxations, uterus pathologies, and pelvic inflammatory disease—each of which was found to be more prevalent in the rural areas. The average number of gynecological pathologies per woman was 2.0.

Again, and as is shown in Table III, the percentage of women with gynecological disorders rose as the number of pregnancies increased.

Table II

The most Frequent Gynecological Diseases among Fertile Women in Sincan and Yenikent, Etimesğut District, 1971

Disease Group	*Semi-urban (Sincan)* *N = 271* *Dis. Frequency (Percent)*	*Rural (Yenikent)* *N = 261* *Dis. Frequency (Percent)*
Cervical Pathologies	82.7	56.3
Pelvic Relaxations	24.0	31.0
Uterus Pathologies	12.9	38.3
Vaginal-Perinal Pathologies	12.2	11.1
Pelvic Inflammatory Disease	11.4	17.2
Mean number of gynecological pathology per woman	2.2	2.0

Table III

Frequency of Gynecological Disorders of Fertile Women by the Number of Pregnancies and Place of Residence Etimesğut District, 1971

Number of Pregnancies	*Semi-urban (Sincan)*		*Rural (Yenikent)*	
	No.	*Percent*	*No.*	*Percent*
1–3	83	60.2	34	55.7
4–6	76	64.5	69	75.0
7–9	67	73.1	52	82.5
10	34	79.4	28	77.8
TOTAL	260*	67.3	252*	72.6

*Women without pregnancy are excluded.

In addition, a similar relationship was found to exist for the increased number of abortions. The overall proportion of women with either physical or gynecological disorders was higher in the rural area than in the urban one, thereby reflecting the poorer health conditions in the rural parts of Turkey. (Table IV).

According to the findings of the above-mentioned studies, the following explanations should be considered. Physical and genital diseases among women aged 15 to 44 years are closely related to the fertility level. A high

Table IV

Outcome of Physical and Gynecological Examinations of Fertile Women by Place and Residence Etimesğut District, 1971

Examination	*Semi-urban (Sincan) Pathologic Percent*	*Rural (Yenikent) Pathologic Percent*
Physical	68.4	95.0
Gynecological	68.3	73.6
Number of Women Studies	271	261

number of pregnancies will eventually lead to a high number of births and/or abortions. In Turkey, the underlying reason for the health problems of married women at fertile ages are: the absence or inadequacy of pre-natal care; undiagnosed or untreated conditions during pregnancy; having a delivery or an abortion without the assistance of trained health personnel and under unsanitary conditions; short intervals between pregnancies; and starting work shortly after a delivery or an abortion. For example, insufficient nutrition during pregnancy or during the lactation period can cause anemia, and if it is not prevented or treated, the condition can worsen during future pregnancies especially if they are at short intervals. It is quite normal, and expected, to observe pelvic relaxations or inflammatory diseases in women who have had difficult deliveries under unsterile conditions and without the help of trained health personnel.

The seriousness of female health problems in Turkey can be illustrated by focussing on a comparison of the age-specific death rates for Turkish men and women and the corresponding death rates for females in Sweden (Fişek, 1978). The death rates in Turkey for females between the ages 15 to 44 years are much higher than the corresponding rates for males (Fig. 1). In other words the health status of women in this age group is poorer than that of men.

A comparison of Turkish material mortality rates with those of Sweden further emphasizes the importance of this problem. In 1968, the estimated maternal mortality rate for the cities and towns in Turkey was 11.4 per 10,000 live births, however, in the same years the corresponding rate for Sweden, a developed country, was 0.9 per 10,000 live births. Thus, the maternal mortality rate in Turkey is thirteen times higher than that in Sweden. In other words, in Turkey, for every 10,000 live births 13 mothers die, whereas, in Sweden, for every 10,000 live births only 1 mother dies. The rate for Turkey would be much higher if the data on maternal death rates in the rural areas, where conditions are worse, could be obtained. Since 92% of the deliveries in Turkey are still done in homes without the help of trained personnel, high maternal mortality and widespread problems related to pregnancy and deliveries are expected results.

It has been long debated whether or not there is such a problem as high fertility in Turkey. To answer this, it is sufficient to review the findings of the National Demographic Surveys. In a recent demographic survey carried out in 1973, 68% of the married women under 49 years of age reported that the ideal number of children that they would like to have was 3 or less. The mean ideal number of children was found to be 2.6 whereas the mean number of actual pregnancies was 4.6 (Tezcan, 1975). The difference between these two figures leads us to assume that a good number of pregnancies were carried to term, but that a significant number were ended by abortion.

In Turkey, it is illegal to end pregnancies with abortion in cases other than where there is a threat to maternal life (health reason), or of delivering a malformed child (eugenic reason). However, reality does not suit

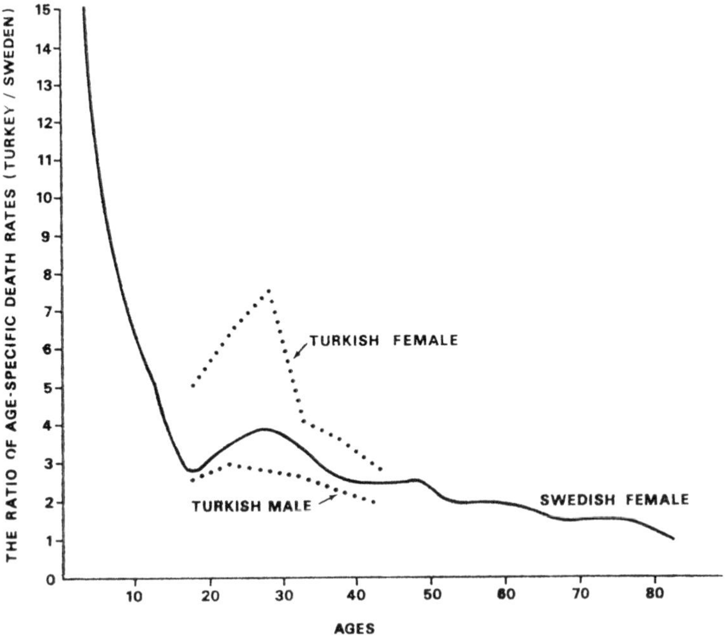

Fig. 1. Comparison of age specific death rates of Turkey and Sweden

the laws. According to the findings of several studies conducted since the late nineteen fifties, illegally induced abortions have been widely practiced by Turkish women, and this practice is one of the most serious health hazards threatening them today.

The abortion studies carried out in Turkey can be divided into two main categories: (1) Hospital-based abortion studies, and (2) Community-based abortion studies that were carried out in either local communities or nationally representative samples. The indices obtained from all these studies are generally termed 'total abortions'. This includes spontaneous as well as induced abortions.

The hospital-based abortion studies revealed that approximately 30% of the women interviewed had had at least one abortion during their reproductive lives. (Table V). The average number of abortions per

Table V

Hospital Based Abortion Studies in Turkey

Author and Reference No.	*Year*	*Place*	*Women Studied Number of*	*Abortion per Woman*	*Proportion of Women having had an Abortion*
Burak (5)	1955–1960	Ankara	5,000	1.1	30
Esendal (8)	1953–1957	Ankara	1,948	1.8	–
Erenus (*ä*)	1966–1967	Ankara	1,388	1.9	29
Baysal (3)	1970	Istanbul	168	2.0	–
Bölükbaşı (4)	1974	Ankara	469	1.1	–

women was between 1 and 2 in different studies. In other words, each woman studied had resorted to one or two abortions of some kind in their past. Although these figures do not reflect the real magnitude of the problem in Turkey, they are still useful in that they give a crude idea about the extent of the issue being studied. The community-based studies, on the other hand, clearly indicate that abortion has been widely practiced, and that it is an individual and community problem in Turkey.

The major findings of the local community-based abortion studies are outlined in Table VI. The first study was carried out in 137 Central and Western Anatolian Villages to study and obtain information on maternal and child deaths and abortion. One-third of all the women studied reported having had at least one abortion during their marital lives. (Table VI). This averaged out to 15 abortions per 100 live births. The second and third studies, also shown on Table VI, were conducted in the rural and semi-urban areas of the Etimesğut District. There, about half of the women interviewed had had one or more abortions, and, on the average, one abortion per woman, or 20 abortions per 100 live births. In other words, 17% of all the pregnancies were ended by abortion. The fourth study in Table VI was conducted on a sample in the city of Ankara where 43% of the women interviewed revealed that they had had at least one abortion, corresponding to an average of one abortion per woman. An important point in Table VI worth mentioning is that a higher proportion of the women living in Ankara—a large city—ended their pregnancies with abortion (27%) than those living in the rural or semi-urban areas (16—17%), and that there were more abortions per 100 live births in the metropolis (38 abortions per 100 live births) than in the other areas (15—20 abortions per 100 live births in rural, and semi-urban areas).

Table VI

Community Based Local Abortion Studies in Turkey

Author and Reference Number	*Year*	*Place*	*Number of Woman Interviewed*	*Abortion Indices*			
				Abortion per 100 Pregnancies	*Abortion per 100 Live births*	*Abortion per Woman*	*Proportion of Woman having an Abortion %*
Fişek (9)	1959	137 villages in central & western Anatolia	7,082	–	14.5	–	29
Güven (12)	1971	Yenikent–Etimesğut	261	16.3	19.8	0.9	47
Egemen (6)	1971	Sincan–Etimesğut	271	17.1	20.9	0.9	41
Akin (2)	1975	Ankara	396	27.0	38.0	1.0	43

The abortion indices obtained through national samples are presented in Table VII. The first three studies were primarily concerned with the collection of demographic data and they also included some questions on abortion. The first national study to focus on the abortion problem was carried out in 1975 by Tezcan. While the total abortion indices shown in the first three columns of Table VII do not differ much from one study to the other, it is interesting to note that the proportion of women with induced abortion increased from 7.6% in 1963 to 13.9% in 1975 (almost

Table VII

Community based Nationwide Abortion Studies in Turkey

Author and Reference Number	Year	Number of Women Inter-viewed	Abortion Indices			
			Total Abortion per 100 Live births	Total Abortion Per Woman	Proportion of Women having any kind of abortion %	Proportion of Woman having Induced Abortion
Özbay (15)	1963	5,100	–	–	–	7.6
Fişek (10)	1968	3,068	17.2	0.7	32.6	10.2
Kişnişci (14)	1973	4,581	17.3	0.6	33.1	–
Tezcan (19,20)	1975	1,521	17.2	0.7	33.1	13.9

doubling within the past twelve years). This clearly indicates that a higher proportion of women are ending their unwanted pregnancies with induced abortions as compared to the past.

Tezcan's more detailed information on induced abortion in Turkey reveals that 14% of the married women, under 44 years of age, have had one or more induced abortions. Of these women, 44% have had one, 29% have had two, and 27% have had three or more induced abortions.

In tables VIII, IX, X, XI and XII the induced abortions indices are presented according to certain socio-demographic characteristics. They can be summarized as follows:

The proportion of women with induced abortions increases with the size of the place of residence (Table VIII) and with the woman's educational level (Table IX). The proportion is greatest among those women with 3—4 living children (Table X); among those living in nuclear families (Table XI); and among those who have at one time or another practiced family planning (Table XII).

In view of the above findings, the following explanations might prove useful:

. Women who live in the cities and/or women with a higher educational level are more highly motivated to limit their family size than those who do not have these characteristics.

. Women with 3—4 or 5—6 living children seem more determined to end their unwanted pregnancies by induced abortion than those with 1—2 or 7 and more living children. Probably, women with 1—2 living children have not yet reached the desired family size, whereas those with 7 or more living children are less motivated and just accept every unwanted pregnancy as the will of God.

. Women who live in nuclear families are probably more independent in their decisions and more influential on their spouses in convincing them to end an unwanted pregnancy by induced abortion.

Table VIII

Induced Abortion Indices by Place of Residence TURKEY, 1975

Place of Residence	Proportion of Women with Induced Abortion %	Number of Induced Abortions		
		Per 1000 Women	Per 1000 Pregnancies	Per 1000 Live births
Metropolis	24.5	592.4	147.3	197.3
Urban	17.8	370.8	82.0	99.3
Rural	4.6	99.8	20.6	23.2
TOTAL	13.9	303.7	66.6	79.2

Table IX

Induced Abortion Indices by Education of Women TURKEY, 1975

Education of Women	Proportion of Women with Induced Abortion %	Number of Induced Abortions		
		Per 1000 Women	Per 1000 Pregnancies	Per 1000 Live births
Illiterate	8.3	169.7	32.8	37.2
Primary School	18.7	438.1	113 4	145.7
Secondary school or More	36.3	745.1	246.0	374.4
TOTAL	13.9	303.7	66.6	79.2

Table X

Induced Abortion Indices by Number of Living Children Turkey, 1975

Number of Living Children	Proportion of Women with Induced Abortion %	Number of Induced Abortions		
		Per 1000 Women	Per 1000 Pregnancies	Per 1000 Live Births
1–2	11.1	210.9	99.7	133.2
3–4	19.8	466.2	184.8	133.6
5–6	16.6	377.2	59.9	69.5
7 or More	12.0	247.9	26.7	29
TOTAL	13.9	303.7	66.6	79.2

Table XI

Induced Abortion Indices by Family Type Turkey, 1975

Family Type	*Proportion of Women with Induced Abortion %*	*Number of Induced Abortions*		
		Per 1000 Women	*Per 1000 Pregnancies*	*Per 1000 Live births*
Nuclear	16.8	374.5	74.4	89.0
Extended	9.1	186.8	49.5	58.0
TOTAL	13.9	303.7	66.6	79.2

Table XII

Induced Aboration Indices by Use of Family Planning Turkey, 1975

Use of Family Planning	*Proportion of Women with Induced Abortion %*	*Number of Induced Abortions*		
		Per 1000 Women	*Per 1000 Pregnancies*	*Per 1000 Live births*
Ever	21.0	610.0	127.2	162.0
Never	6.7	159.6	33.4	38.3
TOTAL	14.7	322.4	67.3	80.1

Women who have used some kind of contraceptive method will, of course, be more highly motivated to limit the size of their families as compared with those who have never used any type of method. If the contraceptive method that these women use should fail, they will then be more determined to end an unwanted pregnancy with an abortion. Other data collected by Tezcan revealed that:

93% of all induced abortions were done during the first three months of pregnancy.

73% of the induced abortions were done by dilatation and curretage, 18% were done by injection or oral medication.

64% of the induced abortions were performed by private physicians, 14% were done in hospitals, and 19% were done either by untrained local midwives or the women themselves.

In 89% of the induced abortions, women had the approval of their husbands, 3% had abortions though their husbands disapproved, and 7% had them secretly.

Among the most common reasons given for having an induced abortion, 37% reported excess number of children, 23% short pregnancy intervals, 21% economic reasons, and 9% reported other reasons.

Recommendations

After presenting the most common health problems affecting married Turkish women between the ages of 15—44 the following preventive measures are not only logical but necessary:

Antenatal care:

— Married women at fertile ages should be visited at regular intervals by trained health personnel during their pregnancies in order to diagnose and treat problems related to early pregnancy, or general health problems.

Deliveries under sanitary conditions:

— All deliveries, even those at home, should be assisted by trained health personnel. In addition adequate health services should be readily available in case any complications should occur.

Postnatal care:

— Dissemination of effective family planning information and contraceptive devices, and regular check-ups for those women who are using any one of the various contraceptive methods in order to treat any complication that might occur.

Change in abortion laws:

— If being in good health implies the social wellbeing of individuals, then it should be the right of a woman to end her unwanted pregnancy for social reasons, such as excess number of children, short intervals between pregnancies, economical or marital problems and so on. In reality, women practice abortion for social reasons anyway. Thus, the abortion laws should be changed so that women may obtain legal induced abortions for social reasons as well as for medical and eugenic reasons in hospitals, under sterile conditions and at less cost.

Periodic screenings:

— As resources permit, periodic screenings of women at fertile ages should be done for early diagnosis and treatment of health problems.

Health education:

— Continuous health education for young girls and women on general health, reproductivity, and motherhood should be given.

The reference list of this chapter is on page 319

AYŞE BAYSAL

NUTRITIONAL PROBLEMS OF TURKISH WOMAN

Introduction

Malnutrition is a major problem in the world today. Some of the adverse effects of malnutrition are a high rate of infant and child mortality, stunted physical growth and mental development, specific nutritional deficiency diseases, low resistance to infectious diseases, reduced physical capacity for work and susceptibility to chronic-degenerative diseases. Today, while millions of people are fighting death and disease caused by chronic starvation and malnutrition, others are putting their lives in jeopardy at early ages with faulty or over nutrition.

Malnutrition mostly affects children and women. In some countries, malnutrition kills more children than malaria and tuberculosis combined. The infant mortality rate is 120—160 per thousand in developing countries while it is 10—20 in developed countries. In most of these cases, malnutrition was either a primary (7%) or a secondary cause (46%) of death. Among the 0—6 age group, from 4 to 46% show signs of growth retardation. In the developed countries, iron deficiency anemia affects 10 to 25% of the female population whereas in the developing countries 6 to 17% of the men, 15 to 50% of the women and 20 to 70% of the children suffer from it.[1]

In Turkey, malnutrition is one of the most serious public health problems. The infant birth rate is 145 per thousand. The average incidence of malnutrition among the preschool age group is 20%. This rate, however, is much higher in some regions and among certain groups. Anemia is a problem for 20 to 60% of the child and female population. In the adult female population, obesity resulting from faulty nutrition is another health hazard.

In this paper, we shall examine the nutritional problems commonly observed among Turkish women, their underlying causes and the measures which should be taken to alleviate them.

[1] L. R. Brown, "Death at an Early Age". *UNICEF News*, Issue 85—3, 1975. Also see: J. M. Bengoa, "The Problem of Malnutrition". *WHO Chronicle*, 28—3, 1974.

The Nutritional Problems of Turkish Women

An individual's nutritional requirements vary according to his or her age, body size and physical activity. For women, there is the added dimension of pregnancy and lactation. A normal women, doing a moderate amount of work requires 2200 calories daily, 60 gr. of protein, 22 mg. of iron, 500 mg. of calcium, as well as a certain amount of vitamins and other minerals (Table I). If the woman becomes pregnant or is lactating, these amounts must be increased, otherwise her own health status and that of her child will be adversely affected.[2]

Table I

Energy and Nutrient Requirements of Women In Different Physiological Conditions

Energy and Nutrients	*Average Daily Requirement*		
	Normal Woman	*Addition for Pregnancy*	*Addition for Lactation*
Energy—K calories			
1. Light work	2000	150	700
2. Moderate work	2200	150	700
3. Over moderate	2550	150	700
4. Heavy work	3000	150	700
Protein—g	60	5	15
Iron—mg	22	5	5
Calcium—mg	500	500	500
Vitamin A—IU	5000	1000	3000
Thiamin—mg	0.9	0.1	0.4
Riboflavine—mg	1.2	0.2	0.4
Niacine—mg	14.0	1.0	5.4
Vitamin—C—mg	50.0	30.0	30.0

There are various ways of determining the nutritional status of an individual or a community. The most common ones are:

1. Measurement and comparison of growth, development and body status with the standards.

[2] A. Baysal, *Nutrition*. Hacettepe University Publications. Pub. No. A/13 (Sec. Ed.) 1977.

2. Clinical examinations to determine whether there are signs of nutritional deficiencies.
3. Laboratory analysis of the levels of nutrients or their metabolic by-products in the body fluids.
4. Statistical analysis of the mortality and morbidity rates in different age groups.
5. Survey of nutritional habits and practices.
6. Identification and analysis of food consumption levels.

Research data employing the above methods to determine the nutritional status of Turkish woman is quite limited. However, according to the limited scientific data available, the most important nutritional problems affecting Turkish women are: iron deficiency anemia, endemic goiter mainly resulting from iodine deficiency, dental caries and several vitamin deficiencies. In addition to these, a good number of pregnant and lactating women are underweight while another segment suffers from obesity. Although there is not much research data on the subject, there is a high probability that many of the women who have had quite a few children while their diets were inadequate or unbalanced, suffer from osteomalacia (a disease caused by calcium deficiency).

The Problem of Anemia

Anemia is caused by a deficiency in any one of several nutrients, the most important of which is iron deficiency. In order to determine the presence of iron deficiency anemia, the levels of hemoglobin, hemotocrits, transferrin saturation and serum iron are checked. In Turkey, the most widely used measure is the hemoglobin count.

The Turkish Nutrition-Health Survey was conducted to determine, among other things, the prevelance of anemia in different age and sex groups.[3] The survey revealed that approximately half of preschool children, pregnant and lactating women have anemia problems (Table II). Very few adult males are anemic. When examined by region, the incidence of iron deficiency anemia was found to be highest in the Black Sea area (Table III). In terms of urban/rural residence, the villages registered the higher rate (Table IV).

[3] *Nutrition in Turkey: A Report on the National Nutrition-Health and Food Consumption Survey*, Ankara, 1977.

Table II

Incidence of Anemia in Different Sex and Age Groups (percents)

Age and Sex	*Severe Degree*	*Mild Degree*	*Total*
0–60 month male	17.3	33.3	50.6
0–60 month female	14.4	32.7	47.1
5 years and over male	4.3	20.9	25.2
5 years and over female	6.8	21.5	28.3
pregnant woman	16.1	35.1	51.2
lactating woman	8.6	32.6	41.2

Table III

Incidence of Anemia by Region (percents)

Age and Sex	*Aegean-Marmara*	*Black Sea*	*Central*	*Medi-terr.*	*East-S. East*
0–60 month male	44.5	82.1	33.0	65.3	41.4
0–60 month female	37.9	76.1	32.6	65.2	46.0
5 years and over male	7.6	70.4	21.5	19.8	27.0
5 years and over female	20.4	72.2	29.4	41.7	20.6
pregnant woman	36.9	88.1	46.3	54.8	47.7
lactating woman	29.4	75.0	36.4	49.3	28.2

Table IV

Incidence of Anemia by Type of Residence (percents)

Age and Sex	*Metropolitan*	*City*	*Town*	*Village*
0–60 month male	51.1	48.8	50.9	53.1
0–60 month female	50.0	41.3	50.6	54.0
5 years and over male	12.4	25.0	28.5	28.6
5 years and over female	24.0	32.0	36.8	42.3
pregnant woman	39.2	51.0	70.5	51.8
lactating woman	33.3	47.0	42.6	37.3

The results of another survey carried out on a population of 2000 in the 5—25 age group, including children, soldiers and villagers in the Ankara area, showed that village women, more than men, suffer from anemia (Table V).[4] When place of residence is taken into account, rural women have a higher frequency than urban ones. Age was also found to be an important factor in this survey. According to the findings, the highest incidence of anemia exists among children in the 5—9 year age group. The prevelance of anemia in this survey, however, was generally lower than that in the National Nutrition-Health survey. The reason for this difference is that pregnant and lactating women were not included in the second study. Also, students and soldiers are, for the most part, well-fed groups when compared to the general population.

Table V

Incidence of Anemia According to Different Parameters (percents)

Living Place	*According to hemoglobin level*			*According to hemotocrit level*			*Percent of iron deficiency according to transferrin saturation*		
	Man	*Woman*	*Total*	*Man*	*Woman*	*Total*	*Man*	*Woman*	*Total*
Rural	7.4	14.2	11.6	2.7	7.9	6.0	31.3	29.8	30.4
Urban	11.6	10.7	11.4	17.2	15.9	16.5	4.8	13.9	8.5
General	11.1	11.4	11.4	15.3	14.2	14.7	13.9	22.4	18.2

A survey carried out on university students in the 17 to 24 year age group proves this observation. The results of this survey indicate that 6.62% of men and 9.73% of women have iron deficiency anemia.[5] Other surveys carried out in the villages near Ankara, however, have shown that 42 to 66% of the pregnant and 20 to 38% of the nonpregnant women have iron deficiency anemia.

All of this evidence is presented merely to dramatize the fact that the incidence of anemia is much higher in women who have poor and inadequate diets, as is the case in the rural areas. It is also much higher for those who are undergoing the physiological conditions of pregnancy and lactation. When one considers the high percentage of Turkey's population living in villages and its high birth rate, it is no wonder that anemia is the most serious nutritional problem affecting its women.

[4] A. Çavdar, A. Arcasoy, S. Gözdaşoglu, Ş. Cin, J. Erten, *Anemia, Iron Deficiency and Trace Elements in Turkish Children and Youth.* TBTAK-AÜ. Tıp Fakültesi Çocuk Sag. ve Hst. Kliniği Araştırmalarından, Ankara, 1976.

[5] M. K. Işıksoluğu, *The Prevalence of Iron Deficiency Anemia Among University Students and the Factors Affecting it.*, Ph. D. Thesis. Hacettepe University, Ankara, 1975.

The Clinical Signs of Nutritional Deficiency

According to the National Nutrition-Health survey (Table VI), the percentage of women who have dental caries, endemic goiter and anemia is much higher than men. Table 1 shows the distribution of clinical signs by region and type of residence. The incidence of dental caries is highest in the Aegean-Marmara Region and lowest in the Black Sea Region where endemic goiter and clinical signs of anemia are much more frequent.[6]

The incidence of vitamin B_2 deficiency, which is the most frequently observed vitamin deficiency among Turkish people, is much higher in rural women than in urban ones. Since this survey was carried out in the summer, when more fresh fruits and vegetables are consumed, the incidence of vitamin C deficiency is low.

Table VI

Clinical Signs of Nutritional Deficiencies

Clinical Signs	*Percent of Person with Signs*			
	over 5 years female	*Pregnant woman*	*Lactating woman*	*over 5 years male*
Vitamin B_2 deficiency	4.7	2.1	4.0	5.1
Vitamin C deficiency	2.9	2.1	2.1	2.1
Dental caries	40.0	30.0	33.8	24.6
Endemic goiter	9.1	13.8	15.4	3.3
Anemia	4.0	7.5	5.1	1.5
Adema in the leg	2.0	4.9	1.0	0.6

Another survey[7] carried out in a low-income district of Ankara and the surrounding villages, similarly showed that the percentage of village women who have signs of vitamin C deficiency is much higher in winter than in summer (Table VIII). This can be partially explained by the fact that most fruits and vegetables in Turkey are seasonal crops. Although more is being done in the field of year-round cropping, the harvests are limited and often beyond the means of the average consumer.

[6] O. Köksal, "*The Problems of Endemic Goiter in Rize, Trabzon and Giresun*". Beslenme ve Diyet Dergisi, 1—15, 1972.

[7] A. Baysal, "*Changes in Nutritional Status by Season and Region*". Beslenme ve Diyet Dergisi, 4—20, 1975.

Table VII

Clinical Signs of Nutritional Deficiencies in Woman Over 5 in Different Region and Area of Residence

Region, Clinical Signs	*Percent of Person With Signs*			
	City	*Town*	*Village*	*General*
1. Aegean-Marmara Region:				
Vitamin B_2 deficiency	3.2	4.2	10.1	3.6
Vitamin C deficiency	1.3	0.0	0.3	0.9
Dental caries	64.0	60.0	55.0	62.0
Endemic goiter	6.0	13.2	7.1	6.6
Anemia	3.5	4.3	5.9	3.1
2. Black-Sea Region:				
Vitamin B_2 deficiency	5.3	6.7	12.6	8.7
Vitamin C deficiency	2.5	1.5	2.8	2.5
Dental caries	25.0	14.0	21.0	23.4
Endemic goiter	19.7	44.5	18.3	22.1
Anemia	13.4	1.0	14.2	13.6
3. Central Region:				
Vitamin B_2 deficiency	2.2	3.4	6.5	3.4
Vitamin C deficiency	7.6	6.7	9.5	7.8
Dental caries	35.0	34.0	26.0	32.5
Endemic goiter	5.2	5.4	6.2	5.4
Anemia	2.6	5.8	5.0	3.3
4. Mediterranean Region:				
Vitamin B_2 deficiency	5.7	3.2	11.1	6.8
Vitamin C deficiency	1.2	0.8	2.0	1.4
Dental caries	43.0	26.0	26.0	31.8
Endemic goiter	7.8	15.3	15.5	10.4
Anemia	2.4	3.7	2.8	2.7
5. East and S. east Region:				
Vitamin B_2 deficiency	1.6	6.1	7.5	4.4
Vitamin C deficiency	0.3	0.0	0.1	0.4
Dental caries	35.0	28.0	26.0	30.3
Endemic goiter	9.0	8.4	3.4	7.1
Anemia	0.1	0.0	0.2	0.1

The underlying cause of endemic goiter is iodine deficiency. Since iodine is deficient in the soil and water in some regions, the foods produced in these areas also are deficient in iodine. Thus, people eating these foods develop endemic goiter in time. The underlying causes of dental caries are high consumption of refined carbohydrates, low intake of foods high in phosphate, protein and calcium and the low concentra-

Table VIII

Some Clinical Signs of Nutritional Deficiencies in Woman Over 5 By Season

Signs	*Percent of Person With Signs*			
	City		*Village*	
	Winter	*Summer*	*Winter*	*Summer*
Vitamin B_2 deficiency	8.0	3.0	4.0	9.0
Vitamin C deficiency	9.0	8.0	11.0	4.0
Dental caries	86.0	no data	84.0	no data
Endemic goiter	1.0	no data	1.0	no data
Anemia	3.0	5.0	3.0	6.0

tion of fluoride in the water. Low intake of foods rich in vitamin B_2 and faulty cooking methods are the main reasons for the high incidence of vitamin B_2 deficiency signs.

Body size

Body size is related to nutritional status. The results of the National Nutrition-Health Survey related to body size are shown in Table IX. As can be seen in this table, among the 12—16 year of age group, the percentage of girls under standard height and weight is 4 and 20, respectively.

The percentage of underweight and underheight girls increases at the age of 17. This is indicative of the fact that especially in the rural areas women marry and become pregnant at an early age; the foods consumed meet only the requirements for pregnancy but not for growth. In a study in the İstanbul area, it was shown that the growth rate of girls in a high socio-economic section of the city is comparable with that found in America while the growth rate of girls in a low socio-economic section of the city and the villages is retarded.[8] In general, it may be said that after 17 years of age, there is no increase in the height of Turkish women.

In general, Turkish women tend to be shorter than women in the Western Countries. After growth in height has stopped, excess calories are deposited as fat, physical fitness declines and weight becomes a problem.

[8] C. Gürson, O. Neyzi, *The Nutritional Status of Children in the Istanbul Region.* Besin Simpozyumu, TBTAK Publication Ankara, 1969.

Table IX

Mean Weight and Height of Girls Aged 12 to 17 Years and the Percentage Below Standards

Age	*Mean Height cm./ft.*	*Below Standard %*	*Mean Weight kg./lb.*	*Below Standard %*
12	146.5/4.48	4.9	39.9/ 87.78	18.2
13	150.6/4.94	3.2	45.1/ 99.22	19.3
14	153.8/5.05	0.8	49.6/109.12	12.4
15	155.4/5.10	4.9	51.9/114.18	20.3
16	155.6/5.10	4.8	52.9/116.38	20.9
17	153.1/5.02	16.1	51.8/113.96	25.2

Table X

Weight Status of Adult Men and Women by Height

Sex	*Mean Height cm./ft.*	*Mean Weight kg./lb.*	*Under-Weight %*	*Nor-mal %*	*Over Weight %*	*Obese %*	*Over Weight Obese %*
Men	168/5.18	64.7/142.34	7.3	58.7	26.4	7.6	34.0
Women	153/5.02	58.3/128.26	3.2	32.7	38.5	25.6	64.1

The results of a survey conducted in Ankara and the surrounding villages revealed that 54.6% of the women in the low socio-economic sections of the city and 36.5% of the women in the villages are overweight. The main cause appears to be high carbohydrate intake coupled with decreasing physical activity. It is interesting to note that young village women are not overweight as they work in the field and at the same time are responsible for the household chores, child birth and child care. When they become middle aged women and hand the heavy field work over to their daughter-in-laws, weight then becomes a problem.

Food Habits and consumption

It is impossible to determine exactly the food intake of an individual woman. In food consumption surveys, usually the amount and the kinds of foods consumed daily by the family are determined. Table XI summarizes the Turkish Nutrition-Health Survey's findings on food consumption levels for families in various regions of the country. The amount and kinds of foods recommended for adequate and balanced nutrition are also included in this table. As can be seen the meat group which is the best source for iron and vitamin B_2, is consumed the least in the Black Sea Region where the incidence of anemia and vitamin B_2 deficiency signs are highest.

The consumption level of main food groups varies with the place of residence. Table XII shows that meat consumption is also very low in the villages.

Table XIII shows the energy and nutrient intake levels of urban and rural families. According to this table, animal protein, vitamin B_2 and vitamin A are lower in the diets of village families than families living in the cities.

Table XI

Food Consumption Level in Turkey By Region (G/Person/Day)

Food Groups	*Amount Recommended*	*National Average*	*Aegean-Marmara*	*Black Sea*	*Central*	*Mediterr.*	*East S. East*
1. Bread	300	402	391	366	407	392	442
Other cereals	100	91	70	150	90	91	100
2. Milk-yoghurt	230	79	72	84	64	72	127
Cheese	30	24	30	21	21	18	23
3. Meat, poultry, fish	56	55	67	40	58	45	45
Egg	25	9	10	8	13	6	5
D. Legumes	25	10	13	5	13	9	3
4. Potatoes	75	32	32	50	40	26	15
Fresh vegetable	225	289	318	272	245	313	248
Fresh fruits	230	222	252	127	177	280	211
5. Fats	20	19	20	15	22	17	18
Oils	20	19	31	20	14	15	4
Sugar	40	36	38	42	41	26	31

In general, dietary iron is not adequate to meet the iron requirement of women in the child bearing age bracket. This is a primary factor for the high incidence of iron deficiency anemia among females. Although the iron intake of villagers seems higher than other groups, the actual amount of utilizable iron in their diets is low. The absorption of iron from cereals, and especially unleavened bread (yufka) consumed largely in the villages, is relatively low.[9]

[9] N. Aykut Şenyüz, *The Utilization of Bread Iron in Human beings and Factors Effecting it*. Ph. D. Thesis, Hacettepe University, Ankara, 1976.

Table XII

Consumption Level in Turkey of Food Groups in Different Areas (G/Person/Day)

Food Groups	*Amount recommended*	*National Average*	*Metropolitan*	*City*	*Town*	*Villages*
1. Bread	300	402	374	395	406	445
Other cereals	100	91	80	76	93	135
2. Milk-yoghurt	230	79	60	63	86	108
Cheese	30	24	31	23	20	19
3. Meat, poultry, fish	56	55	90	55	50	19
Egg	25	9	12	8	12	6
D. Legumes	25	10	18	7	4	8
4. Potatoes	75	32	37	30	25	34
Fresh vegetables	225	289	320	300	268	244
Fresh fruits	230	222	215	249	218	175
5. Fats	20	19	25	18	18	16
Oils	20	19	24	18	16	16
Sugar	40	36	43	36	36	30

Table XIII

Daily Energy and Nutrients Intake In Turkey

Energy and Nutrients	*Avarage Intake*				
	National	*Metropolitan*	*City*	*Town*	*Villages*
Energy-Kcal	2291	2430	2208	2207	2336
Total protein—g	68.0	72.9	64 1	64.1	69.1
Animal protein—g	18.0	26.5	17.7	17.6	12.7
Carbohydrates—g	369.1	358	355.4	362.9	412.0
Fat—g	62.4	77.7	62.9	55.9	47.7
Calcium—mg	362.4	358.4	332.8	356.8	428.8
Iron—mg	14.6	14.6	14.1	13.9	15.8
Vitamin A-IU	3752	4876	3224	3772	2564
Vitamin B_1-mg	1.82	1.75	1.73	1.74	2.09
Vitamin B_2-mg	1.03	1.15	1.00	1.00	0.97
Niacine—mg	16.08	17.29	15.60	15.67	15.79
Vitamin C—mg	105.9	118.7	111.3	102.2	82.6

Women are affected more by the inadequate intake of nutritients than men. There are two reasons for this. First, although the nutritional requirements of women increase due to pregnancy and lactation, there is no addition to their diets. As shown in Table XIV, the majority of rural women have 4 or more children and they are breast fed for a long period of time (Table XV). However, according to Tables XVI and XVII most women do not supplement or fortify their diets during these critical periods.

Table XIV

Distribution of the Women with Preschool Age Children Who Are Pregnant or Lactating

Area of Residence	Women Surveyed	Preg-nant %	Lactat-ing %	Percentage of Women With Children 1	2	3	4	5	6+
City (Low socio-economic)	229	15	32	16	16	20	12	13	23
Villages	264	9	31	11	12	20	10	12	35

Table XV
Periods of Lactation

Area of Residence	No of Lactation	Percentage of Women 3 month and less	4–6 month	7–12 months	13–18 months	19 months longer
Metropolitan	15.6	11.2	38.6	20.6	10.2	3.8
City	9.7	6.8	30.3	28.8	18.7	5.6
Town	8.7	6.1	27.5	31.2	21.3	5.1
Villages	4.8	4.4	22.8	28.4	29.2	10.4
General	9.7	7.1	30.0	27.2	19.7	6.4

Table XVI
Percentage of Women Taking Additional Foods During Pregnancy

Area of Residence	Percentage of Women Milk Group	Meat Group	Egg	Veg-Fruit	Other	None
Metropolitan	4.6	0.2	0.2	2.8	1.8	90.4
City	2.0	0.6	0.1	1.9	1.8	93.6
Town	2.3	0.9	0.0	1.1	2.5	93.2
Village	1.0	0.3	0.0	0.8	1.4	96.5
General	1.9	0.6	0.1	1.6	1.6	94.2

Table XVII
Percentage of Women Taking Additional Foods During Lactation

Area of Residence	*Percentage of Women*					
	Milk Group	*Meat Group*	*Egg*	*Veg-Fruit*	*Other*	*None*
Metropolitan	3.6	0.5	0.2	2.8	1.6	91.2
City	2.0	0.7	0.1	1.9	1.6	93.7
Town	2.4	0.9	0.0	1.1	2.0	93.6
Villages	1.0	0.3	0.0	0.8	1.3	96.5
General	2.1	0.6	0.1	1.7	1.6	93.9

Table XVIII
Meal Serving Practices

Area of Residence	*Percentage of Families*	
	Common Plate	*Separate Plate*
Metropolitan	29.2	70.8
City	64.1	35.9
Town	71.9	29.1
Village	95.0	5.0

Second, the meal serving practices and the differences in social status between men and woman in Turkish society play an important role in this matter. Table XVIII indicates that in most village families, all the family members eat their meals from one common plat. In many families, the men eat their meals first, then the women eat whatever is left. In such situations the men get more and better quality food than the women. Furthermore, if the men do not like the poor quality food prepared at home they go to a restaurant. Women, however, are not given this opportunity.

Table XIII shows that the daily carbohydrate intake per person is higher in metropolitan families than in other groups, One of the reasons for this, and for the high percentage of obesity in small towns and some parts of the cities, is the "Kabul Günü" (reception day). At these meetings women consume large amounts of cakes, cookies and pastries. Since they have less physical activity than village women, bear fewer children and breast fed them for shorter periods, these added calories add to their nutritional problems.

Measures for Combatting Nutritional Problems

1. Since women are not independent variables, real efforts to solve their nutritional problems should center around upgrading society as a whole. A majority of Turkey's population lives in poverty. Serious steps must be taken to improve their socio-economic status. If such steps aren't taken, efforts to combat malnutrition, or any of their other problems, will remain meaningless.
2. Most women in Turkey lack nutritional knowledge. Because they lack the knowledge and are ignorant of the nutritional values of different foods and the nutritional needs of various age and sex groups, adequate balanced diets cannot be planned. Furthermore, some of the traditional preparation and cooking methods cause nutritional losses. In order to correct this situation, emphasis must be given to nutrition education. Nutrition education should be included in school curriculums in mass-media programs and in the activities of public health and their related organizations. Personnel working in these organizations and in the schools should have nutrition training during their schooling and as a part of their in-service training. Nutrition education can realize its objectives if it is treated as a public health service and a "must" in curriculums.
3. In some countries, the problem of iron deficiency anemia and endemic goiter were improved by enriching cereals with iron and salt with iodine respectively. Such processes are worth a serious try in Turkey. However, to date, they have never been realistically put into effect.
   Since bread making is controlled by the city or municipality, the enrichment of bread with iron in cities should be easy. Most village people, however, use home-made breads. There, people should be taught to use the leavening process as this improves the utilization capacity of iron in wheat.
4. The production of foods with high nutritive value should be emphasized. For example, the production of poultry and milk which are more economical than other animal products should be encouraged to improve diets deficient in animal protein.
   Thanks to advertising, the production and consumption of cola drinks, candies, cookies, chewing gums have increased drastically. These substances should be considered harmful for health and nutrition and the resources spent on them should be used for the production of milk and other foods with real nutritional value. One could buy an egg with

the money that is spent for two chewing gums. In a developing country like Turkey, the governmental regulated mass-media should not encourage people to spend on useless consumption items. In short, it should work for their betterment, not their destruction.

PART TWO

LABOUR FORCE PARTICIPATION, EDUCATION, PLANNING

Last fall Hasan went to Germany. I said to myself, Hanife girl, if one road out of a thousand goes to Germany and if you don't find that road you're an ass, you have to find that road. You have to get to Germany, they say they are giving tons of money to the workers, who cares whether the workers are virtuous or not, it is enough to be strong, see how strong I am, you double dealer Hasan, see how I am going to pile up the money, and then one day I'll dress up like the wife of the governor and sit in a car, boy take me to the factory where that bumpkin Hasan works. When Hasan sees me he will be surprised, then getting fresh he will say Hanife, crazy girl, what are you doing here, I've missed you so much, I won't let him in my car, he will have tears in his eyes like rain drops, I won't let him in my house. Hasan will be madly in love, he will sleep at my doorstep. Girl, let me have a little bit, I can't sleep any more. He will bring his mother from the village to ask for my hand; you wretched peasant, you ox, I am going to marry the governor, moreover the governor of the Germans, I'll tell him.

Sevgi SOYSAL, from her short story *HANIFE*
Translated by Nilüfer Reddy

The child left the mother, and began to walk on the cobblestone road rimmed by a wall. The janitor woman had already pulled a chair they hadn't noticed to a spot near a scaffolding which they hadn't seen either —and she had started knitting. At the bend of the road, the child turned and looked back. At the outer gate, the mother stood smiling under the rain.

FÜRUZAN, *Parasız Yatılı*,
Transl. Talât Sait HALMAN

INTRODUCTION

The basic characteristics of developing countries can be grouped under several headings. With few exceptions their population structure is characterized by such demographic factors as high fertility, excessively high maternal and infant mortality, a high proportion of the population between the dependent ages of 0—15, uninterrupted internal and external migration, poor health conditions and serious nutritional deficiencies. The various data presented in the first subsection confirms this kind of typicality.

Similarly, a second group of common denominators characterize their pattern of labor force participation, employment and education. In most developing countries, the bulk of the labor force is engaged in the agricultural sector and the active female population is almost exclusively employed there. In these nations, industrialization, urbanization and technological innovations promote sex segregated employment opportunities, which, in effect, exclude women from the labor market. The small percentages of wage earning women are mostly concentrated in the service sector in marginal activities. Education issues related to literacy, primary school attendance, vocational training, technical and higher education seem to be the most decisive factors reinforcing sex discrimination. Again, education is closely related to class affiliation. Thus, continued efforts to achieve rapid economic development without the necessary structural changes only serve to reinforce the existing disparities.

Besides these general considerations, a cultural dimension has to be added. In almost all Moslem countries, the archaic and patriarchal family structure, particularly in rural areas, has successfully resisted the effects of industrialization. This resistance has sharpened the difference between rural/urban life styles. Accordingly, when tradition is a determining factor, production relations remain unchanged and women to a large extent are excluded from extrafamilial activities. This seems particularly true in Moslem countries where institutional prescriptions optimize the responsibility of kin units to make explicit economic provisions for all female relatives regardless of their marital status. This kind of situation can eliminate from a woman's life the need to be economically self sufficient. Statistics indeed confirm this trend. In most of the Middle Eastern and North African Islamic societies only about 5 percent of the adult women are employed in the non-agricultural sector. In Turkey this rate has reached 11 percent. In Latin American countries, by contrast, a large percentage of the women are employed, but close to 40 percent of them work as domestic servants.

All the authors in this subsection have dealt with questions related to Turkey's recent industrialization pattern and the direction to which it will orient its potential female labor force. Kazgan and Şenyapılı, using a critical frame of reference, clearly show that class oriented education systems are bourgeois in nature. Because of this, it is very unlikely that women in general (Kazgan) will secure more and better employment opportunities in the formally organized sectors and that (Şenyapılı) "gecekondu" women, in particular, will find a way of escaping marginal activities.

It should be noted that women's entrance into non-agricultural jobs —unless they belong to the professional group—depends on factors which are independent of their will. Irrespective of the economy in a particular region, the employment of men is given priority. If there are no industrial jobs, men will occupy the tertiary ones. For better or for worse, male employment determines the level and degree of female employment possibilities.

Furthermore, the work world's sex roles and the distribution of jobs based on these roles, particularly during periods of industrial development, has led to the everyday use of the concepts "men's jobs" and "women's jobs". What are the unwritten laws governing this distribution of work between men and women? To a large extent it may be said that, when a particular kind of work declines in value, it is left to women. The converse is also true: when an area of work becomes female dominated, it declines in value. To a large extent this might explain the inferior level of women's wages.

The well known economist, Kazgan, has not only dealt in detail with the employment, occupational structure and wage scales of Turkish women, but has established a correlation with their educational achievements as well.

Özbay's excellent essay points out the important relationship between rural urban residence and the benefits derived from educational opportunities, the development of occupational preferences among children, and the interaction between education, marital and work status. Finally, Özbay touches upon the important issue of the "feminization" of employment, which thus far has not become a matter of public opinion concern in Turkey.

Şenyapılı's essay, clearly demonstrates that fast, unequal urbanization gives rise to serious problems especially for women even if they are not aware of them. Ester Boserup has repeatedly stated that the activities of women in developing countries are radically altered when they move from rural to urban areas as most of the subsistence activities they performed in the rural area, cannot be carried out in urban surroundings. Hence, women are left with more time for non-domestic activities. Yet, when economic pressure, for example, the insufficient income of the family head, inflation or other such reasons, forces them to seek employment, they usually become victims of development, because 1) family obligations make them less mobile than men, 2) their occupational choices are more narrowly limited by custom, 3) they usually have less education and training and 4) even without these handicaps, they often face sex discrimination. The Turkish data provided has largely confirmed this trend.

Actually, all three authors (Kazgan, Şenyapılı, Özbay) imply that the maintenance of the traditional family, where women function in a subsistence economy and where their access to the marketplace is short circuited, is predominantly a normal consequence of the capitalistic system. Thus, a significant change can only logically come about with a basic modification of the social order.

In Turkey, as everywhere, the integration of women into the development process as equal partners with men—a goal inherent in almost every plan—is confronted with serious obstacles. Some of these obstacles are political, others attitudinal. Resistance to women's greater participation in economic and political life is usually stronger among the groups most exposed to rapid social change and most ambivalent about it. Still other obstacles are conceptual, for example, the employment of women is widely considered "supplementary" to that of men. Another misconception is the relation between men's and women's work. The "unpaid family worker" is an example of this concept. Finally, planners need to understand the extent to which important changes in women's work occur in terms of class formation. The time is ripe for Turkey's planners, politicians and opinion markers to concentrate on such debatable issues as the promotion of feminine occupation versus the democratization of vocational training, the conceptualization of education policies in light of women's dual roles and its relationship to capitalist production, and the elimination of sex stereotypes as a precondition for democratic socialization. Whether the dynamics of Turkey's multiparty system will be able to tackle in the near future a problem of such magnitude remains to be seen.

GÜLTEN KAZGAN

LABOUR FORCE PARTICIPATION, OCCUPATIONAL DISTRIBUTION, EDUCATIONAL ATTAINMENT AND THE SOCIO-ECONOMIC STATUS OF WOMEN IN THE TURKISH ECONOMY

The status of women, like that of any other social group is determined by the economic development level of the country in which they live in, by the social class to which they are affiliated and by the cultural values that prevail in that society. The identification of Turkey as a developing economy and its cultural value system derived basically from the Islamic creed are succinct indicators as to where the status of its women lies. But, recall that this country is characterized by a dual economy, implying at one and the same time, the existence of a deep cleavage that separates one social stratum from the rest. Amongst the various meanings that one may ascribe to the term "social duality", one is based on sex with males at the progressive end and females at the bottom echelons of the social framework. This distinction is not, however, as categoric as the term implies; for, in the upper social strata, the discrepancy between the socio-economic status of the two sexes narrows then widens as one moves down the social ladder, reaching its maximum in peasant families which still constitute the majority (60 percent) of the Turkish population. Also, as the economy develops and social transformation accompanies (p.c.) per capita income rise, the status of women undergoes a radical change within all social strata ameliorating in most but worsening, even if only temporarily and relatively, in others.

In the following paragraphs, the socio-economic status of Turkish women, as well as its change over time, will be studied in light of their participation in productive activity. The extent to which and the ways in which they become involved in the production of goods and services outside the narrow confines of their homes will help to demonstrate at least one aspect of their relative socio-economic standing with respect to males.

I. Female Labour Force Participation

a) History of the Entry of Women into Market Activity

Human beings pave the way to their personal freedom and welfare and simultaneously contribute to socio-economic progress when they assume tasks in the productive process. It is true that they are also charged by nature with a reproductive (biological) assignment—that is to keep the human race going. But, when one of the sexes, namely males, undertakes the former productive duty and women are left with the latter (reproductive) charge, a social division of labour based on sex ensues, freezing the socio-economic status of both. Up till the late 19th century, such a rigid division of labour—as dictated by the religious social ethic—defined (Moslem) Turkish society. Except for rural women participating in field work on the family plot and the women engaged in domestic services in the houses of the rich, the rest of the female population was totally precluded from economic activity in the market. It was only in the late 19th century that women made their first appearance in the labour market as teachers in girls' primary schools under the influence of Western ideas which were then only assimilated by the upper social class. This was followed, about two decades later, by women's entry into factory work as a result of the pressure exerted on the labour market by the continuum of wars. It should be noted that both the first (professional) and the second (factory) type of female market activity met with opposition. However, in both cases, socioeconomic forces weighed more heavily than the teachings of religious ideology. Thus, even though negligible in terms of numbers, women's entry into market activity implied a significant breach with the rigid cultural value system of the past.

The Atatürk reforms aimed at giving women equal legal rights and equal opportunity in education as well as in employment. But deprived of the necessary economic foundations, the reforms brought no immediate betterment in the work opportunities for women. Nevertheless, when added onto the secularization of the State, they facilitated a further encroachment upon the sex role assignment of Koranic teachings. They also initiated an impulse towards economic development and modernization, which in turn, additively raised the educational requirements of women, particularly in terms of labour force membership.

In the post World War II years, this impetus was further strengthened as contacts with the industrialized world gained momentum, as the exchange economy evolved further, and as the economic welfare of the masses improved under the impact of industrial development. All this is not to say, however, in the hundred years since women first entered the labour market, they have taken considerable strides towards equality in working with males. It is true that there have been some notable changes both in women's educational attainment and their rate of participation in economic activity. Nonetheless, one may say in this respect that the current status of women in this country is presumably inferior to that in other developing countries (with approximately the same p.c. income) where cultural values areat least neutral with regard to sex roles.

b) Women in the Labour Force in Contemporary Turkish Society

In a basically peasant society—as the major part of Turkey is still defined—where small farms operated by unpaid family labour harbour approximately three fourths of the agricultural population, female labour force participation (LFP) generally tends to be high, particularly when and where labour-intensive technology is employed. Men, usually operate the agricultural equipment and machinery while women perform the manifold manual tasks, particularly during the harvest season.

In the post World War II years, Turkey started from a stage of socio-economic development where over 80 percent of the population was actively engaged in agriculture, of which women made up over 50 percent (Table I and IV). If unpaid female family labour, making up 90 percent of the active females, is included in the total labour force figures, the obvious result is an extremely high LFP rate for women (81.5 percent of the women aged 15 and over). In this case, women would appear to have an almost equivalent (47 percent) contribution to production with men. But, in the 1950's less than 4 percent of active females were employed in the non-agricultural occupations where wage remuneration is prevalent. It is true that the urban labour force was as yet small (17 percent) due to the low degree of urban-industrial development.

To fully assess the changes that have occurred with the integration of women into society's productive activity, it will be necessary to study their LFP rate in the non-agricultural sectors side by side with total economic activity. This is because, the quarter century from 1950 onwards marks this country's transition from a traditional society to an urban-industrial one and a significant transformation is likely to emerge in the course of this process. In addition, sheer figures on unpaid family labour fail to be very reliable indicators of the actual LFP rate.

First, a few words are in order on the female LFP rate inclusive of unpaid family labour in agriculture. It may be observed in Table I and Table II that both time series and cross-sectional data trace a backward-bending supply curve of female labour as p.c. income rises. The more than doubling of p.c. income in the course of industrial development since 1950, has been accompanied by a halving in the share of active women in the labour force. A striking consequence of this evolution has been a substantial decline in the overall rate of LFP for the population as a whole. Note that women have constituted a small and almost constant proportion (on the order of 10 percent) of the non-agricultural labour force; but, as the latter's percentage share of the total active population continued to rise, so did the share of females engaged in non-agricultural occupations (from 3.5 percent to 10.4 percent). See Table I.

If the metropolitan cities of Turkey and other large urban centers are considered as the examplary social targets to which other provinces

Table I

Labour Force Participation of Women (Age 15 Years and Over) 1950–1975 in percentage

	Total Labour Force			*Non-Agricultural Labour Force*			
	Active females out of females age 15 and over	*Active females in total labour force age 15 and over*	*Total active population in population age 15 and over*	*Active females as % of total (both non-ag.) age 15 and over*	*Non-ag. female labour as % of active females*	*Total non-ag. labour in total active population*	*p.c. income in 1968 prices (TL)*
Years	%	%	%	%	%	%	
1950	81.50	47.0	88.4	10.0	3.5	17.0	1848
1955	72.0	43.1	83.7	9.9	3.9	19.8	2349
1960	65.3	40.3	79.6	9.3	4.7	26.5	2550
1965	56.2	37.9	74.1	7.1	4.0	28.2	2879
1970	45.3	37.5	60.1	10.8	10.0	34.8	3507
1975	37.0	35.2	51.8	11.0	10.4	37.8	–

Source: Population Census Data, State Institute of Statistics (SIS), Ankara; for p.c. income, State Planning Organization

will evolve as the process of socio-economic development proceeds, the same tendency is further strengthened. In Istanbul, the largest metropolitan center, the female LFP rate (inclusive of agriculture) stands at the minimum with only 16.5 percent of the female population (aged 15 and over) engaged in economic activity. If the six largest urban centers

Table II

Labour Force Participation Cross-sectionally (1970). Percentage of Males and Females Age 15 and Over

Three Metropolitan Centers	*M* %	*F* %	*Literacy rate (F)*	*Graduation from some school (F)*	*LFP of migrants to urban centers %* *M*	*F*	*Degree of socio-econ. development (Index)*
			as % of females 6 years and over				
Istanbul	73.7	16.5	71.8	55.7	74.5	16.0	250.6
Ankara	72.8	29.8	67.2	49.6	70.9	18.1	204.8
Izmir	79.1	34.0	68.5	51.0	75.7	23.8	166.3
Other Large Centers							
Adana	75.3	39.1	54.4	34.8	77.5	19.6	127.5
Bursa	83.1	44.8	63.6	44.8	82.0	23.7	105.4
Eskişehir	76.6	38.5	60.0	51.4	74.9	18.6	118.7
Total		50	40	25.1			

Source: For population characteristics, *1970 Population Census Data;* for degree of socio-economic development of provinces, Dr. Barlas Tolan, *Türkiye'de Iller itibariyle Sosyo-Ekonomik Gelişme Endeksi (1963–70)*, State Planning Organization, Ankara 1970, (mimeo).

are ranked in decreasing order according to their degree of socio-economic development, the LFP rate for women tends to rise as the magnitude of the former declines; that is, the two variables appear to be inversely correlated (Table II). (Simpler calculated cross-sectionally between the indexes of socio-economic development of 37 provinces and their female LFP rate yields a coefficient with a negative sign: $r = -0.883$). Thus, cross-sectional data traces a backward bending supply curve of female labour in the same way as time series data if unpaid family workers are included in the work force statistics. This contrasts sharply with the positively sloped female labour supply curve in industrialized societies with an approximately 6—10 fold higher level of p.c. income.[1]

Nevertheless, the assertion that the female LFP rate has been declining in the transitional stage from a basically peasant society to an urban way of living rests on the assumption that women employed without remuneration as unpaid family members in agriculture are full-time workers. Unless, of course, data are available with respect to work intensity of male and female labour in farming operations, this assertion rests on shaky grounds.[2] If, however, underemployment in Turkish agriculture is a real phenomenon and if it is associated exclusively with unpaid family labour, then, we should not equate a woman working without remuneration in agriculture with either an urban female or male wage worker. Therefore, to say that "the backward bending supply curve of female labour stems from the substitution effect being outweighed by the income effect"[3] as the economy develops, in the style of economics textbooks, would be utterly meaningless for systematic errors in measurement distort the results.

Even if systematic errors in measurement are involved in the observed backward-bending supply curve of female labour, it is nevertheless true that Turkish women occupy a relatively unimportant place (on the order of 11 percent) in the urban labour force and this place has not changed remarkably over time. Since about 85 percent of the urban women of working age remain out of the labour force, a social division of labour

[1] For example, in the U. S. A., the LFP rate of women (as percent of all workers) has evolved as follows: 17 percent in 1890, 22 percent in 1930, 29 percent in 1950, 33.3 percent in 1960, 37.1 percent in 1968. "Handbook on Women Workers: 1969", U. S. Department of Labour, p. 10 (This rate exceeds 40 percent in the early 1970's.)

[2] All over the less developed world, the inclusion of women (working as unpaid family members) in the agricultural labour force introduces an element of error or instability in interspatial or intertemporal comparisons. For, some countries always record them within the labour force while others do not; but also, a country may include them within the labour force in one census yet leave them out in another. In Turkey women working on the family plot without remuneration are always recorded in the census data as a part of the work force; thus no inconsistency arises in time series analysis of agricultural employment; however, intercountry or intersectoral comparisons may yield misleading results. (See E. Boserup, *Women's Role in Economic Development*, New York, 1970, p. 75—76).

[3] The text book explanation of the backward bending supply curve of labour as derived from orthodox economic theory is the following: "As real wages rise, people demand more of all goods and services — under the proviso that their income elasticities are positive — inclusive of leisure. This is the income effect of the rise in real wages. But the rise in the wage rate assumes the labour supply curve to be a function solely of its own wage rate whereas in the case of women, this is not true.

based on sex still appears to be an outstanding feature of Turkish urban society.

In effect, the high incidence of marriage and the high fertility rate[4] (Table III) support this argument: never married women above 25 years of age account for only four percent of the total female population. This percentage does not vary even in the urbanized localities with a population exceeding 10,000. When this figure is coupled with the high fertility rate even in urban centers (with the exception of a minority who are well-educated), it becomes apparent that woman's major occupation is taking care of the house and the children, especially in view of the low degree of mechanization of household chores in a developing country.

Table III

Occupational Distribution of Female Labour (as % of Total Labour in the Occupation) 1970–75

Occupations where female employment is maximum	*Females as % of total* %	*Occupations where female employment is minimum*	*Females as % of total* %
Agriculture	50	Mining	4
Tobacco Industry	57	Construction	1
Textile-Apparel	30	Furniture	3
Food-Beverages	25	Metals	2
Chemicals	22	Car Industry	2
Electrical Machinery	17	Machinery	3
Teaching	34	Petro-Chemicals	3
Banking	34	Transport-Communications	3
Medical Profession	30	Salesman and Related workers	1
Physicists, Chemists and related workers	20	Protective services	1

Source: *Population Census Data*, SIS

In other words, even if sex role assignment ceases to be completely determined by the social ethic imposed by religious dogmas, but rather by other social factors, the outcome is more or less the same: household

[4] The negative association between the incidence of marriage and labour force membership is a well-known universal phenomenon. But what is not so well-known is the direction of causality. Do women enter working life because they have remained single despite their will or do they remain single deliberately in order to pursue a career seriously and to reject the division of labour based on sex?

activity appears to be the primary occupation for an overwhelming proportion of urban women and preclusion from productive market activity determines their socio-economic status.

c) *Turkish Women Working Abroad*

As of 1975, there were 632 thousand women in the country engaged in non-agricultural occupations. In addition to these there were 147 thousand women working abroad in Western Europe. Thus, the total number of women working with remuneration in secondary and tertiary industries rises to 779 thousand. It is interesting to note that although women constitute only 11 percent of the labour force in urban occupations in the domestic economy, their percentage share stands on the order of 17.6 in total Turkish labour abroad. Based on this, one may allege that when the opportunity arises for receiving a higher wage rate and/or when relieved of the pressure exerted on them by the traditional cultural value system, Turkish women readily enter the labour market and that a relatively higher proportion of women are beginning to reject their sex role assignment as their sole occupation. It appears that a totally different social environment, such as exists in Western Europe, creates a different set of incentives for women and alters their attitude towards household and market activity. However, it should be noted in passing that in one of the major labour recruiting countries in Western Europe, namely Western Germany, female labour makes up 30.2 percent of all foreign labour coming mainly from such Mediterranean countries as Italy, Spain, Greece, Yugoslavia and Portugal in addition to Turkey.[5] But, despite the existence of numerous factors favourable to inducing women to enter this labour market, Turkish women have failed to attain the high LFP rate of women from other Mediterranean countries.

[5] Duncan Miller, Ihsan Çetin, "Migrant Workers, Wages and Labour Markets", Istanbul University, Faculty of Economics, Institute of Economic Development, Istanbul 1974, p. 7, Table 2.

II. Occupational Distribution of Female Labour

a) *Nature and Degree of Occupational Concentration*

Social differentiation between males and females is perhaps in no category as striking as it is in the case of the occupational distribution of women. At one extreme women constitute a relatively important share in the least qualification demanding industries and operations and at the other extreme, they appear to carry an almost equivalent significance with male labour in the most sophisticated occupations. That is, in some sectors, women occupy a non-negligible place in economic activity whereas in others they are almost non-existent.

Table III shows the nature of occupational concentration by listing in one column the activities in which female labour weighs heavily and by contrasting this in the next column with the sectors where women's role is quasi nil. Agriculture, light manufacturing industry (tobacco, textiles-apparel, food-beverages, packaging of chemicals) and certain subdivisions of service industries are typically "feminine" occupations. Women make up no less than one fifth of the labour force engaged in such activities; but their percentage share rises to one third in the respectably feminine services, namely teaching, banking and the medical profession. Their share is equal to or greater than one half in agriculture and the closely related tobacco industry. In contrast, women have hardly entered, until recently, the physically demanding occupations such as mining, construction, the heavy industries and the service industries which involve close contact with male clientele, i. e. trade and related services, transport, communications, and the protective services. They constitute at most four percent of the labour force in mining[6] and even less in the remaining fields. Note that all of these activities are either 'unfeminine' in a purely physical-biological sense (mining, construction and heavy-industries) or 'unfeminine' in an ideological sense (the service industries). In other words, sex segregation reinforces the observed character of occupational concentration which defines the female labour force.

---

[6] Since women of all ages are banned by the Labour Law from employment underground, women work not in the production process but in other departments of the mining industry.

As to the *degree* of occupational concentration: suffice it to say that over 88 percent of the active women are engaged in agriculture whereas a little less than 4 percent and 8 percent are employed in industry and services respectively. A comparison of Table III with IV shows that, even though (or because) a small proportion of women work in non-

Table IV

Occupational Distribution of Labour Force by Sex (Male and Female) 1955–1975 in percentage

Occupation	*1955*			*1965*			*1970*			*1975*		
	M	*F*	*Total*	*M*	*F*	*Total*	*M*	*F*	*Total*	*M*	*F*	*Total*
Agriculture	46.6	53.4	100	50.4	49.6	100	49.5	50.5	100	50	50	100
Industry	87.1	12.9	100	94.4	5.6	100	83.4	16.6	100	88.5	11.5	100
Services	92.4	7.6	100	97.4	8.6	100	90.8	9.2	100	87.4	12.6	100

Source: *Population Census Data*, SIS

Table V

Occupational Segregation Index of Women (1955–75)

Year	*Index*
1950	32.05
1960	33.80
1965	32.25
1970	36.65
1975	39.95

Source: *Population Census Data*, SIS

agricultural sectors, occupational concentration is remarkably high. But what is more remarkable is that occupational segregation appears to rise over time rather than the reverse. The index in Table V indicates that the percentage of active females that would have to shift occupation to have the same distribution as the active males has risen from 32.05 in 1950 to 39.95 in 1975.[7] This stems from the fact that women are channelled into almost the same occupations over time whereas men are

[7] For the computation of the index of occupational segregation (See, M. H. Stevenson, "Relative Wages and Sex Segregation by Occupation" in *Sex, Discrimination and the Division of Labour* (ed. Cynthia B. Lloyd) Columbia University Press 1975.

spread over an increasing number of varying activities. For example, while women constituted 24 and 27.6 percent of the labour force in banking and teaching activities respectively in 1963, their percentage share has risen to 35 by 1973. However, if this index is interpreted as one of occupational segregation in an *ex post* sense, its origin should be searched partly in the relatively lower qualifications of women and partly in the social value system. The former female characteristic, however, is partly a result of the latter's ethical prejudices. As will be discussed in the following paragraphs it too has firm economic underpinnings.

b) *Occupational Concentration, Real Wages and Social Security Coverage*

The occupations in which female labour is concentrated are in general characterized by low earnings, the typical examples being agriculture and the light industries. Since they are the major source of Turkey's principle export products, they are open to competition in the world market in contrast to the highly protected domestic industries listed in the second column of Table III, which produce import-substitutes. Whereas the former pays low wages, on account of relatively low competitive prices the reverse is true for the latter: prices incorporating monopoly rents provide a source of high wage payments in essentially male industries. In effect, the relative wages of female labour in occupations covered by Social Security regulations have varied in general between two thirds and four fifths of male wages between 1955—74 (Table VI). This differential may be explained on the basis of various female attributes: first, as will be shown later, the labour qualifications of women are fairly low. Secondly, the Turkish Labour Law bans the employment of women in the physically toilsome but high paying sectors such as mining, construction and the heavy industries;[8] therefore, a legal barrier exists on the entry of women into the high-wage sectors; hence their cumulation in the remaining. Thirdly, the following simple correlation coefficients calculated between the percentage of female labour employed in the 19 subsectors of manufacturing industry and some explanatory variables yield some clue as to the underlying causes of relatively low

[8] Article 68 of the Turkish Labour Law (No. 1475) stipulates that male minors and women regardless of age are banned from employment underground and underwater; and the latter also on night shifts. In addition, this ban also exists on the perilous and toilsome or poison yielding activities on the grounds that women may be hampered from undertaking their reproductive engagements.

Table VI

Index of Total Workers (1955 100) and Percentage of Female Workers and Daily Relative Earnings of Women Covered by Social Insurance: (All Turkey)

Years	*Total (1955 100)*	*Employment Female*	*Female (Numbers)*	*Average Daily Wage Female/Male*	
				Total (1955 100)	%
1955	100	12.2	64.892		65.3
1960	116.5	11.3	70.036		67.9
1965	168.0	11.6	104.278		81.4
1970	246.3	8.9	117.284		91.8
1974	337.6	9.2	152.316		74.7

* Refers to average daily wages of workers covered by Social Insurance. Hence, they should not be considered as representative of relative female wages for Turkey in general.

Source· *Social Insurance Institute Data;* Istatistik Yıllığı, SIS

female wages: simple r calculated between the percentage share of female labour in the manufacturing activity and capital per worker stands at —0.375. This bears evidence on the concentration of women in the relatively more labour intensive manufacturing sectors. Simple r calculated between the former variable and the percentage of workers covered by collective bargaining within the subsector stands at—0.35 indicating the existence of an inverse, though not too strong, association between the two variables. Thus, in so far as female labour in manufacturing industry is concerned, they appear to be engaged more or less in the more competitive low wage sectors where capital per worker is relatively less and the degree of unionization is low. In the service industries as well (leaving the sophisticated medical professions aside) where female labour constitutes no less than one third of the labour force, e. g. teaching and banking activities, salaries are low in relation to their educational requirements. As to the social security coverage of female workers, even as late as the mid 1970's only about nine percent of the workers covered by social insurance were female (Table VI). Note also that about five percent of the active women engaged in non-agricultural activities are in the 12—14 year age group and therefore are legally excluded from social security coverage.[9] In addition to female minors women engaged in home or small industries are employed clandestinely so that they

[9] Social Security coverage starts with the age 15.

escape social statistical records. Hence, neither in terms of relative wages nor in terms of social security coverage may the figures above be considered as representative of female labour conditions in non-agricultural activities.

To dwell on relative wages and social security coverage in non-agricultural activities and to ignore the working conditions of women in agriculture would, obviously, be misleading since an overwhelming proportion of active women (88 percent) are employed in the latter sector without remuneration. This topic will be dealt with at length in connection with the employment status of women. At this point, suffice it to say that about 30 percent of the wage workers in agriculture are women, i. e., their percentage share in agricultural wage labour is triple that in non-agricultural activities. Since agriculture, the lowest paying sector in the economy,[10] is still outside the coverage of the Labour Law, and social security provisions, one may rightfully conclude that women are for the most part engaged in low wage, labour-intensive competitive industries and are only minimally covered by social insurance provisions.

III. Employment Status of Female Labour

a) *In Agriculture as Unpaid Family Member*

For the majority of working women, employment status is determined by their occupational distribution. Of the active females who are engaged in agricultural activity, 88 percent, only 1.5 percent are wage employees. The remainder toil under the status of "unpaid family member". That is, the overwhelming proportion of rural female labour carry on productive activities as a natural extension of their household duties, as daughters or sisters at one stage of their lives and as wives or mothers at the next. The fact that 86.6 percent of active females (1975) are employed without remuneration (Table VII) implies that these women are deprived of reaping the direct fruits of their labour in the form of personal monetary gains; but rather, the return from their work accrues to the male head of the family, viz., the father or the brother in early ages and the husband later on. A direct corollary of the way in which the return from their labour is distributed is their restricted influence on its spending pattern.

[10] Net-value-added per capita of working population (inclusive of unpaid family members) in agriculture stands at one fifth of that in non-agricultural occupations.

Table VII

Distribution of Active Population by Employment Status in percentage

Years	*Employee*		*Employer and workers on own account*		*Unpaid family labour*		*Total*	
	M	*F*	*M*	*F*	*M*	*F*	*M*	*F*
1955	22.3	3.8	48.3	4.7	29.4	91.4	100	100
1960	30.2	4.9	48.1	7.0	21.7	98.1	100	100
1965	32.8	5.9	48.4	4.5	20.8	91.2	100	100
1970	38.4	10.2	40.2	7.6	21.3	82.9	100	100
1975*	38.1	9.4	39.3	3.7	21.9	86.6	100	100

Source: *Population Census Data*, SIS

* Figures for 1975 refer to active population aged 12 and over whereas the coverage for previous censuses is different: they cover active population aged 15 and over.

Therefore, the rising share of wage plus self-employed work among women should be considered as a relative improvement in their socio-economic status assuming that, in so far as they can have access to the return from their work in the form of monetary gains, they are relatively better off. This is particularly true if they are able to make independent spending decisions for at least one part of their income.

The employment status of rural women also helps to explain the underlying causes of some of the social customs that still prevail in rural Turkey, which in turn serve as a meaningful indicator of the socio-economic status of peasant women. One such social custom is the payment of a bride price by the husband's family to that of the bride. In so far as the unpaid female family worker is considered a capital good yielding flow services over her life time by working in the fields as well as in the household, such a social custom has firm economic underpinnings.[11] Note that the custom of paying a bride price still survives in parts of rural Turkey where the extended family system has not yielded its place to the nuclear family[12] and/or where labour-intensive farming operations

[11] Bride price may also be regarded as a compensation paid to the bride's family for the loss of a free farm hand. This custom prevails in other Islamic societies as well, but it also carries traces of an old Turkish custom which envisaged the payment of a price for the bride as a peaceful way to the enactment of the marriage contract. Nihat Aytürk, "Kadın ve Başlık Sorunu", *Milliyet*, July 21, 1977.

[12] The association between family systems and payment of a bride price has been treated very well in Serim Timur, *Türkiye'de Aile Yapısı*, Haccettepe Üniversitesi, Ankara 1972, Table 37.

require a large number of free farm hands to reduce costs.[13] Labour intensity is high not only in agricultural productive operations but also in the carrying out of household chores. Deprived of most of the modern household facilities and gadgets and still living at the margin of the exchange economy, rural women have to toil hard to run the house, e. g., bringing water from a distant water fountain or bringing wood from the forest, or preparing animal dung to be used as fuel or preserving food for future use, etc. When added to the high fertility rate among rural women, then it stands to reason that peasant women are wellworth the bride price which is paid for them. Ideologies rarely linger very long after their economic foundations disappear. Thus, this custom loses its stronghold as mechanization reduces the demand for labour in agricultural operations and as rural families migrate to urban centers. It almost completely disappears in the metropolitan centers, where the nuclear-family system prevails.

Another custom closely related to the economic role of women in agriculture under labour-intensive technology concerns polygamic marriages. In the ultimate analysis, polygamic marriages serve almost the same purpose as that implied in the paying of a bride price: to reduce costs of agricultural production by increasing the number of free farm hands and to cope with the drudgery of household chores. Obviously, polygamic marriages multiply the amount of free labour not only by increasing the number of housewives, but also by duplicating or tripling the number of children that are born to the family. However, it is impossible to back the argument concerning the wide prevalence of polygamic marriages in rural Turkey, either in the recent past or the present with the available statistics. Population census data shows only 2—5 percent of married women in excess of married males, over the last half century when population censuses have been regularly held.[14]

In view of the heavy physical toil that rural women have to shoulder,

---

[13] Under labour-intensive technology, labour intensity per unit of output or per unit of capital is high. A large peasant family with a high number of free farm hands whose sole cost lies in the subsistence requirements paid out of the family income and at least partly produced by the family, therefore, contributes to keeping costs of production low.

[14] It may well be that polygamic marriages are hidden from the officials collecting the census data since they are legally banned. Similarly, payment of the bride price is also banned by law. The Timur study shows that 53.1 percent of families on a country wide scale received a bride price when marrying off their daughters. Therefore, official population census data cannot be sufficient proof of the small incidence of polygamic marriages in rural Turkey.

one may argue that migration to towns involves a substantial amelioration in their socio-economic status and welfare. For, no matter how poor urban amenities may be in the squatter housing districts of large cities where migrants settle, not only is the exchange economy more fully developed but also better organized public services are an integral part of urban life. Also, no matter how hard wage work may be because of its rigid discipline, women can definitely exercise better control over the spending pattern of their money wages; and when covered by one of the social security institutions, they are rid of depending on a male family member to provide for them in old age or in case of sickness. But, recall that only a small proportion of urban women, including female migrants, are within the labour force (Table II); hence the advantages associated with urban work are realized by only a small proportion while dependency continues in other forms for the majority.

b) In Non-agricultural Activities as Self-employed or Wage Worker

If one may attribute a superior socio-economic status to wage work and self-employment than to family work without remuneration, then it may be said that the status of women has been ameliorating overtime. Whereas only 8.5 percent of the active women enjoyed such a status in mid 50's, this percentage rate has risen to 13 by 1975 (Table VII).

Nevertheless, three considerations appear to be relevant in relation to the preceding observation. First, the improvement in the employment status of women, even though valid, has not been significant enough to involve a radical change in their socio-economic status. Secondly, if within work with remuneration, self-employment is accorded a higher status relative to wage labour, active females in non-agricultural occupations may be considered worse off as the former status has remained constant but wage work has risen in a relative sense. Finally, since being an employer implies a status at the higher rungs of the social ladder in a bourgeois society, one may say that very few women succeed in enjoying such a privilege. Women are employed for the most part by men, be it without remuneration as unpaid family member or in return for wages; but the reverse is not valid. A female employer is a "rare bird". Indeed, their numbers are so few that we have deemed it unnecessary to open a new column in Table VII for this purpose, but have lumped them together with the self-employed.

In short, one may say that the "second sex" attribute of women is well confirmed by their employment status: almost never employing males but always employed by them, and this most of the time without remuneration.

IV. Educational Attainment of Women and the Female Labour Force

a) Low Degree of Educational Attainment

The relatively lower socio-economic status of women in general and of rural women in particular is on the one hand reflected by and on the other hand explained by their low degree of educational attainment. The prevailing social value system well reinforced by economic considerations creates a vicious circle of "relative backwardness" for women which hampers any possibilities of their catching up with males.

If the literacy rate is taken as an index of the capacity to absorb new knowledge and skills and to manipulate technologically advanced equipment or to carry on market activity in general, one may say that not only are women less qualified than males in a relative sense, but also in an absolute sense for more than half are unfit to carry out all but the most simple manual tasks. Even in recent years (1975), the female literacy rate (aged 6 and over) has stood at only 48 percent. Since the modern sector demands some non-traditional skills and qualities of their workers, illiterate, unqualified women are *ipso facto* eliminated from the occupations with better employment conditions and are lumped either in traditional agriculture or in traditional urban occupations, or they remain at home as housewives.

Women's relatively lower degree of educational attainment persists invariably at all levels of education. Undeniably, in terms of absolute increases, a tremendous improvement has been recorded in the educational achievement of females and males over the last three or four decades. But, both in terms of school enrollment and in terms of the number of graduates, the discrepancy between the sexes has narrowed only slowly. It has narrowed most in terms of the literacy rate and at the primary school level, but least at the higher education levels. Of the total number of graduates, females constitute a little less than 40 percent at the primary school level, about 30 percent at the secondary school and lycee levels and 20 percent at the university level. That is, the percentage of females that drop out of educational institutions rises *pari passu* with the level of schooling.[15]

b) Educational Attainment and LFP Rate of Women

The relatively lower level of educational attainment within the female population may be considered on the one hand the cause of their low rate of labour force participation (leaving out those working without remuneration) and on the other hand its consequence. The argument that a low degree of educational attainment underlies the low LFP rate of women may be supported on the basis of data with respect to both variables. For example, as the female LFP rate rises concomitantly with the level of educational attainment, one may conclude that it is this factor that lies behind the former female attribute. It may be seen in Table VIII that the rate of entry into the non-agricultural labour force rises from 1.3 percent in the case of illiterates to 5 in the case of primary school graduates, to 12.5 for secondary school graduates, to 30 for the lycee graduates, to 56.2 in the case of graduates from vocational schools and goes up to 70 percent for university graduates.[16] It is true that this neat picture is somewhat distorted when agriculture is brought into the picture and entry into the total labour force is considered; for, the LFP rate of illiterates and primary school graduates rises on account of their concentration in agriculture. But, since they are employed as family members without remuneration and their agricultural activity is a natural extension of their household engagements, the concept of 'LFP rate' in a strict sense has in fact little relevance to their particular situation. The neat trend and its casual effect on the LFP rate that emerges in the last column of Table VIII is therefore what needs to be explained.

The economic rationale that underlies the observed trend is simple and clear: investment in education is one of the determinants of the alternative cost of a woman's household activity. The higher the level of education the higher this cost. Hence, the higher the level of foregone

[15] For detailed analysis of education and its impact on women see: Ferhunde Özbay, "The Impact of Education on Women in Urban and Rural Turkey", p. 160—180.

[16] This scale appears to hold in the case of women in the U. S. as well where LFP rate rises from 19 percent for married and 78 percent for single women with less than four years of schooling, to 61 percent and 94 percent respectively for those with more than 17 years. E. James "Income and Employment Effects of Women's Liberation", in *Sex, Discrimination and the Division of Labour*, Ed. C. B. Lloyd.

Table VIII

L.F.P. among School Graduates at each Educational Level
(Females aged 12 years and over in 1975)

School Level	*In female population aged 12 and over number of graduates (000)*	*In L.F. in total activities (000)*	*2/1 %*	*In L.F. in Non-ag. activities*	*3/1 %*
Illiterates	(8.583.3)	(3.678.8)	(42.9)	(114.5)	(1.3)
Primary	4.595.7	1.622.8	35.3	218.5	5.0
Secondary	525.8	85.6	16.3	65.7	12.5
Lycee	240.4	77.6	32.3	72.0	30.0
Vocational	193.1	110.8	57.4	108.5	56.2
Higher	67.9	48.5	71.4	47.0	70.0
Total	5.622.9	1.945.3		511.7	

Source: *1975 Population Census Data*, SIS

earnings in case the women gives up market activity. But recall that women are also productive in the home and can produce a variety of goods and services instead of buying them in the market place. Their labour force participation therefore implies the incurring of a cost in the form of foregone home produced income in kind. This cost is particularly high in developing countries inclusive of Turkey where, on account of the relatively low degree of industrialization and marketization of the GNP, a non-negligible proportion of the latter is produced within the home. That is, the market activity of women also has a cost in the form of foregone income in kind. However, if women give up their household activity altogether or if they shoulder both market and non-market activities simultaneously, their attitude with respect to the wage incentive will not be identical. In the poor urban working class families, women carry on both tasks at one and the same time. Hence, the market wages of women contribute a net addition to family income whereas in the case of better educated women a handsome deduction needs to be made from market wages to arrive at the net addition. Since even this net addition is expected to rise in concurrence with the level of education, the higher the level of educational attainment, the higher the percentage of women who participate in the labour force. Therefore, one would not be at fault to conclude that the low level of educational attainment of Turkish women is the principal underlying cause of their low rate of LFP.

But the converse of the argument advanced in the preceding paragraph appears to be no less true; that is, the low LFP rate of women may be sorted out as the basic economic reason why women are educated less than males. Again, assuming that social choice depends solely on economic calculus, a rationale may well be adapted to fit such an argument. Since investment in education is expected to yield a return over the lifetime of the individual, the lower the LFP rate of women, the lower will be the expected return both for the family and for society at large. Families will find it more profitable to educate their sons rather than their daughters who are expected to assume their role in the social division of labour based on sex. This is particularly true when education at higher levels than primary school is involved. In effect, low income families cannot afford to finance educational expenses when this is considered a "consumer good", i.e., education is considered only to yield a direct non-monetary satisfaction to the individual or the family rather than an investment expenditure that will yield monetary returns. Therefore, the low LFP rate of women in wage work, one may contend, is the basic determinant of the low degree of education that families are willing to finance in the case of their daughters. Hence, the current division of labour, by determining the income expectations of families, entails the recurrence of the same pattern in the future.

Whether cause or effect, such rational decisions definitely underlie the observed parallel between education and the LFP rate of women. But to this should also be added the impact effects of the cultural value system which defines the role of women in terms of motherhood, and confines their activity to the house. It is difficult to assess to what extent such dogmas enter into decisions to educate girls less than boys or in the preclusion of even the educated women from wage employment, even in the large metropoles. It is also difficult to say whether it is only after receiving an education at least at the vocational school level, that women can rid themselves of such dogmas and can revolt at the role imposed on them by society, or at the hegemony of the male head (husband or father) of the family. That education contributes to the psychological as well as the socio-economic emancipation of women is well supported by a survey we conducted among 179 female university students in Istanbul. Only 13.4 percent of the surveyed group replied that the permission of the husband or the family would be called for if they were to apply for a job, whereas 53.6 percent replied that they would personally decide whether to be gainfully employed in the future or not.[17] But no matter

[17] For the results of this survey see Gülten Kazgan "Türkiye'de Kadın Eğitimi ve Kadın Çalışması", *Toplum ve Bilim*, Yaz, 1978.

which standpoint one takes in this regard, one decisive conclusion is that, the LFP rate in non-agriculture of the non-educated and little or medium educated women is extremely low, but rises somewhat at higher levels of schooling.[18]

In conclusion, it is worth noting that the urban female labour force appears to have a peculiar distribution with a heavy bottom consisting of unqualified women who definitely come from the low income urban class; and a rather heavy top with qualified women who, it is equally certain, come from the better income families[19]; but there is an indentation in the distribution in the semi-qualified category. This sets a clear contrast to the distribution pattern of female workers in the industrialized countries where the semi-qualified working women weigh heavily in the labour force.

V. Consequences of the Characteristics Observed in the Female Labour Force

a) Of Declining LFP Rate Over Time

The substantial decline observed in the LFP rate (inclusive of agriculture) for women over time as urbanization *cum* industrialization proceeds, involves various types of social and direct costs to the economy. Even if one may allege that the standard of living of female rural migrants in large urban centers improves as the heavy physical work they had to undertake in the villages substantially declines, the costs are nonetheless there. In addition, a multiplicity of vicious circles are created which entail the recurrence of some undesirable tendencies in the society.

The dependency ratio[20] rises not only because of the increasing pro-

---

[18] The said survey revealed that only 55.9 percent of girl students have been enrolled in the university with the decisive purpose of preparing themselves for a career in the future whereas 26.2 percent replied that they will base their decision whether to work or not on the income position of the family, ibid.

[19] Only 11.7 percent of girls competing in university admittance exams come from rural areas, i. e., the poorest section of the society. On the other hand, the ratio of the succeeding candidates to the competing candidates is directly proportional to the income of the family. Tevfik Çavdar, Demet Tünay, Tuna Yurtseven, *Yüksek Öğrenime Başvuran Öğrenciler (1974—75): Sosyo Ekonomik Çözümleme*, DPT Ekim 1976, Ankara, Table 30, p. 36.

[20] The term "dependency ratio" implies the number of dependents per thousand of active population.

portion of minors (children aged 15 and under) in the total population on account of the high fertility rate, but also because of the shift to inactivity of females aged 15 and over. In Table IX it may be observed that over the two decades between 1950—70 the rate of growth in the latter dependency ratio has been much faster than in the former. The two taken together implies that urban males have to shoulder increasing economic responsibilities stemming from an economically inactive wife as well as from her high fertility rate. In addition, a loss of income is

Table IX

Dependency Ratio: Age Group 0–14 (Male and Female) and Inactive Females Age Group 15 Years and Over

Year	*Ratio of Dependence*	
	Children Male and Female Age Group 0–14	*Inactive Females Age Group 15 Years and Over*
1950	0.713	0.197
1970	0.859	0.393

Source: For age group 0–14, DPT *Toplumsal Yapı Araştırması, 1950–70* Table 3, Ankara 1977, for inactive females age group 15 and over, *Population Census Data.* Dependency ratio implies the number of dependents per (000) of active population.

involved in two senses: on the one hand because in urban areas women contribute less to the production of goods and services within the home, and on the other because of their discontinuation of directly productive activity.

Available data suggest that there appears to be a statistically significant negative association between female employment in the urban sector and fertility rates [21]—whereas urbanization *per se* does not affect it to any appreciable scale.[22] This argument may be supported using the

[21] Activity in such traditional occupations as agriculture or the home industries; differ in their impact on fertility rates from employment in the modern sector. More precisely, the former does not appear to exert any pressure to reduce the number of children whereas employment in the modern sector does. Baran Tuncer, *Ekonomik Gelişme ve Nüfus*, Hacettepe Üniversitesi Yayınlari, Ankara 1976, p. 136.

[22] Educational attainment of female population appears to be of utmost significance in relation to reducing fertility rates, (Table X) so does employment in the modern sector; while no significant negative association has been established in population studies between urbanization *cum* industrialization and this rate. See, B. Tuncer, op. cit., p. 114—142.

Table X

Fertility Rates, LFP and Educational Attainment of Women (Average Live Births per Woman)

Educational Attainment	*Average Live Births*	*LFP and Literacy*	*Average Live Births*
		A) *Rural*	
Illiterate	4.2	Non-Literate Non-Working	4.3
Literate, no diploma	3.2	Literate, Working	3.6
		B) *Urban*	
Primary School	2.8	Literate and Working	2.3
Secondary School, Lycee,		Working	2.3
Vocational	2.0	Currently Working	2.9
University	1.4	Never Worked	3.5
		Non-Literate and Non-Working	4.0
		C) *Metropolitan Cities*	
		Currently Working	2.7
		Never Worked	2.8

Source: For the first column, Serim Timur, "Socio-economic determinants of differential fertility in Turkey", Hacettepe Institute of Population Studies, Ankara 1971. For the second column, Hacettepe Nüfus Etüdleri Enstitüsü, *1968 Aile Yapısı ve Nüfus Sorunları Araştırması.*

data in Table X which shows that the fertility rate dips down to the minimum in the case of urban and literate (and highly educated) women who are engaged in gainful activity while no appreciable decline is observable in the case of urban but non-literate and non-working women. But, if urban women constitute such a small proportion (on the order of 11 percent) of the non-agricultural labour force, then the expectation that the fertility rate will record a substantial decline as the country is further urbanized is not likely to be born out by facts. One may also speak of the existence of a vicious circle in relation to the high fertility rate and the ratio of dependence: inactive urban females contribute to the sustaining of a high fertility rate hence increase the dependency ratio on two counts, namely their own non-activity as well as their high fertility rate. But, as the annual rate of population increase is sustained at a high level (2.5 percent p.a.) employers can afford to be extremely selective in their choice of employees because of the rising pressure on the labour market which has approximately 1 million new entrants each year. Available job opportunities fail to meet the demand for jobs[23]; hence women with lower qualifications than males (at the given wage rate) drop out of the labour force. Thus, the cycle of "high female dependency ratio, high fertility rates, high dependency ratio" tends to repeat itself in the low income urban families.

Investment in females for the formation of human capital—be it in the form of formal education or migration or on the job training, all appear to have low yields. Even if primary school education is considered as a *sine qua non* of "good citizenship" and even if a better educated female population definitely creates external economies (better education of children, better household services, greater possibility to help the husband in various ways etc....), investment in higher education must yield a return to compensate its cost to the family and to society. Since there are fairly rigid capacity limits, at least in the short-run, in educational institutions, the enrollment of a larger number of girls implies that a corresponding number of boys will have to be left out. This case is most explicit in the case of the university admittance exams, whereby a predetermined number of students are admitted depending on the number of points they make in the exam. The case is no less valid for vocational schools which have also recently embarked upon the implementation of admittance exams on account of the high number of applicants that exceed capacity limits. Thus, society looses the increased additions to national income expected to be contributed by better educated males who are certain to remain in the labour force throughout their working life time. In contrast, 44 percent of the female vocational school graduates and 30 percent of the female university graduates remain out of the labour force with consequent losses in national income.[24]

A vicious circle is also operative at this point, impeding improvement in the educational attainment of the female population: the high rate of leakage into inactive life among female graduates creates the expectation that this state of affairs is likely to continue in the future. Consequently, both families and society at large stand less ready to invest in the educa-

---

[23] After 1973 when Turkey's prospects of sending labour to Western Europe dimmed following the economic slump, the unemployment rate is estimated to have risen to 15 percent of the active labour force.

[24] The rate of return on education at various levels of schooling has been estimated as follows: the technical secondary school: 21—23 percent; the lycee 23—25 percent; private rate of return on university 25—27 percent; and social rate of return 8—9 percent. Anne Krueger, "Turkish Education and Manpower Development: Some Impressions" in *Essays on Labour Force and Employment in Turkey—1971* (ed. D. R. Miller), p. 249.

tion of women than men. But as noted previously, the LFP rate of women appears to rise concurrently with the level of educational attainment. Thus, a higher female LFP rate is hampered by the expectation that this rate is likely to remain low.

A similar consequence ensues in the case of migration. Since LFP rates are low among female migrants to urban centers (Table II), mostly illiterate or barely literate women remain behind in the village where they carry on agricultural activity at subsistence levels in addition to taking care of the children. For example, according to the 1970 population census, women constitute 49.4 percent of total population, but their percentage share rises to 51.2 in the villages and declines to 46.6 in the cities.[25] This has an important consequence both for agricultural productivity and for women. When agriculture becomes the reservoir of illiterate women, concentrated mostly in subsistence production, low productivity and low income persists without any possibilities for improvement. On the other hand, one cannot deny that an urban social setting, in addition to formal schooling, provides the background for self-improvement and for acquiring new skills. Thus, the relatively low rate of female migration implies that such possibilities are also relatively less for women. Here, the trade-off between the continuation of low productivity subsistance production by women and the possibilities for their self-enhancement is obvious; so is the vicious circle in the perpetuation of the relatively backward female characteristics. The low LFP rate of women in urban areas, in addition to their low literacy rate and formal schooling, is a major set-back in their migration to towns; but if and when they remain in the village, the possibilities for self-enhancement are hampered. Consequently, one may say that the two important types of investment, i.e., education and migration to build up human capital, are undertaken on a lesser scale in the case of females relative to males, on account of the former's low LFP rate in urban areas.

The same holds no less true in the case of on the job training. The low LFP rate of urban women implies the prevalence of a high labour turnover rate. Moreover, the average working life time of women, i.e., the time span between their entry into the labour force and their retirement age is shorter than that of males, as stipulated by law. Hence, employers find it more profitable to invest in male workers than in females since the

[25] The discrepancy between the male and female share of urban population is largest in the relatively less developed provinces of Eastern Anatolia and smallest in the three metropolitan centers. In the former region, women constitute about 40 percent of city population while in the latter their percentage share approximates the national average.

expected rate of return following their training will be less, the labour turn-over rate will be higher[26] and their average working life-time will be shorter. Consequently, the labour characteristics of urban women appear to be a crucial hindrance in the way of increasing the third type of investment, *viz* on the job training, in the same way as it hinders the others.

Starting from the preceding premises, one may ask why the high LFP rate of rural women does not act as a counterbalancing factor and be conducive to a higher rate of investment in women. If the flow of migration had been from the city to the village, rather than the reverse, the high LFP rate of rural women would have created the required incentives for making a larger investment in them. But, economic growth is accompanied by urbanization and the LFP rate of urban women is low and has remained low.

b) Of the Distribution of the LFP Rate with Respect to Education and Occupation

An overwhelming proportion of females within the labour force (95 percent in agriculture and 50 percent in non-agriculture) are unqualified on the basis of our classification, hence are employed in general, in simple manual operations. As studied in the previous section, investment in these women to build up human capital is low and is likely to remain low. That is, once poor and unqualified, they are likely to remain so throughout their lifetime.

However, another peril, namely unemployment awaits such women in the course of economic development as technology improves and as simple manual tasks are replaced by machinery. In effect, the shifts in the percentage share of women in industrial employment between census years are derived by and large from technological changes. Similarly, agricultural mechanization embarked upon in the immediate post World War II years is now being extended to encompass harvest operations (e.g. in cotton picking) with the resultant decline in the demand for female labour in particular. Recall that, on the other hand, the dynamic subsectors of manufacturing and other industries employ a low percentage

[26] Since unqualified women work under the pressure to augment family income, at the cost of doing heavy work at home and outside, they drop out of the labour force as soon as the family's economic bottlenecks are solved. Their high fertility rate is another factor which increases the labour turnover rate.

of female labour except in the packaging or administrative departments.[27] Thus, few jobs are likely to be generated in new industries as women are eliminated from the traditionally feminine occupations such as agriculture and the traditional or non-dynamic sectors of the manufacturing industry.

It may be argued that the tertiary sector which has been growing even at a faster rate than the secondary sector will generate a large number of jobs for women as well as for men, as has been the case in the recent past. As a reminder let us re-emphasize the fact that services employ to a large extent (41 percent) qualified women. Moreover, in some service industries which employ unqualified or semi-qualified workers (e.g. restaurants, cafeterias, coffee houses, car repair shops, intra or inter city public transportation, service stations, etc.), women have yet to make their entrance. It is, however, not very likely that women themselves will be very willing to take up jobs in the traditionally male occupations that would accord them less prestige. Hence, one presumption is that qualified women will go on flowing into the basically feminine services; but for the remainder, particularly the unqualified or even semi-qualified women, job prospects even in the tertiary industries do not appear to be too promising. Hence, the expectation of an increasing unemployment rate, particularly in the low income strata of society amongst non-qualified women.[28] The adverse effect of technological development on income distribution is thus likely to make itself felt by killing off jobs for the uneducated and untrained women in labour-intensive operations on the one hand and by not generating new prospects on the other.

Another adverse impact on income distribution comes directly from the distribution pattern of female labour with respect to education. This is because (leaving agriculture aside) the LFP rate of urban women rises in direct proportion to educational attainment and because the level of schooling girls receive is for the most part directly associated with the income level of the family. That is, better educated women who by and large come from the relatively higher income strata are more likely to join the labour force and contribute to family income. But, in the low income families girls are hardly given an education beyond the primary

---

[27] The term "dynamic sectors" implies those industries which under the impact of a high income elasticity of demand for their products and a rapid technological change witness a high growth rate.

[28] A typical example relevant to this argument is the mechanization of household chores in the high or medium income families which obviated the need for employing permanent house maids.

school and even when they are educated at the secondary school or the lycee levels, they are less likely to join the labour force. This latter point implies that at levels of schooling which girls are likely to receive in the low income strata, families bear the cost of education (in the form of foregone income and school expenses) but are less likely to reap its fruits.

Data from the university admittance exams may be introduced to support the preceding argument: girls competing in the university entrance exams make up 22.4 percent of the total candidates; but girls from rural Turkey, i.e., from low income families presumably, constitute only 2.6 percent of the total and 11.7 percent of the total number of female candidates (as against 51 percent of rural population that is female).[29] In addition, further data indicate that the ratio of the succeeding students to the competing candidates rises in direct proportion to the income of the family except in the highest income stratum.[30] Thus, one may conclude that it is improbable for girls from the low income rural areas to move to an upper social class by receiving a university education and by making a career. That is, once a girl is born to a low income peasant family, the probability that she will remain so appears to be much higher than the probability of her moving to an upper class, at least by her own efforts.[31] But "to her who hath, more riches will be bestowed" seems to be the expectancy in the case of girls from better income families. They receive not only better formal education, but also by contributing to family income open up the way for moving to a still higher social class. Add onto this, the differing fertility rates of the former and the latter group of women, then the worsening effects on income distribution presented in the preceding paragraphs will be more clearly revealed. Social tendencies thus tend to cumulate on top of each other, in the same direction, rather than one compensating the impact effects of the other.

---

[29] Tevfik Çavdar, Demet Tünay, Tuna Yurtseven, op cit., p. 17, Table 3.

[30] This decline is associated with the high income farmers' and industrialists' children. In all probability, at such a high income level where capital income instead of labour income provides the source of economic welfare, the incentive to move up to a higher class by making a career declines or disappears. Nevertheless, this does not appear to be the case for students coming from other social strata. T. Çavdar, et. al., op. cit.

[31] Note that in the case of the male members of society, social mobility is much higher. Again data from the university admittance exams may be brought in to support the argument: male candidates from rural areas constitute 35.7 percent of total male competitors and 27.7 percent of total (male plus female from both rural and urban areas) candidates. This latter percentage stands only at 2.6 for rural female candidates. T. Çavdar, et. al., op. cit.

Prospects of marriage should also be introduced to complete the foregoing picture of the divergent trends in the destiny of women from the lower and upper social classes. This concerns the prevalence of "intra social class" marriages and the almost non-existence of "inter social class" marriages. In other words, women from the better income families enjoy a higher probability of improving their socio-economic status because they are more likely to receive a better education, and consequently are more likely to be committed to a career. In addition, they are more likely to marry the better educated and the higher income members of their own social class, and to give birth to a reasonable number of children. The same factors tend to cumulate in the opposite direction in the case of low income, particularly the rural women and hamper the relative improvement in their socioeconomic status. Thus, social duality tends to perpetuate itself in the case of women, even if undeniably there are leakages from the bottom to the top and even if the welfare of women, as a whole social entity, ameliorates as a function of urbanization and modernization.

FERHUNDE ÖZBAY

THE IMPACT OF EDUCATION ON WOMEN IN RURAL AND URBAN TURKEY

The education offered to women in Turkey today neither improves their social status nor does it enable them to play a more productive role in society even though, in the Republican era, the educational services and the female population benefiting from these services have increased.

The results of the 1975 Census show that 52% of the women aged 6 and over are illiterate (SIS, 1976). Among the women aged 11 and over only about 33% have a primary school education (Table I). The proportion having a secondary level of education is negligible (7%). University education, on the other hand is a luxury for women; only about 5 out of every one thousand women have graduated from institutions of higher education. When compared to the male population, women especially at the university level, are the least represented (Table I).

Table I

Distribution of Population by Last School Graduated from and Sex (Ages 11 and over) 1975

School	*Female (1)*	*Male (2)*	*Ratio (1)/(2)*
Non-graduates	59.6	34.1	1.75
Primary school	33.0	50.3	.66
Junior High	3.7	7.6	.49
Vocational School at junior-high level	0.1	0.2	.50
High School	1.7	3.5	.49
Vocational School at high-school level	1.4	2.4	.58
College	0.5	1.9	.26
TOTAL	100.0	100.0	
Population Sample	13,914,654	14,252,172	

Source: SIS, *The 1975 Population Census 1% Sampling Results*, 1976, (Başbakanlık: Ankara), pp. 6–7, Table 4.

Educational Inequality

The educational services not only are insufficient, but certain classes or groups tend to benefit more from these services than others. Class privileges in education particularly affect the female population.

The educational services are not able to cope with the requirements of the increasing population, even at the primary school level (Başaran, 1974). This situation is amplified at the level of higher education; in the 1974—75 academic year, only 16% of the applicants were accepted in the universities. (Çavdar et al., 1976).

The nation-wide distribution of these limited services is contradictory to the principle of equal educational opportunity which is based on laws. The educational programs are concentrated in the urban areas, especially in the large cities, both quantitatively and qualitatively, whereas they are quite insufficient in the rural areas where the majority of the population lives.[1] In the rural areas where educational services are the least sufficient, education further differentiates according to the varying socio-economic development levels of the rural settlements. (Özbay and Balamir, 1978).

Even in the urban areas, the educational services are not able to meet the needs of the urban population. Further, the criteria used to select the students who will benefit from the limited educational opportunities is class bound. Thus, the chances of succeeding in schools and on entrance examinations are low among the children whose families belong to the lower socio-economic groups (Çavdar et al., 1976).

Sex discrimination in education is observed in both the rural and the urban areas and in every age group (See Fig. 1). In the rural areas, the sex differential is higher for the younger generation than it is for the older one. This trend may be explained by the priority men have in benefiting from the increasing educational services. In the urban areas, however, the sex differential is gradually decreasing among the younger generation. This decrease not only exists at the primary school level, but is also noticeable at the junior high school level. While the ratio of female junior high school graduates aged 65 and over, to their male counterpart is 22%, the same ratio for the 15—19 age group is 86%.

[1] In censuses, settlements with a population of less than 10,000 are defined as the rural. The 1 % sampling results of the 1975 census show that 59 % of the total population live in rural areas. (SIS, 1976).

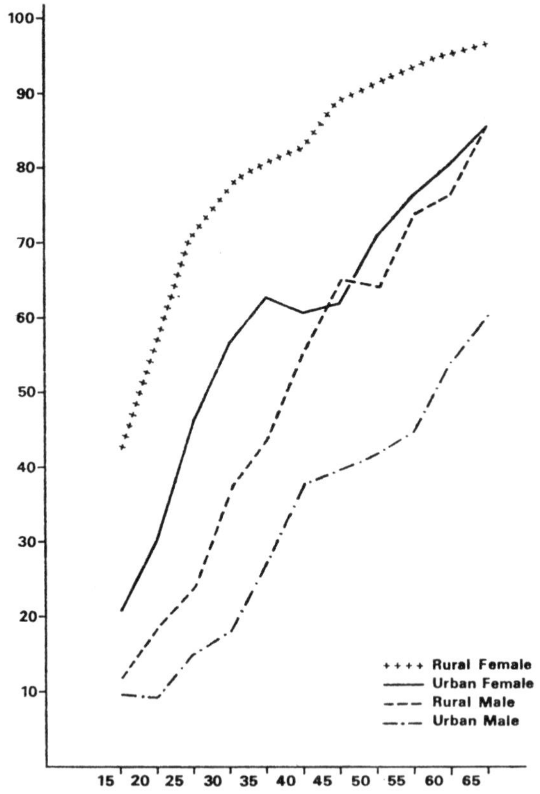

Fig. 1. In 1973 Distribution of the Non-Graduates in Urban and Rural Areas by Sex and Age Groups (Ages 15 and over)

The sex differential in benefiting from educational facilities reaches its peak in the rural areas where these facilities are the least sufficient. (Table II). Within the rural areas, the ratio of female students to male students is higher for villages with a high socio-economic development level and an external orientation than it is in underdeveloped villages. (Özbay and Balamir, 1978).

Within the urban areas, there is no sex differential among the families with a high socio-economic status (Kağıtçıbaşı, 1975). Sex discrimination increases as the socio-economic status of the families declines. Çavdar et al., 1913).

Table II

Distribution of Population in Urban and Rural Areas by Last School Graduated from and Sex (Ages 15 and Over) 1973

	Rural					
	Unstandardized Rates			*Age Standardized Rates*		
School	*Female (1)*	*Male (2)*	*Ratio (1)/(2)*	*Female (3)*	*Male (4)*	*Ratio (3)/(4)*
Non-Graduates	73.0	41.0	1.78	62.8	31.4	2.00
Primary	24.3	48.6	.50	30.7	55.5	.55
Secondary or higher	02.7	10.4	.26	06.5	13.1	.50
Total	100.0	100.0		100.0	100.0	
	Urban					
Non-Graduates	52.0	25.1	2.07	43.6	19.7	2.21
Primary	32.7	46.9	.70	37.9	50.3	.75
Secondary or higher	15.3	28.0	.55	18.5	30.0	.62
Total	100.0	100.0		100.0	100.0	

Source: 1973 Survey Person Cards.

Employment and Education

The Turkish female labour force consists mainly of women who have not finished any school. Most of these uneducated women are employed in the agricultural sector. (Table III). When the educational level of women is controlled, the highest rate of labour force participation is observed among the college graduates. However, their proportion of the employed female labour force is only one percent. The graduates of vocational and technical schools at the high school level follow the college graduates in terms of their labour force participarion. High school graduates having the same level of education as those from vocational schools, have a lower participation rate. Similarly, those who have graduated from vocational schools at the junior high level are proportionally more employed than the junior high school graduates. It seems that education, which provides individuals with practical and defined skills has some impact on labour force participation.

Table III

Distribution of Female Population by Last School Graduated from and Employment Status (Ages 12 and over) 1975

School	Employed	Not Employed	Total	Population Sample
Non-Graduate	50.1	49.0	100.0	7,913,364
Primary School	36.4	63.6	100.0	4,454,068
Junior-High	15.4	84.6	100.0	521,594
Vocational School at Jr. High Level	34.0	66.0	100.0	13,530
High-School	32.1	67.9	100.0	239,475
Vocational School at High-School Level	57.2	42.8	100.0	192,331
College	71.4	28.6	100.0	67,093
Total	44.1	55.9	100.0	13,401,455

Note: Unknowns are excluded from the analysis.
Source: SIS, *1975 Population Census, 1% Sampling Results, 1976*, (Başbakanlık: Ankara), pp. 6–7, 24–25.

According to the 1975 Population Census, there are 13.4 million females aged 12 and over, of which 44% are employed. Ergil, in her earlier studies, pointed out that female labour force participation declines from 72% in 1955 to 51% in 1975.[2] The reason for this decline could be the gradual removal of the female labour force from the rural agricultural sector.

Labour Force Participation in Rural Areas

The estimated figures for female labour force participation are lower in the social surveys than in the censuses. The difference between the two sources of data is particularly eminent in the rural parts of the country. According to the results of a village survey conducted by the State Planning Organization (SPO) in 1968, only about 11% of the women were reported as working. (Yurt, Ergil, Sevil, 1971), whereas in the 1975 Census, 39% of the total female labour force was employed in the agricultural sector. The difference between the census figures and those of

[2] Ergil defined the economically active population as those 15 years and over. The 1975 Census results on the other hand, considers 12, the minimum age limit for the economically active population instead of 15. Taking the age of 15 may have increased the proportion of labour force participation for 1975, but the difference is negligible. (Ergil, 1977).

the survey may have been due to the questions asked. In the SPO Village Survey the "main job" was requested. The respondents may have considered being housewives their main job although they may have also worked on the farms.

According to the results of the 1973 nation-wide survey conducted by Hacettepe, the female labour force participation rate was estimated to be 20.6%. This proportion rose to 25.3% in the rural areas (Peker, 1978). This too was a lower estimate when compared to the census results. The difference may have again been due to the different definitions of employment.

In the 1973 Survey, emphasis was placed on the definition of work which brings cash money. Most probably, family members who work on their own or a relative's farm without any wage were underestimated in the 1973 Survey.

In addition to different definitions, the surveys or the censuses may contain errors. Nevertheless, we do not face the same problem when estimating the employment status of males.[3] Therefore, it can be argued that there is a large degree of uncertainty about female labour force participation, especially in the agricultural sector.

In 1975, Hacettepe conducted another survey in 25 villages. In order to overcome the definition problem, all possible activities for rural women were listed; and the respondents checked the one they regularly performed. The activities were grouped in the following way: (i) government official; i. e. primary school teacher, nurse, midwife (indigenous midwives who have not been trained for this occupation were also included in this group), (ii) sewing, needle work, or weaving for money, and other non-agricultural activities which were not specified in the first group, (iii) waged agricultural laborers, (iv) self employed persons working on their own farm or garden, or doing husbandry for themselves. The continuity and the amount of time devoted to these activities were not taken into account.

Moreover, a woman chose an activity according to the above order. Thus, if a woman did more than one activity, it could not be shown in the tables. Further, since the very order of the activities gave priority to the "non-agricultural" types, it is a possibility that the agricultural activities were underestimated. Although, the results cannot be general-

[3] Labour Force Participation among males was estimated to be 76.1% in the 1975 Census (SIS, 1976), and 69.8% in the 1973 Survey (Peker, 1978). The difference is relatively small.

ized for rural Turkey, some interesting references can be drawn from the findings. The results indicate that a great majority of the women in the 25 villages (87%) are involved in some kind of economic activity (Table IV). Those who work for cash money represent 28%. Since husbandry was also considered an agricultural activity, the proportion of family workers participating in agriculture was higher than expected (58%).

Table IV

Distribution of Women in 25 Villages by Economic Activity, Education and Type of Community 1975

Economic Activity	Non-Graduates "Developed" Villages	Non-Graduates "Under-Dev." Villages	Total	Primary School Graduates "Developed" Villages	Primary School Graduates "Under-Dev." Villages	Total	Grand Total
Prim. school teacher, midwife, nurse, etc.	1.5	.3	.7	2.4	4.9	2.7	1.1
Other non-agric. activities, sewing etc.	11.4	13.9	13.0	13.7	11.5	13.4	13.1
Waged agric. worker	18.5	10.5	13.3	18.3	13.1	17.6	14.1
Husbandry and farming, independent	64.9	54.6	58.3	59.7	44.3	57.4	58.1
Housewife	3.7	20.7	14.6	5.9	26.2	8.8	13.0
Total	100.0	100.0	100.0	100.0	100.0	100.0	100.5
Number of People Surveyed	676	1,214	1,890	371	61	432	2,322

Source: The 1975 Hacettepe Village Survey, Person Cards.

Female economic activities in this village survey showed some peculiarities with respect to the women's level of education and the socio-economic development level of the communities in which they lived. When the type of villages is controlled, it is observed that the non-graduates work more in agriculture than the primary school graduates. Since the waged agricultural workers are mostly concentrated in the "developed" villages, the observed relationship between education and agricultural occupations declines in the overall analysis.

Except for occupations like teaching or midwife, the non-agricultural activities do not vary by educational background. This may be due to the general grouping of this category which includes both the low status activities such as housework and those which require certain skills like sewing. Another important point in this survey is that in the "developed" villages 96% of the women are involved in some kind of activity other than housework, whereas in the "underdeveloped" villages this percentage drops to 79%. This may be explained by the work possibilities in the villages.

The 1973 Survey data was also used to compare the relationship between labour force participation and education in rural and urban areas. The findings which are summarized in Table V reveal that education attainment is not related to labour force participation in the rural areas.[4]

Again according to the 1973 data, the proportion of women who work in agriculture decreases as their level of education increases. This is also supported by the 1975 Survey data. Agricultural activities among the secondary or higher school graduates are negligible. It is possible that the majority of these women come to the rural areas from outside, sent by the government, such as teachers, midwives or the spouses of government officials, etc., and this may be why their proportion in agriculture is small. Increasing levels of education and departure from agricultural activities do not show a significant trend. Moreover, the proportion of primary school graduates is also low. Thus, it cannot be argued that the education of women has a direct impact on the occupational structure in the rural areas.[5]

Limited Job Opportunities in the Non-Agricultural Sector

It is observed that female labour force participation declines rapidly in the urban areas among the non-graduates and primary school graduates when compared to the rural areas. This is to some extent due to the fact that many of the females who migrate from village to urban areas have little or no education, and are only experienced in agricultural work. As there are no agricultural activities in the cities, they tend to break away from the labour force.

[4] If this proportion were similar to that of the census, participation in the labour force would increase with increasing levels of education.

[3] According to the 1975 Survey, primary school graduates are more eager to move to cities than non-graduates: 15% of the non-graduates and 22% of the graduates reported that they were planning to migrate to a city in the future. It is possible that education has an indirect impact on the occupational structure because of geographical mobility.

In general there is a positive relationship between education and labour force participation in the urban areas (Table V). Secondary school graduates work three times more than the rest of the women. However, only 28% of the women among the secondary school graduates work. Due to the limited job opportunities in the non-agricultural sector, finding a job is not only related to educational attainment but also to sex.[6]

Since men, more than women, are expected to be the breadwinners of the family, society accepts sex discrimination in hiring men as opposed to women with the same educational background. In order to end these discriminatory hiring pactices, it is not suggested that educated women

Table V

Distribution of Female Population by Education, Employment and Occupational Status in Urban and Rural Areas (Ages 15–64) 1973

	Total Women					
		Urban			Rural	
Status	*None*	*Prim.*	*Second.*	*None*	*Prim.*	*Second.*
Working	9.1	9.4	28.4	23.9	26.3	22.4
Not Working	90.9	90.6	71.6	76.1	73.7	77.6
TOTAL	100.0	100.0	100.0	100.0	100.0	100.0
	Working Women					
Occupation						
Agriculture	29.5	10.1	–	92.1	84.3	4.7
Non-Agric.	64.5	89.9	100.0	9.7	15.7	95.3
TOTAL	100.0	100.0	100.0	100.0	100.0	100.0

Source: The 1973 Survey, Person Cards.

be given priority in the job market. In such a case, the unequal access to education enjoyed by certain groups could reflect itself more, particularly in the professional structure. As mentioned earlier (Kağıtçıbaşı, 1975), the most educated women in Turkey come from families with a higher socio-economic status than the men with the same level of education.

[6] In 1973, 59% of the male graduates of secondary schools (15—64 age group) were working. Among the men in this age group, the students reduced the male labour force participation rates. (SIS, 1976).

A logical approach to this problem should incorporate the expansion of educational opportunities for women.

The differences between the female labour force participation rates and those of the males are much more significant among the uneducated or less educated groups. In the urban areas, while only 9% of the women in these groups are employed, 82% of the men with the same level of education are working. One of the most important problems affecting female labour force participation in the urban areas is that of competition. There, women have to compete with men for the limited job opportunities, and educated females have almost no power in competition.

Jobs Towards Which Females are Directed

Another problem which women in urban areas face with respect to labour force participation is related to the kinds of jobs they do. Women with no education or primary school education tend to work in food production or as dress-makers, etc., although their proportion in these jobs is less than that of the men. (SIS, 1976). Alternative jobs such as servants in homes, or working as prostitutes, are always open to uneducated women. These jobs, of course, have a very low social status. (See Erten, 1978, for problems of prostitutes).

Among the vocational schools at the secondary school level, the girls' vocational schools have the highest proportion of students (Tayanç and Tayanç, 1977). These schools teach the role of being a housewife instead of preparing them to productively participate in society.

At the university level, as Tayanç stated, "girls have a tendency to choose the kind of education which directs them towards service jobs rather than towards the production of goods". (1977, p. 139). According to the 1975 Census if agricultural occupations are not taken into account, graduates from universities or vocational schools are mainly in the occupational category of "scientists, technical, professional and related jobs". This category also includes occupations like teachers, nurses and midwives. University graduates, on the other hand, work mostly in the fields of literature and law rather than in the sciences and medicine. (Tayanç and Tayanç, 1977). Again, according to the 1975 Census, graduates of junior high and high schools work mostly as clerical personnel. Whatever their educational level, women are less represented in trade, administrative and mamagerial jobs, and in all industrial occupations except manufacturing. (SIS, 1976).

Women who were made to work as unwaged family workers in the rural areas are excluded from the occupations that provide political and economic power in the urban areas. The educational system functions to support this biased structure instead of correcting the unbalanced situation which exists between the sexes. Female oriented occupations are clearly identified in every part of society and are also reflected in the preferred occupations of the mothers for their children.

Preferred Occupations for Children

In the 1973 Survey, married women aged 15—49 were questioned about the occupations they would prefer for their daughters and sons. In both urban and rural areas, one fourth of the mothers wanted their daughters to be teachers. The second most preferred occupation stated was that of housewife. This was a less desired status for urban mothers (8%), but in the villages 21% of the mothers wanted this status for their daughters. 17% of the mothers in the large cities wanted their daughters to become medical doctors. In places with less than 2,000 population, this percentage was very low (3%), but rather high (14%) for the occupations of nurse or midwife. In general, except for the occupation of housewife, mothers wanted their daughters to become teachers, nurses or midwives, dress-makers, M. D.'s, and pharmacists, in this order. The preferred occupations for sons were more varied. Mothers mostly stated occupations like medical doctors, teachers, engineers or architects, government officials and army officiers. Mothers' preferences for their sons showed some differences by rural-urban residence. Urban mothers preferred their sons to become medical doctors, or engineers, whereas village mothers mostly wanted their sons to become teachers.

Although the occupation of 'teacher' does not have a very high status in the village, the women perhaps associated this profession with the urban occupational structure and therefore stated it.[7] In the villages, mothers did not think of farming as an occupation for their children, as if to say "anything but a farmer". Again, mothers did not mention professions like engineers, technicians, administrators and university professors for their daughters.[8]

[7] According to the SPO 1968 Village Survey, a village teacher is not counted as one of the most powerful, respected leaders in the villages. (Yurt, Ergil, Sevil, 1971).

Education, Marital and Work Status

In Turkey, working women also carry the main responsibility for househ old chores and child rearing.[9] Thus, the working woman's load is much heavier in comparison to that of a man.

Since the number of child-care facilities are very limited and expensive, it is very difficult for women to work outside their homes even if they do have an education. Many women solve this problem by working at home, i. e. as dress-makers. According to the 1973 Survey of currently married working women in the reproductive age group, 92% stated that they had jobs outside their homes. However, 43% of the women living in small towns (with a population of 10,000 to 25,000) stated that they worked at home. Although working at home for money does give economic power to a certain extent, it isolates the woman from thc external world. In the long-run she will not be able to develop herself, and with the spread of technology (i. e., confection will take the place of hand-made clothes) such jobs will die out.

Married women with little or no education have less of a chance of working than other women, especially single women. The results of the 1973 Hacettepe Survey support this statement. Among the uneducated single women, one out of every five is working. This figure, however, is only 8% among the currently married. Among the primary school graduates, the lower percentage working is again found among the married women. (Table VI). Job opportunities for married women without any education are limited for various reasons. Such women can only work in low status jobs. Husbands whose recognized duty it is to protect the honour of their families, may not let their wives work at such jobs. More important, the women must find a place to leave their children when they start to work. If the women succeed in finding a suitable place for their children, very often their perspective wages will not be enough

[8] These professions are not only male oriented but also require long years of training (especially university professors). Boserup mentions that in developing countries families do not want their daughters to study for a long period of time since in that case, it would be difficult to find them proper spouses. (Boserup, 1970). According to observations made this line of thinking is also valid in Turkey.

[9] In families with a higher socio-economic status, women do not generally work, and their domestic responsibilities are fulfilled by helpers. Such women only are mentioned because they use the limited educational facilities more than the others. Emphasis should be given to other women who are in the majority.

Table VI

Employment Status of Women by Education and Marital Status in Urban Areas (Ages 15–64) 1973

	Marital Status		
	Single	*Married*	*Widow-Divorced*
Non-Graduates			
Working	19.7	8.0	13.2
Not Working	80.3	92.0	86.8
TOTAL	100.0	100.0	100.0
Primary School Graduates			
Working	14.9	7.3	16.6
Not Working	85.1	92.7	83.4
TOTAL	100.0	100.0	100.0
Secondary or Higher School			
Working	26.7	31.4	30.4
Not Working	73.3	68.6	69.6
TOTAL	100.0	100.0	100.0

Source: 1973 Hacettepe Population Survey, Person Cards.

to cover the daycare fees.[10] Thus, while heavy household responsibilities affect the work lives of women on the one hand, employers who are insensitive to this situation, affect it on the other.

Regardless of their marital status[11] women work proportionally more as their level of education increases. (Table VI). It may be possible that in the beginning single women work in order to increase their chances of finding a good spouse, but after marriage they work with the aim of helping the family income. The 1973 Hacettepe Survey results indicate that 60% of the married women aged 15—49 work in order to make a

[10] It is generally believed that most families in the lower socioeconomic groups live in extended households and that the elders take care of the children. Timur has shown that most families in Turkey are nuclear and that family types do not show much difference according to urban occupations.

[11] Although domestic responsibilities are rather low for single women, at the secondary education level their participation in the labour force is smaller than that of the married, widowed, or divorced women. It is mainly due to the fact that some of the single women are still attending school.

living. Those who work only because they like to is small, only 8%. "If you did not need money, would you still work?" 33% of the same women replied positively when asked this question. In other words, two thirds of the married women work to help the family income and they tend to stop working as their economic situation improves.

The proportion of women who stop working after marriage is high. Again, in the 1973 Survey, 35% of those who were working earlier, left their jobs because they got married. 18% reported that they stopped working after having a baby. Urban women are more likely to stop working because of marriage. According to this Survey, 5% stopped working because their husbands did not allow them to work. In villages with a population of less than 2,000 no woman reported that she stopped work because of her husband's refusal to permit it.

The 1973 Survey clearly shows that regardless of the woman's educational level, female labour force participation is affected by the roles of housewife and mother. This is more important for urban women. Therefore, it may be argued that unless the responsibilities related to child care and domestic duties are shared by men and the State, it will be difficult for women to use their education to improve themselves and to participate in the labour force.

Education and Marriage

The relationship between education and marriage in Turkey has not been analyzed in detail. The 1973 Survey suggests that with the increasing level of education, age at first marriage is increasing. A delay in the age at first marriage is especially high among women who have secondary or higher level of education (Table VII).

According to the census results, it was estimated that the mean age at first marriage (SMAM) increased on a nation-wide basis between 1955 and 1965. (Yener, 1969). The 1973 Survey and the 1975 Census results indicate that the increase is continuing. Rural/urban estimates of SMAM in 1960 were 18.86 and 20.24 respectively. It is observed that in 1973 the mean age at first marriage increased especially in the rural areas where it was found to be 20.07. In the urban areas this figure was 20.96.[12]

[12] The mean age at first marriage (SMAM) was estimated from the proportion of singles in each age group. Therefore, it is higher than a direct estimation which is based on the reports of married women. In 1973, the mean age at first marriage was found to be 17.7 among married women ages 15—49 (Kunt, 1978).

In general, a delay in marriage may be due to the increasing educational attainment of the females. It may also be due to factors within the urbanization and modernization process. Since earlier analyses are lacking, it is impossible to interpret the rural/urban differences in age at marriage by educational level in detail.

Table VII

Mean Age at First Marriage (SMAM) of Female Population in Rural and Urban Areas by Last School Graduated from 1973

School	*Urban*	*Rural*
Non-Graduates	18.61	19.17
Primary School Graduates	20.81	21.46
Secondary or Higher School Graduates	26.41	25.42
TOTAL	20.96	20.07

For the estimation technique of mean age at first marriage (SMAM) see Hajnal, 1953.

The increase in the mean age at first marriage in the rural areas may be explained by young male out-migrants who want to be educated in the urban areas. (Yener, 1977).

Education and Fertility

The relationship between education and fertility has concerned social scientists for a long time. Population surveys in Turkey which have been carried out more frequently since the 1960's, agreed that there is a negative relationship between education and childbearing in the country.[13]

In 1968, this subject was analyzed in detail using the Family Structure and Population Problems Survey data. At that date, illiterate women had 4.2 mean numbers of live births, whereas primary school graduates had 2.8 mean numbers of live births, and university graduates had 1.4 mean numbers of live births (Timur, 1977). Such differences in fertility by educational levels existed both in urban and rural areas. However, as the differences in fertility patterns sharpened in the urban areas, they

[13] An evaluation of such findings from different studies was made by Oppenheim and her colleagues (1971).

became relatively small in places with less than 2,000 inhabitants (Table VIII).

One of the intermediate factors which affects differential fertility by education is age at first marriage. As mentioned above, educated women marry later and thus reduce their number of childbearing years.

Table VIII

Mean Number of Live Births by Education and Place of Residence, Turkey (Married Women Ages 15–44) 1968*

Women's Level o Education	3 Largest Cities	Type of Place			Total
		City	Town	Village	
Illiterate	4.1	3.8	4.3	4.3	4.2
Literate	2.5	3.1	3.1	3.8	3.2
Primary School Graduates	2.6	2.7	2.6	3.2	2.8
Secondary or Higher School Graduates	1.9	2.9	–	–	2.1
TOTAL	2.7	3.2	3.8	4.2	3.9

* The means are standardized by the duration of marriage.
Source: (Timur, 1971, Table 5, p. 13).

Besides age at first marriage, differential contraceptive use by education may also be responsible for the fertility variations. Fişek, using the 1973 Hacettepe Survey results, pointed out that educated women use contraceptives more than uneducated women. (Fişek, 1978). However, education may not be the predominant cause of the existing fertility differences by level of schooling. The meaningful relationship found between education and childbearing, marriage, work status, etc., may in fact be partly due to the unusual educational opportunities for women in various socio-economic groups. The impact of education per se should be discussed with a multiple variable analysis technique. In this study such an analysis could not be realized.

The Importance of Education to Women

In the 1975 Hacettepe Survey, married women between the ages of 15—49, were asked their opinion of the statement: "There is no need for rural/urban women to receive an education". About 40% of a total

Table IX

Need of Education According to Village Women 1975

"It is not necessary for women to receive an education and have an occupation"	*Non-Graduate*	*Primary School Graduate*	*Total*
For Rural Women			
True	824 (43.6)*	94 (21.8)	918 (39.5)
Undecided	165 (8.7)	33 (7.7)	198 (8.5)
False	901 (47.7)	305 (70.6)	1,206 (51.9)
TOTAL	1,890 (100.0)	432 (100.0)	2,322 (100.0)
For Urban Women			
True	702 (37.1)	75 (17.4)	777 (33.5)
Undecided	190 (10.1)	31 (7.2)	221 (9.5)
False	998 (52.8)	326 (75.5)	1,324 (57.0)
TOTAL	1,890 (100.0)	432 (100.0)	2,322 (100.0)

Source: The 1975 Hacettepe Village Survey, Female Cards.
* Number of individuals (percent of total).

of 2,322 women thought that this statement was true for rural women. (Table IX). Whereas 9% were undecided or felt that the need depended upon certain circumstances. This negative attitude towards educating rural women varied with the educational attainment of the women. Only 22% of the primary school graduates saw no need for rural women to receive an education whereas this percentage doubled among the non-graduates. In other words although 71% of the educated women considered education a must for rural women, more than half of the uneducated ones saw no need for it.

Although village women do not know urban life very well, they are able to draw a slight distinction between urban and rural educational needs in the sense that urban women need an education more than rural ones.

The rural women's desire and their need to have an education and an occupation varied depending upon the environmental conditions in which they lived. The importance of the environmental conditions becomes more meaningful when their own conditions are controlled.

Table X

Need of Education for Women in "Developed and Underdeveloped" Villages 1975

"It is not necessary for women to have an education and to have an occupation"	"Developed" Villages N 12		"Underdeveloped" Villages n 13	
	Non-Grad.	Prim. School Graduate	Non-Grad.	Prim. School Graduate
For Rural Women				
True	180 (26.6)*	78 (21.0)	644 (53.0)	16 (26.2)
Undecided	63 (9.3)	28 (7.6)	102 (8.4)	5 (8.2)
False	433 (64.1)	265 (71.4)	468 (38.6)	40 (65.6)
TOTAL	676 (100.0)	371 (100.0)	1,214 (100.0)	61 (100.0)
For Urban Women				
True	151 (22.3)	63 (17.0)	551 (45.4)	12 (19.7)
Undecided	66 (9.8)	27 (7.3)	124 (10.2)	4 (6.6)
False	459 (67.9)	281 (75.7)	539 (44.4)	45 (73.4)
TOTAL	676 (100.0)	371 (100.0)	1,214 (100.0)	61 (100.0)

Source: The 1975 Hacettepe Village Survey, Female Cards.
* Number of individuals (percent of total).

In the 1975 Survey, villages were grouped into one of two categories depending upon their degree of urban contact and their socio-economic development level. With their own environmental conditions in mind, educated and uneducated women in both these groups were again asked to consider the statement: "there is no need for rural/urban women to receive an education". In the developed villages, the educated and uneducated women had similar attitudes (Table X). The majority of both groups thought that rural women needed an education. However, in the "under-developed villages", there was a significant difference of opinion. It would appear that uneducated women change their attitudes towards education to a great extent under different environmental conditions.

In the so-called "underdeveloped" villages, the number of women who have graduated from primary school is small. A more detailed analysis may show that the majority of such women came from other villages or cities. It may be argued that environmental factors not only determine the relative importance of personal characteristics, like education, but they also have a direct impact on behaviour and attitudes. The environmental influence is such that the person acts as if these conditions were his own. In rural Turkey it was found that women's fertility patterns varied according to the type of village they lived in as well as by their educational attainment. (Özbay, 1975).

Despite the 1975 Village Survey results pointing out that an important proportion of women do not believe in the need to educate women, the 1973 Survey results indicate that the majority of mothers (ages 15—49, currently married) want their daughters to have an education. In places with less than 2,000 inhabitants, only 10% of the mothers did not want their daughters to have any education (Table XI). Moreover, in the same places, 1% of the mothers wanted only a religious course for their daughters. It is assumed that this percentage is actually higher, but for one reason or another was not reported. If the two survey results are compared, it may be said that in the rural areas the negative attitudes shown towards women's education change when their own conditions, particularly their daughters' education, are concerned. Some of the mothers in villages who wanted their daughters to be educated, did not have any idea of how much education would be most desirable. (31%). About half of the mothers in the villages preferred primary school education for their daughters.

In the cities, especially in the large cities, mothers desired a higher level of education for their daughters as compared to the village mothers. In Ankara, Istanbul and Izmir all the mothers wanted their daughters to have some education. Those who preferred primary school education only were fewer than those in the villages (12%). 43% of the mothers in these cities wanted a college education for their daughters.

On the average, mothers indicated college or primary school education as being the levels of education most desired for their daughters. Vocational schools took third place on the preference list. In the rural areas, mothers desired primary schools the most; their desired preference for vocational schools was as high as for colleges.

The preferred educational level for daughters actually indicates the functions and the problems of the educational system in Turkey. A desire for a primary school education only, may show, on the one hand the relatively high aspirations of uneducated mothers, but on the other, it may also show how unnecessary it is to invest more in women's education in Turkish society. In the villages, only 6% of the mothers wanted their sons to have a primary school education. The rest wanted higher education for the boys. Sex discrimination in education actually has bases in the social system.

A college education was desired for boys in all the areas without a doubt. For girls, this was only valid in the urban areas. Junior high and high school educations were neither desired very much for girls nor for boys. This once more definitely reflects the fact that secondary schools do not provide individuals with any practical, defined skills which can be utilized in their economic life.

Conclusion

Using various data and simple techniques, we have tried to determine the impact of education on women in urban and rural Turkey. The reader, at this stage, may be disappointed for neither are all the factors that positively or negatively influence women in the field of education fully explained nor could even the partial effect of education on women be clearly shown.

Education is obviously a viable and decisive means of orienting the masses towards change in a short time. But, it can do this only when the educational system itself is established on healthy grounds. In Turkey this is not the case. Instead of inducing social change and mobility, education as an institution protects the existing and, in many respects, the traditional structure. Thus, one should not expect this system to foster any significant advancements in the field of women's development.

The differences observed among women at various educational levels, must not be interpreted as the sole result of education. In the relationship between two variables, even if time favours education, as in the example of education and work status, one cannot state precisely which of the variables influences the other as indeed the relationship is reciprocal. Also, a possibility exists that both variables are influenced by another important, often omitted factor, that being environmental conditions. As highlighted in this study, "environmental conditions" or the woman's social class, may not have solely influenced her educational level, but also her work conditions, profession, age at marriage, fertility, contraceptive use, and even her attitude towards education.

It is presumed, however, that education, especially profession oriented education, has an effect on increasing social mobility. But, so few women have received this kind of education that according to some, they are negligible in the system, and their parade effect impedes a comprehensive approach to the relevant problems of the majority.

A set of appropriate measures must be taken to give way to the development of all individuals, men and women. This set of measures must include the expansion of educational opportunities for women, especially in the rural areas; getting rid of the bottlenecks in the system from the primary level upwards; giving more emphasis to profession oriented secondary education instead of to the classical junior high or high school type; the introduction a contemporary, technical, production oriented curriculum into these schools; the provision of fellowships, credits and free boarding facilities; and an accelerated adult education program.

A set of appropriate measures in the field of education must also take into consideration the problems in the social, economic and political spheres. Such a comprehensive approach must be taken if educational problems are to be handled in a relevant manner and if the problems concerning women observed at present are to be solved.

The reference list of this chapter is on page 320

AYŞE ÖNCÜ

TURKISH WOMEN IN THE PROFESSIONS: WHY SO MANY?

I. Introduction

This paper addresses itself to an intriguing "puzzle": the high incidence of women in the two most prestigious professions in Turkey, namely, law and medicine. One in every five practicing lawyers in Turkey is female. One in every six practicing doctors is again female. This is puzzling in view of the fact that law and medicine have traditionally been bastions of male exclusivity in Western industrialized societies, and until recently, very few women have been able to penetrate their strongholds (Epstein, 1970; Theodore, 1971). Unlike some of the less prestigious professions, such as nursing or education, schools of law and medicine in these countries have long been considered the province of the male species, and despite the rapid move towards sexual integration in professional schools, women doctors and lawyers will find themselves a conspicuous minority for years to come.

The high incidence of women practitioners in law and medicine in Turkey appears anomalous not only in contrast to the patterns observed in the West but also when cast against the high rates of illiteracy in the female population and the low levels of labor force participation in urban areas of the country. Women constitute about 10 percent of the urban labor force in Turkey (Kazgan, 1978), and approximately half of the women above the age of 15 in Turkey's urban areas have never finished primary school (Özbay, 1978). How then, can we explain the high proportion of women in such prestigious professions as law and medicine?

In the following pages, first an attempt will be made to document the phenomenon in question more fully by presenting some figures on the distribution of women practitioners in law and medicine. "Is the high incidence of women in these professions a relatively new trend? Is it a growing trend? Does it exhibit regional variations?" In the first part of the paper, questions such as these will be discussed. The second part of the paper will be devoted to a discussion of alternative explanations;

i.e. the question of Why? Here, available information and clues to be gained from existing social science research will be combined to pose possible answers at alternative levels of explanation.

Turkish Women in Law and Medicine: Some Facts and Figures

The access Turkish women enjoy to the most prestigious and skilled professions should be considered within the context of overarching regional and economic inequalities. The proportion of female lawyers ranges from 21 percent in the more urbanized and economically developed provinces to 8 percent in the least developed ones. Thus, not only are there more lawyers in the developed regions of the country, but also a higher ratio of females among them.

Table I

Distribution of Lawyers in Turkey: 1975

Provinces	*Total Lawyers Listed*	*Female Listings*	*Female Listings As Percent of Total*
Developed (16)	12,305	2,590	21.05%
Intermediate (24)	2,049	212	10,35%
Less Developed (27)	1,116	89	7,93%
Totals	15,470	2,891	18.69%

Source: Union of Bar Associations.

When the three largest metropolitan centers of İstanbul, İzmir and Ankara are considered seperately, the disparities are even more striking. 60 percent of all lawyers in Turkey are practicing in three metropolitan centers and one out of every four of these is female.

The large advance Turkish women have made in law careers is basically a metropolitan phenomenon. It is also a post World War II phenomenon. Records of the İstanbul Bar Association, the oldest and largest in Turkey, indicate that the first female lawyer registered in 1936. But, until 1960, the proportion of female lawyers remained below 10 percent, after which time, steady and substantial increases became noticeable.

The entry of women into the medical profession in substantial numbers is again a post-World War II phenomenon. Until the 1940's, there

Table II

Membership Distribution of the Istanbul Bar Association: 1960–1978

Years	*Total Lawyers Listed*	*Female Listings*	*Female Listings As Percent of Total*
1960	2,192	279	12,72%
1965	2,956	541	18.30%
1970	3,615	822	22.74%
1975	5,670	1,562	27,55%
1978	6,513	1,859	28.54%

Source: Records of The Istanbul Bar Association.

was only one faculty of medicine in the country, and it was attached to the University of İstanbul. By 1950, despite the establishment of a second school in Ankara, only about 10 percent of the diplomas granted annually were received by women. By 1970, this proportion had risen to about 25 percent.

Table III

Distribution of Medical School Diplomas: 1945–70

Years	*Total Number Of Diplomas Granted*	*Diplomas Granted to Women*	*Women Grantees As Percent of Total*
1945–50	2,368	276	11.66%
1950–55	2,677	300	11.21%
1955–60	2,461	389	15.81%
1960–65	2,573	550	21.31%
1965–70	3,281	820	24.99%

Sources: DIE, *Milli Eğitim Hareketleri: 1927–1966*, Yayın No: 517. Saglık ve Sosyal Yardım Bakanlığı, *Türkiye Sağlık Istatistik Yıllığı: 1964–1967; 1968–1972*, Yayin No: 413; 444.

Official statistics on the numbers and distribution of physicians in Turkey do not record sex distinction. We therefore lack accurate data on the proportion of female physicians in the professional labor market. An estimate based on the available information regarding medical school diplomas granted and the global figures on total numbers of physicians, indicates that women constitute around 15 percent of the total number of physicians in the labor market.

Table IV

Estimated Proportion of Female Physicians in the Professional Labor Market: 1955–70

Years	*Total Number Of Physicians*	*Estimated Number of Female Physicians**	*Female Physicians As Percent of Total*
1955	7,077	824	11.6%
1960	9,826	1,185	12.0%
1965	10,895	1,662	15.2%
1970	15,856	2,245	14.1%

* Estimate based on female graduation data for the 1926–70 period, using method of moving averages and assuming that survival period is 26 years for a new graduate.

As in the case of lawyers, overarching regional inequalities exist in the distribution of physicians in Turkey. In 1975, 70 percent of all physicians were practicing in the most developed and urbanized provinces of Ankara, İstanbul and İzmir. It would be safe to assume that the percentage of female physicians in these three provinces considerably exceeds the global estimate of 15 percent.

The figures cited above indicate that the access Turkish women enjoy to the prestigious professions of law and medicine is equal, if not wider than that of their counterparts in such highly industrialized Western countries as the U. S. A. or France. In the U. S. A., for instance, only 3 percent of the lawyers (White, 1967) and 6 percent of the physicians are female; in France women constitute 15 percent of the physicians (Silver, 1973). We have no information on the question of the occupational success Turkish women are able to achieve in these fields and how it compares with that of men. Research on women lawyers and physicians in the advanced industrial societies of the West indicates that they tend to be concentrated in the lowest paid and prestigious specialties (Safilios-Rothschild,1972). For instance, women lawyers specialize in trusts and estates, domestic relations; while women physicians are found mostly in pediatrics and, to a lesser extent, gynecology. Furthermore, women very infrequently reach the higher ranking administrative positions, and they tend to work fewer hours. It is possible that these characteristics are equally applicable to Turkish women in law and medical careers. In any case, the fact remains that Turkish women are able to enter the professional labor market in proportions that compare favorably with the most advanced Western industrialized societies.

Alternative Levels of Explanation

The range of work opportunities Turkish women enjoy in the professional labor market is wider than that in the most industrialized societies of the West. But Turkey is not unique in this respect. A number of other Third World countries which have become rapidly integrated into the world market in recent years, or are in the process of doing so, such as Mexico, Argentina, Greece, Costa Rica, India, etc., provide women with more options in the professional labor market than do the most industrialized Western societies. Cross-national studies indicate that in the capitalist societies (as opposed to state-socialist), there is a curvilinear relationship between the level of industrial and economic development and the range of options open to women in professional careers. At intermediate levels, there are higher proportions of women in professional schools and also in the professional labor market than at either extreme. In such countries, law, medicine and dentistry constitute a "cluster" of occupations that appear as Women's options (Safilios-Rothschild, 1971; 1972).

Facilitating Mechanisms

The by now classical argument advanced to explain this trend is as follows: upper and upper-middle class urban women in developing countries can exercise a great number of choices and thus become much more "emancipated" than their counterparts in highly industrialized countries, due to the existence of overarching class inequalities. Rapid rural-urban migration and scarcity of factory employment result in a large pool of unskilled female labor in the large cities, which upper class women are able to exploit. Professional and marital roles become compatible because: a) domestic labor is available at prices that can be afforded by upper and upper middle class families and b) although most families are nuclear and neolocal, the extended family network can be relied upon for child rearing tasks. Thus, wives' mothers or inlaws, in combination with hired help, can solve the problem of the working mother (Safilios-Rothschild, 1971).

In its broad outlines, evidence from the Turkish case fits this argument very well. Professional women come from predominantly urban upper- or upper middle class backgrounds. Access to university education, the prerequisite for entry into the professions, is largely a function of the class inequalities in Turkey. And, higher education consolidates class position more often among women than among men. This is well demonstrated by the findings from a recent survey of applicants to the centrally administered university examinations. The salient findings from this survey can be summarized as follows (Çavdar, Tümay, Yurtseven, 1976):

—22.6% of all applicants were female; 28% of those who passed were females.
—30.3% of the total applicants were from rural areas. Of the applicants from rural areas only 8.7% were females.
—31% of the applicants and 47.6% of those who passed the entrance examinations were from the largest metropolitan centers (İstanbul, Ankara, İzmir). 54% of the females who passed the examinations were from these three metropolises.
—In terms of their fathers' occupation, the percentage of farmers and laborers among the applicants was 35%. Alternatively, the proportion of civil servants and professionals was 26%. Among female applicants, these proportions were 18% and 38% respectively. Students coming from civil service or professional families are twice as likely to pass the examinations as the applicants whose fathers are laborers or farmers.
—Secondary school graduation points do not seem to make a difference in terms of performance on the entrance examinations.

The evidence reported above not only demonstrates that entry into the university system is largely a function of geographical and economic inequalities; but also that it consolidates these inequalities much more strongly in the case of women than men. The findings of more delimited studies, investigating the socio-economic background of students in specific professional schools, point in the same direction. For instance, two separate surveys of Ankara University Law Faculty students both indicate that approximately fifty percent come from civil service or professional backgrounds in terms of fathers' occupation (Abadan, 1961; Field, 1964). Furthermore, the proportion of female students who come from such backgrounds is higher than males (Field, 1964).

While there is little dispute that upper-class women enjoy wide access to professional education in Turkey, evidence on the discrepancy between their educational opportunities and the extent of their professional achievements is much more scanty. According to the official figures of the State Statistical Institute, 70 percent of women who have completed higher education are working, in contrast to 32 percent of those who have completed lycee education. So, seven out of ten women who have received some sort of higher training are in the labor force. But we know nothing about the process of selectivity that occurs in the transition from professional schools to the labor market. Whether women in the professional labor market are less likely to be married; whether they have fewer children; whether they are more likely to be working part-time—on these and a host of other questions, we have no information. The lack of data on these specific questions does not invalidate the general argument, however. Given the virtual absence of well staffed child care centers, professional women who are married and have children have to rely upon third persons to perform household and childrearing tasks. "Transient extended" or "modified extended" families, ie. families where one grandparent is living with the nuclear family are quite common in large Turkish cities, ranging between 13 to 17 percent of total families (Timur, 1972; Kâğıtçıbaşı, 1977). And, although most families are nuclear and neolocal, the functions of the extended family continue in terms of exchange patterns (Kâğıtçıbaşı, 1977). Finally, and most important, a ring of squatter settlements around large metropolitan centers constitute a pool of cheap female labor which can be relied upon for domestic labor.

It is difficult to deny the importance of such facilitating mechanisms as the availability of relatively cheap domestic labor and the prevalence of "transient extended" or "modified extended" families, if not in terms of residence, then in terms of exchange patterns. But in explaning why in such "developing" countries as Turkey, law medicine and dentistry constitute a "cluster" of occupation that tend to appear together as women's options, they offer only a partial solution. What needs to be kept in mind is that in the advanced industrial societies of the West, women *do* enjoy considerable access to the professions; but they tend to cluster in the middle ranks. The characteristic pattern observed in such countries as the U. S. A. or France is a tiny participation of women in the most skilled and prestigious professions, such as law and medicine, *but* a very considerable presence in such middle level professions as teaching and public administration. To give an example, in France, 55 percent of lycee instructors were women in the school year 1968—69 (Silver, 1973). The comparable figure for Turkey in the school year of 1972—73 is 35 percent, indicating a sizable discrepancy (DIE, 1977, p. 102). But in the most skilled and prestigious professions, this discrepancy disappears. As indicated earlier, 15 percent of physicians both in France and Turkey are women. It is difficult to account for this pattern solely in terms the presence or absence of such facilitating mechanisms as the availability of hired help or prevalence of modified extended families. Crucial differences in the historical evolution of the prestigious professions need to be taken into account.

Difference in the Historical Evolution of Prestigious Professions

Historically, medicine and law are oldest, the 'Classical' professions in advanced industrial societies of the West. Their growth in the second half of the nineteenth century is associated with the rise to power of an urban middle class, which not only provided an expanding demand for these professional services but also supplied recruits for the growing ranks of professionals. The association of law and medicine with middle-class power marked them as 'gentlemanly professions' and also provided the basis from which they made persistent use of the political process to gain special privileges from the state (Carr-Saunders and Wilson, 1933). Through the creation of autonomous organizations to control standards of entry, performance and conduct in the profession and the legalization of this monopoly power by state registration, they achieved a degree of self-regulation, which has become the yardstick against which the "professionalization" of all other occupations is measured (Johnson, 1972).

The ideology of professionalism associated with self-regulation emphasizes the highly skilled and complex nature of professional services, and the inability of the client to assess their quality. To protect the public against malpractice, control of entry by satisfying examinations and training requirements as well as the supervision of performance and conduct in the profession, needs to be regulated by the professional group itself. Only the members of the professional community can judge the competence of one another. This ideology of collegiate control and communtity solidarity is inculcated during lengthy periods of training and close supervision within an apprentice system. Similar experiences of entry and socialization, reinforced by networks of communication, contact and referral among practitioners serves to maintain it.

An important by-product of the degree of self-regulation achieved by the classical professions of law and medicine over the past hundred and fifty years has been the enhancement of their status and earning powers. The rising entry requirements and the strict professional norms regulating the behavior of members with respect to fees, advertising etc., have served to limit entry and restrict competition in the profession. Thus, the classical professions of law and medicine have evolved into self-perpetuating systems; elite groups with restricted entry and tight-knit unity (Lees, 1966; Jamous and Peloille, 1970). Today, the lengthy and costly training requirements involved, coupled with the importance of social connections in the professional world to become established in private practice, continue to pose formidable barriers which only those well placed in the social pyramid can surmount.

In Third World countries by contrast, the growth of professions is a much more recent phenomenon. The rapid creation of a "trained elite", able to supervise the introduction of advanced industrial techniques into previously "underdeveloped" countries, has been a major aim of governments. To meet this pressing need, technical and university education has been expanded rapidly. Such rapid expansion of elite cadres with specialized higher and technical education is not possible without a large infusion of individuals drawn from backgrounds of manual or present origins—unless women from the upper reaches of the social hierarchy begin to enter professional schools. The restricted patterns of entry and the relatively tight knit unit exhibited by the most skilled, prestigious and high-income professions in the Western industrial societies is a product of the self-regulatory systems which have evolved over the past hundred and fifty years. While professional associations and state registration have also been introduced in the Third World countries, it is difficult to maintain self-perpetuating elite recruitment patterns under conditions of rapid expansion in professional education. The evidence from the Turkish case indicates that despite the rapid expansion of professional education over the past fifty years, the proportion of university students drawn from manual or peasant backgrounds remains limited. This is in part because women from professional and white-collar origins have begun to enter professional schools in substantial numbers.

The argument which emerges here is as follows: under conditions of rapid expansion, the elite recruitment patterns into to most prestigious and highly remunerated professions are maintained by the admission of women from the upper reaches of the social hierarchy. Women from elite backgrounds are much more acceptable and less threatening than upwardly mobile men from humbler backgrounds who are likely to be more competitive and achievement oriented. The admission of women serves to maintain closure by keeping it a family affair, so to speak.

Given the importance of professional contacts and referrals in such fields as medicine and law, women with family connections in the elite world find it much easier to establish themselves in the job market than men from manual and peasant backgrounds.

This argument, emphasizing the maintenance of closure in elite recruitment patterns does not of course negate the importance of the facilitating mechanisms discussed previously. It does, however, offer a more macro level explanation of why such facilitating mechanisms are called forth.

Changes in the Sex-linked Stereotypes of the Professions

The two arguments presented above, although they represent different levels of explanation, both lead to predictions in the same direction: the rate of "feminisation" of the prestigious professions in Third World countries will decline. The reasons why such a trend might be expected to occur are obvious: the circumstances which foster the entry of large numbers of women from elite backgrounds into the professions are to some degree historically specific, involving as they do the rapid expansion of the professions and the hothouse creation, bolstered by state policies, of a new professional-technical elite cadre. The facilitating mechanims which enable women to reconcile professional and marital roles, on the other hand, do not entail a radical redefinition of marital roles. The availability of third persons to perform household and childrearing tasks constitutes a transitional type of solution which cannot continue when the daughters of working women will want to work and when hired help becomes more scarce and expensive as more lower class urban women enter the organized labor market. Thus, both of the arguments presented above lead to the conclusion that the proportion of females in the prestigious professions will become stabilized in the near future, or perhaps decline.

One development which casts doubt upon such a prediction involves the changes in sex-linked stereotypes in the professions. Perhaps it would be more correct to talk about the absence of sex-typing, rather than changes therein. The recency and rapidity which characterizes the growth of professions in the Third World countries not only renders them more 'open' but also frees them from traditional sex-linked stereotypes. The state sponsored political ideology concerning women's equality with men; coupled with sizable proportions of women actually able to enter the prestigious professions, inhibits the institutionalization of sexual stereotyping. In the advanced industrial societies of the West, law and medicine still remain stereotyped as "masculine", despite women's greater participation in recent years. The redefinition of an existing and traditional "masculine" image is a lengthy process. In the Third World countries by contrast, the expansion of prestigious professions is a much more recent phenomenon; their newness in the cultural context means that the socialization process which labels these professions as 'deviant' careers for women has not occurred. Under these conditions what determines the desirability of a particular profession for women is the nature of the work involved. Such professions as law, medicine or dentistry provide maximum flexibility and a satisfactory and highly remunerative source of work, since the practice of these professions can be limited for some years to only certain hours of the day, those hours being chosen on the basis of a schedule best suited to the needs, for example, of a mother with young children. The pattern of sex-linked stereotypes which emerges as a result, varies from those attached to various professions in many of the advanced Western industrial societies. Depending of the popular image of the work involved, certain professions become desirable choices for women, despite the fact that men largely predominate in them.

A number of studies on the occupational aspirations of female students and of their parents in Turkey, indicate that medicine and pharmacy, for instance, have become defined as highly desirable occupations for women. A study on the occupational aspirations of lycee students in İzmir, one of the three largest metropolitan centers, reveals that nearly half of the females in the sample aspire to the prestigious professions and among these medicine is accorded the highest preference. Male students also aspire to the professions but engineering is the most favored (Uysal, 1970). A wider national survey conducted in 1973 (Özbay, 1978) indicated that in large cities, 17 percent of mothers want their daughters to be medical doctors.

This channelling of the occupational aspirations of women to the prestigious professions and the institutionalization of cultural definitions which label them as desirable careers for women countervails the expectation that the proportions of females in these professions will stabilize or decline. It is possible that elite women in the Third World countries will in the near future have to compete with men of similar backgrounds, given the fact that the conditions which have facilitated the rapid expansion of professional-technical cadres in these countries are to some degree historically specific. Even where university education continues to expand rapidly, entry into the most prestigious and highly remunerated professions is likely to become more difficult and competative. But to the extent that these professions have acquired a 'feminine' image, the key social determinant of selectivity will be class background, rather than gender.

A decline in the availability of third persons to help with childrearing and household tasks is again possible. But, elite women have the power basis from which they can make persistant use of the political process to generate governmental action in providing more and better services such as nursery schools and kindergartens for working mothers. Also, it is difficult to see how an acute market demand on the part of a group with substantial buying power could fail to stimulate private investments in schools and child care centers of acceptable quality.

SUMMARY AND CONCLUDING REMARKS

This essay has mainly focussed on the question of why there are so many Turkish women in the prestigious professions. 'Many' is a relative term of course and if equal proportions of men and women are meant by it, then Turkish women in law and medicine are very few indeed. But when the over all rates of female participation in the non-agricultural labor force are taken as the base, then female lawyers and physicians in Turkey are conspiciously numerous.

Also, the level of participation of Turkish women in the professions compares quite favorably with the most advanced industrial societies of the West; this being the case only in the highest ranking professions and not in the middle ranks.

In cross-national perspective, countries where women enjoy equal or wider access to the prestigious professions than Turkey fall into two groups: Third World countries at 'Intermediate levels of development' and state-socialist societies. In state-socialist countries, the presence of women in the professions is part of a wider patterns of high female labor force participation. In 'developing' Third World countries by contrast, women enjoy access to the prestigious professions despite the characteristically low rates of participation in the non-agricultural labor market. A particular combination or configuration of conditions needs to be taken into account to explain this phenomenon.

One common characteristic of women entering the prestigious professions in the Third World countries is that they come from elite backgrounds. In Turkey, available evidence indicates that women in the highest ranking professions are predominantly drawn from urban, professional or civil service backgrounds. The elite background of professional women is significant from two points of view. First, within the context of overarching class inequalities in developing countries, the ready availability of lower class women as domestics in private homes "emancipates" upper class women to pursue professional careers. Secondly, in the face of deliberate state policies aimed at the rapid expansion of professional cadres, maintenance of elite recruitment patterns is only possible through the infusion of women. Thereby women from elite backgrounds are encouraged to enter the prestigious professions, restricting the options available to men from manual or peasant backgrounds.

This particular combination or configuration of conditions which enables women from elite backgrounds to enjoy access to the prestigious professions are to some extent historically specific. But at the same time, the cultural definitions which label a number of prestigious professions as desirable and acceptable options for women are becoming institutionalized. To the extent that such cultural definitions tend to be enduring, the prestigious professions in the Third World countries are not likely to develop into strongholds of masculine dominance.

The reference list of this chapter is on page 321

TANSI ŞENYAPILI

A NEW COMPONENT IN METROPOLITAN AREAS

The 'Gecekondu Women'

1. Introduction

During the nineteen sixties, world capitalist markets grew rapidly in size and strength. Their growth was due to several factors, such as the development of production technology, the Vietnam War and the independent or joint entrance of the Third World countries (i. e. OPEC) into world markets. Concomitant to the enlarging markets, a need to increase the labour force appeared, but the existing capitalistic mode of production remained the same.

In such a situation, if profits are to constantly increase, the remuneration for labour should be closely controlled. Therefore, the rational action for the capitalist is to increase his labour pool from the periphery whenever possible. That is, he keeps the organized, skilled, experienced labourers in the center of his labour pool and he fills the periphery with semi-skilled, unskilled or skilled but inexperienced, unorganized labourers among whom the labour turnover is high. The most basic common denominators between the center and the periphery are lost. Although both ends of the pool economically function as complementary components, socially they are dual. For the capitalist, the advantages of retaining an unintegrated and, in this sense, peripheral labour force are that the capitalist pays less, labour turnover is high therefore organization is delayed and, as Marx mentioned, this group and the 'reserve' labour force to which it is more integrated, act as a means of holding down the wage increases of the central group.[1] An example is the Third World labourers abroad who cannot be integrated into the central pool (in this case the skilled, organized domestic workers of the foreign country in question). The women's rights campaigns that have gathered momentum since the last decade should be interpreted within the same context, as they too aim at channelling women into the peripheral forces of the labour pool.

The common element in the campaigns conducted in different countries

---

[1] K. Marx and F. Engels, *Nüfus Sorunu ve Malthus* (Population Problem and Malthus). Ankara: Sol Yayinlari, 1976.

at different levels of development is that they are mostly promoted by the bourgeoisie who in formulating their proposed solutions assume a constant socio-economic framework. Yet, within the bourgeoisie, class proposals dependent on transformation of the socio-economic framework have also been developed.[2] Thus, the women's rights problem is viewed from two different angles: from a socio-economic point of view and as a competitive sex battle. The proponents of the latter approach start from different premises like 'women should first gain sexual independence' or 'women's rights can only be obtained by legal reforms'. Both, however, usually agree on a common package of proposals: the level of female education should be increased, women should enter the business world more extensively and there should be equal pay for equal work.

In this study, we assert that the problem cannot be solved in such a context. Let us pose the problem in the framework of the Third World countries citing examples from Turkey. In this framework industrial and service sectors are based on technology which is mainly imported, obsolete, expensive and inadequate. Therefore, the economic functioning of these sectors is dependent on keeping labour remuneration cheap. Entry into foreign markets is limited due to conditions upon which the Third World countries have no bargaining power. The domestic market is limited due to production difficulties and low, unequally divided incomes.

In such a framework, retaining a low level of labour remuneration is as important as retaining an ever-enlarging domestic market. Thus, women are encouraged to join the cheap, mobile, unorganized sections of the labour pool, on the one hand, and ground is laid, on the other, to channel their increasing incomes into the consumer market.

As long as the socio-economic structure is the same, it will continue to impose a specific value system in which the primary role of woman is to be a good wife and mother. Again, within this unchanging framework women will enter the labour market no to contribute to the achievement of a national goal but to solve the economic problems of the family or to achieve a higher level of consumption. Therefore, women will interpret 'work' as a temporary evil to be suffered until the family overcomes the bottleneck at the expense of a 'shameful' neglect of her primary role.

---

[2] Notable examples in Turkey are:
F. Tayanç and T. Tayanç, *Dünyada ve Türkiyede Tarih Boyunca Kadın*, Ankara: Toplum Yayınları, 1977. A. Altındal, *Türkiye'de Kadın*, Istanbul: Havass Yayınları, 1977. S. Tekeli, "Siyasi Iktidar Karşısında Kadın" *Toplum ve Bilim*, Autumn, 1977.

As a result, labour turnover in the female group will be high; women will be concentrated in certain work branches 'feminizing' them; and specialized training will not be necessary. Even if women enter new economic sectors, they will still perform less specialized work, and the principle of equal pay for equal work will never be realized. Since sex segregation is observed in most aspects of social life, the organization of female labour to protect their rights will be delayed.

The proponents of the proposal that the level of female education should be raised and more expansive work channels should be provided (although it is never explained why and how these proposals will be accepted and realized) further propose that supplementary social services should be provided. Yet, in Third World countries the needed social consciousness and the surplus to pay for such services (home help, 'day care' for young children, care of school children, afterschool care and health services accessible to all social strata) are not developed. The few available services are 'sold' to higher income groups at high charges. Labour organizations with bargaining power are needed to exert pressure on employers to provide such services for them. Yet, general labour policies in these countries coupled with the fact that female labour is mainly engaged in less specialized work and that it cannot get organized, prevent the formation of bargaining power on such services.

Further, even if the decision to raise women's level of education is realized within the existing framework, low income Third World women still will not be able to afford long years of classical, bourgeoisie education which has no functional relation to their social environment. Moreover, they will not be able to compete with students from upper social classes and their number of failures or drop outs will increase. Middle class and high income group children will continue to attend universities as usual, but due to the influence of social conditioning, their increased education will mainly be used for more specialized and luxurious consumption.

In summary, as long as the social and economic infrastructure and its derivative value systems and consumption norms remain constant, measures to promote women's liberation will remain superficial 'reforms'; manual work will continue to be belittled; and women, in addition to their traditional primary role of wife and mother will have to work 6 to 8 hours a day outside their homes in unsatisfying, unwanted and tiring jobs. Thus, posing the problem in Third World countries in a context of constant socio-economic background will only contribute to the increased exploitation of women.

2. The 'Gecekondu'

In accordance with the discussion above, the problem of the 'gecekondu woman' should be evaluated within her own social class. The reason being that social class affiliations determine the time, the location and the pattern in which a woman will market her labour. Therefore, the gecekondu woman should not be studied as a separate, independent entity but rather within the context of her own class or group affiliation. Our purpose here is not to review the descriptive or evolutionary material related to gecekondus, but to present the reader with a few basic economic determinants and their derivatives so as to comprise a brief socio-economic framework in which to evaluate the subject.[3]

The 'gecekondu' environment can be studied in an abstract-concrete spatial trilogy.[4] The typical migrant member of the gecekondu forms economic and social relations which in turn constitute coordinates of n-dimensional abstract spaces.[5] He also builds a physical environment for himself in easily observable and measurable physical space. In this study, we assume that relations in economic space are the independent variables and that relations in other spaces are the dependent ones. Further assumptions are:

—The transition of the migrant from unorganized to organized urban work is not realized in a clear, single-step passage. Instead, the migrant draws a pendulum-like curve moving among jobs in the section of urban work space reserved for him, according to his skills, experience and social relations in hopes of landing a permanent and secure job.[6]

---

[3] Information on gecekondus in Turkey may be obtained from: M. B. Kıray, "Squatter Housing, Fast De-peasantization and Slow Workerization in Underdeveloped Countries". Paper presented at the 7th World Congress of Sociology, Varna, September 1970. I. Tekeli, *Bağımlı Kentleşme* Ankara: Mimarlar Odası Yayınları—18, 1977. K. Karpat, *The Gecekondu.* Cambridge: Cambridge Univ. Press, 1976. E. Kongar, "Altındag Gecekondu Bölgesi" *Amme Idaresi Dergisi*, 6 : 3, Eylül 1973.

[4] T. Şenyapılı, "Kent Yaşantısıyla Bütüleşmemiş Kentli Nüfus Sorununa Çok Yönlü Bir Yaklaşım Denemesi" Unpublished Ph. D. Thesis, 1977. Economic Space concept is discussed in:
F. Perroux, "Economic Space: Theory and Applications" in J. Friedmann and W. Alonso, *National Development and Planning.* Cambridge: The M. I. T. Press, 1966. Social Space concept is discussed in:
B. J. L. Berry and F. Horton, *Geographic Perspectives on Urban Systems.* New Jersey: Prentice-Hall, Inc., 1970.

[5] In both surveys about 90% of the sample population turned out to be migrants.

[6] T. Şenyapılı, "Integration Through Mobility". Mimeo, 1977.

—The migrant cannot explore all urban work space, that is, all urban jobs are not open and suited to his qualifications and background. Therefore, the pendulum-patterned mobility curve is drawn only among those work areas open to him. Mobility is horizontal not vertical, and it does not provide upward class mobility.

Thus, the migrant draws a mobility curve between the points where his skill, experience, social relations and exogenous employment opportunities intersect, until he settles in economic space in a 'satisfying' job. Relevant inquiries have shown that gecekondu dwellers appraise the characteristics of urban economic space very realistically. When asked about their occupational preferences, they never mentioned white collar professional jobs that involve upward social mobility. The majority pointed out that, in their opinion, a 'satisfying job' was becoming a small entrepreneur. Such a position would give them the freedom to determine their own work conditions, 'to become a boss' and the chance to adjust their incomes according to the rate of inflation.

Thus, gecekondu dwellers, although they do not use scientific methodology, data and terminology, appraise their situation within the limits of their socio-economic affiliations.[7]

The mobility curve drawn in economic space has repercussions in other spaces. The one-to-one relation in physical space is the building process of the gecekondu itself. The importance of owning a house has been discussed in the past. This process is just as important as having a secure, continuous job from the point of view of settling in economic space.

Contrary to the habitat and environment building processes of other social classes, the gecekondu construction process is spread over time and is realized in evolutionary stages. This process is dependent on the economic mobility curve. As his economic condition gets better, the gecekondu dweller develops his house, adds new rooms, facilities, even stories. If he slips back into low paying, unorganized marginal work, construction stops, rooms may be sublet, or the house itself may be sold to help the migrant get to a higher point on the mobility curve. When the migrant settles in economic space, the construction process is completed. From this point on, if the building is more valuable than the land on which it stands, it may be transformed into a multi-story structure to bring rent income. If, however, the land is more valuable and if

[7] Şenyapılı, "The Relevance of Small Entrepreneurship in the Third World Countries—A Case Study: Turkey". Mimeo, 1977.

there is surplus capital, it may be sold and the owner may move elsewhere, perhaps to a better neighborhood.

In social space, the new urban relations formed in the city are realized under the area defined by the mobility curve drawn in economic space. This is to say, the migrant's rural and kinship based relations continue but his new social contacts in the city are work based. His new friends are his fellow workers. As he moves from one job to another, he forms new social relations in the form of small islands, each on his own socio-cultural and economic level.

The gecekondu woman, like her spouse, is part of the peripheral labour force in the sense that she too cannot find employment in the formal, organized urban sectors. She shares the general characteristics of this labour force in that she is uneducated, untrained, unskilled and inexperienced. Concomitant to the specific peripheral place she occupies in urban economic space, she too—like her social group—will form primary social contacts with other gecekondu women, and, in correlation with the dictates of her own class, she will consider material possessions, especially real estate and durable goods, insurance against the insecure future.

3. A New Component in the Metropolitan Areas—'The Gecekondu Women'

We have briefly discussed the economic (peripheral-essentially mobile, unorganized, untrained labour force in low-paying jobs) and social (confined to its own socio-cultural group) dimensions of the gecekondu population. Demographic characteristics of this population indicate the existence of a generally young group.[8] Two surveys conducted in 8

[8] The data presented in this paper was collected in two survey studies. The survey in Istanbul was made in the context of the project 'Unintegrated City in City' directed by the author and financed by the Centre For Environmental Studies of London. The Istanbul survey involved a sample of 1134 interviews made in 5 gecekondu neighborhoods (Gültepe, Zeyrek, Eminönü, Gaziosmanpaşa, Istinye). The survey was conducted in 1976.
The second survey was made in 3 gecekondu neighborhoods in Ankara (Akdere, Tuzluçayır, Yıldız) in 1977. This survey was conducted in the context of the second year design studio of the Department of City and Regional Planning of the Middle East Technical University. The students were supervised by the author and a colleague. The Ankara survey sample consisted of 708 interviews. In both surveys the sample was selected by a systematic sampling method. On the other hand, neither survey aimed at collecting specific data about gecekondu women. Therefore the data presented in this paper is derived from the questions asked to collect information related to the specific hypotheses about the gecekondu population.

gecekondu neighborhoods in Istanbul and Ankara show that the average age of the male heads of household is 40.1 and the average age of their wives is 35.8 (Table I). When checked against their date of arrival in the

Table I

*Average Ages and Age Differential between Husbands and Wives**

	1	2	3	4	5	6	7	8	9
Gültepe	350	1,690	39.1	34.0	83.8	5.6	10.6	5.6	3.5
Zeyrek	150	710	41.1	36.6	78.9	3.8	17.3	5.6	4.2
Eminönü	200	934	39.7	34.9	79.5	12.4	8.1	7.0	3.0
G.O.P.	400	1,815	44.0	40.0	85.0	4.0	11.0	7.0	4.0
Istinye	34	192	37.5	33.4	71.0	3.2	25.8	5.9	2.0
Tuzluç ayır	200	1,027	39.2	35.1	86.2	5.0	8.8	6.4	2.2
Yıldız	254	1,266	39.0	36.0	76.1	9.8	14.1	5.9	2.8
Akdere	252	1,297	41.2	36.3	78.4	7.2	14.4	7.4	3.5

1—Number of famillies interviewed
2—Sample population
3—Average age of husbands
4—Average age of wives
5—Percentage of families where husbands are older
6—Percentage of families where wives are older
7—Percentage of families where husbands and wives have the same age
8—Average age differential when the husband is older (years)
9—Average age differential when the wife is older (years)

* Gültepe, Zeyrek, Eminönü, Gaziosmanpaşa, Istinye, are districts in Istanbul; Tuzluç ayır, Yıldız, Akdere are districts in Izmir.

city, it was realized that these people are in general the children who migrated to the cities with their parents around 1955. The young age average is significant as it denotes the existence of a group with potential to integrate into urban life and enter the labour force.

Survey data further shows that in the gecekondu neighborhoods, families with 2, 3 and 4 children constitute the majority (Table II). The average family size is 4.72 in Istanbul and 5.22 in Ankara. These values are higher than urban family size (4.6) but lower than rural family size

(6.2). 72% of the families interviewed in Istanbul and 77% of the families interviewed in Ankara were nuclear.

Other demographic characteristics of the gecekondu family are: only 7% of the households in the Istanbul survey and 3% of the households in the Ankara survey consisted of bachelors. In both surveys, only 1% of the families had female heads of household, all of whom were widowed, middle-age women. Only 0.4% of the couples were divorced. In general, husbands were older than wives (79.4% of the couples in Istanbul, 79.5% of the couples in Ankara). The average age differential, when the husband is older, is 6.2 years in Istanbul and 6.6 years in Ankara. When the wife is older, the average differential falls to 3.3 years in Istanbul and 2.8 years in Ankara. In the majority of the couples (80%), both husbands and wives were born in the same province.

Table II

Distribution of Number of Children (percentage of families)

	No Chd.	*1 Ch.*	*2 Chd.*	*3 Chd.*	*4 Chd.*	*5 Chd.*	*6 Chd.*	*7 Chd.*	*8 Chd.*	*Total*
Gültepe	9.4	17.2	29.1	21.8	12.5	5.6	2.5	1.9	–	100
Zeyrek	10.5	17.3	30.1	18.8	11.3	6.7	3.0	2.3	–	100
Eminönü	8.6	16.0	25.3	23.5	14.2	5.6	5.6	1.2	–	100
G.O.P.	26.5	2.2	34.5	22.1	9.7	3.6	1 1	0.3	–	100
Istinye	–	19.0	31.2	21.9	3.1	6.2	6.2	6.2	6.2	100
T. Çayır	7.0	15.4	20.7	27.1	17.0	9.0	2.0	1.0	1.0	100
Yıldız	9.8	18.4	25.2	19.7	14.5	9.4	1.7	0.9	0.4	100
Akdere	5.0	13.4	22.7	22.3	20.6	7.6	5.9	2.5	–	100

The surveys did not inquire about age at time of marriage. Yet, the fact that most of the daughters beyond 20 years of age who still lived with their parents were widows, implies that the general age of marriage is around 18—20. Mothers give birth to their first children at an average age of 22 and, in general, the intergenetic interval is about 3 to 3.5 years (Table III). Thus, an average gecekondu woman who has her first child at the age of 22 fulfills her reproductive cycle in about 10—15 years.

Table III
Intergenetic Intervals (years)

	1–2 child	*2–3 child*	*3–4 child*	*4–5 child*	*5–6 child*	*6–4 child*	*7–8 child*	*XX*
Gültepe	3.5	2.9	3.5	3.5	3.0	2.2	–	21
Zeyrek	3.9	3.2	2.8	2.8	2.5	2.7	–	22
Eminönü	3.7	3.1	2.5	2.6	2.8	4.0	–	21
G.O.P.	4.0	4.0	4.0	3.0	3.0	4.0	–	22
Istinye	3.0	3.8	2.7	3.4	2.5	3.5	2.0	22
T. Çayır	3.3	3.4	3.5	3.5	3.1	1.7	3.5	21
Yıldız	3.7	4.2	2.8	3.4	2 8	1.8	3.0	24
Akdere	3.5	3.3	3.2	3.1	2.9	3.4	–	21

XX – Average age of mothers at the birth of fiist child

The fact that the values found in the Istanbul and Ankara gecekondu areas are very close suggests the existence of universal characteristics among the gecekondu population. In general, the gecekondu population is a migrant one. Furthermore, it is young and does not display symptoms of anomie. People in the gecekondu area lead regular family lives, their families tend to be nuclear, and they are reducing in size. Female gecekondu dwellers marry young and start having children at an early age. Their reproductive cycle is short. Data related to the demographic characteristics of the female indicates the existence of a young and sizeable labour potential in the gecekondu areas.

When we consider the quality of this potential female labour force, a distinction appears between mothers (wives of the heads of household) and daughters. The majority of mothers are illiterate (48.7% in Istanbul and 50.5% in Ankara), and in the literate group the percentage of those who attended schools beyond the primary level is very small (Table IV). However, almost all of the daughters attend primary schools and some daughters attend higher educational institutions (Table V). This shows that the daughters are definitely more educated than their mothers. Thus, the educational advantage enjoyed by the male population, observed in Table VI, will be changed towards equalization of the differences

Table IV

Level of Education of Heads of Household and their Wives

		1	*2*	6	*4*	*5*	*6*	*7*	*8*	9	*10*	*11*	*12*	*13*
Gültepe	F	45.7	5.0	42.2	3.4	1.6	0.6	1.2	–	–	0.3	–	–	100
	M	16.4	4.9	53.3	4.0	7.5	5.2	6.1	0.3	–	1.4	0.3	0.6	100
Zeyrek	F	47.4	8.3	37.6	1.5	0.7	3.0	0.7	0.7	–	–	–	–	100
	M	19.5	9.4	53.7	5.4	5.4	4.0	1.3	1.3	–	–	–	–	100
Eminönü	F	60.5	–	30.9	1.2	4.3	1.9	1.2	–	–	–	–	–	100
	M	34.5	0.5	48.0	4.5	4.5	4.0	2.0	0.5	–	1.0	–	0.5	100
G.O.P.	F	35.0	4.6	51.4	1.6	6.3	0.3	–	0.5	–	0.3	–	–	100
	M	16.2	5.8	55.3	3.3	12.7	1.8	3.1	–	–	1.8	–	–	100
Istinye	F	54.8	–	35.5	9.7	–	–	–	–	–	–	–	–	100
	M	23.5	–	58.8	2.9	5.9	5.9	–	–	–	2.9	–	–	100
Istanbul	F	44.7	4.3	42.9	2.4	3.6	0.9	0.7	0.3	–	0.2	–	–	100
	M	20.2	4.9	53.3	4.0	8.5	3.6	3.5	0.5	–	1.3	0.08	0.3	100
T. Çayır	F	53.7	5.3	4.3	32.4	2.1	0.5	–	–	–	1.6	–	–	100
	M	8.5	4.8	60.0	4.3	6.4	2.6	8.5	1.1	–	1.6	–	1.6	100
Yıldız	F	41.9	7.3	36.3	3.4	2.1	0.9	2.6	0.4	–	5.1	–	–	100
	M	8.5	6.1	53.4	2.0	10.5	3.6	6.9	0.4	–	8.5	–	–	100
Akdere	F	55.8	4.7	29.2	6.4	1.3	–	2.1	–	–	0.4	–	–	100
	M	13.2	6.4	62.1	3.0	4.7	3.0	1.7	0.9	0.9	1.3	–	3.0	100
Ankara	F	50.2	5.8	24.6	12.8	1.8	0.5	1.7	0.2	–	2.4	–	–	100
	M	10.1	5.8	58.5	3.0	7.3	3.1	5.4	0.8	0.5	4.0	–	1.5	100

1—Illiterate
2—Literate, not school graduated
3—Primary sch. grad.
4—Primary sch. drop out
5—High sch. grad.
6—High sch. drop out
7—College grad.
8—College drop out
9—College student
10—Univ. grad.
11—Univ. drop out
12—Univ. student
13—Total

in the near future. However, it must be pointed out that the pattner of increased education is concentrated at the primary and high school levels and not at the college or university level.

In summary, the young girls in gecekondu areas are subjected to a short (5 to 8 years) formal education which cannot be integrated with the life style and intellectual level of their environment. When formal education terminates, the young girl is subjected to the specialized capitalist culture via the mass media. The most popular mass medium in the semi-literate gecekondu environment is the T. V. In addition, the girls read photo-comics, magazines that relate romantic love stories

Table V

Percentage of Attendance to School in Each School Age Group

		1	*2*	*3*	*4*	*5*	*6*	*7*	*8*
	(F) Attend.	78.8	75.0	68.4	82.1	61.4	95.6	100.0	95.7
9	Not attend.	21.2	25.0	31.6	17.9	38.5	4.4	–	4.3
	(M) Attend.	84.4	88.0	78.0	83.8	81.2	100.0	100.0	100.0
	Not attend.	15.6	22.0	22.0	16.2	18.8	–	–	–
	(F) Attend.	32.2	22.2	21.2	28.0	16.7	61.1	57.8	56.9
10	Not attend.	67.8	77.8	78.8	72.0	83.3	38.9	42.2	43.1
	(M) Attend.	42.4	30.0	35.0	49.3	–	71.4	73.2	72.4
	Not attend.	57.6	70.0	65.0	50.7	–	28.6	26.8	27.6
	(F) Attend.	12.5	18.2	13.6	19.3	–	43.5	45.7	17.6
11	Not attend.	87.5	81.8	86.4	80.7	–	56.5	54.3	82.4
	(M) Attend	15.0	5.0	8.8	27.3	22.2	48.1	48.8	45.5
	Not attend.	85.0	95.0	91.2	72.7	77.8	51.9	51.2	54.5
	(F) Attend.	0.6	–	–	–	–	25.0	28.6	7.4
12	Not attend.	99.4	–	–	–	–	75.0	71.4	92.6
	(M) Attend.	0.3	11.4	2.1	6.5	–	26.2	19.2	12.1
	Not attend.	99.7	88.6	97.9	93.5	–	73.8	80.8	87.9

1—Gültepe
2—Zeyrek
3—Eminönü
4—G.O.P.
5—Istinye
6—T. Çayır
7—Yıldız
8—Akdere
9—Primary sch. age group
10—High sch. age group
11—College age group
12—Higher edu. age group

through pictures. The photo-comics constitute simple reading matter, coupling minimum reading with visual material. Structurally, the stories presented have fable-like simplicity. Women in the gecekondu area are affected and oriented more by this culture than permeates through the mass media, exploiting their basic desires in simple, understandable terminology, symbols and images, than they are by the alien bourgeoisie culture given in public schools.

This specific culture that affects the lives of gecekondu women can be summarized as follows: The underlying aim is to stimulate women to more and more intensive and extensive consumption. Several value judgements are imposed to lead women to this aim. Among them, the importance of vertical mobility is underlined (alienation from her own class). Yet, it is emphasized that the only way for women to achieve

Table VI

Comparison of Level of Wives' and Husbands' Education (in percentages)

	1	*2*	*3*	*4*
Gültepe	49.7	4.4	45.9	100,0
Zeyrek	42.9	8.3	48.8	100.0
Eminönü	36.4	3.7	59.9	100.0
G.O.P.	37.9	4.4	57.7	100.0
Istinye	42.9	8.3	48.8	100.0
T. Çayır	61.5	1.1	37.4	100.0
Yıldız	62.4	3.4	34.2	100.0
Akdere	59.1	3.1	37.8	100.0

1—% of families where husband's education level is higher
2—% of families where wives' education level is higher
3—% of families where the couple's level of education is equal
4—Total

vertical mobility is through marriage. In order to make a match which will provide vertical class mobility, a woman should be beautiful (beauty is only achieved by the use of cosmetics, and by closely following the current fashion), she should be clean and fastidious (achieved through detergents, household gadgets) and she should be obedient.[9] She should remain in the background and never compete with her husband intellectually. The indication of vertical mobility is luxurious consumption.

[9] Television advertisements are very revealing in this aspect. They feature men who read, drink, smoke, drive, participate in sports, dress dictinctively and make decisions. Incidentally, no ad has ever shown a woman reading a book or a newspaper so far on Turkish T. V. On the other hand, women wear fashionable clothes, use lots of cosmetics; they knit, wash dishes, clean floors, do the laundry, take care of children, brag about their possessions. A very recent T. V. ad featured a husband setting aside his newspaper to chide his wife who has returned from shopping carrying two packages although he has told her to buy only one item. The problem is solved when she tells him that one item was given by the shop as a bonus. Thus, even shopping decisions are made by the husband.

Girls may work, yet only in specially feminized jobs an the aim is to be able to make a match of the type explained above.

The question is how realistic is this image? Can gecekondu girls really marry into higher class families? The answer lies in the pattern according to which the gecekondu family occupies urban economic and social spaces. In economic space, gecekondu families are not severely segregated from the middle classes. It is obvious that the two classes—middle and lower—differ in income and occupation. However, since gecekondu families constitute a demographic majority in the metropolitan areas, their participation in the consumer market must be encouraged if the market is to enlarge. Therefore, several mechanisms are provided to ensure their increasing participation.[10] Despite the low incomes found in the gecekondu neighborhoods, there were almost as many expensive durable consumer goods in these houses as there were in the middle class ones. The young gecekondu girls are loyal followers of the latest fashion.

We can thus conclude that the gecekondu family under stress for integration into urban life participates in this channel, the only channel for integration offered by the urban society, willingly and completely.

Against this integration channel that the system deliberately offers to lower income classes, a sharp segregation is observed in social space. Although lower and middle class families share the same consumer goods, they never share their social lives. It has already been mentioned that segregation in the economic business area is reflected by social 'islands' in social space. Within this context the female gecekondu population remains introverted in her own group. Marriages are thus realized in inner rural-based or work-based groups. In summary, the vertical mobility aim transmitted to lower income women via the public media is never realized in the real sense of the concept, and the gecekondu women, bound by their social and economic affiliations, are rarely able to move upward socially.

Thus, formal public education, even if the girls go as far as the univer-

[10] One example is the man who drives a domestically manufactured car, carrying around a wide assortment of goods which range from lingerie to clothing. His customers are for the most part residents of gecekondu districts and they usually do not have credit standing. He sells on minimum monthly installments. The customer's name, address and the debt are recorded in a notebook. No signature, no guarantee nor any formal procedure are required. If the debtor cannot pay the installment for a month or so, the seller does not press him because he would rather wait and not lose a customer since he cannot legally prove that the transaction took place. Also, cheap replicas of goods sold in expensive shops are displayed in the streets on folding portable tables (işporta) and in suitcases.

sity level, cannot affect or orient their lives because it is designed to suit the requirements and dictates of the upper classes of a socially and economically stratified society. Conversely, T. V. and simple reading material which penetrate the socially hungry gecekondu environment, effectively impose a consumption oriented value system which leads to needless cravings, unsatisfied desires, alienation from one's own class, and consequent unhappiness among women.

Having observed the existence of a potential female labour force and its quality, the question is whether this labour enters urban economic space, and if it does, where and how. We have divided the answer into two different time periods; the 1950—70 time period when women in gecekondus performed an important function in urban economic space and the nineteen seventies when we surveyed the area.

In the fifties, a migration of unprecedented volume consisting mainly of unskilled, illiterate, former villagers hit the cities. Yet, in that period, neither the investments nor the industry nor the service sectors were sufficiently developed. Therefore, urban economic space was not ready to accept and employ them. Slowly towards 1955, under the influence of inflationary economic policies and emphasis on show-case type urban investments, employment opportunities appeared in the marginal sector for gecekondu labour and jobs opened in the service sector for educated middle class women. This in turn gave rise to the only possible work area for the illiterate, unskilled gecekondu women—the houses of middle class women.[11] This new labour market brought two groups of women from different socio-cultural classes face to face in a new exploitation environment. The middle class women established a clear-cut exploitation order on the gecekondu women. The terms of work were never publicly or legally determined. An oral, one-sided work agreement was made by declaration of the terms of work by the female employer. The female employer undertook no responsibilities for her employee, and she provided her with no work security whatsoever. The gecekondu women performed heavy, dirty work for long hours in return for insufficient pay, degrading treatment and leftover food and clothing. This situation went on until national and urban investments achieved a level where they could foster new employment opportunities for large groups of marginal, factory and service workers and small enterpreneurs in urban areas.

[11] The houses of the newly rich middle class families who yearn to copy the style of living of the established rich upper class households may also be added. Increasing urban construction has also opened up doorkeeping jobs.

The most suitable and eager candidates for these jobs were the gecekondu males. Thus, until the demand was formed for male gecekondu labour in urban economic space, the gecekondu woman had to work under all sorts of conditions, providing channels of participation for the middle class women in the service sector.

Under changing economic conditions, while more and more middle class women entered clerical and other service work, the gecekondu women withdrew to their homes or entered the less specialized branches of the urban service sector which required minimum training or work experience. Their daughters also preferred to work in several branches of the service sector. Thus, although the contemporary civilized society still has not displayed regulatory attempts to eliminate female labour exploitation in the maidlaundress type of work, the changing supply and demand balance has given bargaining power to the gecekondu women. Today, this house service is termed a temporary evil to be suffered if and when the gecekondu family faces an economic bottleneck, but the terms of work are now open to discussion and bargaining by both sides. In general, the whole area of maid-laundress service tends to be closing down as a possible female employment area.[12] Accordingly, when we entered the gecekondu areas in 1976—77, the number of women engaged in this type of work was surprisingly low (Table IX).

One point which should be underlined is that this work area pitted women of two different classes against each other, provoking and encouraging them to exploit each other. Thus, a resentful environment was formed between the two classes of women, further severing relations. Further, the fact that gecekondu women entered middle class houses and observed middle class living closely, stimulated new cravings, hopes and aspirations which remained unsatisfied thus causing further unhappiness among gecekondu women.

When we surveyed a section of the gecekondu population in urban economic space in 1976—77, we found that women were basically confined to their homes. As discussed earlier, increased demand for the typical type of labour found in the gecekondu areas—labour which has occupational mobility and a low level of skills, experience, and training—has drawn men and young boys into the market, lightening the economic burden of the family. Since girls tend to marry young and family size is

[12] Today with the withdrawal of the gecekondu women from housecleaning jobs, this area is being taken over by the wives of doormen to a certain extent. These women usually perform daily cleaning jobs for tenants in the same building.

Table VII

Activity and Dependency Ratios[1]

	Activity Ratio			*Dependency Ratio*
	Female	*Male*	*Total*	
Gültepe	2.7	46.2	26.5	699
Zeyrek	3.4	57.0	33.0	581
Eminönü	1.8	52.8	31.0	586
G.O.P.	5.1	52.1	30.1	529
Istinye	–	42.7	24.4	621
T. Çayır	4.7	41.0	24.0	448
Yıldız	4.3	43.5	24.8	729
Akdere	1.8	50.0	25.3	665

1—Activity ratio: $\frac{\text{No. of working people}}{\text{Total population}}$

Dependency ratio: age groups—$\frac{(0-14)+(65)}{(15-64)}$ activity ratios are given in percentages whereas dependency ratios are in thousands.

gradually reducing, gecekondu women are not compelled to work full time. In general, they venture into the labour market temporarily, whenever economic bottlenecks arise. Thus, out of 1,450 women in the age group 15—64 in the Istanbul survey, only 81 (5.5%) and of the 952 women in the same age group in the Ankara survey, only 60 (6%) were working (Tables VII—VIII).

The pattern of female participation in urban economic space is a replica of the pattern discussed in Section II. The gecekondu women, as their men, are allowed to explore only a certain section of urban economic space—that section which contains low-esteemed, low-paying, unorganized jobs in which unsatisfactory work conditions discourage enthusiasm for further work (Table IX). Table IX shows that the highest position a women can reach in the urban white collar scale is teaching. There was one exception—a female chemist who was the wife of a school teacher in Ankara. A difference appears in female occupational distribution in Istanbul and Ankara. Istanbul houses several industrial complexes

Table VIII

Economically Active Population by Age Groups and Sex (in percentages)

		0–14		*15–64*		*65*		*Total*	
		F	*M*	*F*	*M*	*F*	*M*	*F*	*M*
Gültepe	Employed	–	2	5	75	3	19	3	46
	Not working	100	98	95	25	97	81	97	54
Zeyrek	Employed	0.0	3	6	82	–	43	4	57
	Not working	100	97	94	18	100	57	96	43
Eminönü	Employed	0.0	2	2	75	4	57	1	53
	Not working	100	98	98	25	96	43	99	47
G.O.P.	Employed	0.0	2	7	76	4	5	5	52
	Not working	100	98	93	24	96	95	95	48
Istinye	Employed	–	–	–	66	–	–	–	43
	Not working	100	100	100	44	100	100	100	57
Total (Istanbul)	Employed	0.0	2	5	76	3	29	3	51
	Not working	100	98	95	24	97	71	97	49
T. Çayır	Employed	–	–	8	73	15	17	5	41
	Not working	100	100	92	28	85	83	95	59
Yıldız	Employed	–	–	8	70	5	50	4	44
	Not working	100	100	92	30	95	50	96	56
Akdere	Employed	–	0.0	3	75	–	17	2	47
	Not working	100	100	97	25	100	83	98	53
Total (Ankara)	Employed	–	0.0	6	73	1	19	3	44
	Not working	100	100	94	27	99	81	97	66

around which many of the existing gecekondu neighborhoods have been developed. For most gecekondu women, immediate employment possibilities opened up in these complexes. As a result, about 72% of the working women in Istanbul were employed as factory workers. By contrast, Ankara has an economic space more specialized in bureaucratic and service functions. Therefore, 47% of the working women were employed in some type of clerical work.

The results of a household labour force survey conducted by the State Institute of Statistics in 107 Turkish cities in November 1969, resembled the female employment pattern in the gecekondu environment[13]. According to this survey, 52% of the female household members were housewives and only 6% were employed. Whereas 47% of the male household members were employed. Of the employed labour force, 88% were male and only 12% were female. According to the distribution of employed

[13] D. I. E., *Türkiye Istatistik Cep Yıllıgı*—1976 (Statistical Pocket Book of Turkey—1976). Ankara: Devlet Istatistik Enstitüsü Matbaası, 1976.

Table IX
Occupational Distribution of Female Members of the Household
(Istanbul)

	Wife	*Daughter*	*Son's wife*	*Mother*	*Female relative*	*Total*
Factory worker	14	35	5	1	3	58
Clerk	1	4	–	1	2	8
Teacher	1	–	–	–	–	1
Salesgirl	–	2	–	–	–	2
Dressmaker	–	1	1			2
Hairdresser	1	1	–	–	–	2
Model	–	1	–	–	–	1
Janitor	2	–	–	–	–	2
Apprentice	–	1	–	–	–	1
Maid-servant	1	1	–	1	1	4
Total	20	46	6	3	6	81

(Ankara)

	Wife	*Daughter*	*Son's wife*	*Mother*	*Female relative*	*Total*
Factory worker	1	1	–	–	–	2
Clerk	16	12	–			28
Teacher	8	1	–	–	–	9
Nurse	3	–	–	–	–	3
Salesgirl	–	1	–	–	–	1
Profession	1	–	–	–	–	1
Janitor	8	1	–	–	1	10
Maid-servant	2	–	–	–	–	2
Agriculture	–	–	–	1	–	1
Apprentice	1	1	–	–	–	2
Secretary	–	1	–	–	–	1
Total	40	18	–	1	1	60

and unemployed household members by their last economic activity in November 1969, 29% of the employed females were engaged in the agricultural sector, 29% were employed in the manufacturing sector and 31% were employed in the service sector. 24% of the employed females were family workers (engaged in family business mostly without pay).

Thus, the present employment pattern of the women in the gecekondu reflects a general withdrawal from the urban labour market and a tendency to enter unorganized, low-paying, unspecialized jobs. This specific pattern reflects the function and the consequent bargaining power the gecekondu labourer has in the urban economic market.

4. The Conclusion

The points emphasized in this study can be summarized as follows:

The problem of women's rights cannot be studied as an entity separate from the socio-economic structure of the society. The social, economic and cultural problems of a woman differ in nature according to the social class to which she is affiliated. These specific affiliations determine the range of alternatives open to her in economic space. In turn, the pattern and nature of the place occupied in economic space determines the general level and nature of relationships encountered in socio-cultural and physical spaces. Therefore, the topic of discussion—the gecekondu women—should be defined in the context of her own socio-economic group—the gecekondu. Likewise, proposals developed to improve women's position in the society should be based on comprehensive approaches originating from the socio-economic structure.

In the specific framework of the Third World countries, unless basic changes are introduced in economic and social spaces, proposals like encouraging women to work, increasing the level of their education, and the concomitant provision of social services will not work. When women of all social stratas decide to work, they choose a spot in economic space according to their socio-economic backgrounds. Thus, well-educated, highly skilled upper class women with influential social connections will land in well-esteemed, well-paying bureaucratic jobs, while women from lower classes will enter low-esteemed manual or service work. Again, women from lower classes will neither be able to afford long years of formal education nor highly inaccessible social services. Furthermore, women from lower classes, especially the gecekondu women who comprise a high percentage of the female urban population, will join 'peripheral' labour force as there is immediate demand for her type of labour in that labour market and she will be subjected to further exploitation due to the basically unorganized, marginal nature of this section of the labour force.

Moreover, society's traditional emphasis on woman's primary role of 'wife-mother' will cause further psychological stress due to the conflicting dual roles women are expected to perform in their houses and at work. Thus work, in general, will never be a source of social unification, equalization and satisfaction. For most women, it will be a solution for individual family problems when all other alternatives are exhausted, to be suffered until the problem is solved or retirement time arrives.

Within this framework, that is at the level and pattern of development of many Third World countries, the present predominant function of lower class women—in Turkey the gecekondu women—is to substantially contribute to the enlargement of the consumer market. Compared to the life of the gecekondu family in the rural areas before migration to the city, life in the gecekondu environment is far superior. Men work less, women in general. do not work, children benefit from education and other urban services. This obviously is the comparison made by especially the male members of the family. The women, although deeply aware of the superiority of the family's present condition, are also familiar with middle class living standards. Consequently, the gecekondu woman not only wants to take roots in the city but also wants to raise her family's standards of living to that of the middle class. She, more than her husband, is sensitive to integration into urban life and is therefore open to consumption stimulants and relevant consumption norms, the only integration channel that the system offers this class. It is she who identifies upward mobility with material possessions and it is she who pushes for acquisition of real estate, consumer goods, modern gadgets and is tolerant towards children who want to follow the latest urban fashions.

In the near future with the enlargement of the capitalist market and the favorable medium created for women to enter work, the gecekondu women will join the urban work force. Yet, the point is that as long as the present development pattern, rate and level is retained, she, in general, will join the peripheral urban work force.

What might be a comprehensive approach taking into account the socioeconomic background? Starting with education, on-the-job training must be emphasized instead of classical formal education; and classical education must be underlined with vocational training so that the boys and girls who cannot afford formal education and who have to go to work as soon as they finish primary school, will be able to advance into careers. Formal education should offer areas of specialization and training to students from all social classes which orient them to manufacturing types of work instead of solely to bureaucratic service work.

Concomitant changes are needed in economic space based on changing development, organization, pattern and rate. More should be done to develop national technology instead of basing the economy on imported technology and consumer goods oriented industry. Within this framework, women's work conditions should be readjusted considering not only female physiology but their differing socio-economic backgrounds as well. An equalizing medium is needed if equal wages are to be paid.

In this sense, work should not be a situation in which men and women from different classes are pitted against each other,—one class always controlling the other—but rather one where differences blend.

Certain changes are also necessary in socio-cultural and physical spaces if income accruing from production is not to be channelled into the consumer market. This involves a readjustment of standards, including those in physical space. Social services should be made available to all social classes and luxurious consumption should be limited. A change of attitudes and norms, reflected from the alphabet books to the T.V. ads, is necessary to upgrade manual work, to achieve a more unified society and to change women from self, home decorating machines to productive elements in the society.

Even these extremely brief proposals show that a transformation in the socio-economic background is necessary if lower class women are to enter the work forces and free themselves from economic and social exploitation. If not considered in a comprehensive framework, the gecekondu women as new components in Turkish metropolises will never be a fully effective part of the labour force and they will always be subjected to increasing levels of exploitation.

PART THREE

CONTINUITY AND CHANGE IN SEX ROLES

GOLDENHILL

(Goldenhill is a shantytown built behind Ankara. All its residents have dreams until daybreak. Here you will read only one young girl's dream.)

She has dreams about a husband:
A fine gentleman with a fair salary.
They get married and move to the city.
They receive mail at their new address:
Happy Nest Apartments, the basement.
The flat they live in is cosy like a box.
No more outside work to do laundry or wash windows;
The dishes she has to wash are her own.

A baby is born to them, a bundle of joy.
They buy a used cart too.
Outings in the morning to the Kızılay Playground
So that little Yılmaz could play in the sandbox
Like those upperclass children.

Orhan Veli KANIK, *Altındag*
Transl. Talât Sait HALMAN

INTRODUCTION

Gender differentiation is more ancient, more stable and more widespread than any other type of social differentiation. It appears in all known economic systems and political orders. But, the extent to which gender constitutes a differentiating element in society varies considerably, culturally and historically.

Sex roles can also be understood in terms of ideologies. According to the traditional and romantic sex role ideologies, politics belongs to the male role. This is particularly true in countries where sex segregation is nourished by the cultural system. The Marxian sex role ideology is based on the principle of total equality of men and women in society, including the work and political spheres. The radical sex role ideology in Scandinavia proceeds further than the Marxians and the early suffragettes by trying to bring about changes in the man's role, as well. It encourages men to accept some traditionally feminine responsibilities, like child care and housework. The goal is the total integration of the sexes. The women power or liberation movement in the United States is based on the notion of men and women's conflicting interests. It assumes that integration is not possible, but that revolt and fight are necessary to bring women into power. Its goal is woman power.

Muslim societies have generated a cultural understanding which is explicitly based upon sexual inequality, both in public and in the family. In Islamic culture (and in many pre-Islamic Mediterranean cultures as pointed out by Germaine Tillion), male honor is closely linked to female purity. This requires virginity for the unmarried, fidelity for the married, and continence for the divorced or widowed. This conception of honor means that the behaviour of an individual woman affects not only her own reputation, but that of all her male kin. The logical consequences have been in general terms, men assume all public roles, and women assent to the domestic ones.

Since Turkey began to implement over fifty years ago a very comprehensive set of legal reforms aiming to abolish in all spheres sex segregation, especially after the speeding up of urbanization, industrialization and migration, important changes in sex roles have taken place in Turkish society.

These changes cover a broad range. They stretch from a complete adherence to a progressive, even militant code of behaviour and values to a mild, conventional, slow type of adjustment. It is important, however, to take notice of the centers of continuity and those of rapid change. The three papers in this subsection, due to their different methodological approach, might indeed shed light on this fascinating subject. While Kıray, through a meticulously embroidered piece of anthropological research, enables the reader to take notice of the subtleties with regard to small town women's versatile modes of behaviour and its impact on the family structure, consumption patterns and choice of education, Kandiyoti's essay represents a different kind of data. Her intergenerational survey—the first of its kind undertaken in Turkey—reveals continuity even in upper middle class mothers. Their relatively strong attachment to exclusively feminine social relations, networks, and activities may be used as an indicator of "modern conformism". This tendency is interestingly contrasted with the emotionally more detached, ego-oriented daughters, who, among others, have apparently partly discarded from their mental trousseau, the imperative concept of virginity. Altıok, a literary critic, attempts to describe the evolution of the images of women projected through fiction starting with the late Ottoman Empire up till the present day.

Sex roles being closely related to class structure, Turkey's rapidly developing capitalist economy and its needs are indeed promoting fast changes in social life too. The most relevant examples can be derived from internal and external migration, where the intrusion of a new consumption pattern forces a redistribution of sex roles. The degree of this lasting or only transitional emancipation depends largely on time and residence.

Yet, the impact of all these changes have so far only partly touched large segments of Turkey's female population. This also explains why public discussion similar to Western societies, is not invited on topics like the determination of sex role distribution and the problem of individual aspirations for equality. The answer lies partly in the fact that during the early phases of capitalism, selected issues, for instance the exploitation of unpaid family members in rural areas, the continuation of the bride-price institution, and the employment/family problems of migrant women workers abroad, occupied an important place in public discussion, while problems such as quasi-egalitarianism, covert differentiation, the need for self-awareness, role heterogeneity remain so far undiscussed. Even so, the impact of legal reforms in the past and the steady challenge Turkey's democratic system is offering, have no doubt increased in Turkish society the humanization of family relations, classrooms and the work world. It is from these changes that women are deriving their share of equity.

FÜSUN (ALTIOK) AKATLI

THE IMAGE OF WOMAN IN TURKISH LITERATURE

The reader must not be misled by the title and think that this is an attempt to present a thorough study of the development of woman's image in Turkish literature going back centuries ago beginning with the "Divan" and "Folk" literatures. Such a study can only be achieved with the collaboration of historians of literature and sociologists and, even they would need the assistance of experts in other branches of the humanities. Besides, this writer is neither a historian of literature nor a sociologist, but merely a teacher of philosophy whose specific interest lies in literary criticism. Nor will this essay deal with the structural, formal or esthetic problems of literature. This essay is simply an effort to bring to light the way in which various Turkish writers have dealt with 'women' in various literary periods. By doing so, it is hoped that some light—if not an objective and exhaustive one, going deep into the roots—will be shed particularly on the changes and transformations Turkish woman underwent just before and during the Republican period.

To efficiently accomplish this objective, we shall dwell almost entirely on fiction, that is novels and short stories. Poetry rests greatly on image and possesses a peculiar structural wholeness of its own. Such characteristics, especially the structural wholeness, might render it difficult to carry out this kind of a study as then the focal point would become an analysis of content rather than the topic defined above. Naturally, images of women appear in poetry too, even though they may not be directly involved in the problems of 'women'. Generally, what we see in poetry is not the woman herself, but the way the poet sees her.

Before taking up various images of woman in narrative, let us take a glance at an essay entitled: "The State of the Beloved" by Cemal Süreya, an eminent contemporary Turkish poet. In this essay, which effectively illustrates the various images of women in Turkish poetry, Cemal Süreya relates the evolution of this image, which may be summarized as follows:

In the "Divan" poetry, the beloved is an 'idea' isolated from what is human, and existing merely in the realm of aesthetics. This attitude towards the beloved stems from the slavery of women. The "beloved" has no name. She is supposed to possess all the virtues a poet can conceive.

A movement which began with the "Tanzimat" period (1860—1895) brought a certain amount of reality to poetry, no matter how vague that reality might be. Here, love is pushed to the background and naturally so is woman. Yet, even if in the background, the beloved is a human being. She is the beloved of the Ottoman aristocrat who enjoys a position in the ruling class.

Later, in the "Servet-i Fünun" (1896—1908) poetry, the beloved appears as a weak, pale, sickly creature wrapped in clouds, whom the romantic bureaucrat admires from a distance. Aesthetics negate reality. In love poems, only prostitutes exhibit life. Life is filthy and therefore it must be avoided. The beloved is an "eternal virgin".

Passionate love finds its way into poetry for the first time with Yahya Kemal and Ahmet Haşim. Woman is now alive and really feminine.

In "Hececi" (Syllabic meter) poetry, 'woman' is identified sometimes with an aristocratic or semi-aristocratic lady from İstanbul, sometimes with a peasant girl. The beloved peasant is gay, healthy, beaming and rosy-cheeked. Yet, the poet himself does not address her directly, but rather lets the shepherd Ahmet fall in love with her. He depicts the shepherd's feelings as a third person, as a mere observer.

In Nazım Hikmet's poetry, love is the essential element nourishing poetry and elevating the "human" factor to its highest possible dimensions. Nazım Hikmet was a man of ideology. He was the first Turkish poet to attribute to woman such qualities as friendship and solidarity. The images of 'wife' and 'beloved' unite for the first time in his poems.

In the nineteen-forties a revolution broke out in poetry: ordinary people became the major theme, and thus the beloved began to be chosen from among them. The beloved is now a living human being. She is just any woman. She can belong to any social class: sometimes she is the wife of a driver, sometimes a worker in a tobacco factory, sometimes the educated daughter of a government official. With her virtues, faults, beauty and ugliness, she is a real human being.

In Turkish poetry after 1955, the theme of love and woman gains new dimensions and becomes richer. As social values and prohibitions in Turkish society are based largely upon sexuality, sexual tension between men and women has always been much higher in Turkey than in other countries. Therefore, the avoidance of erotism in Turkish literature up to 1955, was nothing but hypocrisy. This taboo was broken in the post-1955 period.

During the 1940—1960 period, the theme of love in Turkish poetry assumed the form of rebellion against the social system. The new poet who wanted to change the world, identified his beloved with an intimate friend, sometimes even with a comrade in arms; and he saw her as his wife, or alternatively, he saw a "beloved" in his wife.

Having briefly exposed the changes which, according to the poet, C. Süreya, the image of woman underwent in Turkish poetry, let us now pass on to narrative in which the image of woman is made up of different and more complex elements, though in some respects one may draw a parallel with the transformation in poetry.

In order to keep alive the interest of the foreign reader, who presumably may not be familiar with either Turkish women or Turkish literature, quotations from the works which this reader might never be able to read, shall be avoided.

In the pre-Republican period, we observe that narratives are insufficiently developed either in quantity or in quality and that woman and her problems are treated only indirectly or by way of implication. Yet, there are some 19th century writers like Şemsettin Sami, Sami Paşazade Sezai and Nabizade Nazım, whom we may consider pioneers in bringing the various problems concerning women to the agenda and in creating certain female images though these are not sufficiently clear. These writers are among the first names in the history of the Turkish novel and short story.

Şemsettin Sami's *Taassuk-u Talat ve Fitnat* (The Love of Talat and Fitnat) (1872), considered to be the first Turkish novel, is worth mentioning here in that it exposes the snags about marital customs, i.e. the role of go-betweens. This novel is doubtlessly a primitive one, not only from a literary, but also in terms of it's analysis of the problems involved.

Sami Paşazade Sezai's novel entitled *Sergüzeşt* (Adventure) (1889), which also indirectly deals with the problems of woman, exposes and reproaches the injustice suffered by a slave girl. The problems arising from the slave-odalisque institution in Ottoman society were also taken up by writers in later periods.

The last of the pioneers was Nabizade Nazım with his novel *Zehra* (1896). He, too, did not go beyond the typical İstanbul families, evening entertainments and cruises on the Bosphorus. Although Nabizade Nazım is considered the first realistic novelist, his women are still vague figures, rather than fully developed characters.

Let us now take a glance at the later pioneers, namely Halit Ziya Uşaklıgil, Hüseyin Rahmi Gürpınar and Halide Edip Adıvar.

Halit Ziya Uşaklıgil, a significant Turkish novelist, published his works over a considerably long period of time, from 1892 to 1924. The main types of women appearing in his novels are the upperclass ladies of Istanbul whose greatest virtue is their chastity. Frivolous women, ambitious to find their way into upper class family circles, sometimes succeed in upsetting the so-called happy lives of the virtuous people, and the romantic, dreamy, sad and sensitive young ladies. In his short stories, Halit Ziya describes generally the oppressed, life-defeated nurses, maids, cooks and half-slave little girls serving the families in the *köşks*[1] and *konaks* of İstanbul.

Hüseyin Rahmi Gürpınar was a prolific writer, who published novels, short stories and plays during the years 1889—1943. He approached the problems of women—naturally the women of his time—and he even tried to get to the core of these problems. However, these problems, instead of being reflected in the behaviour of the women characters themselves, are exposed by the writer in those parts of the novel where the author indulges in expressing his own ideas as if he were writing an article. His women are mainly back-street types, ignorant, superstitious and excluded from men's world. Although he sometimes depicts educated, enlightened types of women, conscious of their lower status and of their humiliation by men, he simply uses them to express his own ideas about the equality of men and women and to criticise the morals and even the laws of his time. In general, however, his women are ardent defenders of the inequality between the sexes, which the author himself opposes.

Another novelist whose approach to the problems of women and whose women characters are of particular interest is Halide Edip Adıvar. She mainly concerned herself with the recognition of women's rights and their emancipation. As she began writing in the pre-Republican period and continued to do so during the period of Atatürk's reforms, the problems she approached and the images of women she created show great variety. For instance, we come across the images of nationalistic women, modernized women, women with a strong personality, women rising up against oppression, and idealistic women striving to educate the masses. However, her inconsistent ideological tendency, vacillating between pan-Turkism and pro-Americanism, or Turkish nationalism and the ideal of Westernization, prevented her from basing her analyses and her proposed solutions on solid ground, even in *Sinekli Bakkal*, which is believed to be her most important work, where she tries to combine these ideologies into an original synthesis.

The majority of the writers during the first decades of the Republican

[1] Special names given to the mansions of the upper-class Ottoman families.

period laid emphasis not so much on the socio-economic aspect of the transformations brought about during this period, as on the superstructures, such as morals, values and beliefs, or to put it more properly, on the inconsistencies in the superstructures.

Among these writers one may mention Reşat Nuri Güntekin, Yakup Kadri Karaosmanoğlu, Peyami Safa and even Ahmet Hamdi Tanpınar, who continued to deal with the same *problematique* during the years that followed. These writers who differ so greatly in their literary merits as well as in their world outlook, show a strange resemblance with regard to their images of women. This resemblance may be explained by the turbulent transition process that was taking place. The old patriarchal, feudal or semi-feudal family family relationships based on male domination were being transformed into the Republican period's modern family concept in which women would enjoy, at least under the law, the possibility of directly participating in production and, to a certain extent, the blessings of education and freedom. Thus, in their narratives, the tendency and efforts towards Westernization are criticized and even condemned. The generous, hospitable, chaste and faithful Ottoman woman is longed for. The family institution and morals—which always means sexual morals when women are involved—are believed to be in danger. In Reşat Nuri, this danger can only be avoided in a rather idealistic and even populistic way, i.e., by means of the image of a young virtuous girl devoted to an ideal. With the exception of *Çalıkuşu*, which reflects this optimistic approach, Reşat Nuri also saw woman under the threat of degeneration and moral disintegration. This degeneration and woman's role therein appear along much more pessimistic lines in Yakup Kadri and Peyami Safa. For the latter, it is the Islamic values themselves that were shaken. In his novels one comes across daughters of respectable families dragged into prostitution. For him, the only way out is to return to Islamic values and to stick to them.

Yakup Kadri maintains that women, already desperate and dependent, could not remain intact in the midst of this moral degeneration; they would come to place beauty and charm above chastity; their flamboyance and recklessness would lead them to complete ruin and they would end up fallen women. Such women are depicted in his works. Selim İleri, a contemporary literary critic, points out that Yakup Kadri created an infernal sexual medium since he identified sexuality with sin, and summarizes his attitude as follows: "In Yakup Kadri's works events and people are under the yoke of moral collapse. The economic reasons for this collapse (the 1883 Trade Agreement and the İttihat Terakki's

(Union and Progress) attempt to create a national bourgeoisie that resulted in the appearance of war profiteers and blackmarketeers) are not dealt with directly. Effects rather than causes are given emphasis. Causes are investigated from a critical realistic observer point of view and are projected into his novels as mere results. For instance, Seniha, the heroine of Yakup Kadri's novel *Kiralık Konak* (A Mansion for Rent), who becomes a slave to the *nouveau riche* social circles, pays for her beauty and flamboyance with her exhaustion as a human being. Seniha is a result, of the *Konak* way of life.

Yakup Kadri's complaint about "our moral values being affected by Rococo, just like our clothes and furniture" is typical of the view which identifies modernization with Westernization and holds both equally responsible for the degeneration of the value-system. The identification of social change with degeneration inevitably led all these writers to approach the theme of woman from the standpoint of a moral *problematique.*

Even Ahmet Hamdi Tanpınar, who continued to publish his works long after 1949, discussed the dilemma of Eastern and Western cultures and created the image of woman indulging in a "strenuous fight against the centuries-old family values", his image replaced the woman of the past, who was deprived of personality.

Consideration of problems in the context of the dialectic integrity of the 'social' and the 'individual', a recent phenomenon in Turkish literature, assumed significant dimensions especially in the last twenty years. It is only in recent Turkish literature from Orhan Kemal onwards, that women undergoing the process of emancipation are depicted with their economic, social, intellectual and psychological background.

It is important to point out here that the writers, in whose works we see sound and realistic female characters, possess a conscious, assimilated world outlook which is no longer eclectic, inconsistent or idealistic in the philosophical sense of the term. They all share an essentially socialistic world outlook, irrespective of their differences with regards to models or strategies.

It is again in the last twenty years that regional differences and class distinctions between women, both in novels and short stories, have become meaningful. The factors that determine the images of women from different social strata in rural and urban regions, i.e., peasants, workers, petit-bourgeois intellectuals, have become crystal clear only in the second half of the first fifty years of the Republican period. Woman with her economic, social, psychological, intellectual and sexual aspects, has now found her way into our literature. Consideration of the 'social' and the 'individual' in the context of their counteraction, treatment of morals and superstructures in general, without being isolated from their infrastructural foundations, have rendered it possible for woman to be reflected in literature not as a mere "idea", but as a full-fledged, real human being. Thus, the theme of woman has become concrete enough to be the subject of sociological, psychological and philosophical studies.

The image of the 'woman worker' was introduced into our literature by Orhan Kemal. The state of women who participate in production and the additional dimensions of their being oppressed, stemming from their being 'the other sex', could only be brought to light from a class-consciousness point of view. Orhan Kemal was the first representative of this approach in Turkish literature.

Women living in rural areas, that is peasant women, became a major theme in the novels of Yaşar Kemal and Fakir Baykurt. Baykurt's *Irazca* and Yaşar Kemal's *Meryemce* have become the prototypes of woman in village literature. The hard-working, suffering Meryemce, struggling against injustice side by side with men, is utterly hopeless vis-a-vis the social mechanism based on exploitation. The author stresses the fact that Meryemce is not only an oppressed, lifebattered peasant woman, but also as a loving, respectable mother. As a matter of fact, in works depicting village life, woman's role as mother is of primary importance.

Similarly, Fakir Baykurt's Irazca is a mother above all. We first see her as a firm, brave woman amidst a life full of hardships, having the upper-hand in the family with her son, daughter-in-law and grandchildren. Later, when her son moves into town, she is left all by herself with everything around her upside down. Like Baykurt in Irazca, almost all the modern Turkish writers see woman as a natural human being, not an artificial creature.

Before passing on to literature dealing with urban life, I would like to take a brief glance at the short stories of Bekir Yıldız, who depicts South-East Anatolia and its mores. The way he sees women of South-East Anatolia, where the remnants of traditional, feudal or semi-feudal relations are most intense, is explained as follows by Hilmi Yavuz, a well-known Turkish literary critic. "Bekir Yıldız analyzes the attitude of Anatolian people towards the mores which fully dominate their spiritual life. His masculine characters are not unconsciously resigned to the mores. It is the women who cannot rise against them, or at least who fail to make any effort towards changing them. In Bekir Yıldız's stories the difference between the male and the female attitude towards these mores is of utmost importance. He points out that women in the patriarchal, primitive rural society are utterly weak and insecure and have no alternative other than blind submission to the mores. This is symbolized in the short story entitled *Kara Çarsaflı Gelin* (The Bride in Black) by the heroine who turns over her daughter to the family of the man murdered by her husband as a sort of atonement. In fact, it is only the men who fight against the harshness of the mores".

Let us now turn to the urban women in Turkish literature over the last decade. The major characteristic of this period is that the images of woman have been drawn from the most part by women writers. Thus, after Halide Edip, who failed to go beyond creating vague images, women are once again seen through the eyes of women, but this time in an entirely new light.

The question of the freedom of women in the Atatürk period, pursuant to the proclamation of the Republic and the reforms related to women's rights is analyzed in depth in Adalet Ağaoğlu's novel, *Ölmeye Yatmak* (Lying Down to Die), published in 1973. The heroine of the novel, Aysel, who is an Associate Professor, reflects upon the transformation process of and the crises experienced by the intellectual women of Kemalist Turkey. In her personality, we find an analysis of the conflict between the pro-Western ideology and the values of the traditional family institution based on the individual/society dialectics. Hilmi Yavuz approaches the novel as follows: "The problem of woman's freedom in *Ölmeye Yatmak*, in the given historical period, gains a pulpable dimension in the conflict between the institutions of education and family. The family institution, which expresses the traditional ideology and the educational institution, which expresses the pro-Western Republican ideology creates conflicts in a manner which leads to the perception of the problem of woman's freedom as a tragic phenomenon. The structural duality finds its expression in Aysel's personality as a contradiction, which she experiences in full detail..".

Other aspects of the problem appear in the works of Nezihe Meriç, Leyla Erbil, Füruzan and Sevgi Soysal.

Nezihe Meriç, in her novel *Korsan Çıkmazı*[2], describes a provincial girl who leaves her closed family circle and goes to İstanbul for education. The heroine, in spite of her fears and hesitations trys hard to get to know the world and to develop her personality through her own experiences. We come across a different type of woman in Meriç's short stories. She is

[2] The name of a street in Beyoglu, Istanbul.

again a provincial woman settled in a city: womanly, loving, helpful, gay, optimistic and a source of happiness for all the people around her.

Leyla Erbil brings the image of a woman who is capable of critically looking at man and of seeing him with all his faults and weaknesses, and of opposing him when he tries to oppress her, both intellectually and sexually. For this angry, sophisticated petitbourgeois woman, the discrimination between the sexes has lost its sharpness to such an extent that one might even think that the imbalance would change in favour of women!

In Füruzan, we see two major types of women. The first is the "fallen woman" in brothels or the poor back-street girl whom poverty forces to sell her body to rich but disgusting middle-aged men in movie-theaters or in beach cabines. Prostitution is now taken within its social and economic context; not as a question of crisis of values or moral degeneration, as the previous writers had seen it. Füruzan does not neglect the psychological and emotional aspects of the individual when she deals with prostitution as a socio-economic problem. The second type of woman in her stories is the *mother struggling to* bring up and educate her child, all alone amidst all sorts of deprivations. She describes the misery of the poor from the angle of class-consciousness without indulging in "tearful sentimentality".

Sevgi Soysal introduces the type of woman in revolutionary action, searching for a light in the political darkness of oppression and persecution following the 12th of March, 1971.[3] Never leaving aside her very peculiar irony, she discusses in her novels and diary how theoretical accumulation should be made use of, and what results might arise in practice from the petit-bourgeois intellectual's participation in the struggle for socialism. The image Sevgi Soysal creates is that of a woman who embarks on political action, who fights side by side with man and who is condemned to imprisonment.

In conclusion, it may be said that the images of woman created by the writers who in the last decades introduced to the Turkish literature the individual/society dialectics and the totality of the human beings, are contemporary and realistic images. This point may be of secondary importance from a purely literary and artistic point of view. However, it assumes primary significance if considered as a subject for analysis in the realm of the social sciences.

---

[3] The 12th of March, 1971 is the day, when the political process was temporarily "put on ice" by a military intervention and the proclamation of martial law.

SELECTED BIBLIOGRAPHY

Alangu, Tahir—*Cumhuriyetten Sonra Hikaye ve Roman* (Novels and Short Stories in Republican Period), Vols. 1, 2, 3. Istanbul, 1968.

Berkes, Mediha—"Hüseyin Rahmi Romanlarında Aile ve Kadın" (Woman and Family in Hüseyin Rahmi's Novels) in: *Dil ve Tarih Cografya Fakültesi Dergisi*, Vol. III, No. 19.

Kudret, Cevdet—*Türk Edebiyatında Hikâye ve Roman 2*. (Novels and Short Stories in Turkish Literature 2.), Varlık Y., 1967.

Naci, Fethi—*On Türk Romanı* (Ten Turkish Novels). Ok Y., Istanbul 1971.

Ileri, Selim—*Çağdaşlık Sorunlari* (The Problems of Contemporaneity), Günebakan Y., Istanbul, 1978.

Kandiyoti, Deniz—"Toplumsal Değişme ve Kadının Yeri" (Social Change and Woman's Place), in: *Bogaziçi Üniversitesi Dergisi*, Vols. 4—5, 1976/77.

Sőnmez (Doğramacı), Dr. Emel—"Turkish Women in Turkish Literature of the XIXth Century" in: *Hacettepe Bulletin of Social Sciences and Humanities*, Vol. 2, Nos. 1 and 2, 1970.

Sönmez (Doğramacı), Dr. Emel—"The Novelist Halide Edip Adıvar and Turkish Feminism" in: *Die Welt des Islams*, XIV, 1—4.

Sűreya, Cemal—Şapkam Dolu Çiçekle (My Hat Full of Flowers), Ada Y., Istanbul, 1976.

Yavuz, Hilmi—*Roman Kavramı ve Türk Romanı* (The Concept of Novel and Turkish Novel), Bilgi Y., Ankara, 1977.

DENIZ KANDIYOTI

DIMENSIONS OF PSYCHO-SOCIAL CHANGE IN WOMEN: AN INTERGENERATIONAL COMPARISON

INTRODUCTION

The nature of legal and political changes affecting women since the foundation of the Turkish Republic have been the focus of considerable attention (Inan, 1962; Taşkıran, 1973; Abadan-Unat, 1963, 1967). However, social scientists have long been questioning the extent to which these changes have fundamentally altered women's lives. Thus, the number of studies directly or indirectly stressing the structural determinants of women's status in the process of social change have steadily increased (Timur, 1972; Kıray, 1964, 1976a, b; Başaran, 1971, 1974; Abadan-Unat, 1977; Çitçi, 1974; Kâğıtçıbaşı, 1977; Kandiyoti, 1977a, b). On the other hand, women's perceptions of themselves, of their sex-roles and the nature of the subjective pressures that bear upon them have not been the subject of much investigation[1]. Did the process of social change really have an impact on women's self-concepts, role expectations and attitudes about work and marriage or did it merely produce superficial adjustments without fundamental psycho-social change? This is the question we would like to address ourselves to, albeit in a very limited way. The method of intergenerational comparison was adopted to achieve this goal and a group of female students at Boğaziçi University were compared to their own mothers.

The psychological concepts which form the theoretical basis of intergenerational comparisons are drawn from four areas of the psychology of women. These are; a) Achievement orientation in women b) sex-role stereotypes c) sex-role standards and d) patterns of socialization. Thus, the type and extent of intergenerational change will be assessed by examining differences in achievement orientation, sex-role stereotypes, sex-role standards and socialization patterns. It has also been necessary

[1] A lot of insights on this question can be found in the work of a new generation of women writers, reflecting upon their own experiences. An examination of this work, however, remains outside the scope of this paper.

to test the cultural relevance within the Turkish context of psychological variables assumed to produce consistent differences between the sexes. To that effect, a control group of male students at the same University were compared with the same-age females. However, comparisons between the sexes will be left out of the scope of this paper and references will be made to some basic findings only when strictly necessary. The method of our research, the descriptive characteristics of our research sample and a definition of our psycho-social variables will be briefly discussed before the presentation of our intergenerational findings.

METHOD

The data of our research was collected in two phases. The first phase which took place in June 1977 consisted of a questionnaire survey of a sample of 470 students (190 female, 280 male) from Bogaziçi University, studying at the Faculties of Engineering, Business Administration and Arts and Sciences. The second phase, carried out in October 1977, covered a sample of mothers selected on a matched-pairs from the sample of female students. The major issue at this stage was to draw an adequate sample of mothers and the matched pairs technique was favored as a means of keeping all factors other than generational differences constant. The women University students were requested to write their full address in the part of the questionnaire dealing with their residence characteristics. These addresses were then checked against the records of the University Registrar and all errors and incomplete addresses were corrected. It was found that a great majority of students (88%) had reported Istanbul, Ankara or Izmir addresses. 91 of these were Istanbul addresses, 76 were Ankara and Izmir addresses and finally 23 were distributed throughout other regions in Turkey and abroad. In order to avoid loss of subjects and to minimize error it was decided that the questionnaires should be administered in interview form. Given the time and cost constraints imposed by the interviews the study was limited to Istanbul respondents only. The interviews were carried out by four female psychology students with previous experience in field work, who were trained again for the purposes of this study. Home calls, preferably with previous telephone appointments, were made and a net return of 82 interviews was obtained with a sample loss of 9 respondents.[2] The data analysis

[2] Sample loss was due to cases of out-of-town travel, address change and death.

was carried out at the Bogaziçi University Computing Center, using the Statistical Package for the Social Sciences (SPSS).

Mothers and Daughters: Descriptive Characteristics of the Research Sample

As we went from a sample of University students of generally high socio-economic status, to the sub-sample of mother-daughter pairs who are Istanbul residents only, the middle, upper-middle class nature of our research sample became even more evident. Studies of women in Turkey have so far mainly concentrated on rural and small town populations (Kandiyoti, 1977). Our knowledge about middle-class urban patterns which are less accessible to research is therefore more limited. Yet, this is the part of the female population which has had the greatest opportunity to benefit from the Republican reforms and hence would be particularly interesting to investigate. One of the characteristics of our sample is that it represents that section of the female population quite adequately as will be seen from the discussion that follows.

An examination of the mothers' own family backgrounds reveals that 54% are from Istanbul, Ankara or Izmir, without a history of prior geographical mobility, and hence at least second generation urban. Those mothers whose families lived in small towns or smaller places of residence remain at 11%, and there is only one mother of rural origin (1,2%). The education level of mothers' parents can be considered quite high, especially according to the standards of their generation (22% of fathers are University graduates, and 18% of mothers are high school graduates). Mothers' fathers' occupations are also in prestigious areas such as professional careers (6.1%), commerce (%24.4), civil service (12.2%) and the army (12.2%). Therefore, with regards to their background characteristics it could be said that these mothers were in a position to take advantage of the educational and other opportunities made available to women after the Republic.

The figures in Table I give us a fairly good idea about the educational breakthrough that took place in this generation. The proportion of mothers who have attended or completed a University education is 30% as against 1,2% in their mothers' generation. The total proportion of women who have had a high school education or above is 60% in the mothers' generation, as against only 18% in their own mothers' generation.

Table I

Level of Education

		Mother	*Own Mother*	*Husband*
1. No schooling	N	2	13	0
	%	2.4	15.9	0
2. Attended primary school	N	0	5	0
	%	0	6.1	0
3. Graduated from primary school	N	4	22	3
	%	4.9	26.8	3.6
4. Attended secondary school	N	2	6	1
	%	2.4	7.3	1.2
5. Graduated from secondary school	N	14	18	1
	%	17.1	22.0	1.2
6. Attended high school	N	4	3	2
	%	4.9	3.7	2.4
7. Graduated from high school	N	32	14	8
	%	39.0	17.1	9.8
8. Attended University	N	3	0	4
	%	3.7	0	4.9
9. Graduated from University	N	21	1	63
	%	25.9	1.2	76.8

The average age of mothers in our sample is 49—50 and their husbands' age is 55. Their modal age of marriage is between 21—23, and their modal age of first motherhood is between 24—26. Their average number of children is 2,3. These demographic characteristics also seem to be in keeping with their high socio-economic status.

The ways in which the mothers met their husbands range from traditional arranged marriages to marriage through mutual consent by meeting in school or work contexts (Table II). The mothers who have married through intermediaries either directly by arranged marriages or more indirectly through arranged "chance" meetings, are in the majority (68,3%). The proportion of those who have made their own choices is 31.7%.

An examination of the mothers' social lives, aside from their socio-economic and demographic characteristics, should provide us with important insights regarding their family dynamics and give us clues about the socialization context of their daughters. It is a well known fact that relationships between spouses may vary from quasi-total role segregation and parallel social lives to role complementarity and almost total sharing of social lives (Bott, 1957; Rainwater, 1965; Komarovsky, 1967).

Table II

Ways of Meeting Marriage Partners

1. Arranged marriages	N	29
	%	35.4
2. Marrying with relatives	N	4
	%	4.9
3. Meeting through organized get-togethers in a family or acquaintance context	N	23
	%	28.0
4. Meeting in school or a professional context	N	12
	%	14.6
5. Meetings in other contexts leading to mutual consent marriages	N	14
	%	17.1

Students of the family in Turkey have generally stressed role segregation, the separate worlds of the sexes and the "duofocality" of the family (Kıray, 1964; Fallers and Fallers; Timur, 1972; Olson-Prather, 1976). The degree to which this model of family life applies to our urban middle-class sample is, of course, open to question. The mothers' familial and social lives have been assessed by focusing on three different areas: their professional lives, their leisure activities and their degree of participation in family decision-making.

The number of working mothers (12%) represents only a fraction of University graduates (26%), indicating that having a professional life remains a minority phenomenon. The proportion of mothers who are house-wives with no prior employment history is 48%. The others were unable to continue working after their marriage or the birth of their first child. All the women who decided to stop working were involved in what can be considered traditional female occupations (teaching, secretarial work, sewing etc.), whereas those who are currently employed are either professionals or in the academic career.

Mothers' leisure activities have been evaluated along two axes considered to be of theoretical significance. The first is the degree to which leisure is spent within primary groups or secondary organizations (such as clubs and associations); the second is the degree to which leisure is sex-segregated or shared with husbands. It is possible to see specific combinations of these two dimensions in different cultures and social classes. Both the lives of women in Turkey (Fallers and Fallers, 1976; Kıray, 1964; Mansur, 1972; Benedict, 1974) and those of the Western working class (Young and Willmott, 1957; Rainwater, Coleman and Handel, 1962; Komarovsky, 1967) present examples of intense primary group, sex-segregated socializing. In contrast, the Western middle-class presents a picture of both greater participation in voluntary associations as well as a higher gravitation towards the husbands' work connections as a social context (Papanek, 1973a). Indeed, where the social and geographical mobility of the couple is high, it is harder for women to sustain their own primary ties (such as family, school mates, old neighbors etc.). Thus, they become automatically more dependent both on their husbands' network of social relations and on the secondary organization of whichever community they may be living in.

The position of the mothers in our study may be considered an intermediate one with regard to the axes defined above. Membership in voluntary associations exists to a certain degree (38%); however, the prestige function of such membership seems to be more salient than the actual social functions. Unlike the traditional model, mothers do share a lot of social activities with their husbands. However, these shared activities which remain limited to evenings and week-ends in no way impede the cultivation of their own social circles and primary groups by women independently of their husbands. As was pointed out earlier, the mothers' profile of geographical mobility is rather low. It is hence easily possible for them to maintain a network of social relations predating their marriages. In fact, when mothers were asked who they spent most of their time with, most (87.8%) mentioned family, relatives, neighbors and former class mates. Those who mentioned their husbands' social circle remain at a low 3.7%, and 8.5% mention their own professional circle as their source of most frequent social contact.

There are increasing suggestions that women who are not exclusively dependent on their husbands and other males for their self definition have greater psychological freedom and clearer ego boundaries (Chodorow, 1974). If that is a criterion to be taken seriously, our middle class mothers seem to be at the cross roads since they keep a delicate, but so far advantageous balance, between traditional prerogatives and more modern participation patterns.

As can be seen from Table III, joint decision making is the dominant pattern of intra-familial decisions. Whether or not mothers' statements reflect the actual authority patterns within the family, they certainly give us an idea about what their values and normative preferences are. It is thus possible to say that mothers view themselves as equals in intra-familial decision making.

After this brief presentation of the general characteristics of the mothers' generation, it should be sufficient to remind ourselves that the younger generation are students at Boğazici University with ages ranging between 19 and 24, sharing the same socio-economic background.

Table III

Intra-Familial Decision-Making

		Father's decision	*Joint decision*	*Mother's decision*	*Other (children etc.)*
1. Decisions about	N	22	35	25	0
children's pocket money	%	26.8	42.7	30.5	0
2. Decisions about	N	10	49	15	8
children's formal education	%	12.2	59.8	18.3	9.8
3. Decisions about	N	14	42	25	1
children's discipline	%	17.1	51.2	30.5	1.2
4. Shopping decisions for	N	20	46	16	0
expensive items	%	24.4	56.1	19.5	0
5. Decisions about outings	N	15	50	14	3
and recreation	%	18.3	61.0	17.1	3.7
6. Decisions about traveling	N	12	56	10	4
and holidays	%	14.6	68.3	12.2	4.9
7. Daily shopping decisions	N	6	8	66	2
	%	7.3	9.8	80.5	2.4

Psycho-social Concepts and Indicators

It was previously pointed out that intergenerational comparisons would involve achievement orientation, sex-role stereotypes, sex-role standards and socialization patterns. In this section, a brief discussion of how these concepts were operationalized for the purpose of our study, will be offered.

Achievement Orientation in Women

The psychodynamics of women's achievement related behavior is undoubtedly one of the most controversial topics in the psychology of women. The controversy which was sparked off by contradictory sex-related findings in experimental research (Veroff, Wilcox and Atkinson, 1953), was followed up by different attempts at explaining women's achievement motivation (Field, 1951, Garai and Scheinfeld, 1968).

One of the most debated points of view on this subject has been Horner's (1970, 1972) hypothesis on the Motive to Avoid Success (M-s) or "fear of success". According to this view women's success, especially in male-dominated fields, is a source of inner conflict, a major component of which is fear of rejection through loss of femininity. Thus, being successful entails an approach-avoidance conflict, a psychological barrier which many achievement oriented women may seek to resolve by seeking refuge in traditional feminine roles. Using an open-ended sentence with a theme of scholastic success in a very male-dominated field (i.e. medicine) Horner found that female subjects have significantly more numerous responses stressing the negative consequences of success (65%) than male subjects (10%).

Attribution theory which emphasizes cognitive influences upon behavior stresses the fact that women seem to possess an attributional framework which is incompatible with success. Indeed, important sex differences have been found regarding the attribution of causality for success and failure (Deaux and Elmswiller, 1974; Bar-Tal and Frieze, 1973; Fricze, 1975; Taynor and Deaux, 1973). Women's success seems to be more frequently attributed to luck, both by themselves and others, whereas the same level of performance in men is significantly attributed to ability. Thus, women's success is associated to external (luck) and thus less dependable causes, whereas men's is more often attributed to internal (ability or effort) causes which are more stable and psychologically satisfying. The same type of difference is reported on Rotter's (1966) scale of internal vs. external locus of control. Finally, Tangri (1975) proposes a somewhat different approach to the same subject. She suggests that women tend to define their own identities as a function of who their husbands will be rather than what they are or plan to be. Thus, definitions of the self are often left open until marriage clarifies which role will be appropriate. Tangri suggests that a woman's description of her ideal husband can be a useful projective device to assess her achievement motivation, since her own strivings are likely to reflect themselves upon such a description. Two measures are obtained from descriptions of the ideal future husband. The first is Implied Demand Character of the Wife's Future or Wife's Demand, and reflects the extent to which the woman's description implies an expectation of leadinga demanding, productive life. The second is called Demand Character of the Future Husband or Husband's Demand and implies the degree to which the husband is described as being high in demand himself. Women higher in Husband's Demand were expected to have lower occupational aspirations and to be more traditional since they are assumed to project their achievement needs on their husbands. On the other hand, women who are high on Wife's Demand were assumed to be more achievement oriented themselves. Tangri supported these assumptions by showing that women who scored high on Wife's Demand were likelier to be role innovators in terms of career choice (i.e. choose occupations with less that 30% women in them).

All three points of view were incorporated in our research. Horner's concept of fear of success was included through an open-ended sentence adapted to the Turkish context.[3] Causal attributions of success and failure were also assessed by asking members of both generations whether they attributed their own successes or failures to luck (external factor) or effort and ability (internal causes). Finally, descriptions of the ideal husband were obtained and scored for level of demand by means of a rating scale, in line with Tangri's procedure. Apart from these measures, inspired by the literature, mothers were asked to comment on the meaning of being "a successful woman".

Sex-Role Stereotypes

Each culture has its own stereotypes of masculinity and femininity which exert pressures on their members towards conformity. Rosenkrantz, Vogel, Bee, I. Broverman and D. Broverman (1968) constructed a Sex Role Stereotype Questionnaire consisting of bi-polar adjectives by means of which they established the pervasiveness and consensus producing qualities of such stereotypes, as well as the greater social desirability of characteristics ascribed to men. Another important finding is that sex-role definitions are implicitly and uncritically accepted to the extent that they are incorporated into the self-concepts of both men and women. Moreover, women tend to perceive themselves in more stereotypic and unfavorable terms (McKee and Sherriffs, 1959). In addition to the pervasiveness of sex-role stereotypes their resilience and persistence

---

[3] Horner's open-ended sentence mentioned success in a pre-med class which has no counterpart in the Turkish educational system. Besides male monopoly of the medical profession is also a typically American phenomenon. The sentence we selected instead is as follows:

> "When Fatma, who was an excellent student, specialized in her field and got appointed as the vice-president of a large firm....

This formulation was favored since a managerial position in business can be considered very challenging for a woman in Turkey.

Table IV

Distribution of Average Stereotype and Social Desirability Scores of the Sex Role Stereotype Scale

	Average stereotype score	*Average social desirability score**
Emotionality	3.93	2.31
Cool headedness	2.06	1.84
Hardness	1.90	3.76
Faithfulness	3.82	1.75
Independence	1.72	1.60
Softness	3.76	2.39
Ambition	2.33	2.52
Self sacrifice	3.83	1.95
Having wide interests	2.44	1.61
Being affectionate	4.09	1.69
Realism	2.48	1.53
Talkativeness	3.50	1.89
Family-orientedness	3.87	2.13
Initiative	2.14	1.91
Submissiveness	3.88	4.23
Self confidence	2.32	1.24
Warmth	3.62	2.74
Agressiveness	2.18	4.37
Neatness	3.73	2.32
Domination	1.92	3.26
Feeling superior	2.06	3.47
Rigidity	2.24	3.86

* Low average scores denote higher social desirability. Low average stereotype scores indicate masculinity.

through time has also been reported. In a study carried out on two generations of women in Toronto, Simmons and Turner (1974) found that despite important changes in sex role standards, women's self-concepts as defined through stereotypic adjectives remained strikingly similar across generations. Similar results were found in a pilot study using the same method in Istanbul (Kağıtçıbaşı and Kansu, 1977). Thus, self-definitions appear to be an important element of continuity despite behavioral change.

Since a tool of the type developed by Rosenkrantz et al. (1968) was not already available in Turkey, it had to be constructed for the purposes of our study. In order to achieve this goal our first step was to ask a sample of 56 female and 80 male students to write an open-ended description of what they considered to be typically male and female attributes. Those attributes which were repeated at least twice constituted a list of 78 adjectives. This list was administered to two groups of students, the first of which was asked to indicate on a 5-point scale the degree to which these attributes characterized men or women (N = 142); the second group was asked to rate the degree of social desirability of each attribute (N = 73). Thus, a mean stereotype and social desirability score was obtained for each adjective. After a first elimination on the basis of mean scores, adjectives were factor analyzed to insure unidimensionality and only those adjectives which fitted the factorial pattern were retained. This led to the adoption of a 22 adjective list covering 10 female and 12 male attributes. These adjectives were incorporated into the questionnaire in a way to insure a balanced and non-systematic presentation of male-female attributes as well as social desirability scores (Table IV). This list was used for three different purposes:

a) Assessing self-concept by using the adjectives for self description in both generations.
b) Assessing how mothers and daughters perceive their own mothers by using the adjectives to describe their mothers.
c) Assessing the degree of stereotypic identification of the sexes by asking both generations to evaluate the degree to which they think these attributes characterize men and women in general.

Sex-Role Standards

By sex-role standards we mean standards of behavior considered appropriate for men and women within a given culture. It is widely accepted that these standards exhibit great variation between cultures, sub-cultures and generations. This indicator can be considered a normative one since it addresses itself to the question of acceptable behavior for men and women. Sex-role standards are assessed in this study through ten attitude statements specifically designed to cover a wide range of issues. Thus, four items deal with pre-marital sex and discipline standards, three items stress attitudes to women's work and self-development, and another three items cover authority relations within the family. The degree of agreement of respondents with the statements in question is elicited by a 5-point scale.

Socialization Patterns

It is widely accepted that gender identity gets established through a process of differential socialization which has very early origins. Undoubtedly, part of the continuity of sex-role definitions is a function of continuities in socialization and behavioral expectations. In our study, continuity across generations could be assessed only indirectly by asking mothers and daughters to evaluate the degree of importance which certain areas of socialization carried in their own upbringing. An eight item question covering critical topics such as academic achievement, strict discipline, family affection, independence etc. was rated for degrees of importance along a 5-point scale. In addition, an attempt was made to assess patterns of interaction and identification within the family by asking respondents to state who they felt closest to and more similar to in the family, and whom they considered the most powerful family member.

Intergenerational Comparisons

The concepts and indicators outlined above will constitute the basis of intergenerational comparisons and will be dealt with in the same order.

Achievement Related Indicators

a) *Mothers' Definition of the "Successful Woman"*

Before comparing mothers and daughters, we would like to discuss the connotations that the expression "successful woman" carries for mothers. 32.9% of mothers define the successful woman in exclusively domestic terms as a "good mother and wife". 23.2% stress being socially active and useful to the community alongside being accomplished housewives. 25.6% see being able to combine a career with household duties as a criterion of success. Finally, 12.2% stress being self-sufficient and self-fulfilled persons as the ultimate goal. Apart from this last exception, all mothers insist on not compromising their qualities of good spouse and mother, whatever their other achievements may be. It is, thus, possible to conclude that mothers have developed new role strivings without making any fundamental changes in their traditional housewife expections. Their criteria of success are therefore quite difficult to live up to.

b) *Fear of Success*

It was assumed that mothers who seem to have set themselves rather stringent criteria of traditional housewifeliness would react more unfavorably, or at least more non-committally to the open-ended sentence with a theme of professional success. However, no differences were observed between generations in this respect (Table V) and fear of success responses remained in the minority for both mothers and daughters. The presence of responses by mothers, whose own marriages were mainly arranged, indicating that they considered professional success as a means of broadening all of women's options, including marriage, were particularly interesting and in conflict with Horner's assumptions about anxiety over loss of femininity. If we add the fact that comparisons between the sexes carried out in the earlier part of our study had not revealed any differences in terms of fear of success, the cross cultural applicability of this concept becomes questionable. It would seem reasonable to suggest that the different modes of control of female sexuality by different cultures are likely to produce corresponding and specific

Table V

Responses to the Open-Ended Sentence on the Theme of Professional Success

		Daughters N: 82	*Mothers N: 82*
1. Responses stressing psychological satisfaction and personal happiness	N	48	52
	%	58.5	63.4
2. Responses stressing material rewards	N	5	4
	%	6.1	4.9
3. Ambiguous responses leading to eventual success	N	10	7
	%	12.2	8.5
4. Responses stressing personal unhappiness and feelings of emptiness	N	7	13
	%	8.4	15.6
5. Fears of social rejection	N	5	3
	%	6.1	3.7
6. Unclassifiable responses	N	7	3
	%	8.5	3.7

psychological consequences. An approach which I shall briefly label as the Fallers-Papanek hypothesis suggests for instance that when the transition to modern occupations occurs from a starting point of strict segregation between the sexes as in Turkey and the rest of Middle East, women may in fact experience greater psychological freedom than their Western counterparts. Fallers and Fallers (1976) in their study of Edremit report that women who are self-sufficient and psychologically more independent of men in their segregated worlds have less difficulty in separating their professional and sexual identities in a work situation. Papanek who worked in Pakistan makes very similar observations (1971, 1973b). It would seem that the confusion between sexual and professional identity is most likely to occur in societies or parts of societies where women are in free competition with each other on the marriage market. Where family control over female sexuality is stricter and marriages are arranged, the concern over femininity does not seem to appear as acute. In fact, external constraints may take the place of psychological barriers and render them unnecessary. It would of course be interesting to study the effects of increasing sexual permissiveness in Turkey's large urban centers from the point of view of its consequences for women's psychological make-up.

c) *Causal Attributions of Success and Failure*

As can be seen from Table VII, mothers' causal attributions of both success ($x^2 = 15{,}71$, p .001, $\gamma = -.25$) and failure ($x^2 = 6{,}50$, $p = .038$, $\gamma = -.31$) are significantly more external than their daughters'. Compar-

Table VI

Causal Attributions of Success and Failure

Success		*Daughters N: 82*	*Mothers N: 82*	*Failure*	*Daughters N: 82*	*Mothers N: 82*
1. Luck	N	2	18	1. Bad luck	17	24
	%	2.5	22.0		21.0	29.3
2. Ability	N	23	13	2. Lack of	3	10
	%	28.4	16.0	ability	3.7	12.2
3. Effort	N	56	51	3. Lack of	61	48
	%	67.9	62.0	effort	75.3	58.5
4. Not known	N	1	0	4. Not	0	0
	%	1.2	0	known	0	0

isons between the sexes had not produced any significant differences in this respect. This finding can be partly accounted for by the fact that the daughters have an academic framework to which they can directly relate their successes and failures, whereas the mothers are mainly housewives whose very standards of success are different.

d) *Demand Characteristics of Ideal Marriage*

Daughters' expectations of self-development and a demanding life (Wife's Demand) are significantly higher than their mothers' expectations[4] ($x^2 = 13,77$, $p = .0081$; Table VII). There is, however, no significant difference between generations regarding Husband's Demand. According to this, mothers are more traditional women who expect vicarious achievement through men.

Table VII

Demand Characteristics of Marital Future

		Wife's Demand		*Husband's Demand*	
		Daughters N: 82	*Mothers N: 82*	*Daughters N: 82*	*Mothers N: 82*
1. Very low demand	N	9	19	5	1
	%	10.9	23.2	6.1	1.2
2. Low demand	N	44	25	12	14
	%	53.7	30.5	14.6	17.1
3. Moderate demand	N	11	21	35	26
	%	13.4	25.6	42.7	31.7
4. Higher demand	N	10	5	20	26
	%	12.2	6.1	24.4	31.7
5. Very high demand	N	2	1	4	4
	%	2.5	1.2	4.9	4.9
6. Uncertain	N	6	11	6	11
	%	7.3	13.4	7.3	13.4

Thus, mothers who try to conciliate traditional and newer roles are more external in their causal attributions of success and failure and more

[4] Mothers' expectations were obtained by asking them to describe the ideal husband they would want for their daughters. The demand characteristics were rated in the same way.

traditional in their demand characteristics. There is, however, do difference between generations in terms of fear of success and psychological barriers in that sense seem to be absent.

Sex Role Stereotypes

a) *Mothers' and Daughters' Self-Descriptions*

We have already discussed findings indicating the effect of sex-role stereotypes on self-concept (Rozenkrantz et al., 1968; McKee and Sheriffs, 1959) and their intergenerational continuity (Simmons and Turner, 1974; Kâğıtçıbaşı and Kansu, 1977). In the light of these findings we would have expected to find considerable similarity between the generations' self-descriptions. However, as shown in Table VIII there

Table VIII
Intergenerational Comparison (T-tests) of Self-Descriptive Evaluations

	Daughters' average	*Mothers' average*	*t*	*p*	*Comment*
1. Emotionality	2.00	1.68	2.27	.025	M > D
2. Cool headedness	2.78	3.01	−1.10	–	nd
3. Hardness	3.58	3.46	.69	–	nd
4. Faithfulnsss	1.87	1.32	4.59	.000	M > D
5. Independence	2.17	2.82	−3.81	.000	D > M
6. Softness	2.34	1.98	2.41	.017	M > D
7. Ambition	3.19	3.59	−1.97	.050	D > M
8. Self sacrifice	2.07	1.48	4.94	.000	M > D
9. Having wide interests	2.44	2.37	.38	–	nd
10. Being affectionate	1.95	1.40	4.96	.000	M > D
11. Realism	2.03	1.81	1.62	–	nd
12. Talkativeness	2.43	2.30	.70	–	nd
13. Family-orientedness	2.26	1.24	7.52	.000	M > D
14. Initiative	2.89	3.18	−1.59	–	nd
15. Submissiveness	3.98	3.08	5.51	.000	M > D
16. Self confidence	2.15	1.89	1.83	–	nd
17. Warmth	2.01	2.09	−.55	–	nd
18. Agressiveness	4.13	4.36	−1.57	–	nd
19. Neatness	2.86	2.46	3.39	.001	M > D
20. Domination	3.89	3.58	1.66	–	nd
21. Feeling superior	3.53	3.87	−1.87	–	nd
22. Rigidity	4.04	4.26	−1.45	–	nd

Note: M D: greater for mothers; D M: greater for daughters; nd: no difference.

was no such evidence of similarity. The major reason for significant discrepancies was not the masculine attributes but the feminine ones which were emphasized systematically more in their self-descriptions by the mothers. Mothers defined themselves as softer, more submissive, more faithful, more affectionate, more emotional, more family-oriented and neat. These attributes fit in very well both with their own image of a good mother and with the stereotypic mother. The fact that daughters' self concepts are different can partly be accounted for by their being University students with high S-E-S characteristics. This context is evidently less conducive to anticipatory socialization for motherhood, which could also explain the differences with other findings in the literature. The question which is of true relevance to us here is whether the daughters will be able to sustain their different self concepts or whether they will grow more like their mothers when they marry, and more importantly, have children. It is our contention that even if the differences do get smaller, the gap between the daughters and their mothers will remain larger than that between the mothers and their own mothers. The reasons for this contention will be discussed throughout the following paragraphs.

b) *Mothers' and Daughters' Description of their Own Mothers*

Both mothers and daughters were asked to describe their own mothers by means of the adjective list. When the daughters' self-descriptions are compared to the description they give of their mothers, important differences are seen. Daughters see themselves as being more independent, coolheaded, ambitious and realistic than their mothers, and having wider interests. They also attribute feminine characteristics to their mothers significantly more than to themselves. In contrast, mothers' definitions of themselves and their own mothers is so similar as not to yield any significant results (Table IX). It thus seems that unlike the daughters' dissimilarity between their self-concept and mother description, the mothers exhibit greater continuity with the previous generation. Indeed, the comparison between the daughters' and mothers' description of their own mothers reveals they are strikingly similar (Table X). It is interesting to note, however, that mothers have described their own mothers as significantly more dominating, rigid and superior feeling, whereas their daughters have described their mothers as softer, neater and more family-oriented. These differences in perception may very well reflect the changing attitudes of two generations of women (grandmothers and mothers) vis a vis their own daughters. These differences will be stressed further whilst discussing socialization.

Table IX

Comparisons of Mothers' and Daughters' Self-Descriptions of their Own Mothers (T-test)

	Comparison between daughters' self descriptions and descriptions of own mother			*Comparison between mothers' self descriptions and descriptions of own mother*		
	t	*p*	*Comment*	*t*	*p*	*Comment*
1. Emotionality	2.19	.032	Mg	1.30	–	nd
2. Cool headedness	– 2.06	.042	Sg	– 1.41	–	nd
3. Hardness	.94	–	nd	.32	–	nd
4. Faithfulness	5.16	.000	Mg	.00	–	nd
5. Independence	– 6.99	.000	Sg	– 1.03	–	nd
6. Softness	4.21	.000	Mg	– 1.60	–	nd
7. Ambition	– 2.00	.048	Sg	– .37	–	nd
8. Self sacrifice	7.16	.000	Mg	1.84	–	nd
9. Having wide interests	– 4.19	.000	Sg	– 3.81	.000	Sg
10. Being affectionate	4.41	.000	Mg	– .63	–	nd
11. Realism	– 2.94	.004	Sg	– 3.75	.000	Sg
12. Talkativeness	.88	–	nd	– 1.00		nd
13. Family orientedness	9.82	.000	Mg	– 1.74	–	nd
14. Initiative	– 1.66	–	nd	– .54	–	nd
15. Submissiveness	5.83	.000	Mg	.23	–	nd
16. Self confidence	.00	–	nd	– 2.68	.009	Sg
17. Warmth	1.59	–	nd	.84	–	nd
18. Agressiveness	– 1.79	–	nd	2.24	.028	Mg
19. Neatness	6.81	.000	Mg	1.22	–	nd
20. Domination	– .38	–	nd	1.80	–	nd
21. Feeling superior	– 1.29	–	nd	3.03	.033	Mg
22. Rigidity	– 3.48	.001	Sg	1.92	–	nd

Note: Mg: greater for own mother; Sg: greater for self; nd: no difference.

c) *Mothers' and Daughters' Evaluations of Sex Role Stereotypes*

As can be seen from Table XI, there is consensus between generations on 12 out of 22 adjectives in the list. Whenever consensus does not exist, this is because mothers tend to define both male and female attributes in more extreme terms than their daughters do. In other words, despite considerable consensus, mothers seem to exhibit a more stereotypic system of attribution of characteristics to the sexes.

Table X
Comparisons between Daughters' Mother Descriptions and Mothers' Mother Descriptions

		Daughters' mother description	*Mothers' mother description*	*t*	*p*	*Comment*
1.	Emotionality	1.73	1.51	1.57	–	nd
2.	Cool headedness	3.14	3.34	– .89	–	nd
3.	Hardness	3.71	3.42	1.48	–	nd
4.	Faithfulness	1.29	1.33	– .52	–	nd
5.	Independence	3.18	3.03	.72	–	nd
6.	Softness	1.82	2.25	– 2.59	.011	DMg
7.	Ambition	3.58	3.69	– .55	–	nd
8.	Self sacrifice	1.28	1.32	– .37	–	nd
9.	Having wide interests	3.04	3.02	.11	–	nd
10.	Being affectionate	1.48	1.47	.06	–	nd
11.	Realism	2.53	2.47	.30	–	nd
12.	Talkativeness	2.28	2.43	– .77	–	nd
13.	Family-orientedness	1.16	1.38	– 2.55	.012	DMg
14.	Initiative	3.15	3.30	– .69	–	nd
15.	Submissiveness	3.21	3.02	.91	–	nd
16.	Self confidence	2.15	2.28	– .76	–	nd
17.	Warmth	1.81	1.89	– .52	–	nd
18.	Agressiveness	4.36	4.05	1.91	–	nd
19.	Neatness	2.06	2.47	– 1.97	.050	DMg
20.	Domination	3.82	3.12	3.34	.001	MMg
21.	Feeling superior	3.70	3.28	2.15	.033	MMg
22.	Rigidity	4.43	3.98	3.05	.003	MMg

Note: DMg: greater for daughters' mothers; MMg: greater for mothers' mothers nd: no difference.

Sex Role Standards

Mothers are consistently and significantly more conservative than their daughters in all respects (Table XII). Attitude items have been submitted to a Guttman scaling procedure whereby priority rankings of the items were obtained. Table XIII shows the rankings of the items, all worded in the traditional direction, together with their percentages of acceptance and rejection. Alongside the clearly higher percentages of rejection of the daughters, they also have a different priority ranking. The area where mothers and daughters seem to differ most strikingly is that of premarital sexual standards, the issue of virginity in particular. While 84% of mothers believe that virginity until marriage is a must this

Table XI

Evaluations of Sex-Role Stereotypes by Mothers and Daughters (T-tests)

		Daughters average	*Mothers' average*	*t*	*p*	*Comment*
1.	Emotionality	3.96	4.07	− .83	−	nd
2.	Cool headedness	2.16	1.81	2.38	.019	M+
3.	Hardness	2.07	1.68	3.03	.003	M+
4.	Faithfulness	3.75	4.04	−2.05	.042	M+
5.	Independence	2.11	1.85	1.84	−	nd
6.	Softness	3.72	4.10	−2.95	.004	M+
7.	Ambition	2.46	2.32	.94	−	nd
8.	Self sacrifice	4.04	4.01	.27	−	nd
9.	Having wide interests	2.66	2.58	.54	−	nd
10.	Being affectionate	3.95	4.04	− .67	−	nd
11.	Realism	2.58	2.57	.05	−	nd
12.	Talkativeness	3.37	3.74	−2.72	.007	M+
13.	Family-orientedness	3.81	3.86	− .40	−	nd
14.	Initiative	2.11	1.93	1.30	−	nd
15.	Submissiveness	4.09	4.19	− .89	−	nd
16.	Self confidence	2.66	2.26	3.14	.002	D+
17.	Warmth	3.34	3.79	−3.40	.001	M+
18.	Agressiveness	2.07	2.15	− .58	−	nd
19.	Neatness	3.96	3.79	1.02	−	nd
20.	Domination	1.96	1.68	2.05	.042	M+
21.	Feeling superior	2.14	1.78	2.57	.011	M+
22.	Rigidity	2.34	1.86	3.32	.001	M+

Note: D+: daughters more extreme; M+: mothers more extreme; nd: no difference.

percentage drops to 38% for daughters. In addition, while 45% of mothers believe that women should avoid responsible positions and jobs this proportion is of 11% for daughters. Nonetheless, the fastest changing norms between generations seem to be in the area of premarital sex. Despite important differences in magnitude, items having to do with authority relations in the family and women's roles as wives and mothers keep a similar ranking for the two generations and do not exhibit the discrepancies we witness for premarital standards.

Table XII
Intergenerational Comparisons of Sex Role Standards (T-tests)

Item:	*Daughters' average*	*Mothers' average*	*t*	*p*	*Comment*
1. It is generally preferable for women to avoid jobs involving serious responsibility (such as managerial roles)	4.43	3.30	5.76	.000	Mt
2. Young people should make every effort to accommodate their families' preferences in selecting marriage partners	4.36	3.21	6.04	.000	Mt
3. A woman should quit her job if it seems detrimental from her husband's and children's point of view	2.43	1.75	3.75	.000	Mt
4. It is in no way a must for a woman to remain a virgin until she marries (a)	3.50	1.84	8.44	.000	Mt
5. A woman should always know how to make concessions and ease tension in order to avoid entering into conflict with her husband	3.52	2.01	7.96	.000	Mt
6. It is only natural that stricter discipline standards should be applied to girls than boys of the same age	4.31	3.50	4.07	.000	Mt
7. A woman should give priority to her interests and self-development even at the expense of familial harmony	2.80	1.85	4.57	.000	Mt
8. Women cannot be really happy unless their husbands can, at times, assert their authority and have the last word	3.28	2.97	1.35	–	nd
9. A man helping with housework seems slightly funny to me	4.53	3.90	3.57	.001	Nt
10. In the final analysis, a girl's pre-marital relations jeopardize her chances of finding a suitable husband in the future	4.01	3.47	2.67	.008	Mt

N.B.: The averages of items (a) and (b) have been calculated after reversing them. Lower values denote a more traditional outlook, whereas higher values indicate a more liberal outlook.

Mt: mothers more traditional; nd: no difference.

Table XIII

Ranking of Sex Role Standard Items by Guttman Scaling

Item nb:	*Daughters' ranking** *Acceptance* %	*Daughters' ranking** *Rejection* %	*Item nb:*	*Mothers' ranking*** *Acceptance* %	*Mothers' ranking*** *Rejection* %
3. Woman should quit job if detrimental for family	81	19	3. Woman should quit job if detrimental for family	87	13
7. Woman should not give priority to her own interests at the expense of harmony	64	36	4. Virginity until marriage is a must	84	16
8. Husbands must be somewhat authoritarian	55	45	7. Woman should not give priority to her own interests at the expense of harmony	84	16
5. Women should make the concessions in relations between spouses	44	56	5. Women should make the concessions in relations between spouses	82	18
4. Virginity until marriage is a must	38	63	8. Husbands must be somewhat authoritarian	55	45
10. Pre-marital relations jeopardize chances for a good marriage	30	70	1. Women should avoid responsible jobs	45	55
6. Stricter discipline standards should be applied to girls rather than boys	15	85	2. Families' wishes must be met in choosing a marriage partner	43	57
2. Families' wishes must be met in choosing a marriage partner	12	88	10. Pre-marital relations jeopardize chances for a good marriage	39	61
1. Women should avoid responsible jobs	11	89	6. Stricter discipline standards should be applied to girls rather than boys	34	36
9. It is funny for men to help with housework	88	93	9. It is funny for men to help with housework	24	76

* Coefficient of reproducibility = .81.
** Coefficient of reproducibility = .76.

Socialization Patterns

We have already discussed the fact that mothers and daughters define themselves differently and wondered whether these differences did really correspond to differences in their psychological make-up or whether they merely reflect age-related role expections. Undoubtedly, age is an important factor accounting for such differences. However, it is inasmuch as we can identify differences in socialization between generations that we can take them more seriously.

Table XIV

Intergenerational Comparison (T-test) of the Importance Attributed to Certain Dimensions in Socialization

		Daughters average	*Mothers' average*	*t*	*p*	*Comment*
1.	Respect to parents	1.79	1.69	.73	–	nd
2.	Family affection	1.90	1.73	1.27	–	nd
3.	Academic success	1.96	2.58	– 3.49	.001	D > M
4.	Strict discipline	3.21	2.68	2.62	.010	M > D
5.	Making one's own decisions	2.00	3.01	– 5.49	.000	D > M
6.	Hiding one's feelings	3.21	3.17	.23	–	nd
7.	Independence	2.51	3.41	– 5.30	.000	D > M
8.	Responsibility	1.65	2.43	– 5.03	.000	D > M

Note: D > M: more important for daughters; M > D: more important for mothers; nd: no difference.

Table XIV indicates that there are important intergenerational differences in their perceptions of their own socialization. Daughters evaluate the importance attached to their academic performance, their capacity to take responsibility, to make their own decisions and to be independent significantly more highly than their mothers. The mothers' perception of strict discipline, on the other hand, is significantly higher. Even dimensions such as respect to parents, family affection and hiding one's feelings which do not produce significant t-test results exhibit very different correlation patterns for the two generations. For instance, respect to parents is significantly related to affection ($r = .35$, $p = .001$) and independent of strict discipline for daughters. The opposite is true of mothers, where respect is independent of affection ($r = .05$), but closely correlated to strict discipline ($r = .47$, $p = .001$). The importance given to hiding one's feeling is positively correlated with strict discipline (r = .35, p = .001) and negatively related to independence and responsibility (r = −.27, p = .013; r = −.22, p = .048) for mothers. These correlations are different both in sign and degree for daughters where there are no significant relations of this type. Mothers seem to exhibit a more consistent pattern of respect, restraint (hiding one's feelings) and constraint (not being independent, not taking responsibility etc.) and project an image of more traditional family atmosphere.

For daughters family affection is unrelated to discipline (r = .02), negatively related to hiding one's feelings (r = −.21) and positively related to making their own decisions and taking responsibility (r = .15, r = .33, p = .002). For mothers, on the other hand, we see positive relations between family affection strict discipline and hiding one's feelings (r = .11, r = .14) whereas there are negative correlations between affection, making their own decisions and taking responsibility (r = −.15, r = −.11). The low correlation coefficients do not warrant any conclusions although the directions of the signs remain interesting. Evidently, mothers perceive affection in a more restrictive context, whereas daughters relate it with a more permissive one.

The distribution of family members felt closest to, most similar to and most powerful is shown on Table XV. There are significant intergenera-

Table XV

Distribution of Perceptions of Closeness, Similarity and Power among Family Members

		Close		*Similar*		*Powerful*	
		Daughters N: 82	*Mo-her N: 82*	*Daughter N: 82*	*Mo-ther N: 82*	*Daughter N: 82*	*Mo-ther N: 82*
1. Mother	N	43	33	26	18	16	19
	%	52.4	40.2	31.7	22.5	19.5	23.2
2. Both mother and father	N	12	8	11	7	11	5
	%	14.6	9.8	13.4	8.8	13.4	6.1
3. Father	N	6	16	32	41	38	49
	%	7.3	19.5	39.1	51.9	49.4	59.8
4. Other family members (brother, sister etc).	N	20	25	12	14	11	9
	%	24.4	30.5	14.6	17.5	13.4	11.0
5. Not known	N	1	0	1	0	6	0
	%	1.2	0	1.2	0	7.3	0

tional differences with respect to family members who one feels closest to (x^2 calculated excluding the category "other persons", $x^2 = 6.57$, $p < .05$). A higher proportion of daughters (52,4 %) rather than mothers (46,4 %) have selected their mothers as their closest family member. Both generations mainly report greater similarity to their fathers (51,2 % for mothers, 39,1 % for daughters) and perceive their fathers as the most powerful figure in the family (59,8 % for mothers, 40,4 % for daughters). Although mothers' percentages are higher there are no statistically significant differences. Both mothers and daughters exhibit the tendency to see themselves as more similar to family members they describe as more powerful ($tau_b = .22$, $p = .015$ for mothers; $tau_b = .18$, $p = .039$ for daughters). The importance of attributed similarity to the father stems not from its basis in reality, but in that is represents an identification choice or rather, preference. This finding is particularly surprising, and may even seem conflicting for mothers in view of the previously established similarity between mothers' description of themselves and their mothers. It is well to remember, however, that self-descriptions are based on the masculinity-feminity dimension only, and that there is little reason for women who seem to have internalized the traditional standards of good motherhood to be different from the previous generation in that respect. It nonetheless remains a fact that there is a great social gap between the mothers' and their own mothers' generation from the point of view of their social lives and familial relations. If we reflect upon the life styles mothers lead, it seems very doubtful that their mothers could have been very adequate role models. Their differences in terms of educational level, relations with spouses and social aspirations have probably meant that they have not taken their mothers as their criteria, and hence have chosen to identify with members of the family they perceived as more effective.

In conclusion, it is possible to say that the major breakthrough from a social point of view has taken place in the mothers' generation. However, mothers are in a special phase of social transition. While their education is quite high (especially compared with their own mothers) and their level of employment is non-negligible, their ways of meeting their marriage partners have been quite traditional and their definition of the "successful woman" attempts to conciliate traditional and newer demands. It seems apparent that despite the considerable social changes in the mothers' generation, these have not been able to change their traditional expectations which are rooted in their own socialization in any fundamental way, but have just added on some new roles. In this respect, psychological continuity with the previous generation would hardly seem surprising. It seems ironical that it is when we look at our University students who seem to share more similar social worlds with their mothers whom they could have more easily adopted as role models, that we find what seems to be a higher degree of psycho-social change. This brings to mind the possibility that although the social changes which mothers have undergone may not have changed their own sex-role expectations fundamentally, they might have made a different orientation to their daughters possible, reflecting itself in their socialization practices. The degree to which these seemingly different socialization practices have produced results which will stand the test of time is a crucial issue which could be further explored through a longitudinal study of our research sample.

The reference list of this chapter is on page 322

MŰBECCEL B. KIRAY

THE WOMEN OF SMALL TOWN

In Turkish small towns, three distinctively different types of women emerge. As far as their essential relationships are concerned, i. e. those with family members or other women in the community, they don't differ one from the other. Their lifestyles, however, do display a great deal of variation. The first group consists of the women in the poorer families who work, at one time or another, on the farms or gardens surrounding the town. Like peasant women, they are less sex-segregated. They work hard both at home and outside, and are therefore more integrated into the community. The other group is made up of the wives civil servants, lawyers, doctors and the few other professionals who came from outside and settled in small towns. The third and largest group fall somewhere in between these two. They are the wives, mothers and grown up daughters of the traders, artisans, shopkeepers, fishermen and people who make up the town. These women are extremely segregated from men and, consequently, from the community. As they are free of such distorting factors as the sophistication gained from education upper class status or city life, an investigation of their lives reveals the critical aspects of woman's role and her function in Turkish society.

In this paper, we shall discuss the women in Eregli, a small town on Turkey's western Black Sea Coast. We will concentrate on these women's intra-familial relationships as their most important roles are fulfilled within this context; consumption patterns; and family problem-solving since regardless of their standard of living, solutions are reached only with the coordination and labour of the womenfolk in the house. We shall also look at something called "women's leisure" which in reality is her relations outside the home. Finally we shall discuss gainful employment and education as a way of acquiring skills, for these women stand on the crossroads of change and have the potential to decrease the segregation and particularism of the women's world in Eregli.[1]

---

[1] Eregli is a town on the Black Sea coast. When the material was collected in 1967 it had a population of 8,815. It is a district seat as well as secondary center in the province's most important coal mining area, and functions as a coal port. Most important of all, however, it is an exchange point for the relationships between villagers and townpeople.

Women in the Family

In Eregli families tend to be small and nuclear. We do not know what the large extended families in Eregli were like before. However, recent studies on the history of families show that they were never very large which may be the case for our town as well.[2] Only about one-tenth of the families in Eregli have the characteristic composition and function of a patrilineal joint extended family, where the father, mother, married sons, their wives, and their children, as well as their unmarried sons and daughters live as a single unit. Another one-fourth of the families, although not all conforming to the classic patrilineal extended family type, are variations of this pattern. In all these cases, the father's traditional powers of authority and control were passed on the son. Most important of all was the high rate of nuclear families consisting of only one married couple and their unmarried children. More than 60% of the independent units were found to be such nuclear families. It should be noted that almost another one-tenth of the families included the wife's parents, a situation which is highly irregular in terms of traditional patterns. There was yet another family type which can be termed 'distorted'. Here various relatives, from either the father's or mother's side live together.

In order to better understand such diversified family arrangements and the place and role of the women in them, let us briefly examine the interaction of the members within the various types. Both mothers and fathers show great affection but at the same time firmness to their daughters and young girls. The mother-daughter relationship is a particularly intimate one from the moment the latter leaves school. The female child is constantly with her mother when doing house work, as a companion on excursions and as a close friend in times of crisis. While fathers are affectionate and may be proud of their daughters, their relationships to them differ greatly from that of mother-daughter or father-son, in that it is a spontaneous relationship based partly on affection and partly on indifference until her marriage. If a daughter has a problem prior to marriage she solves it with the help of her mother. Her brother may also help, but his attitude would tend to be authoritarian and intolerant. It is the mother who negotiates with both the father and the brother to

[2] Peter Paslett and Richard Wall (Eds.). *Household and Family in Past Time.* Cambridge University Press, 1976. See the introduction.

settle issues that concern her daughter. The mother's role as mediator is becoming particularly important and difficult as the present-day girls' demands increase because she spends more time with her girl friends, dresses differently, goes to school or wishes to work in an office. If and when a daughter starts to show a preference for a young man, no matter how innocent it may be, the reactions of her father and brothers may be very definitely negative and prohibitive. At this time she looks to her mother to find an accomplice. While the girl may show anger, nervousness and grief, her mother tries to do all she can to hide her daughter's behaviour under the cover of their intimacy and friendship. To hide their permissiveness towards daughters, mothers appear to play the role of angry old women towards their husbands and sons. Today, it is only through the mother that any permissiveness is allowed in a girl's behaviour. Marriage is a small town girl's primary aim. When she marries, she goes to live in a different place often among total strangers, in close, intimate and, in some cases, basically hostile circumstances. This can be a very difficult experience for her. However, by participating in their mothers' lives, girls learn to accept the idea that they will have to adapt themselves to their husband's family, and that they will become second class members in that strange environment. This is a thoroughly different socialization process from that of boys, who are constantly reminded that they will eventually replace their fathers in the important position of control and decision-making. Indeed, almost from childhood sons are given a privileged status. As a result of their different socialization patterns, girls are always able to adjust to adverse circumstances more easily than boys.

In Eregli little pressure is put on girls regarding choice of marriage partners. Today, there is no question of marriage between two young people who do not know one another, and conditions are such that they always have a chance to seek out and speak to each other. The type and intensity of relationships may vary from simply observing one another in the street, in shops, at the cinema or in the park, to actually having a secret affair. In more conservative families, special occasions are arranged when the boy and girl can see each other from a distance. In families where both sexes visit together, the boy and girl are given as many opportunities as possible to speak to one another. In all the accepted and unaccepted modes of contact, the mother plays the most important role, and during this time children communicate with their fathers only through their mothers.[3]

After marriage, the husband-wife relationship is quite a varied one in Eregli. It is still true to say that the wife is completely subservient to her husband, especially when the latter's relatives live under the same roof. However, as the years go by, the wife's status rises, she becomes less subservient and more independent. In fact, she gradually becomes the central figure in the family as her children grow up, marry and have children of their own.

In the typical artisan-trader families of the town, husbands and wives still live in separate worlds. Husbands do not spend much time at home and wives have no chance of participating in the husbands' world outside. Many husbands never talk to their wives about their work life outside the home. And women rarely bother them with household problems or the minor troubles of children. This brings about the special independence of women's personalities observed in sex segregated societies both in Africa as well as in Turkey.[4]

This kind of segregation, however, definitely seems to be lessening among the younger generation with higher incomes. Visiting other families in the evening with wives, going on picnics or to movies in mixed company, travelling together are all new patterns that have emerged during the last ten to fifteen years. More important perhaps is the companionship between men and women that has recently became more noticeable in Eregli nuclear families. In many interviews, husbands openly asserted that in all critical situations they nowadays prefer their wives' advise. The increasing number of nuclear family units, as well as the rivalry and competition among traders and artisans has helped to bring man and wife together. What path this trend will follow in the future is yet to be seen.

The focal relationship in classic Turkish families is that of father-son since it serves to perpetuate the multifunctional structure of the family. Traditionally a family strongly desires sons. After childhood, the father takes care to see that his sons find jobs or learn the family trade; that

[3] On the socialization of girls see also Mübeccel Kıray: "The Family of the Immigrant Worker" in Nermin Abadan-Unat (Ed.) *Turkish Worker in Europe*. The Hague: EJJ. Brill, 1976.

[4] See Lloyd and Margaret Fallers: Sex Roles in Edremit in *Mediterranean Family Structures*, J. G. Peristiany (Ed.). Cambridge University Press, 1976. Also Ester N. Good: *Context of Kinship: An Essay in the Family Sociology of the Gonja of Northern Ghana*. University of Cambridge Press, 1972.

suitable girls are found for them to marry, and that, at the end of his active years, the welfare of his family can be entrusted to them. Thus, commencing a new domestic cycle. Because of change, such relations have become less rigid. Conflicts have arisen and sons have begun to rebel. During times of change, frictions and crises are to be expected and, to some extent they do exist. This is where women, and mothers particularly, step in and facilitate the change by playing the very important new role of buffer between father and estranged son. In many cases, this conflict does not become serious, and the mother steps in to calm the two parties by acting as a mediator between them. She intercedes on her son's behalf, sometimes even to the extent of sharing his guilt. In a household, the mother alone is in a position to judge the severity of the dispute and the feasibility of a solution since it is only the mother who directly and intimately interacts with everybody. The husband, the son, the daughter or the daughter-in-law will act only through her.[5]

For a women under these circumstances, the most important relationship in the family is the one with her son. At the beginning, as a bride, she is an outsider and is always made to feel so. Her status is low, and no matter how good a daughter-in-law she is by any standard, she will only receive final recognition when she has given birth to a son. It is not until then that she gains higher status and feels herself to be accepted by her husband and his family. As a result, all her hopes and fears, and her plans for the future are concentrated and expressed in the love she shows for the growing boy. A mother can always rely on her son to protect her and defend her interest in intra-family disputes and fights, particularly against the father. The son is the second to the father in authority and in influence within the home, and a mother would never consider severing her ties with him or becoming less affectionate towards him. Generally, in a conflict between his wife and mother, the son will take his mother's side and is expected to do so. If a choice has to be made "the stranger's daughter" (el kızı) or daughter-in-law, does not stand a chance. Today, this mother-son relationship is also undergoing changes. In many cases, mothers and sons unite in rejecting the father's authority, not only to prevent his arbitrary decisions as in the past, but also to force him to accept new modes of behaviors or new values. Such conflicts become crucial when women's two other spheres of life are in

[5] For a more detailed analysis of the role of mothers see also Mübeccel Kiray: "New Role of Mothers" in J. G. Peristiany (Ed.). *Mediterranean Family Structure*. University of Cambridge Press, 1976.

question, namely consumption and leisure. When new and expensive household items such as radios, refrigerators or electric irons are desired, or when a father refuses to permit his woman to go to the cinema or to open-air concerts in the park, or to purchase new styles of clothing, or more importantly when he will not accept his wife's open participation in the making of some crucial family decision, sons usually take their mothers' side.

However, sons who change their behaviour towards their fathers also begin to change their actions towards their wives and mothers. Consequently, a mother can no longer always count on her supreme power over her daughter-in-law if her son starts to take his wife's side against her. This causes constraint in mother-son relations. As yet, it is too early to determine exactly how these changes will affect the cherished traditional roles of women.

Consumption and Women

It is a truism, of course, that home is women's domain. In this domain, next to intrafamily relations, women's important role of coordination and decision-making can be seen in the consumption patterns of the family. Changes in consumption patterns also change many other relations of the women. New income levels and the rate of earning money also change the values attached to consumption and wealth. In fact, one can readily assert that consumption for the house, with decisions about food, clothing, and furniture purchases as well as decisions about which of these should be processed and prepared in the house is the most important and definitive economic activity of small town women. When change occurs, the patterns that emerge at certain stages become rather significant. Differences in the consumption patterns of men and women appear, indirectly indicating their different status within the culture.

Eregli is not a rich community. Household standards range from subsistance level to a standard that is comparable to the upper limits of the middle classes in large Turkish cities. As this is a cash economy, cash is provided by the men of the house and the basic items—food, clothing, and furniture—are bought with the wife's planning on a weekly, seasonal or yearly basis. Along with this, small amounts of cash are given to women for daily purchases from nearby stores or weekly open markets since they do not frequently shop in the main streets and markets of the town. Going out requires the husband's permission; at least he has to be informed. The income for the family earned by the men, is divided into two parts, one for family consumption at home and the other for the husbands' own consumption outside the family. Men reserve rather large amounts for their own consumption as they frequently eat out and do their own shopping for clothes. Their spending for pleasure, cigarettes and drinks may consume large amounts of their budgets.

Concerning household furnishings it is possible to distinguish differences arising from family status and/or traditional versus modern trends. In low income families the furnishings are few and old-fashioned. The mattresses and quilts, the floor coverings, which are woven from left over pieces of material called "çul", and a few utensils complete the setting. In the middle and higher income groups, the furniture changes from divans to upholstered armchairs or sets of sleeping, dining and living room furniture with considerable importance given to traditional carpets and modern tulle curtains. No matter what the level or style, women choose the household furnishings after gaining the hard-earned approval of their husbands. The furnishings and household items that can be bought with the wives' savings, such as sheets, towels, or small kitchen utensils, are the result of long and difficult planning. Decisions regarding the purchase of expensive items, particularly modern appliances such as sewing machines, refrigerators or washing machines are made solely by the men because they are very large items for Eregli budgets. The priorities in such purchases are interesting. Because they are the expenditure saving machines, sewing machines and refrigerators are bought first and the really labour saving ones, such as washing machines, come much later. This is a pattern that will be observed again and again in all aspects of consumption. The labour women put into washing clothes, for example, is simply not considered work. Such an omission gives way to a type of mutual help pattern among the women of a neighborhood. Those who have any labour or expenditure saving devices are visited frequently by those who do not, thus the facilities in one house are shared with others.

It can generally be said that in Eregli the new consumption patterns and the increased consumption, particularly in household goods and furnishings, often cause tension between women and men. That tension is not evident when clothing is in question. The life style of small town women does not require them to change their dressing habits which are simple and subdued. Besides, the values attached to them never allow them to be extravagant enough to attract attention in public.

In the low income brackets, this tension usually centers around a new model radio since women, who are always at home, listen to it more than men. In the higher income brackets, the demands vary a lot. However, more expensive home improvements such as installing a new bathroom or rebuilding the kitchen are not made easily. This is not because financing such changes is prohibitive, but because these facilities involve women's comfort and it is very difficult to make men see their necessity.

Food items and meals are the least affected after incomes rise above the middle brackets. Women tend to use economical cooking methods by preparing simple dishes of dried beans, chick peas, cracked wheat or noodles, at most with some ground meat added to them. Only one dish is prepared per day even in the upper income brackets. To give taste, tomato paste and onions are added. The women improve the food by putting a great amount of labour into its preparation. Stuffed vegetables, different kinds of pies (börek) and noodles are the cheap but labour consuming dishes of the Eregli families. The food served, even in the wealthiest families, is all prepared by the female members of the family, including the food for daily consumption and that for ceremonial occasions, such as weddings and circumcision ceremonies. The food served at such occasions is much fancier, but again requires a lot of work by the women. Women, of course, can only enjoy a festivity, be it a holiday or wedding, only after everybody, particularly the men, have been served and pampered.

Another aspect of the relation between women's labour and food processing and preparation can be observed in the amount of processed food bought from outside. Nowadays, home made bread, which used to be a major job for women, has been almost totally abandoned and commercial bread has taken its place. However, all other types of food making and preserving are still the women's duty. Staple foods such as noodles and cracked wheat, and foods which add flavour to the diet, such as tomato paste, pickles and jams are still mostly prepared at home.

The labour put into food preparation is not the only significant factor in understanding the relative place of men and women in the subject of food consumption. The general pattern, particularly among artisans, traders and shopkeepers—that is among the men who work in the town—is to eat outside whenever possible. The restaurants are meeting places for men, who gather around tables, eat and drink alcoholic beverages until late at night. As long as income was limited, and was not changing, such outings were limited. Now that the town is changing and incomes have improved, this old custom is gaining a new dimension. Men are eating out more frequently and also eating much better meals than their families. Thus only a limited amount of the increased income is spent on the family as a whole. Large amounts of money are reserved for a man's personal consumption and food consumption particularly, outside of the home. It has also been observed that when men do not "like" the food prepared at home, the usual traditional simple dishes consumed by wife and children, they go out and have more extravagant dishes, such as broiled meat and other delicacies in the restaurants. Thus, increased income for many families has led to double standards in food consumption in addition to double standards in sex behaviour.

Similar trends can be observed in men's clothing. Clothes are now ready made. In very few families women still sew men's underwear or shirts. Men can have suits custom made or more recently, buy them ready made. Again, partly because of the possibility of buying or ordering clothing from outside, partly because the cost is met by the men themselves, and also because culture puts no restrictions on men's apparel, they are much better dressed than the women.

Women, on the other hand still sew many of their own undergarments. Ready made garments, particularly those made of synthetic fabrics, and undergarments have started to appear and young girls want them for their trousseaus. In fact a most striking aspect of women's clothing in Eregli is the great variety of style, be it traditional or modern. There are no women who cover their faces in the town. Their clothing varies from modern slacks to long black overcoverings (çarşaf). Undergarments have also changed from long rough cotton undershirts to nylon brassieres. The most modern group wears short sleeved dresses, goes around without stockings in summer and with nothing on their heads. The largest group of women, however, wear long sleeves and longish dresses with no particular style. They prefer to wear a jacket or coat in all seasons and wear a scarf around their head. Compared to men's, women's clothing lacks quality, style and modernity. There is no distinct sign of conspicuous consumption in women's clothing in Eregli. This contrasts sharply with larger centers in Turkey and the West. Perhaps this is because the women of Eregli are not "displayed" for status purposes. As a result, women stress home furnishings, ceremonial consumption at weddings, births and deaths to prove the status of the family and underplay their own clothing consumption and leisure. But this preference results in distinct differences in the standards of consumption of men and women, putting women on a lower level. In any case, consumption in Eregli in general means a lot of deprivation and hard work. The women's share in this deprivation and hard work is much greater than the men's.

Leisure

To understand women's life outside the family and home, one has to look at their activities termed "leisure". This, however, must be done with caution, since we are talking about women's life outside the home in a culture where "fun" is frowned upon, and women's honour is valued highly. Women should not be seen in public much, and they should never make themselves conspicuous. Still women, particularly the wives, daughters and mothers of the traders, shopkeepers, etc. go out of their homes basically for what could only be termed leisure. Besides, in small towns there is never a clear differentiation between work and play. As all activities are unorganized and undifferentiated, leisure is also amorphous, both for men and for women.

For women, the most striking leisure activities are endless visits to other women. In the lower income groups, women visit without ceremony. To "drop in", "to come for morning coffee", "to come and sit in the evenings" all cover the same thing. In fact, the home visits of the women correspond to the coffeehouse attendance of the men and both play a role in perpetuating sex segregation. Such visits basically take place in immediate neighborhoods. For the women who are better-off, there are "at home" days when visiting, food and drinks are more formal. Women give more attention to their appearance on such days, and contrary to informal "drop in's", small children are not taken on the visits. Great care is taken, however, to bring grown-up daughters as these visits provide an opportunity to show off eligible young girls. The women who do not have "at home" days consider this way of entertaining "snobbish". But those who have them, consider "dropping in" inconsiderate. Many wealthy merchant's wives, however, have double styles of entertainment for two types of acquaintances.

During the visits women talk, knit or embroider. Sewing together constitutes a special reason for visiting and entertaining. The talk usually centers around births, deaths, weddings, problems of children and housekeeping. They also talk about the movies they have seen or magazines they have read.

Another type of visits, rather important in the life of Eregli women, are ceremonial visits at births, deaths and weddings. They meet in houses where religious recitations, *mevlut*, are given by women who make this their living. In fact, Eregli women find many occasions to have *mevlut* recitations.[6] The *mevlut* prayer tells the story of the life of the Prophet. The poem-prayer was written in the fifteenth century by a Bektasi scholar and poet in Turkish. These *mevluts* are held either as a way of earning god's good will or in order to thank him for a favour. They are always held in cases of death or for the souls of dead relatives. Money is always collected before the meeting to buy *mevlut* candy. The *mevlut* is attended by women of all ages. As the evening or afternoon advances, it turns into any ordinary gathering with much talk and laughter. Sometimes during the summer, the women hold their prayers on the wooded hill where there is the tomb of a saint, Nasrullah Dede. Such an outing is not very different from any picnic in the open air.

They also go in small groups to the park, to movies, particularly open-air movies in the summer, and to a secluded beach for women only. Shopping in weekly open-air markets in the main street is an important affair. The husband's permission is required or he at least must be informed so that there will be no talk about it in the shops. Usually 7—8 year old sons and daughters accompany their mothers visiting a relative or friends who live in other neighborhoods. The small children share the social life of their mother. They go with their mothers to the cinema, shopping, and visiting. Since most men are out of the house at work or in coffeehouses after lunch or supper, children are left with their mothers. In a sense, the children chaperon their elder sisters and mothers. If women go to various places with their children, their honour and respectability remains intact. Indeed, if women go places with their children, particularly their seven-eight year old sons an if there is some religious aspect to the occasion even if it is only a *mevlut*, which is half-secular and may turn into an opportunity for festivity, and if what ever they do takes place in the open air, they are safe, honourable, accepted and comfortable.

It has to be realized that home is basically the place where women work, be it morning, noon or evening. First of all, that place has to be kept clean and orderly; secondly meals have to be ready for every member of the family although they often eat at different times. Thirdly, she is the mediator of all disputes at home so she has to be alert and ready

[6] See also Fatma Mansur: *Bodrum: A Town in the Aegean*. E. J. Brill, 1972. Especially pages 106—108.

to interfere in all types of conflicts within the family. Fourthly, especially during the periods when the husband is at home, şhe has to be ready to respond to all his whims and wishes. So, women never relax at home except in the afternoon, really the only time reserved for herself, and some time in the evening after the husband has left for the coffeeshop and the children have gone to bed.

It is interesting to note that when men are not at home, women spend considerable time listening to all types of programs on the radio. Young girls, who do not have many responsibilities, read popular magazines (such as *Hayat*, *Ses* and *Yelpaze*). The serials and novels attracts their imagination and they enthusiastically talk about them. These magazines circulate from one house to another, to at least six or seven different readers. Among the small town young women there is a conspicuous, vicarious satisfaction in following the romantic stories of big city, upper class society.

Although up to here we have emphasized the segregation of the sexes, it would not be correct to say that this is the only life style in Eregli. Four-fifths of the husbands have taken their wives on trips to İstanbul. Two-thirds of them visit their acquaintances at night with their wives. Half of the heads of household go to the cinema with their wives. In certain gatherings, such as wedding ceremonies and engagement parties, government officials, teachers, upper income professionals and their wives dance together. In general, as the family gets smaller, more participation, interaction and mutual dependence emerges between man and wife. Although this is not equality or emancipation it is at least a first step for women wishing to participate in a larger world and play some role in it, even if not the leading one.

Women's Employment

Women's life outside of the home is traditionally limited to infrequent shopping trips and leisure activities. However, employment and work has started to gain importance in the women's world, or at least in the expectations of the younger generation. Interestingly, many types of work which are age old occupations of the women are not mentioned as "work" in conversation. At the top of this group comes work as maid. Then comes dress-making, and embroidery. All these have been the source of extra income for families for a long time. These jobs are done in houses and do not require a special place of work outside the residential areas.

Primary school teaching is the most prestigious of this group, but among the men and government officials it is looked upon as a second class government job. There are, in the whole town, about fourty women who do cleaning jobs in various government offices, in hospitals, or lawyers' and doctors' offices. These jobs are considered to be different from the work done by house servants. Proper office work and secretarial jobs are very highly regarded by the younger women, and in general the society places them higher in the occupational hierarchy. But there are actually only three typists in the district office and four young girls who work as secretary—clerks in lawyers' offices. All these girls are single. The girls consider office work very desirable and the younger ones want to go to high school in order to be able to get such jobs. They resent their parents' wanting to send them to the Girls Techical Evening School and no longer want to earn a living by sewing or embroidering. There are twenty-one dress-makers in Eregli now. Considering that ready made clothing and underwear are becoming major consumer goods, it is possible that this way of earning a living will die off. On the other hand, the need for more cash for consumption items could lead more members of the family to work for cash income. Ultimately, whether the men see this as the future or not, the young girls are eager to work outside their homes.

To become a primary, or better a secondary school teacher, however, is the first preference of the younger generation. Among all the groups of women working in Eregli, they constitute the largest. There are one-hundred twenty-seven women teachers there. There is only one other professional woman: the gynecologist at the maternity clinic.

In general, the money earned by older women, either in traditional or in professional jobs is kept by themselves. The young girls, however, turn their incomes over to their mothers and the mothers give it to the fathers, another interrelationship where mothers are the coordinators!

Attitudes towards women's gainful employment outside the home are changing fast. A great majority still think that a woman's place, especially a married woman's place is in the home. In fact, more pressure and control are put on married women than younger girls, in regard to gainful work. Among men, different age groups as well as different occupational groups show differences in their attitudes toward women's gainful employment. As one might expect, more than two-thirds of the traditional traders-artisans do not want their women to work outside the home. As for the age groups, the younger ones, 25—35 year old men, perhaps because of infants and younger children at home, and 45—55 year old ones, because they are the husbands of 35—40 year old experienced women with independent personalities, are less tolerant than the others. Education, it seems in this town at least, independent of occupation and age does not make much difference.

While men of Eregli have negative attitudes about working women, they can think of a wide range of traditional occupations such as teaching, midwifery, nursing and sewing for women. They also agree that women could become doctors, judges, engineers, even army officers. Eregli men, while not wanting their own women to work, are realistic enough to recognize that women of other cultures and groups could hold and successfully follow many professions. They pass no value judgements, but accept their existence, perhaps until they are faced with the possibility of a wife or daughter becoming a professional. At this stage none of the artisans or traders can think of women with professions as their wives.

The education of girls shows parallel characteristics to women's work and attitudes towards such work. Almost all of the post-school age girls, sixty percent of the wives of the heads of households, and one-thirds of the female members of the previous generation are literate. But that is all. No further training in any specific skill except dress-making and primary school teaching is thought of as possible employment by the fathers.

The Girls' Evening Technical School offers two year courses in cutting and sewing, artificial flower making, embroidery and lingerie making. Primary school graduates or anyone who knows how to read and write is accepted and there is no age limit. It attracts a wide range of women of all ages from the middle claşs families of traders and artisans. It is interesting to note that while the lower classes aspire to a profession such as primary school teaching for their daughters and take great pains to get their daughters into teachers training schools, middle to higher class artisans and traders are satisfied with giving some skills in refined home economics to their daughters and rationalize their behaviour by saying that if their daughters are ever forced to earn money they can do so by dress-making and embroidery. But as was mentioned before, the girls themselves usually hate these schools and want to go to the secondary school, so that they may one day have jobs in offices. This, of course, is a very alien thought for their parents. The parents rightly do not consider the Evening Technical School a normal school. "It does not matter if my daughter does not go to school, I am sending her to evening courses to learn to sew" or "it is enough for her to learn to sew" are often repeated remarks, again implying that these institutes attract the more traditionally oriented and at the same time create tension and conflict between the generations and sexes.

However, the town, in general is very conscious of education and for a great majority, statements such as "let her go as long as she can" sum up parental attitudes towards children's education. Almost one-third of the parents definitely want their daughters to have a university education, even if it is neither a realistic possibility nor within their means. A fisherman to whom we talked about the conflict said "I can't afford it, but I would like her to go to university. It is a good thing".

While the people of Eregli want to see their daughters educated, they seem unable to formulate their reasons for wanting this. While they feel that "to be educated" is going to be an asset in the future, they have difficulty in describing how. They also have difficulty imagining educated women in the future society. Regarding the education of girls, the majority of responses express a desire to enable girls to adapt to everyday life and to deal with everyday problems. The old expression "girls need not go to school" has given way to "girls must go to school to learn to cope with the problems of life today".

Conclusions

It is clear that it is still very early to expect great changes in the status of women in small towns. The time has not yet come for women to obtain and to occupy strategically important jobs outside their homes, to contribute to the community directly and to deal with their fellow men equally. However, the study of small town women shows other important things. In her home a woman is one of the most important links in the economic activities of the town because her family's consumption patterns are determined by her decisions, actions and coordination. The quality of the daily life of the family springs directly from the roles of women in consumption. In the process of change, however, the differential consumption of the family at home and men outside the home have certain negative effects on home consumption which require further investigation. Another important role of women in small town families is that of coordinator of delicate relations. Women, never passive receivers, show themselves as the most important and skillful coordinators of human relations. It is through their alert and subtle mediation and conciliation that husbands, sons, daughters and others get along within the family. The result is a mature and responsible personality, an independent "women only" sub-culture and a readiness to make many sacrifices for the benefit of various members of the family. It is not yet clear however, how they will enter into the total life of the community and how they will transfer their incredible skills in human relations into interaction in society at large.

PART FOUR

RELIGION AND POLITICAL BEHAVIOUR

ORHAN VELI KANIK

Cımbızlı Şiir

Poem With Tweezers

Neither the Bomb
Nor the Peace Conference.
She's got tweezers in one hand
and a mirror in the other.
What the hell does she care!

—from *I am Listening to Istanbul: Selected Poems of Orhan Veli Kanık*,

Translated by Talât Sait Halman, New York, Corinth Books, 1971, p. 60.

INTRODUCTION

The most widely utilized explanation of sex differences in political participation lies in the political socialization theory. (Hyman, 1959). Political socialization assumes that the political habits of people are formed primarily before adulthood. The differences in the attention that men and women pay to politics result from the same dynamics of childhood learning as other sexual differences. This process of sex differentiation is further accentuated by the dominant stereotypes present in the culture.

The second major school of thought on male/female political differences emphasizes the situational and/or structural factors. Advocates of the situational viewpoint accept the idea that sex roles and cultural stereotypes help shape and perpetuate the differences in the political expression of men versus women.

A modified Marxian model (Heiskanen, 1971) states that the lesser political activity and participation of women is derived in part from the nature of the modern capitalist economy, and in particular, from its need for a large supply of cheap labour and spendthrift consumers. Traditional sex-role ideology is not only a question of cultural lag, a leftover from traditional values, but is also serves the prevailing interests. Also, as the issues concerning economic relationships grow in complexity the content of traditional sex-role ideology is specifically geared to discourage women from participation in politics, i.e. from influencing the prevailing power structure.

This last approach furnishes a convincing argument to explain the strong impact of religious teaching on women and its relationship to political behaviour. As universally observed, strong religious commitment is one of the most stable foundations for conservative voting.

When exploring women's potential preparedness to enter actively into politics, one more dimension has to be taken into account. Related to the concept of marginality, this approach underlines that the woman in politics, because of her ascribed status, is both in the male dominated world of politicians and in that of the unpolitical women.

No doubt the mass media, the omnipotent communication network, and institutionalized or informal religious associations contribute significantly to the reinforcement of sex stereotypes related to participation in public life.

The two essays presented in this subsection while adopting quite different methods and theoretical approaches show a great deal of similarity. They explain why in fast changing societies with strong cultural dualism, women inspite of their highly mobilized vote, still appear to be more a spectator than an actor in politics, consumer rather than producer in mass media usage, tacit follower instead of critical believer in matters of faith.

Tekeli adopting a critical frame of analysis, attempts to furnish a new historical interpretation by qualifying the political emancipation of Turkish women as a complementary action, intended to serve as an "image" for the beautification of Turkey's nascent democratic experience. Tekeli, emphasizing the "symbolic", "selected" and "elitist" value of political rights explains the high degree of marginality with regard to Turkish women politicians, candidates and voters. According to Tekeli, this dependent relation can only be remedied with greater class consciousness, a verdict deserving further discussion especially in light of the concept of marginality.

Sayarı's essay, while re-interpreting certain historical events pertinent to women's emancipation, makes a careful distinction between emancipation and liberation. In her eyes emancipation, especially pertaining to legal status, seems relatively easy to be realized, but genuine liberation particularly in a society imbued with Islamic cultural values, has still a long way to go. Sayari's most interesting thesis is anchored in her observation of the emergence of a counter-elite in present Turkey, such as the cadres around the National Salvation Party, which uses a return to women's traditional status as a political manipulation tool. To what extent this new religious-ideological fostered movement will effect the urban female population depends, among other things, on the growth or decline of political polarization in general.

Finally an important point. It is true that women are able to vote and that they do show a higher political participation rate in rural areas. These facts, however, are not sufficient proof that with this growing participation women are potentially able to alter the power structure.

Research in the domain of politics and religion is still very new. Further progress will require not only good standardized statistics, but also agreement on the choice of the social indicators to be used for such an evaluation.

BINNAZ (SAYARI) TOPRAK

RELIGION AND TURKISH WOMEN

I

The literature on the status of Turkish women has generally been euphoric about the equality of men and women in Republican Turkey. Kemalist reforms concerning legal and political rights of women have been lauded as unprecedented in the Muslim world in terms of women's liberation. Although there has been concern that such reforms have not penetrated the countryside, the liberation of the urban educated woman has been viewed as accomplished.[1]

This acquiescent attitude on the question of women is closely connected to similar analyses-via-euphoria about the modernization of Turkish society. To the extent that modernization was seen as a unilinear process and defined as Westernization, the fallacy of earlier modernization theories was repeated in the Turkish case. Since it was assumed that modernity and tradition are antonymous concepts, societies were seen as moving along a traditional-modern continuum with mutually exclusive phases. Similarly, despite the absence of even rudimentary visions of what is meant by a modern society, the Western model was taken

[1] See, for example, Afet Inan, *Atatürk ve Türk Kadın Haklarının Kazanılması* (Istanbul: Milli Eğitim Basımevi, 1968) and *Tarih Boyunca Türk Kadınının Hak ve Görevleri* (Istanbul: Milli Eğitim Basimevi, 1975); Perihan Onay, *Türkiye'nin Sosyal Kalkınmasında Kadının Rolü* (Türkıye Iş Bankası Kültür Yayınları, n. d.); Kadının Sosyal Hayatını Tetkik Kurumu, *Aylık Konferanslar 1953—1964* (Ankara: Ayyıldız Matbaası, 1967); Tezer Taşkıran, *Cumhuriyetin 50. Yılında Türk Kadın Hakları* (Ankara: Başbakanlık Basımevi, 1973); Kemal Savcı, *Cumhuriyetin 50. Yılında Türk Kadını* (Ankara: Cihan Matbaası, 1973); Ruth F. Woodsmall, *Women and the New East* (Washington, D. C.: The Middle East Institute, 1960) and *Moslem Enter a New World* (New York: Round Table Press, 1936). For comparisons of women's status in urban and rural areas, see Nermin Abadan-Unat, *Social Change and Turkish Women* (Ankara: Ankara Üniversitesi Basımevi, 1963) and "Major Challenges Faced by Turkish Women: Legal Emancipation, Urbanization, Industrialization", *The Turkish Yearbook of International Relations*, XIV, 1974, pp. 20—44.

to be an ideal type in theories of modernization.[2] Hence, in line with this unidirectional view of modernization—unidirectional both in terms of excluding oscillations between the modern and the traditional as well as moving towards the Western experience—the transition of Turkish society from an Islamic empire into a secular, Westernized nation-state received a fair amount of treatment by Turkish and foreigh observers alike as a successful case of nation-building in the right direction.

The approach to the question of women's liberation in Turkey has been influenced by these misconceptions about the nature of the modernization process. Since the inferior status of women in the Ottoman Empire is attributed to the impact of Islam on Ottoman society, it is assumed that women have gained an equal status with men as a result of modernization which, in the Turkish context, is equated with Westernization. The problem with this assumption is that although urban educated women may be Westernized, it is questionable that they are liberated. To be sure, there has been a significant change in the status of women in Republican Turkey, both legally and *de facto*, as compared to the Ottoman period. However, I think that such change is more apparent than real if we talk about liberation rather than the formal guarantee of rights.

This difference between liberation vs. emancipation is crucial in terms of avoiding overenthusiastic assessments of women's condition in Turkish society. Emancipation is a legal issue which is an important prerequisite for the liberation of women. However, just as in any other field of reform, changes in the legal structure are seldom indicative of unidirectional social change. For example, the enfranchisement of women is not very meaningful in a country where women are subservient to the men in their families. Indeed, as a recent survey of Turkish voters shows, within-family voting *en bloc* for the same party is a common pattern among the Turkish electorate.[3] Any assessment of women's role in Turkish society, therefore, has to take into account the interplay between

---

[2] For criticisms of earlier modernization theories along these lines, see Samuel P. Huntington, "The Change to Change: Modernization, Development and Politics," *Comparative Politics*, 3 (April 1971), 283—322 and "Political Development and Political Decay," *World Politics*, 17 (April 1965), 386—430; Joseph R. Gusfield, "Tradition and Modernity: Misplaced Polarities in the Study of Social Change," *American Journal of Sociology* ,72 (January 1966), 351—62; Rajni Kothari, "Tradition and Modernity Revisited," *Government and Opposition*, 3 (Summer 1968), 273—93 and S. N. Eisenstadt, "Breakdowns of Modernization," *Economic Development and Cultural Change*, 12 (July 1964), 345—67.

[3] Hürriyet-Datotek Kamuoyu Yoklaması, 1977.

secular law and Islamic traditions. The changes in sexual roles have historically met with the greatest resistance in Muslim societies. The ambiguous position of the emancipated but unliberated Turkish woman can be understood only if we take into consideration the amalgam of tradition and change in the process of modernization.

II

Throughout history, religious institutions have often collaborated with the state to ensure that the primary occupation of the ruled should be the pursuit of the sacred. Although it is true that religious movements, especially before they become institutionalized, sometimes function as bases of protest against established authority,[4] in general, institutionalized religion has played a significant role in the maintenance of established authority patterns. If this generalization is correct, the impact of religion on the status of women in most societies works in favor of subjugation to male authority. In other words, if religion secures obedience to ruling classes, it performs this function in a double direction in the case of women.

Although there are significant variations of status between women of different classes, I think that relating the question of women's liberation to class exploitation would lead us to confuse class position with unequal status stemming from sexuality.[5] Historically, the inferior position of women in most societies has cut across class lines. In other words, women of both upper and lower classes have been exploited socially, although with varying degrees. In some cases, as in Ottoman Turkey, upper class women have been more heavily subject to social seclusion as compared to, for example, peasant women.[6] The difference between upper and lower class women is that the latter have also been exploited economically, a condition which they have shared, however, with men of the same class. This is not to suggest that the degree of exploitation of men and women

---

[4] For example, many major religions or religious sects originated as protest movements of some kind or another. Cf. histories of Buddhism, Islam, Shi'ism or Sufism. Religion has also played a revolutionary role in the national struggle of many former colonized countries.

[5] For a study of Turkish women which views the problem from a class perspective, see Aytunç Altındal, *Türkiye'de Kadın: Marksist bir Yaklaşım* (Istanbul: Birlik Yayınları, 1975).

[6] See Fanny Ellsworth Davis, *Two Centuries of the Ottoman Lady*. Unpublished Ph. D. thesis, Columbia University, New York, 1968.

holding similar job positions has been the same in terms of wages, work conditions and benefits.[7]

Since the subjugation of women is a within-class rather than a cross-class phenomenon, we have to look for other factors besides class position for depicting the reasons behind the inferior status of women. Religion is, I think, one such factor. It should be noted *in passim*, however, that the religious attitude towards women probably has something to do with the social structure, especially the property arrangements, of the period and the place when the religion in question has emerged.

III

The status of women in Islam, compared to other monotheistic religions, is one of near-complete subjugation to the authority of men. Since the tenets of Islam have not remained at the theological level but have also been incorporated into law, the impact of Islam on women has been doubly restrictive, i.e., at both the social and the legal spheres. Although the advent of Islam somewhat improved the condition of women in Arabia of the time by restricting the practice of polygamy to a maximum number of four wives, by regulating divorce through limiting the repudiation of a wife to no more than three times and by forbidding female infanticide,[8] the fact that Islam assumed the responsibility of such a reform, in the long run, has meant that local customs were carried beyond the boundaries of Arabia and became binding on generations of Muslim women elsewhere as well.

The status of women in Islamic Law is based on the *Koran*, especially the *Nisa Surah* (IV), which lays down the principles that are to be followed in matters of marriage, divorce, parental rights, and inheritance. All these four areas of family law are unquestionably designed to limit the legal rights and social authority of women. What is significant about the *Nisa Surah* from the point of view of Islam's emphasis on male authority is that the only instance where the *Koran* sanctions physical

[7] For a discussion of differences between men and women workers in Turkey in terms of wages, work conditions and other job benefits, see Şirin Tekeli, "Siyasal Iktidar Karşısında Kadın", *Toplum ve Bilim*, 3 (Güz 1977), 69—107.

[8] See Reuben Levy, *The Social Structure of Islam* (Cambridge: Cambridge University Press, 1965), 91—134 and J. N. D. Anderson, *Islamic Law in the Modern World* (New York: New York University Press, 1959), pp. 40—41. Also see *Koran*, IV.

violence against women is when the wife shows disobedience to her husband. The recommended punishment for such offense is beating.[9]

A recent study by Mernissi[10] puts forward an illuminative argument that the inferior status of women in Islam is due to the Islamic view of female sexuality rather than any belief in the intrinsic inferiority of women. She argues that contrary to Western Christian tradition which relates sexual inequality to the inferior biology of women, this inequality in Islamic culture rests on institutional arrangements to check the innate potency of female sexuality. Contrasting Freudian theory with Imam Ghazali's views on marriage, Mernissi concludes that the passive role Freud assigns to women in human sexuality is singularly absent in Ghazali's writings. On the contrary, women are seen as sexually aggressive and able to possess considerable power over men through their irresistible sexuality. Hence, the need arises to contain their power through legal submission and social seclusion if the Muslim *ummah* is to retain its unity and order.[11] As Mernissi puts it, "the Muslim order faces two threats: the infidel without and the woman within".[12]

The Mernissi thesis is, I think, novel in terms of explaining the subjugation of women to male authority in Islam. However, it fails to demonstrate that women are not considered inferior to men in the Islamic view. Sexual power does not, in any way, imply mental capacity. On the contrary, Mernissi's argument is a restatement of the traditional view, dominant at least within the Turkish context, that women use their sexuality to make up for their intellectual and physical inferiority. In fact, so little is the Islamic faith in women's ability for rational reasoning that the *Koran* accepts the testimony of two women as equivalent to the testimony of one man. In addition, the *Koran* explicitly states that men are superior to women[13] and this has been interpreted by some Muslim commentators as proof of divine judgment that women lack mental ability and physical capacity to carry out public duties.[14] Taken in its entirety, therefore, both as religious dogma and a system of law, Islam contradicts its own egalitarian precepts by its unequal treatment of men and women.

---

[9] *Koran*, IV: 38.

[10] Fatima Mernissi, *Beyond the Veil: Male-Female Dynamics in a Modern Muslim Society* (New York: John Wiley, 1975).

[11] *Ibid.*, pp. 1—25.

[12] *Ibid.*, p. 12.

[13] *Koran*, IV: 39.

[14] Levy, pp. 98—99.

IV

The legal and social status of Turkish women during the Ottoman period has been extensively studied. Their legal status was, of course, based on the *Shariah* which had incorporated the basic principles of Islam concerning women on questions of marriage, divorce and inheritance. Similarly, the social life of Ottoman women was also determined by Islamic traditions and customs. Outside of the family, urban women, in general, led a life of near-seclusion with no access to education, work opportunities, recreation in mixed company, or at times, the freedom to go outdoors. Even the color and style of women's veils were subject to limitations by Imperial decrees.[15]

Although from about the beginning of the Tanzimat period (1839—1877) until the end of the century, the status of women gradually began to be questioned, the changes were slower to come. The secularization attempts of the Tanzimat period in the field of education led to the opening of middle-level *(Rüştiye)* and training schools for women. During the Second Constitutional Period (1908—1918), these new educational opportunities further expanded with the opening of high schools *(idadi)* for girls, a university *(Inas Darülfünunu)* and teacher's colleges. At the same time, women began to be employed in hospitals, postal services, laboratories, and other service sectors as greater numbers of working men were sent to the front during the Balkan Wars and WW I. In line with such changes, there was a steady increase of periodicals, journals, and other publications demanding greater freedom for women or attempting to raise their consciousness, in addition to several women's magazines giving information on matters of common interest. The embryonic feminist movement also found allies among the literary circles of Young Ottomans and Young Turks as the women's condition became the subject of several novels, plays, poems, or philosophical writings.[16]

The struggle for women's rights, however, had limited success in changing attitudes towards women. For example, in a women's periodical called *Mahasin* which first began to be published in 1908, the author of an article on the feminist movement argued, in a typical manner, that

---

[15] See Muhaddere Taşçıoglu, *Türk Osmanlı Cemiyetinde Kadının Sosyal Durumu ve Kadın Kıyafetleri* (Ankara: Akın Matbaası, 1958).

[16] Taşkıran, pp. 27—63. Also see Emel Sönmez, *Turkish Women in Turkish Literature of the 19th Century* (Leiden: E. J. Brill, 1969).

women who were able to understand and analyze Darwin's theory of evolution were undoubtedly congenitally malformed.[17] Similarly, in a session of the Ottoman Parliament in 1911, the suggestion of a member that adultery laws imposed unequal punishment on men and women because the law-markers were all men led to reaffirmations of belief that men are superior to women.[18] Likewise, in a session of the National Assembly in 1921, a session which might have as well been a stage comedy, the Assembly members engaged in verbal fights while discussing a planned nation-wide campaign for controlling syphilis when the suggestion was made that unmarried women be also subjected to medical examinations although the owner of the suggestion had modestly limited such examinations to throats and elbows.[19] Again in 1921, the minister of Education, Hamdullah Suphi (Tanrıöver), resigned from his post following an Assembly hearing during which he was criticized for having held a Teachers' Congress with the joint participation of teachers of both sexes.[20]

Even as late as 1936, a prominent educator of the Kemalist period could argue that although women may achieve legal freedom, they are naturally "slaves" in terms of their mental and intellectual capacities.[21] His book on women is, in fact, quite interesting in terms of the distinction I made earlier between emancipation and liberation. Although he starts out by an unquestionable enthusiasm about the "new woman" who has gained her legal and political rights under Kemalist auspices, it turns out that he has rather inadvertedly used the "new women" label. The book is a brilliant example of the traditional Muslim view of women—stereotypical in its assessment of female sexuality culminating in emotional hysteria and intellectual poverty—which is cloaked behind a formal and, for an educator of the Kemalist period, befitting approval of women's emancipation.

V

The Kemalist reforms concerning the legal, political, and social status of women was part of an effort to Westernize Turkish society. A catalogue of such reforms is indeed impressive for a Muslim country:

[17] *Ibid.*, p. 51.
[18] *Ibid*, pp. 46—47.
[19] *Ibid.*, pp. 91—95.
[20] *Ibid.*, pp. 95—96.
[21] Cemil Sena Ongun, *Yeni Kadın* (Istanbul, 1936), p. 70.

The adaption of the Educational Bill of 1924 *(Tevhid-i Tedrisat Kanunu)* which secularized the educational system and provided equal educational opportunities for men and women; the adaption of the Swiss Civil Code in 1926 which outlawed polygamy and gave equal rights to men and women in matters of marriage, divorce, inheritance, and property ownership; the adaption of Western styles in clothing in 1925 which legally allowed women to unveil; the granting of political rights to women in 1934; and finally, the opening of career and employment opportunities for women.

Although such reforms were major steps towards the emancipation of women, their impact on women's status in Turkish society has to be assessed with caution. For one thing, the failure of legal measures in affecting changes in the lives of women living in more closed communities is apparent. For example, the provisions of the civil code concerning marriage, divorce, or monogamy are often evaded in favor of more traditional arrangements that Islam has sanctioned for centuries.[22] Similarly, the education of women has remained limited as the wide gap between literate men and women in census findings demonstrates.[23] Women in most small towns and villages are still secluded socially. Sexual promiscuity of women is a taboo and a question of family honor in rural and urban communities alike although similar behavior of men is not only tolerated but is also considered a sign of virility. The authority of the men is unchallengeable in most families of rural background and manhandling of women is quite common.[24] In short, the success of legal reforms in changing women's condition has been limited to the extent that Islamic beliefs and traditions concerning sex roles have socially remained valid.

More significantly, however, the urban educated women, who have undoubtedly achieved emancipation as a result of the Kemalist reforms, have not fared any better in terms of liberation. They are caught in a role conflict between a self-perception which is modelled by their seemingly equal status with men and an image of themselves whose boundaries are determined by the traditional limits that Islamic society places on

---

[22] See, for example, Serim Timur, *Türkiye'de Aile Yapısı* (Ankara: Hacettepe Üniversitesi Yayınları, 1972), pp. 91—93.

[23] According to the 1970 census, whereas 57% of men are literate, this figure drops down to 33% in the case of women. See Taşkıran, p. 169.

[24] For a first-hand account of some cases in courts involving beating of wives by husbands, see Meliha Çalikoglu, "Ailede Kadının Mevkii", in Kadının Sosyal Hayatini Tetkik Kurumu, *Aylık Konferanslar*, pp. 69—84.

them. They neither have, on the one hand, the security that traditional Islamic society provides for women,[25] nor the opportunity to become truly liberated, on the other. They do not wear veils but are still captive in a society which teaches them to be docile, economically dependent on men, and geared to housework and childraising.

I think that appraisals of the Kemalist reforms concerning women miss the point that such reforms were not designed to change sexual roles but rather had a pragmatic political aim. For example, in order to transform the traditional social structure of Central Asia, the Soviet authorities in the 1920's decided to use Muslim women as a "surrogate proletariat". Through legislation which gave Muslim women unprecedented rights, the Soviet government hoped to mobilize what it saw as the most disadvantaged and therefore potentially the most revolutionary group to strike at the roots of traditional society.[26] Similarly, the French army, during the Algerian War, engaged in a campaign of "liberating" Muslim women in an effort both to enlist them on the side of the French cause as well as shake the traditional structure of Algerian society by preventing cultural solidarity.[27]

The emancipation of Turkish women during the Kemalist period had the similar aim, I think, of strengthening the goals of the Kemalist Republic rather than a revolutionary redefinition of sexual roles. The Kemalist vision of a modern society had the Western model as its parameters. The major goal of the Kemalist movement was to establish a modern nation-state as defined by what I would call its quasi-ideology, namely, Westernization. This quasi-ideology determined the boundaries of what Kemalist reforms would attempt to accomplish. Most of them aimed at transforming Turkish society from an Islamic into a Western setting. Hence, the emancipation of women was a necessary corollary of the Westernization effort. It was a politically expedient means of inducing cultural transformation to the extent that women play an important role within the family in transmitting dominant cultural values to younger generations. It was not, however, an effort specifically directed towards a radical reassessment of sexual roles.

---

25 For life of women in a traditional Anatolian town, see the account by Joyce Roper, *The Women of Nar* (London: Faber & Faber, 1974).

26 See Gregory J. Massell, *The Surrogate Proletariat: Moslem Women and Revolutionary Strategies in Soviet Central Asia, 1919—1929* (Princeton, N. J.: Princeton University Press, 1974).

27 See David C. Gordon, *Women of Algeria: An Essay on Change.* Harvard Middle Eastern Monograph Series, 1968, pp. 56ff157.

Approximately forty years after the Kemalist reforms on women, ambivalent attitudes towards sex differences—ambivalent in the sense of pride in women's emancipation coupled with deep-ingrained beliefs about the superiority of men—still find public expression. For example, none other than a Prime Minister of the Turkish Republic, Professor Sadi Irmak, stated in a press conference during his term of office in 1974 that speaking as a medical authority, it is biologically natural for married men to be polygamous provided that their wives do not find out about it.[28] Obviously, his statement makes no sense from a medical point of view to the extent that it limits this biological need to men, not to mention the fact that it is an irresponsible statement since adultery is against the law. It does make sense, however, when viewed as a prototypical attitude of formally accepting women's rights but tacitly supporting the allegedly intrinsic inequality of women. Even as liberal a man as İsmail Cem, who was the chairman of the state-owned radio and television network during 1974, could make the decision not to allow women news commentators on television under the rather shaky pretext that there is no precedence for it in other countries although he later reversed his decision in the face of opposition from women's associations. What is interesting about this incidence is that when I circulated a letter of protest against Cem's decision at the time, some of the educated women among my friends refused to sign since they felt that women newscasters distracted the attention of men. Here, I think, is a good example to support the Mernissi thesis that the psychological resistance of Islamic societies to the liberation of women is connected to the Islamic fear of female sexuality. It is not only the men but the emancipated women as well who have internalized this Islamic ethic.

Given the constrictions that traditional society places on nationalist elites, especially on such a sensitive subject as sex differences in a Muslim country, it is perhaps unrealistic to expect that the Kemalists could do more towards the liberation of women. However, the reforms that they have accomplished should not lead us into a rather comfortable state of contentment. Neither the minority of women who have benefited from such reforms nor the great majority who have been largely unaffected by them have escaped the bonds of tradition.

---

[28] See *Cumhuriyet*, December 7, 9, 13, 1974.

VI

The cultural persistence of the Islamic view concerning the inequality of women has recently found political expression within the ranks of the National Salvation Party (NSP). Founded in 1972 as an explicitly neo-Islamic party, the NSP has gained an impressive victory in the 1973 election, and although its percentage of the total votes declined in the 1977 election, it has participated as a partner in three coalition governments between 1973—1977.

The NSP's assessment of the problems facing Turkish society centers around its view of history. The major issue that the party leadership has sought to politicize is the question of how and why what was once a powerful empire now ranks among the less developed countries of the world. According to the leaders of the NSP, the answer to that question lies in understanding the relationship between Turkey and the West. The suggested explanation is that the Turks have lost their power and influence because they have alienated themselves from their own cultural heritage while, at the same time, they have failed to industrialize. Their relationship to the West has, therefore, been lopsided. They took from the West what they needed least, namely, Western culture, and they failed to borrow what they needed most, namely, Western technology. In contrast to secular intellectuals who view the decline of the Ottoman Empire as a partial consequence of Islam's conservative role in Ottoman society, the NSP interprets this decline in terms of the foreign cultural influences which penetrated Ottoman society at the expense of Islamic thought and traditions.[29]

Hence, the NSP vehemently criticises the Western orientation of the Turkish elite. These criticisms are especially pungent with respect to family life and social customs. The list is long and includes such details as criticisms of long hair, mini skirts, and pornography (a sculpture of a female nude erected in an Istanbul square was considered pornographic and dubbed "the sculpture of shame" by the NSP and was later lifted from square by an order of the interior Minister, an NSP member, during the RPP*-NSP coalition government in 1974);[30] TV, movie and

[29] See, for example, a series of conferences by the party's leader, Necmettin Erbakan, in *Üç Konferans* (Istanbul: Fatih Yayınevi, 1974). Also see the text of his speech in Erzurum in *Milli* Gazete, September 9, 1973.

* Republican People's Party.

[30] See *Milli Gazete*, March 20, 1974.

theatre programs which are influenced by Western culture; wearing of shorts by women students during gym classes and women's participation in sports; tourist accommodations (the Minister of Commerce in 1974, who was an NSP member in the coalition government, refused to give governmental credit for building tourist resorts on the grounds that foreigners corrupt the morality of the Turkish people;)[31] the mushrooming of nightclubs "where the youth are initiated into drinking and sexual liberty" and, in general, the disappearance of traditional family life.[32]

Most of these issues are connected, in one way or another, to the question of women's role in Turkish society. With the rise of the NSP, we are witnessing the emergence of a counter-elite with a different cultural orientation than that of Kemalist Westernists. From the point of view of women, this new elite is attempting to legitimize traditional sex roles. For example, it is no longer the women of the periphery who dress according to Islamic traditions. The women of the center, e.g., the wives of politicians and professional people within the NSP ranks, are also abiding by them and are radically competing with Western fashions in women's clothing through creating indigenous styles for Muslim women.

Kemalist reforms concerning the emancipation of women have not only failed to penetrate the periphery but are also being challenged at the center. It is unlikely that such challenge will pose any serious threat to women's rights. However, it signifies the extent to which changes in sexual roles accompanying any meaningful liberation of women are difficult to come. The Islamic framework concerning sex differences is operative at both the elite and the mass levels. At the mass level, the Islamic concept of women has never been seriously questioned. At the elite level, the Kemalist center formally rejects the inequality of women although this rejection does not preclude a latent acceptance of the Islamic ethic about female submission to male authority which finds its manifest expression within the NSP.

---

[31] See Milli Gazete, Narch 24, 1974.

[32] For repeated statements of NSP leaders on cultural and social issues, see *Milli Gazete*, which is the party's unofficial daily newspaper.

ŞIRIN TEKELI

WOMEN IN TURKISH POLITICS

Introduction

Women in the Western world struggled fiercely for their emancipation and their political rights. This lasted in some countries for a century and in others even longer. Most of these fights were influenced by the indigenous class struggles that shaped the history of the nineteenth century. The hallmarks of these class struggles, 1789, 1848, 1870 and 1917 were also the hallmarks of the women's emancipation movement in the European countries.[1]

In Turkey, however, women's emancipation was embedded in a process of change that could be rightly called the process of "secularization" and "westernization".[2] We must wait until the late 60's in order to find the links between the two types of struggles in Turkey, whereas they were already observable in France, for instance, during the 1789 bourgeois revolution and especially during the 1848 revolutions which put the bourgeoisie and the proletariat face to face. This of course does not mean that the process of "westernization" which gave the women's emancipation movement its particular nature, was independent of class struggles. It is a fact that the modernization process was the particular form that the class struggles took in Turkey. If they were different from the class struggles observed in the Western world it was due to the fact that the Ottoman Empire was a pre-capitalist social formation. The paradox of the modernization process was that the Ottoman State was led to reform its basic structures to meet the challenge of survival that had been posed by the development of capitalism in Europe. But, this process ended with the complete disintegration of the old social structure.

[1] Luisette Blanquart; *Femmes: l'Âge Politique*, ed. sociales, 1974. Albert Brimo; *Les Femmes Françaises face au Pouvoir Politique*, Monthchretiens, 1975, Sheila Rowbotham; *Hidden From History*, Pluto Press, 1973, Elenor Flexner; *Century of Struggle: The Women's Rights Movement in the United States*, Cambridge, Mass., 1959 Constance Rover; *Women's Suffrage and Party Politics in Britain 1866—1914*, Routhledge and Kegan Paul, 1967.

[2] Niyazi Berkes; *Türkiye'de Çağdaşlaşma*, Bilgi, *Ankara* 1973.

The model that the modern Turkey chose for the reconstruction of its society was in fact based upon the capitalistic production relationships. One of the hallmarks of this transformation was the adoption of the Swiss "civil code" in 1926. This was also a significant date for the women's rights movement. Turkish women got most of their civil and political rights through a process of transformation which was dialectically determined by the class struggles of the Western World. Therefore, Turkish women had no ground to fight in order to gain their rights, which they did in a comparatively very short period of time, whereas the women in the capitalist countries had to struggle for a long time.[3]

We nevertheless believe that unless we study the short but interesting history of this emancipation process, we can not understand the place and the particular role that women play in political life. Therefore, in the first part of this paper we shall try to reconstruct the history of this process. The second part will deal more directly with the modalities of women's participation in politics.

Historical Background of Women's Emancipation Movement in Turkey

Social anthropologists inform us that in the pre-Ottoman nomadic tribes, women were not excluded from social life. They rode horses, went to war, and even participated in decision making.[4] This situation conforms rather well to anthropological findings on other tribal societies. In tribal societies women are not excluded from social life even if their status is some what lower than that of men.[5]

Following the establishment of the Ottoman state and even more so after the conquest of Byzantium which brought the Ottomans in contact with the structures of the Byzantine state, women's place in society changed drastically. The Byzantine Empire was a class society basically made up of slaves who worked on the land and the ruling classes who mainly indulged in governing. The women who belonged to the ruling classes and who lived in cities were secluded in the "harem". This prac-

[3] Tezer Taşkıran; *Cumhuriyetin 50. Yılında Türk Kadın Hakları*, Başbakanlık y. 1973.

[4] Taşkıran; *ibid.*, p. 19, Afet Inan; *Tarih Boyunca Türk Kadınının Hak ve Görevleri*, Milli Eğitim, 1975 p. 49,

[5] Maurice Godelier; "Le sexe comme le Fondement ultime de l'ordre social et cosmique chez les Baruya de Nouvelle-Guinée: Mythe et realité" *CERM*, mimeo, 1976, Rayna R. Roiter; *Toward an Anthropology of Women*, Monthly Review Press, 1975.

tice was later adopted by the Ottoman ruling classes. In the Ottoman "harem" women lived among themselves, coming in contact only with the male members of their family. Their social role was limited to reproduction and domestic labour. In a sense the harem women were "slaves" socially, if not juridically. The harem, as an institution, typically corresponds to what Engels calls the "domestic slavery" of women.[6]

In the sixteenth century, the Ottoman Empire became a theocratic state, from which point on, the "Saray" (Palace) and the "ulema" (theologians) began to interpret the Moslem religion in such a way as to justify the complete exclusion of women from social and economic life. We learn from the "fermans" (decrees) of the sixteenth and seventeenth centuries that women were forbidden to work and that their lives were very strictly regulated.[7] In this sense, women lived in a much worse and backward situation under Ottoman rule than the women under feudalism in Europe.[8]

With "Tanzimat" in the mid-nineteenth century, things started to ameliorate. The Westernized intellectuals and modernized bureaucrats thought that if the Ottoman state was backward compared to the "capitalist" West, women's situation had something to do with it. They started some modest reforms concerning women's status like the abolition of slavery, equal inheritance rights for male and female children, and the right of education for girls beyond primary school. These reforms were limited in scope because they had to comply with the dominant ideology, i. e. the religion, which was opposed to any change in women's status.[9] At the end of the nineteenth century there were a number of teachers' schools; a few lycees opened their doors to the recently "embourgeoised" female populations in the big cities of the Empire; and the first university for girls (İnas Darülfünunu) was opened in İstanbul in 1915.[10]

Then came the wars; the First World War and the National Liberation War. The wars affected the women's emancipation movement more than

[6] Frederick Engels; *Origins of the Family, Private Property and the State*, International Publishers, 1972.

[7] T. Taşkıran, *ibid.*, pp. 20—22. Muhaddere Taşçıoglu; *Kadının Sosyal Durumu ve Kadın Kıyafetleri*, Ankara, 1958 pp. 10—25, Hamide Topçuoglu, *Kadının Calışma Saikleri ve Kadın Kazancının Aile Bütçesindeki Rolü*, Ankara, 1957 p. XXI.

[8] Mary R. Beard; *Women as Force in History*, Collier-MacMillan, 1946 (3. printing) pp. 229—254.

[9] Taşkıran, ibid. pp. 24—37, Berkes, *ibid.*, p. 203.

any of the reforms. Indeed, the wars forced women to go out of their homes to look for work.[11] Further, the government had to recognize the necessity of the female labour-force to the economy. Enver Pasha, the prime minister, himself undertook the mobilization of the female labour-force by forming the "Association to Encourage Moslem Women to Work."[12]

During the National Liberation War, the mass participation of women in public life was a fact. They were active not only economically but were also involved in political manifestations and organizations. They even took an active part in the war.[13]

We know from the Western experience that women's participation in war efforts was the factor which determined the enfranchisement of women in the aftermath of wars.[14] This was not the case for Turkish women. To understand why women had to wait until the 1930's to obtain political rights, we must examine the political structure of the country. The composition of the First and the Second National Assemblies provide us with an interesting starting point. Within both of these assemblies one could observe on the one hand, a minority of "revolutionaries" gathered around Mustafa Kemal who not only led the Liberation War but wanted to put an end to the "ancient regime" and, on the other hand the conservative majority who supported Mustafa Kemal in his efforts for independence but opposed him on any issue that concerned the survival of the old Ottoman system. Women's status was one of the issues that put these two groups against each other very sharply. During the debates on the 1924 Constitution, when a minority representative proposed that women be regarded as "citizens", the Assembly suddenly turned into a battlefield.[15]

The revolutionary minority not only sincerely believed in women's rights but more than that, it thought that this issue could play a strategically critical role in the struggle they had decided to lead against the political and ideological structures of the Ottoman state. If the basis of the Ottoman state was religious authority, and if on the other hand women were "the" social category which was most deeply oppressed by

[11] Taşkıran *ibid.*, p. 41, Taşçıoglu, *ibid.*, 45—46.

[12] *Iktisadiyat Mecmuası* No 23, 27, 29, 1916 No. 55, 1917.

[13] Taşkıran, ibid. p. 74., Inan, *ibid.*, p. 102, 108, 125, Halide Edip Adıvar, *Türkün Ateşle Imtihanı*, Istanbul, 1971 pp. 188—265.

[14] Rover, *ibid.*, p. 207, Mattei Dogan, Jacques Narbonne, *Les Françaises face à la politique*, A. Colin, 1955, pp. 8—10.

[15] *Zabıt Ceridesi* (Minutes of the National Assembly) IV Section, Vol. 28, pp. 222—350, also cf. Inan, *ibid.*, pp. 134—136.

this authority, then the importance of the role that the women's rights movement would play within the struggle of the revolutionaries against the hegemony of the religious authorities was quite evident. We can see a clear formulation of this strategy in the "İnebolu" speech that Mustafa Kemal made in 1925. He said, "let women see the world with their own eyes; and let the whole world see their faces...[16] This was definitely a declaration of war by the revolutionaries launched against the "veil" and the "charshaf". We know that Mustafa Kemal was not alone in recognizing the critical role that such an ideological war played in the revolutionary process. Indeed, as he was starting his war against the "ancient regime", the young Soviet Republic was launching a similar fight against the "veil" to liberate the women of the Central Asian steppes from religious oppression.[17]

The objective of the revolutionaries was to create a modern Turkey. And "modernity" was defined as the social organization prevalent in the West, i. e. the capitalist social formation. The forces of production that the new state inherited from the Ottoman Empire were not developed enough to be historically determining; therefore one had to start with modernizing the super-structures. The new "civil code" adopted in 1926 reorganized civil and property relations on the basis of the model relationships dominant in the capitalist states. This was a great step forward as far as women's status was concerned. At last women acquired the juridical status of "person" which enabled them to enjoy equal rights with men. An achievement as it was, the law nevertheless had its limitations. As was the case for women in "bourgeois" societies, the principal limitation pertained to the organization of relationships within the family. The head of the family would be the husband and the woman was required to obey his will, which meant that a woman needed her husband's approval if she wanted to work.[18]

Let us now briefly consider the process through which women's political rights were officially recognized. This came about in two stages. In the first stage, women were enfranchised for the local elections (1930).

---

[16] *Atatürk'ün Söylev ve Demeçleri*, Türk Tarih Kurumu, 1952, vol. II pp. 210—214.

[17] Serge Zeyons; *La Revolution des femmes*, ed. sociales, 1971 part IV the campaign called „hudjum", pp. 101—110. Also cf. Gregory Massel; *The Surrogate Proletariat. Moslem Women and Revolutionary Strategies in Soviet Central-Asia 1919—1929*, Princeton Univ. Press, 1974 Part II.

[18] Civil Code, articles, 152, 153, 159. See also Ülker Gürkan; „Kadın emeğinin değeri ve evli kadının çalışmasının kocasının iznine baglı olmasının yarattığı sosyal ve hukuki sorunlar" *Hacettepe Sosyal ve Beşeri ilimler Dergisi*, vol. 8 No. 1—2, March—Oct. 1976.

They had to wait another four years for their enfranchisement for the national elections. The structure of the National Assembly had undergone a fundamental change after the 1927 elections so that the Third and the Fourth Assemblies were weighted in Atatürk's favor. The conservative opposition had disappeared and the new majority was ready to recognize women's full equality. One could ask at this point why it took such a long time for women to win political rights.

After the unhappy experience of Terakkiperver Fırka, the Republic became a single-party regime. Critics of this regime, both from within and from abroad were accusing Atatürk of becoming a "dictator". It is not all surprising that only a few days before the recognition of women's enfranchisement for the municipal elections, in a conversation with a foreign journalist Atatürk detested the accusation.[19] We know that during this period women's political rights were not yet recognized in some of the "democratic" countries such as France. It is plausible that Atatürk might have thought that women's enfranchisement would be considered proof of the "democratization" of his regime. Indeed, this was the first step in the process of "controlled" democratization that would lead, at the end of the same year, (1930) to the founding of a second party, the Serbest Fırka.

But, the experiment with the new party was not successful, and it was closed before the 1931 elections. Criticisms continued; and more important pressures mounted as a result of the political transformations that were taking place on the European political scene. At the end of 1932, the National Socialist Party came to power in Germany. And shortly after, the Weimar regime was changed into a one-party dictatorship. Atatürk felt the need to dissociate his single-party regime from that of fascist parties. He in fact gave several speeches in which he underlined the ideological differences that existed between his party and the fascist parties.[20] The women's political rights issue became critical within this context. The Nazi's credo about women was "Kinder, Kirche und Küche". If women's full enfranchisement was recognized at a time when the Nazis were secluding German women out of political life, then this

---

[19] Speech given to Vossiche Zeitung on 21, 24 March 1930. *Söylev ibid.*, p. 98. To see the details of the thesis defended here cf Şirin Tekeli; *Kadının Siyasal Hayattaki Yeri Üzerine Karşılaştırmalı Bir Araştırma*, mimeo, Istanbul, 1977.

[20] Richard J. Evans, *The Feminist Movement in Germany 1894—1937*, Sage, 1976, „The Bitter End", ch. 8. See also, Maria-Antoinetta Macciocchi, „*Elements pour une analyse du fascisme*, Union generale d'editions, 1976, part 6 „Les femmes et le passage au fascisme", for Atatürk's speeches about "nationalism" *Söylev ibid.*, vol. II.

would prove definitely that Turkey's singleparty regime was different in nature from the fascist regime. In other words, women's political rights played an important symbolic role. They symbolized the fact that the Turkish Republic was a democratic regime or, at least, one that evolving in that direction. A further argument that we can bring in favour of this interpretation is the fact that Atatürk was not satisfied with the formal recognition of women's political rights but went as far as to encourage women to participate as candidates in the 1935 elections, the result of which was the election of a high number of women deputies with no counterpart in the Western democracies.

Thus, we are justified to conclude women's enfranchisement was used as a valuable strategic instrument to reach certain goals which were crucial for the image of the new regime. In other words, the rulers were killing two birds with one stone with the intelligent timing of the recognition of women's political rights.

Women In Politics

The history of women's emancipation in Turkey leds us to the conclusion that, on more than one occasion, women's rights issues were used by the political authorities of the new Republic for their symbolic value. The symbolic nature of women's participation in political life will appear also in the second part of this paper. We shall first try to document this and suggest an explanation in the concluding pages of the paper.

a. *Women in the Parliament*

In the first general election (and in the 1937 off year elections) which followed the enfranchisement of women in 1934, 18 women were elected to the National Assembly. Women deputies as a group made up 4.5% of the Assembly. It is interesting to note that, at the same period, French women were not yet enfranchised, and English women who had fought violently for their political rights, attained only a very small representation in the parliament, between 0.1% and 2.4% for the period 1918 to 1935.[21]

---

[21] Monica Charlot; "les femmes et la politique" in *Les Femmes dans la société britannique*, A. Colin 1977, p. 227.

Table I below shows the evolution of women's representation in the Turkish Parliament from 1935 to 1977

As shown in this table, the number and the proportion of women representatives were higher in the one-party era. The lowest number in this era (1946 elections) was still higher than the number of women deputies in later National Assemblies. Why is that so? What is the critical importance of this date? We are inclined to see this date as the turning point after which women's representation lost its once critical and symbolic role. Indeed, after the Second World War, demands and pressures on Turkish authorities to transform the regime into a multi-party democracy increased so much that this democratization process became inevitable. As soon as Turkey became a multi-party democracy, the previous symbolic role played by the women deputies lost its importance.

Table I

Women in Turkish Parliament (1935–1977)

Years	*As-semb.*	*W. Dep.*	*Total*	*%*	*Senate Wom-en*	*Senate Total*	*%*	*Total Wom-en*	*% Parl.*
1935–39	V	18	395	4.5	–	–	–	18	–
1939–43	VI	15	400	3.7	–	–	–	15	–
1943–46	VII	16	435	3.7	–	–	–	16	–
1946–50	VIII	9	455	1.9	–	–	–	9	–
1950–54	IX	3	487	0.6	–	–	–	3	–
1954–57	X	4	535	0.7	–	–	–	4	–
1957–60	XI	7	610	1.1	–	–	–	7	–
1961–65	1	3	450	0.7	2	165	1.2	5	0.8
1965–69	2	8	450	1.7	3	165	1.8	11	1.7
1969–73	3	5	450	1.1	3	165	1.8	8	1.3
1973–77	4	6	450	1.3	3	165	1.8	9	1.5
1977–	5	4	450	0.9	3	165	1.8	7	1.2
Total		98	5367	1.8	14	775	1.8	112	1.8

The evolution of the regime into a multi-party system was fatal for women's representation. It meant two things: first, that the women candidates lost the privilege of being elected quasi-automatically which they enjoyed under one-party rule. Secondly, the competition between the parties for more seats in the Parliament tended to be disadvantageous for women.[22] The conservative ideology of the new born DP (Democrat Party) also had a negative impact upon the women politicans. This conservative attitude towards women was to be inherited by AP (Justice Party) after the 1960 coup. The old "revolutionary" CHP (Republican People's Party) was also forced to change its electoral policy towards women.[23] Presently, there seems to be no difference at all between the two major parties, the more leftist CHP and the more rightist AP, with respect to their electoral attitude towards women. To document this observation, we now turn to an examination of women's candidacy.

b. *Women candidates*

CHP's electoral policy had already changed in 1946. But we shall focus our study on the 1961—1977 period since more systematic data exists for these years. Table II shows the number and distribution of women candidates among the parties.

Table II

Women Candidates (1961–1977)

	Political Party											
Years	*AP*	*CHP*	*CGP*	*DP*	*MP*	*MHP*	*MSP*	*TBP*	*TIP*	*YTP*	*Ind.*	*Total*
1961	9 (2)	6	–	–	–	10 (1)	–	–	–	8	4	37
1965	7 (3)	14 (3)	–	–	8	12	–	–	15 (1)	17 (1)	3	76
1969	6 (2)	12 (2)	11	–	13 (1)	6	–	8	7	22	3	88
1973	5 (2)	6 (3)	13	12 (1)	12	15	1	2			9	75
1977	8 (2)	4 (2)	30	11	–	14	–	1	4	–	3	75
Total	35	42	54	23	33	57	1	11	26	47	22	351

[22] Sandra C. Danforth; "Women's Political Participation in the Ottoman Empire and the Turkish Republic" mimeo, 1975, p. 22 We must note that, except on this particular point, we entirely disagree with the author as to her interpretation of the Turkish data. For a criticism of this paper cf. Tekeli. *ibid.*, pp. 371—375.

[23] Danforth, *ibid.*, p. 22.

* Numbers in parantheses indicate the deputies elected.

This table indicates that there is not a significant difference between the attitudes of the two major parties towards women. A more significant difference appears between the attitudes of these two parties and the other smaller ones. And this has an important impact upon the candidacy of women. Indeed, it seems that those parties which have a higher probability of gaining more seats in the parliament have smaller tendency to favour women candidates, whereas those parties that have a lower probability of gaining seats, show a higher tendency to favour them.

The total number of female candidates is one of the principal political factors which explains the small number of women deputies. The 351 women who became party candidates in the period of 1961—1977, represented only 2.6% of the total number of candidates. When we look at the ratio of handicap factor[24] affecting women candidates, we see that it is not particularly high. This ratio was 2.1 for the entire period which means that a man's chance of being elected is twice as high as a woman's. We must therefore conclude that it is not the relative position of women compared to men which works against them, but rather the absolute weakness of the number of the women candidates. When we look for the particular mechanism through which the handicap factor affects women, we see that it is not the order in which the women appear on each party's list. It is in fact related to the way in which women candidates are distributed among various lists. That is to say, because the powerful parties do not favour women, and because they are rather favoured by the small parties, women candidates are handicaped twice more than men.

Why do small parties favour women more? Table II gives us an interesting hint to the answer. We see that small parties tend to favour women candidates especially in the elections in which they are particularly weak. Consequently, CGP (National Trust Party) in the 1977 elections, and the YTP (New Turkey Party) in the 1969 elections had the greatest number of women candidates. Yet, those two elections were the worst elections in the history of these two parties. In light of these details, we can suggest two different explanations. We can say that a small party

[24] J. F. S. Ross; "Women and Parliamentary Elections" *British journal of Sociology*, No. 4, 1953 pp. 16—17. The handicap factor is defined as the ratio of

$$\frac{\text{women candidates} \times \text{men members}}{\text{women members} \times \text{men candidates}}$$

This ratio was as high as 7.5 in England in 1918, it became 2.1 in 1950's and is actually 1.2 Cf. Melville Currell; *Political Women*, Croom Helm, 1974 pp. 24—25.

tends to favour women's candidacy the most in those elections in which it does not hope to gain many seats in the parliament. Therefore, women's candidacy is favoured rather for its symbolic value. The case of CGP fits this explanation well. This party claimed during the 1977 elections that it was a "real" follower of the "Kemalist ideology", and the large place that this party gave to women candidates in this election was a symbol of this claim. There might still be a more technical kind of explanation. Small parties have a limited membership. In order to be eligible in contest elections, it is required that they present candidates in at least 15 electoral districts and name as many candidates as the number of deputies to be elected in each district. This technical requirement might insert a heavier pressure upon the smaller parties which, to find a way out, tend to name women as candidates, without seriously intending to send them to the parliament.

c. *Women in the Government*

The symbolic role that women politicans kept on playing within the Turkish political system even after the one-party era is clearly shown by the role the two women ministers played.

It is a common phenomenon to find few women who are given responsibility in the government. It is known that higher the level of decision making within the political hierarchy, the less will be women's chance of becoming a member of that body. In England for instance, 310 women became members of parliament during the 1918—1974 period whereas the number of women who were appointed to the cabinet did not exceed 31.[25] In the U.S.A. for the period of 1917—1964, 75 women became members of Congress and only two women served in the cabinet during this period.[26] We find the same picture in Turkey. 69 women served in the parliament from 1935 to 1977 and there were only two women ministers in the cabinet.

What is more interesting to note is the fact that both of these cabinets were formed under exceptional circumstances, which qualify them as extraordinary cabinets. The women members in both of these cabinets played the significant role of "symbolizing" the reformist and "Ata-

[25] M. Charlot, *ibid.*, pp. 241—243.

[26] Martin Gruberg; *Women in American Politics*, Academia Press, 1968 pp. 123, 142.

türkçü" orientations of these cabinets.[27] The case of Mrs. Nermin Neftçi is particularly significant because it vividly illustrates the fact that politics at the highest echelons is rather closed to women's access. Mrs. Neftçi was in fact one of the few women politicians who chose to start her political career with grass roots politics. She worked in the lower echelons of her party (CHP) for many years, she competed with her male collegues at every level, and she succeeded in entering the parliament after some severe struggles. Yet, she arrived at the highest ranks of real political power not because of her past-efforts but due to a coincidence that enable her to become a member of an unusual and extraordinary cabinet. It is ironical to note that parliament did not give this cabinet a vote of confidence thus voiding Mrs. Neftçi, as the Minister of Cultural Affairs, from any political power.

The modalities of women's participation in political life at various levels lead us to the conclusion that women's role and place have always been limited, extraordinary and symbolic. This observation needs to be explained. We can think of two different lines of explanation. One line will lead us to look at some more directly political variables. With this hope, we shall now investigate the social backgrounds that women politicians seem to share as a group.

Social Backgrounds of Women Politicians: Elite Within An Elite

a. *Parliamentarians*

The group of women parliamentarians who served in the period of 1935—1977 share two characteristics in common.[28] The first one is that women representatives form an "exceptionally well educated" group. 68.1% of the women deputies have a university degree, 27.5% of them have graduated from either a lycee or a technical school of the same level, and only 2.9% have a primary school education. The second charac-

[27] The first cabinet in which a woman was appointed as the Minister of National Health and Social Welfare (Dr. Türkân Akyol) was the Erim Government which was formed after the 12 March 1971 military ultimatum. This cabinet was in power for 8 and a half months; Mrs. Akyol and ten other ministers resigned as a reaction to the government's failure to pass the promised reforms. The Second cabinet in which Mrs. Neftçi was appointed as the Minister of Cultural Affairs, served as a care-taker government for 4 and a half months, until a new government was elected.

[28] For a more detailed study of the backgrounds and attitudes of parliamentarian women, Cf. Tekeli, *ibid.*, pp. 363—412.

teristic that they share in common is that a great majority of women deputies are professional women. The proportion of "housewives" is only 8.7%, and the spectrum of professions that the women have is very large.

If we compare the educational backgrounds of women deputies with that of men, we see that women are the much better educated group. Frederick Frey indicates that for the period of 1920—57, 62% of the male deputies were university graduates, 10% were high school graduates, and 11% had less education.[29] The significance of this comparison is clear: male deputies are so well educated compared to the entire population that they form an elite but women are even better educated than they are. And if we keep in mind the fact that the female population in Turkey is less educated than the male population, then it appears that women deputies form a group that it would be legitimate to call the "elite of an elite". This also means that there is practically no similarity between the women representatives and the population that they are supposed to represent. The findings of an interview with women deputies confirm this situation. Within our sample, only about 5% felt that they represented women.

b. *Women representatives in local politics*

On the whole, women's participation in local politics is not very much different from what it is at the national level. But, in a few of the "big cities" like İstanbul women's participation in politics is significantly higher than at the parliamentary level. The proportion of women members who served in the two successive Municipal Assemblies of İstanbul from 1969 to 1977 is 7.7% and 9.8% respectively. What kind of women serve in the Municipal Assemblies? Is there a difference between those women who are elected to the parliament and these local politicians? The social backgrounds of the local politicians are indeed significantly different from those of the parliamentarians. In fact, the majority of the local politicians have a primary school or lycee education, and most of them are housewives. This means that they are more representative of the female population as compared to the parliamentarians.

We believe that the structural difference that exists among local and national women representatives gives us the key to explain why there is

[29] Fredrick W. Frey, *The Turkish Political Elite*, MIT Press, 1965, p. 44.

such a small number of women in the parliament and why they appear to be more successful in local politics.

We must consider two factors which are part of the political culture in Turkish society. One is related to the assumed hierarchy that exists between the different instances where political decisions are made. Parliamentary decision-making is assumed to be more important and more critical, and therefore it has a higher rank in the hierarchy of decision-making bodies. The local political instance is assumed to be less important, less critical and therefore it is placed at a lower level than parliamentary decision-making. The second cultural element that is relevant here is related to the assumed hierarchy that exists among men and women with respect to the decision-making processes in general. According to the dominant authority relationships, men are expected to make decisions, and women are expected to obey them. This general norm has at the level of political decision-making the important consequence that political decisions must be made by men and not by women. Within this cultural context, if some women are involved in politics by overcoming these informal but yet very powerful cultural regulations then the society expects them to have some outstanding qualifications. In other words, those women who are acting against the well established cultural norms of the society are expected to be "exceptional". Exceptionality and over-qualification are the conditions for those women who get involved in politics to be tolerated for their audacity and insolence. Now we can formulate a hypothesis about the differential modes of women's participation in national and local politics. The higher the level of decision-making to which women politicians are aiming at, the higher will be the qualifications required from them; the lower the level of decision-making, the lower will be the qualifications required. This hypothesis attempts to explain why there are so few and so "exceptionally" well qualified women in the parliament, whereas there are more women involved in local politics who are also more representative of the common women.

We believe that this is a more valid explanation compared to what is usually suggested. Indeed, some observers tend to explain the higher levels of women's participation in local politics by the qualitative differences that they find between local and national political decisions. They argue that since the local political decisions are made on more concrete problems of daily life, women with their qualifications as housewives tend to be more interested in these decisions.

This, in fact explains why women participate more in local politics, but it does not explain why, even at this level, women's participation does not exceed 10%, in spite of the fact that 52% of the female population who lives in large cities, like İstanbul, are "housewives".[30]

Women's Participation In Elections

If we turn our attention from those few women politicians to the ordinary citizens, we see that there is a significant difference between men and women with respect to the modalities of their participation in elections. Maurice Duverger in his now classic study on women's participation in political life, formulated two important hypotheses about women's attitudes towards elections. One was concerned with their differential participation rates, and the other with the orientation of the vote. Women tended to vote less compared to men, and they tended to be more conservative.[31]

We tried to verify these hypotheses with the data that we had gathered for the 1973 and 1975 elections in Turkey. We must note before going into the findings of this research that these findings are not conclusive but at most are indicative, due to the limited nature of the data collected.

In order to verify the first hypothesis on the modality of participation, we used the electoral list of four polling stations selected from four different "ilçes" (counties) in İstanbul. The social and economic characteristics of each station were homogeneous and differed significantly from those of the others.[32] The first of our findings confirmed the hypothesis: women voted less than men. Their participation rate was 13.5% lower than men's. Our second finding is related to the differential impact that different "social strata" have upon the participation rates. Bourgeois and peasant women tend to vote less than the petit bourgeois and working class women. The rate of abstention is 17.1% for the first two categories,

---

[30] Cf. A. Brimo, *ibid.*, p. 97. For a valid criticism of this explanation Cf. Dogan, Narbonne, ibid, p. 169—174, especially p. 175.

[31] Maurice Duverger, La Participation des femmes à la vie politique, UNESCO, 1955.

[32] For the methodology see, Tekeli, *ibid.*, pp. 310—318. For similar studies done in France, cf. Pierre Barral, "Pour qui votent les femmes?" in Fr. Goguel, *Nouvelles Etudes de Sociologie Electorale*, A. Colin, 1956, pp. 185—194, Alain Lancelot, *l'Abstentionnisme electoral en France*, A. Colin, 1967 pp. 177—179, Madelaine Grawitz, "l'Abstentionnisme des hommes et des femmes aux Referandums d'Avril et d'Octobre 1962 dans cinq bureaux de vote de Lyon "*RFSP*, vol. XV No. 5, 1965, p. 967.

whereas for the petit bourgeois women, it is 8.9% and for the working-class women, it becomes insignificant (4.5%).

How can we explain this second finding, which is contradictory to some of the findings of Western scholars?[33] We believe that this finding is not in fact as exceptional as it appears at first sight. Indeed, Western scholars generally admit that there is a high correlation between the mode of women's participation in economic life and their voting behavior. Women who work tend to vote more than women who do not. When we look at our sample of women, we notice that they tend to participate in economic life differently in each social class. There are very few women who are economically active in the bourgeoisie, and the peasant women are "unpaid family aids". Most of the women who are working belong either to the petit bourgeoisie or to the working-class. Therefore, it would not be wrong to conclude that because they are more integrated in the global society through work, the petit bourgeois and working-class women tend to vote more.

Our third finding was about a quasi-universally valid observation about women's voting behavior. Married women tend to vote more than bachelors and widows. Married women tend to vote only 8% less than married men. Marriage is "the" institution that determines, outside of work, the political behavior of women. If it were not for marriage, women would vote less than they actually do. Thus, it is marriage that reduces the potentially higher rate of abstention among women.

The tendency among the married couples is to vote together or abstain together. In fact, in 83.8% of the married couples, the behavior of the partners is identical. Within the family, the party who tends to make the decision to vote or to abstain appears to be, mostly, the husband.[34] Among those married people who do not vote as a couple, the number of men who participate in the elections is twice as much as that of women. This demonstrates clearly that the dominant authority relationship in Turkish society is such that the political decisions are seen to be the man's responsibility, and women are expected to obey and follow their husbands' political choice.

Is this attitude valid also for the orientation of the vote. Or if we ask this question somewhat differently, do women follow their husbands' political choice in the secrecy of the voting booth? It is quite difficult to

---

[33] Lancelot, *ibid.*, p. 192—194, J. Mossuz-Lavau, M. Sineau, "Les femmes et la politique, *RFSP*, No. 5, 1976, pp. 929—956.

[34] Dogan, Narbonne, *ibid.*, pp. 92—95.

answer this question. Public opinion polls are not conclusive on this point.[35] We made a small survey on a sample of 96 villages. The findings of this survey show that women generally vote more for "religiously" oriented parties than men do. This complies with the general finding of various research studies done in the western countries, especially in those where the Catholic church is dominant.[36] In our sample, which is based upon the electoral results of the 1973 general elections, peasant women, more than peasant men, tended to favour only three groups: MSP (National Salvation Party) which is a religious and conservative party, TBP (Turkish Unitarian Party) which is a religious-sectarian but rather left-oriented party, and the group of independents. Therefore, it is reasonable to claim that women are more open to religious influences. But it is not so easy to conclude that women are more conservative than men. Their preferential vote for the independents might be a consequence of women's relatively higher sensitivity towards the personality of a candidate rather than to the program of a political party.[37]

Conclusion

We have suggested in the first part of this paper that in the eyes of the political authorities who granted women their political rights, women were to play a "symbolic" role which was crucial for the image that these authorities wanted to create.

A study of the effective mode of participation of women in political life shows that, in reality, women's role in the political system has remained a "symbolic" one. Very few women are politically active, and they seldom play any politically significant role. We have also seen that women are less interested in elections, that they vote less, and that their political choices largely depend upon the influence of two major institutions, namely the "family" and "religion", which are relatively more effective on women than on men.

This leads us to the conclusion that women—that is half of the citizens—do not effectively participate in the political life of the country. They live at the margin of politics. They are not full members of the political

[35] Nermin Abadan-Unat and al. "Kim kime niçin oy veriyor?" Milliyet, Sep. 1975. Kenan Bulutoğlu and al. "İşçiler kime neden oy veriyor?" *Milliyet*, Oct. 1969.

[36] Dogan, Narbonne, *ibid.*, pp. 97—102.

[37] Madelaine Grawitz; "l'Accès des Femmes à la vie politique et la personnalisation du pouvoir" in *Referandum de 1962*, FNSP, 1965.

society, in spite of the formal equality of political rights that they enjoy with men. Why is this so? Why do women believe that politics is not their business? We think that this is the most critical question as the answer to it explains what occurs at the various levels of political participation. Women, in general, believe that politics is not their business; they are inclined to vote less; they are even less inclined to work in the political parties and organizations. There are very few women who take responsibility at the higher echelons of these institutions; there are even fewer women who become candidates for political office and only a handful of women finally succeed in becoming a member of a political decision-making body.

Then, what is most critical to explain is the candid observation which appears to be at the base of this chain of causalities. Why do women believe that politics is not their business? This belief is a part of the political culture of our polity. This political culture is shaped by the ideology of the dominant social classes. This is the political culture that Turkey shares more and more with many other countries in the capitalist world. In order to understand the real mechanisms of this cultural and ideological structure, we must look at the functioning of the social structures that are generally effective in capitalistic social formations. It is the basic social division of labour between men and women that attributes to them their social roles. Men are responsible for production under the capitalist relationships of production, whereas women are responsible mainly for reproduction. This social division of labour creates a separation between the unit of production which is the place of work—a factory or a bureau—and the unit of reproduction which is the family. Women who are primarily responsible for reproduction, live and work in the house. Female domestic labour is a particular form and category of labour.[38] A consequence of their seclusion from the social relations of production is that women are also secluded from the social decision-making processes as well. Men are almost exclusively responsible for social and political decision-making since they are a part of the social relations of production. Political culture reproduces at the level of ideology these basic social relationships. Therefore, it would be surprising if women had felt and behaved other than they actually do in all those societies where the capitalistic relations of production are dominant.

---

[38] Wally Seccombe, "The Housewife and Her Labour under Capitalism" *New Left Review*, No. 83 Jan—Feb. 1973. Jean Gardiner, "Women's Domestic Labour" *CSE Bulletin*, June 1975.

SELECTED BIBLIOGRAPHY

I. Women from the Historical Perspective

Abadan-Unat, Nermin. "Turkey". In: *Women in the Modern World*, Ed. R. Patai. New York, Free Press, 1967.

Danforth, S. "Ideas of 19th Century Turkish Intellectuals about Women in Turkish Society". 1974, 1—53. (Mimeo)

Davis, Fanny (Ellsworth). *Two centuries of the Ottoman lady*. New York, Columbia University, 1968. (Tylers Green, University Microfilms, 1971). 434 L. (Ph. D. Thesis).

Turkish University Women's Association, Ankara. *Women in Turkey*. Ankara, Ajans-Türk Matbaası, 1972. 59 p. (Turkish University Women's Association Pub. No: 7).

Üçok, Bahriye, *Women Sovereigns in Islamic States*. Istanbul, Istanbul Matbaası, 1975. 124 s. renkli planş. (Publication of the RCD Cultural Institute).

II. Women's Rights

Abadan-Unat, Nermin. "Major challenges faced by Turkish women: Legal emancipation, urbanization, industrialization". *Milletlerarası Münasebetler Türk Yıllığı* (Ankara), 14, 1974,

Abadan-Unat, Nermin. "The place of Turkish women in the society". *RCD Ülkelerinde Yürürlükte Bulunan Kanunlar Çerçevesinde Kadınların Statüsü* (Ankara), 12—14 Kasım 1968, II y. (Türkiye Üniversiteli Kadınlar Derneği, Ankara Şubesi, Dışişleri Bakanlığı).

Abadan-Unat, Nermin. "The Modernization of Turkish Women". *The Middle East Journal*, Summer 1978.

Abadan-Unat, Nermin. "Women Movements and National Liberation, the Turkish Case". Paper presented at the 9th ISA World Congress, Uppsala 1978.

Afetinan, A. *The Emancipation of the Turkish Women*. Paris, Unesco, 1962. 63 p.

Atabek, Reşat. "Women in the Turkish Family Law". *RCD Ülkelerinde Yürürlükte Bulunan Kanunlar Çerçevesinde Kadınların Statüsü*. Ankara, 12—14 Kasım 1968. 7 y. (Türkiye Üniversiteli Kadınlar Derneği, Ankara Şubesi, Dışişleri Bakanlığı).

Dönmezer, Sulhi. "La Protection de la famille et les infractions contre la morale sexuelle dans le droit pénal Turc". *Annales de la Faculté de Droit d'Istanbul*, 15(21/22), 1965, 99—114.

Işık, Demet. "The Legal Status of Women". In: *Women in Turkey*. 23—32. (Turkish University Women's Association Publications No: 7).

Jennings, Ronald C. "Women in Early 17th Century Ottoman Judical Records. The Sharia Court of Anatolian Kayseri". *Journal of the Economic and Social History of the Orient* (Leiden), XVIII(1), 53—114.

Magnarella, Paul J. "The Reception of Swiss Family Law in Turkey". *Anthropological Quarterly* (Washington, D. C.), 46(2), 1973, 100—116.

Taşkıran, Tezer. *Turkish Women Rights* (50. Yılında Türk Kadın Hakları), Ankara 1973, Başbakanlık Basımevi, p. 81.

Uluocak, Nihal Erdener. "Legal Status of Turkish Women with Respect to International Convention". *RCD Ülkelerinde Yürürlükte Bulunan Kanunlar Çerçevesinde Kadınların Statüsü*, Ankara, 12—14 Kasım 1968. 7 y. (Üniversiteli Kadınlar Derneği, Ankara Şubesi, Dışişleri Bakanlığı).

III. Political Participation

Abadan-Unat, Nermin. "Values and Political Behaviour of Turkish Youth". *The Turkish Yearbook of International Relations*. Ankara, 1963. 81—102.

Danforth, Sandra C. "Women's Political Participation in the Ottoman Empire and the Turkish Republic. A comparative analysis". Middle East Studies Association Convention. Louisville, Kentucky, November 1975, 1—32.

Daver, Bülent. "Political Rights of Women". *Ankara Üniversitesi Siyasal Bilgiler Fakültesi Dergisi*, 23(4), Aralık 1968, 111—120.

Ergil, Gül. "Analysis of Women Oriented Policy outlines and indirect Implication in the Three Five Year Plans". In: Türk toplumunda kadın. Ed.: N. Abadan-Unat. Türk Sosyal Bilimler Derneği Yayını, Ankara 1979.

Field, Gary R. *Political Involvement and Political Orientations of Turkish Law Students*. Unpublished Ph. D. Thesis, 1964.

IV. Economy and Women

Abadan-Unat, Nermin. 'Implications of Migration on Emancipation and Pseudo Emancipation of Turkish Women". *International Migration Rewiev*, Vol. 11 No. 1, Spring 1977.

Abadan-Unat, Nermin. "Turkish Workers in West Germany. A Case Study". *Ankara Üniversitesi Siyasal Bilgiler Fakültesi Dergisi*, 24(1), Mart 1969, 21—49.

Çiftçi, Oya. "Women at Work". *Turkish Public Administration Review*, No. 2, 1975.

Çulpan, Oya—L. Murty—A. Marzotto. "Division of Labour in the Family: A Comparison of two Centuries". Paper presented at *Western Social Science Association Conference*, Colorado, Denver, 1977.

Işık, Demet. "Social and Economic Rights of the Working Women". *RCD Ülkelerinde Yürürlükte Bulunan Kanunlar Çerçevesinde Kadınların Statüsü Semineri*. Ankara, 12—14 Kasım 1968. Düzenleyen: Türkiye Üniversiteli Kadınlar Derneği, Ankara Şubesi ve Dışişleri Bakanlığının İşbirligi, 12. y.

Kardam, Filiz. *The Industrial Entrepreneur and the Industrial Workers in Adana:* A Case Study. Doktora tezi. London School of Economics and Political Science, 1976. 422 s.

Koray, Tanfer. *Working Women in Turkey*. 1975, University of Pennsylvania. (Ph. D. Thesis).

Kundakçıoğlu, Cihan. *A Survey of Facts and Opinions Concerning the Increasing Number of Working Women in Turkey and its implications on the Problems of Marketing*. Istanbul, 1966. 121 s. (M. A. Thesis, Robert College).

Raj, Mohini Seth. *Modernization of Working Women in Developing Societies*, New Delhi, National Publication House, 1976.

Tanfer, Koray. *Working Women: a Study of Female Labour Force and Determinants of Participation in six Large Cities of Turkey, 1970*. Pennsylvania University, 1975. XXX, 300 y. (Ph. D. Thesis).

United Nations Seminar on the Effects of Scientific and Technological Developments on the Status of Women. *Women in Turkey*. Iaşi, Romania, 5—18 Agustos 1969. 20 y. (Teksir). (Documents U. N.).

Yüksekışık, Nadire. "Women in Science". In: *Women in Turkey*. 33—37. (Turkish University Women Association Publication No: 7).

V. Social Change

Abadan-Unat, Nermin. *Social Change and Turkish Women*. Ankara, Ankara Üniversitesi Basımevi, 1963. VII and 36 s. (Publication of the Faculty of Political Science of the University of Ankara, No: 171—153).

Aswad, Barbara. "Key and Peripheral Roles of Noble Women in a Middle Eastern Plains Village". *Anthropological Quarterly* (Washington, D. C.), 40(3), 1967.

Başaran, Fatma. *Attitudes Towards Towns*. Araştırma (V, 1967)' den ayrıbasım. Ankara, Ankara University Press, 1969. 123—129.

Başaran, Fatma. *A Psycho-Sociological Research about Attitude Changes in Diyarbakır Villages*. Ankara, Ankara University Press, 1969.

Benedict, P. "The Kabul Günü: Structural Visiting in an Anatolian Provincial Town". *Anthropological Quarterly*, Vol. 47, 1974. 28—47.

Davis, Fanny (Ellsworth). *Turkish Women*. New York, Turkish Information Service. (1967), 22 p., illus.

Fox, K.—Greer Litton. "Some Determinants of Modernism Among Women in Turkey, Ankara". *J. MARR and Family* (Minneapolis), Aug. 1973, 520—

Kâğıtçıbaşı, Çiğdem. "Social Norm and Authoritarianism: A Comparison of Turkish and American Adolescents". *Journal of Personality and Social Psychology*, 16(3), 1970, 444—451.

Kandiyoti, Deniz. "Sex Roles and Social Change: A Comparative Appraisal of Turkey's Women". *SIGNS Journal of Women in Culture and Society* (Chicago), 3(1), Fall 1977, 57—73.

Kandiyoti, Deniz. "Social Change and Family Structure in a Turkish Village". In: *Mediterranean Kinship*. Ed.: J. Peristiany, New Hampshire, American Universities Field Staff Press, 1975.

Kandiyoti, Deniz. *Women in Turkish Society*. Seminar report. Istanbul, Mayıs 16—19, Ankara, Türk Sosyal Bilimler Dernegi, 1978. 79 s.

Kıray, Mübeccel. "Small Town Women". *Women in Turkish Society*. Ed.: N. Abadan-Unat. Leiden, E. J. Brill.

Kut, Sema. "Women in the Social Sphere". In: *Women in Turkey*. Ankara, 16—18. (Turkish University Women's Association Publication No: 7).

Magnarella, Paul I. "From Villager to Townsman in Turkey". *Middle East Journal*, 1970.

Mansur, Fatma. "Women in Turkish Society". In: *Women of the Middle East*. Eds.: N. Kiddie and L. Beck. Cambridge, Mass., Harvard University Press.

Roper, Joyce. *The Women of Nar*. London, Faber and Faber, 1974. 179 p. illus.

Schnaiberg, Allen. *Some Determinants and Consequences of Modernism in Turkey*. Ann Arbor, University of Michigan, 1968. (Tylers Green, High Wycombe, University Microfilms, 1970). 357 L. (Ph. D. Thesis).

Suzuki, P. "Encounters with Istanbul: Urban Peasants and Village Peasants". *International Journal of Comparative Sociology* (Leiden), 5(2), 1964, 208—216.

Şahinkaya, Rezan. "Women in Rural Areas". In: *Women in Turkey*. 19—22. (Turkish University Women Association Publication No: 7).

Tüzün, Zerrin. "The Present Social Status of Turkish Women and its Relation with Education". *RCD Ülkelerinde Yürürlükte Bulunan Kanunlar Çerçevesinde Kadınların Statüsü Semineri*. Ankara, 12—14 Kasım 1968, 8 y. (Türkiye Üniversiteli Kadınlar Derneği, Dışişleri Bakanlığı).

U. N. Division of Social Affairs. *European Seminar on the Changing Roles of Men and Women in Modern Society: Functions, Rights and Responsibilities*. Groningen, Netherlands, 28 March—5 April 1977.

Ülker, Hilmi Ziya. "Evolution de la condition féminine en Turquie" (Türkiye'de Kadının Cemiyet içindeki Durumunun Gelişmesi). *Sosyoloji Dergisi* (Istanbul), (15), 1960, 140—152.

VI. Population, Urbanization, Migration, Health

Abadan-Unat, Nermin. "The Place of Turkish Women in Society. Türk Kadının Nüfusunun Toplumdaki Yeri". *Ankara Üniversitesi Siyasal Bilgiler Fakültesi Dergisi*, 23(4), Aralık 1968, 131—158.

Abadan-Unat, Nermin. "Turkish External Migration and Social Mobility". In: *Turkey: Geographic and Social Perspectives*. Eds.: P. Benedict—E. Tümertekin—F. Mansur. Leiden, B. J. Brill, 1974. 362—402 (Social and Political Studies of the Middle East, Vol. 9).

Abadan-Unat, Nermin. "Implication of Migration on Emancipation and Pseudo-Emancipation of Turkish Women". *International Migration Review* (New York), 11(1), Sprıng 1977.

Aybay, Aydın. "A Survey of the Gecekondu act 1966, from the Standpoint of Effective Land Use". *Annales de la Faculte de Droit d'Istanbul*, 23(39), 1975, 203—207.

Berelson, Bernard. "Turkey: National Survey on Populations". In: *Studies in Family Planning*. No: 5, Population Council, 1964.

Cerit, Sevil. *Fertility and Contraceptive Usage in Ankara Gecekondu Areas*. Hacettepe University Faculty of the Graduate School, 1971. 88 p. (Thesis).

Demeny, Paul—Frederic C. Shorter. *Estimating Turkish Mortality, Fertility and Age Structure*. Istanbul, Sermet Matbaası, 1968.

Fişek, Nusret. "Epidemiological Study on Abortion in Turkey". *A Hazard to Public Health*. Ed.: Isam R. Nazer, Beirut, Lebanon, LPPF, 1972.

Frey, Frederick Ward. "The Mass Media and Rural Development in Turkey". *Rural Development Project Report No:* 6. Cambridge, Mass., Massachusetts Institute of Technology, 1966.

Frey, Frederick Ward. "Regional Variations in Turkey". *Rural Development Project Report No: 4*. Cambridge, Mass., Massachusetts Institute of Technology, 1966.

Frey, Frederick Ward. *Rural Development. Research Project Preliminary Report* y. y. and y., 1966. 179 p. Metin teksirdir.

Frey, Frederick Ward. "Socialization to National Identification among Turkish Peasants". *Advanced Seminar in the Social Sciences*. Paper presented at the Abant Seminar, 1966.

Hart, Charles W. M. "Peasants Come to Town". *Social Aspects of Economic Development*. A paper presented at a symposium held in Istanbul, 1964.

Hinderink, J.—M. Kıray. *Social Stratification as an Obstacle to Development: A study of four Turkish Villages*. New York, Praeger, 1970. 248 p., illus., maps.

Kâğıtçıbaşı, Çiğdem. *Cultural Values and Population Action Programs: Turkey*. Prepared for the United Nations Educational Scientific and Cultural Organization. Istanbul, Boğaziçi Üniversitesi Matbaası, 1977. 158 y.

Karpat, Kemal. *The Gecekondu: Rural Migration and Urbanization*. Cambridge, Cambridge University Press, 1976. 291 p.

Goldberg, David—Greer Litton, "Family Planning Observations and an Interpretative Scheme Turkish Demography". *Proceedings of a Conference*. Hacettepe University, Ankara, 219—240. (Hacettepe University Publication No: 7).

Gürkaynak, Ipek. *Impact of Social and Environmental Factors on Fertility Behaviour: Turkey and U. S.* Kansas University (Master Thesis).

Güvenç, Bozkurt. *Family Planning in Turkey*. Ankara, CENTO Organization, 1971.

Kıray, Mübeccel. "Squatter Housing, fast De-Peasantization and Slow Workerization in Underdeveloped Countries". A paper presented at the 7. *World Congress of Sociology*. Varna, Sept. 1970.

Kişnişçi, Hüsnü. "Interrelations between the Socio-Economic Status of Women and Fertility in Turkey". *United Nations Seminar on the Status of Women and Family Planning*. Istanbul, Turkey 11—24 July, 1972. 31 p.

Levine, Ned. "Old Culture—New Culture: A Study of Migrants in Ankara, Turkey" *Social Forces*, 51(3), March 1973.

Levine, Ned. "Rural-Urban Migration and its Effects on Urbanization over the Next Fifty Years". Paper presented to the *Conference on Development Trends in Turkey (1974—2024)*. Ankara, June 10—15, 1974.

Levine, Ned. "Value Orientation among Migrants in Ankara, Turkey: A Case Study" *Journal of Asian and African Studies* (Leiden), 8(1—2), 1973, 50—68.

Mansur, Fatma. *Bodrum. A Town in the Aegean*. Leiden, E. J. Brill, 1972.

Özbay, Ferhunde. "*Differential Fertility in Rural Turkey: Individual and Environmental Factors*. Cornell University, 1975. (Unpublished Ph. D. Thesis).

Özbay, Ferhunde—Frederic C. Shorter. "Fertility and Family Planning in the Etimesğut Rural Health Region". In: *Turkish Demography: Proceedings of a Conference*. Eds.: F. C. Shorter and B. Güvenç. Ankara, 1969. 310 p. (Hacettepe University Publications, No: 7).

Özbay, Ferhunde—Frederic C. Shorter. "*Turkey:* Changes in Birth Control Practices, 1963 to 1968". In: *Studies in Family Planning*. 51, March 1970, 1—7.

Özbay, Ferhunde—Frederic C. Shorter—Samire Yener. "Accounting for the Trend of Fertility in Turkey". Presented in UN/UNFPA Expert Group Meeting on *Demographic Transition and Socio-Economic Development*. Istanbul, 27 April—4 May 1977. (in print).

Schnaiberg, Allen. "The Modernizing Impact of Urbanization. A Causal Analysis" *Economic Development and Cultural Change*. (Chicago), October 1971, 80—104.

Schnaiberg, Allen. "Rural-Urban Residence and Modernism. A Study of Ankara Province, Turkey". *Demography* (Chicago), 7 (1), February 1970, 71—85.

Sergün, Ümit. *Population Increase in Turkey and its Problems*. Reprinted from Review of the Geographical Institute of the University of Istanbul. International ed. 1974—1976, No: 15. Istanbul, 1977, 145—157.

Sewell, Granville H. *Squatter Settlements in Turkey: An Analysis of a Social, Political and Economic Problem*. Massachusetts Institute of Technology, Cambridge, Mass., 1964. (Unpublished Ph. D. Dissertation).

Şenyapılı, Tansı. "Integration Through Mobility". *Orta Doğu Teknik Üniversitesi Mimarlık Fakültesi Dergisi* (Ankara), 3(2), Güz 1977.

Shorter, Frederic C. "Information on Fertility, Mortality and Population Growth in Turkey". In: *Population Index* (Princeton), 34(1), January—March 1968, 3—22.

Shorter, Frederic C.—Belgin Tekçe. "The Demographic Determinants of Urbanization in Turkey". In: *Turkey: Geographic and Social Perspectives*. Eds.: P. Benedict, E. Tümertekin, F. Mansur. Leiden, E. J. Brill, 1974. 281—294. (Social Economic and Political Studies of the Middle East. Vol: 9).

Stirling, Paul. *Turkish Village*. New York, John Wiley and Sons, 1965.

Stycos, J. M.—R. H. Willer, "Female Working Roles and Fertility". In: Demography 4. 210—217.

VII. Family and Sex Roles

Atabek, Reşat. "Woman in the Turkish Family Law". *RCD Ülkelerinde Yürürlükte Bulunan Kanunlar Çerçevesinde Kadınların Statüsü Semineri*. Ankara, 12—14 Kasım 1968, 7 y. (Türkiye Üniversiteli Kadınlar Derneği, Ankara Şubesi—Dışişleri Bakanlığı).

Erdentuğ, Nermin. "Family Structure and Marriage Customs of a Turkish Village". In: *Readings in Rural Sociology*. Istanbul, Boğaziçi University Publication, 1977 84—96.

Fallers, L.—M. Fallers. "Man and Women in Ereğli". Paper presented in the social and anthropological meeting of the *Mediterranean Social Science Council on Family Structure in Mediterranean*. Nicosia, 1970.

Fallers, L.—M. Fallers. "Sex Role in Edremit". In: *Mediterranean Family Structure*. Ed.: J. Peristiany. Cambridge, Cambridge University Press, 1976. 243—260.

Fox, K.—Green Litton. "Another Look at the Comparative Resources Model: Assessing Balance of Power in Turkey Marriages". *J. Marr. and Family* (Minneapolis), 1973, 718—729.

Fox, K.—Green Litton. "Love Match and Arranged Marriage in a Modernizing Nation Mate Selection in Ankara, Turkey". *J. Marr. and Family* (Minneapolis), February 1975, 180—193.

Fox, K.—Green Litton. *Some Determinants of Marital Behaviour in Ankara, Turkey*. Ann Arbor, University of Michigan, 1970. Tylers Green, University Microfilms, 1971. 262 L. (Thesis).

Holmstrom, Engin Inel. "Changing Sex Roles in a Developing Country". *Journal of Marriage and Family*, 35(3), 1978, 546—553.

Kâğıtçibaşı, Çiğdem. "Modernity and the Role of Women in Turkey". In: *Boğaziçi Üniversitesi Dergisi*. Sosyal Bilimler 3(5027), 83—90.

Kâğıtçıbaşı, Çiğdem. *The Value of Children in Turkey, Perspectives and Preliminary Findings*. Tenth Annual Meeting of MESA, Los Angeles, Nov. 10—13, 1976. 29 s.

Kıray, Mübeccel. "Changing Roles of Mothers: Changing Intra-Family. Relations in a Turkish Town". In: *Mediterranean Family Structures*. Ed.: J Peristiany. Cambridge, Cambridge University Press, 1976. 414 p.

Kıray, Mübeccel. "The Family of the Immigrant Worker". In: *Turkish Workers in Europe 1960—1975*. Ed.: N. Abadan-Unat. Leiden, E. J. Brill, 1976.

Kongar, Emre. "Some Comparative Characteristics of Gecekondu Families in Izmir". *METU Studies in Development* (Ankara), (4), Spring 1972, 643—656.

Kudat, Ayşe. "The Migrant Family Children; the Turkish Case". *Migration News*, 26(2), Temmuz-Eylül 1977, 16—22.

Le Compte, William F.—Güney K. Le COMPTE. "Generational Attribution in Turkish and American Youth. A Study of Social Norms Involving the Family". *Journal of Cross-Cultural Psychology*, (4(2), 1973, 175—191.

Levine, Ned. "Divorce in Turkey". *2nd Conference on Demography*. Çeşme, September 29—October 1, 1975. Sponsored by Hacettepe Institute of Population Studies.

Magnarella, Paul J. "Aspects of Kinship Change in a Modernizing Turkish Town". *Human Organization* (New York), 31, Winter 1972. 361—371.

Magnarella, Paul J. "Conjugal Role—Relationships in a Modernizing Turkish Town". *International Journal of Sociology of the Family* (Illinois), 2(2), 1972, 179—192.

Sertel, Ayşe Kudat. "Ritual Kinship in Eastern Turkey". *Anthropological Quarterly* (Washington. D. C.), 44(1), 1971, 35—50.

Sertel, Ayşe Kudat. "Sex Differences in Status and Attitudes in Rural Turkey". *Hacettepe Bulletin of Social and Human Sciences* (Ankara), 4(1), Haziran 1972, 4—79.

Spencer, R. F. "Aspects of Turkish Kinship and Social Structure". *Anthropological Quarterly* (Washington, D. C.), 33(1), January 1960, 40—50.

Stirling, A. Paul. "Land, Marriage, and Law in Turkish Villages". *International Social Science Bulletin* (Paris), 9, 1957, 21—33.

Suzuki, P. "Peasants Without Plows: Some Anatolians in Istanbul". *Rural Sociology* (Urbana), 31(4), 1966, 428—438.

Suzuki, P. "Village Solidarity among Turkish Peasants Undergoing Urbanization". *Science* (New York), 132(3431), 30 Sept., 1960, 891—.

Tezcan, Sabahat. *A Comparative Study of Induced Abortion in Turkey using the Randomised Response Technique Versus Direct Questioning.* School of Public Health, University of North Carolina at Chapel Hill, U. S. A. (Ph. D. Thesis).

Timur, Serim. *Fertility and Related Attitudes among Two Social Classes in Ankara, Turkey.* Cornell University, June 1965. (Unpublished M. A. Thesis).

Timur, Serim. "Socio-Economic Determinants of Differential Fertility in Turkey". *Second European Conference.* Strasbourg, August 1971. (Mimeo.)

Timur, Serim—N. Fincancıoğlu. "Socio-Economic and Demographic Characteristics of Turkish I U D Acceptions". In: *Turkish Demography.* Eds.: F. Shorter, B. Güvenç. Ankara, 1969. (Hacettepe University Publications No: 7).

Toros, Aykut. "Condoms in Turkish Family Planning". *IPPF Medical Bulletin* (London), 7(1), February 1973.

Toros, Aykut. *Some Social and Demographic Correlates of Women who are Reluctant. to Prevent Conception After Achieving Desired Family Size: Tarsus, Turkey, 1969.* 1972, 58 s. (A Thesis).

The Turkish Family Planning Association. *A Historical Review of Activities, 1963—1971.* Ankara, Ayyıldız Matbaası, 1972. 24 s.

Yasa, Ibrahim. "Gecckondu Families in Ankara and Some Problems Regarding the City". *Ankara Üniversitesi Siyasal Bilgiler Fakültesi Dergisi,* 22(4), Aralık 1967, 75—83.

Yasa, Ibrahim. "The Gecekondu Family". *Ankara Üniversitesi Siyasal Bilgiler Fakültesi Dergisi,* 27(3), Eylül 1973, 5—7.

Yasa, Ibrahim. "Traditions of Some Atypical Cases of Marriage in Turkey". *Ankara Üniversitesi Siyasal Bilgiler Fakültesi Dergisi,* 24(1), Mart 1969, 1—19.

Yücel, Asuman. *The Squatter Areas and the Employment Problems with Special Reference to the City of Ankara.* Devlet Planlama Dairesi, 1970.

VIII. Education

Baymur, Feriha. "Women and Education". In: *Women in Turkey.* 7—15. (Turkish University Women's Association Publication No: 7).

Fişek Nusret H.—K. Sünbüloğlu. "The Effects of Husband and Wife Education on Family Planning in Rural Turkey". *Studies in Family Planning,* 9(10/11), Ekim-Kasım 1978, 280—285.

Le Compte, Güney—W. LE COMPTE. "Effects of Education and Intercultural Contact on Traditional Attitudes in Turkey". *Journal of Social Psychology* (Provincetown), 80, 1970, 11ffl21.

Özbay, Ferhunde.—Balamir Nefise. *School Attendance and Its Correlates in Turkish Villages 1975.* Unprinted Report. Hacettepe Institute of Population Studies.

Timur, Serim. "Demographic Correlates on Woman's Education: Fertility, Age at Marriage and the Family". *International Population Conference, Mexico 1977,* 11. 1. 2. International Union for the Scientific Study of Population.

Yenerman, Münevver. "L'éducation Feminine dans les Pays en Voie de Développement". *Mason Dergisi* (Istanbul), 23(13), Ekim 1973, 14—17.

IX. Women and Literature

Doğramacı, Emel. "The Novelist Halide Edip Adıvar and Turkish Feminism". *The World of Islam.* Leiden, E. J. Brill, 14, 1971. 71—115.

Doğramacı, Emel. "Turkish Women in Turkish Literature of 19th Century". *Hacettepe Bulletin of Social Sciences and Humanities* (Ankara), Part I, 2(1), June 1970, Part II, 2(2), Dec. 1970.

Doğramacı, Emel. "Turkish Women in Turkish Literature of the 19th Century". *The World of Islam*. 13(1—3). Leiden, E. J. Brill, 1969.

Doğramacı, Emel. "Ziya Gökalp and Turkish Feminism". *The World of Islam*. (Baskida).

Samurçay, Neriman. "Women in the Fine Arts and Literature". In: *Women in Turkey*. 33—37. (Turkish University Women's Association Publication No: 7).

Sönmez, Emel. "Turkish Women in Turkish Literature of the 19th Century". *Die Welt des Islams* (Leiden), 12(1—3), 1969, 1ffl73.

REFERENCE LISTS

Reference list of Sabahat Tezcan's chapter

Akın, Ayşe, "An Epidemiological Study on the gynecological Complaints, Diseases and their Determinants in Rural Ergazi Area" Thesis Submitted to the Community Medicine Department of Medical Faculty, Hacettepe University, 1970.

Akın, Ayşe, "Ergazi Sağlık Ocağı Köysel Bölgesinde jinekolojik şikâyetler, hastalıklar ve sebebleri üzerine epidemiyolojik araştırma", Hacettepe Üniv., 1970.

Akın, Ayşe. "Abortion Problem from the Health Viewpoint of Women." Thesis submitted to the Community Medicine Department of Medical Faculty, Hacettepe University, 1976.

Baysal, Coşkun. "Criminal Abortions and Family Planning in Turkey." *Medical Bulletin of Zeynep Kâmil* Maternity Hospital, U. 3 : 1, 24–32, 1971.

Baysal, Coşkun, "Türkiye'de kriminal abortuslar ve aile planlaması" *Zeynep Kâmil Tıp Bülteni*, 3.1, 24–32, 1971.

Bölükbaşı, Süheyla. "Demographic and Medical Analysis of 469 Cases of Abortion Admitted to Hacettepe Hospital" Thesis Submitted to Ob.Gyn.Dept, Medical School, Hacettepe University, Ankara, 1974.

Burak, Zekai T. Some Observations on Abortion and Contraceptive Measure in Turkish Criminal Law and General Health Hygiene Law, Ankara, 1960.

Egemen, Ayten. "Determination of Health Status of women in Childbearing ages in Sincan, Etimesğut." Thesis Submitted to the Community Medicine Department, Medical Faculty, Hacettepe University, 1972.

Egemen, Ayten, "Sincan'da 15–44 yaşlar arası evli kadınların sağlik düzeylerinin saptanması ile ilgili araştırma" Hacettepe Üniv., 1972.

Erenus, N. *Abortions*, Gürsoy press, Ankara, 1967.

Esendal, Ahmet. "Controlled Pregnancy, Birth Control and Preventive Medicine." *Journal of Medical Faculty, Ankara University*, 15: 4, 1962.

Esendal, Ahmet, "Ana Sağlığı bakımından güdümlü gebelik, doğum kontrolü ve koruyucu hekimlik", *Ankara Üniversitesi Tıp Fak.* Mec. 15: 4, 1962.

Fişek, Nusret H. "Results of Interviews on Maternal and Childhood Deaths in 137 Villages." *Investigations on Practice of Birth Control in Turkey*, edited by Ragıp Üner, Nusret H. Fişek, Publication of the Ministry of Health No 264, 1960.

Fişek, Nusret H. "Epidemiological Status on Abortion in Turkey" in *Induced Abortion: A Hazard to Public Health*, edited Isom Nazer, Beirut, Lebanon, 1972.

Fişek, Nusret, "Epidemiological Study on Abortion in Turkey", Ed. I. Nazer, *Induced Abortion. A Hazard to Public Health* IPPF, Beirut, 1972.

Fişek, Nusret H. "An investigation on determining the priorities in preventing Diseases in Turkey" *Toplum ve Hekim* No. 1, 1977.

Güven, Sabahat. "Determination of Health Status of Women in Childbearing ages in Yenikent, Etimesğut" Thesis Submitted to the Community Medicine Department, Medical Faculty, Hacettepe University, 1972.

Hacettepe University, Institute of Community Medical 1975. An Account of the Activities of the Etimesğut Rural Health District 1970–1974 Hacettepe Ankara.

Kişnişçi, H.; Akın, A. "An Epidemiological Study on Abortion in Turkey." paper presented at the Second Demography Meeting, Sept. 29–Oct. 1, Çeşme, İzmir Turkey, 1975.

Kişnişçi, H. Akın, "Türkiye'de düşüklerle ilgili Epidemiyolojik bir araştırma", Çeşme, 29.9.-1.10. 1975, Second Turkish Population Congress, 1975.

Özbay, F.; Shorter, F. C. "Turkey: Changes in Birth Control Practices, 1963 to 1968." *Studies in Family Planning*, No. 51, pp. 1–7, 1970.

Özbay F. "Changes in Fertility and in Birth Control Practices in Turkey 1963 to 1973". paper presented at the second Demography Meeting, Sept. 29–Oct. 1, Çeşme, İzmir–Turkey, 1975.

Özbay, Ferhunde, "Türkiye'de 1963, 1968 ve 1973 yıllarında Aile Planlama si Uygulamalarında ve Doğurganlıktakı Değişmeler", Çeşme, 29.9–1.10. 1975, Second Turkish Population Congress, 1975.

Population Census of Turkey, 1% sample results, second print. Prime Ministry State Institute of Statistics page. 1, 1975.

Statistical Yearbook of Turkey, Prime Ministry State Institute of Statistics page. 63, 1975.

Tezcan, Sabahat. "A Comparative Study of Induced Abortion in Turkey using the Randomized Response Technique versus Direct Questioning" Dissertation Submitted to the Department of Epidemiology, School of Public Health, U.N.C. Chapel Hill, U.S.A., 1977.

Tezcan, Sabahat. Some unpublished data on details of induced abortion in Turkey, 1977.

Vital Statistics from the Turkish Demographic Survey 1966–1967, Hacettepe Press, Ankara, 1970.

Reference list of Ferhunde Özbay's chapter

Basaran, İbrahim E., *Türkiye'de Temel Eğitim Sorunları ve Çozüm Yolları*. Not printed. Ph.D. Thesis: Ankara University, 1974.

Boserup, Esten, *Woman's Role in Economic Development*. New York: St. Martin's Press, 1970.

Huvinic, Mayra, A Critical Review of Some Research Concepts and Concerns. *Women and Development, An Annotated Bibliography*. Overseas Development Council. 1–20, 1976.

Çavdar, Tevfik, Tunay, Demet, Yurtseven, Tuna, *Yüksek Öğrenime Başvuran Öğrenciler 1974–75*. Sosyo-Ekonomik Çözümleme. T.C. Başbakanlık Devlet Planlama Teşkilatı. Yayın No. DPT. 1496–SPD. 291, 1976.

Devlet İstatistik Enstitüsü DIE. *Milli Eğitimde 50 Yıl*. Ankara: Devlet İstatistik Enstitüsü, 1973.

Devlet İstatistik Enstitüsü. DIE. *1975 Genel Nüfus Sayımı 1% Örnekleme Sonuçları*. Ankara: Devlet İstatistik Enstitüsü, 1976.

Devlet İstatistik Enstitüsü. DIE. *1975 Genel Nüfus Sayımı İdarî Bölünüş*. Ankara: Devlet İstatistik Enstitüsü, 1977.

Ergil, Gül, *Toplumsal Yapı Araştırması Nüfus ile İlgili Gelişmeler 1950–1970*. T.C. Başbakanlık Devlet Planlama Teşkilatı. Yayın No. DPT: 1607–SPD: 298, 1977.

Erten, Özgül, *Yüzyılımızda Kadın ve Kadınlarımız*. Ankara: Türkiye Yazıları, 1978.

Fişek, Nusret H., Türkiye'de Aşırı Doğurganlık ve Kullanılan Gebeliği Önleyici Yöntemler. *Türkiye'de Nüfus Yapısı ve Nüfus Sorunları 1973 Araştırması* Ankara: Hacettepe Üniversitesi Yayınları. D–25. 97–112, 1978.

Hafnal, J., Age at Marriage and Proportions Marrying. *Population Studies*. 7(2). November. 111–136, 1953.

Kâğıtcıbaşı, Çiğdem, Modernity and the Role of Women in Turkey. *Boğaziçi Üniversitesi Dergisi*. Sosyal Bilimler. 3(5027). 83–90, 1975.
Kunt, Güliz, Aile Yapısı ve Doğurganlık. *Türkiye'de Nüfus Yapısı ve Nüfus Sorunları 1973 Araştırması*. Ankara: Hacettepe Üniversitesi Yayınları. D–25. 133–152, 1978.
Oppenheim, Karen, et al., *Social and Economic Correlates of Family Fertility: A Survey of the Evidence*. North Caroline: Research Triangle Institute, 1971.
Özbay, Ferhunde, *Differential Fertility in Rural Turkey Individual and Environmental Factors*. Not printed. Ph.D. Thesis, Cornel University, 1975.
Özbay, Ferhunde and Balamir Nefise, *School Attendance and Its Correlates in Turkish Villages 1975*. Unprinted report. Hacettepe Institute of Population Studies, 1978.
Peker, Mumtaz, Türkiye'de Insangucünün Bazı Özellikleri. *Türkiye'de Nüfus Yapısı ve Nüfus Sorunları 1973 Araştırması*. Ankara: Hacettepe Üniversitesi Yayınları. D–25. 13–48, 1978.
Tayanc, Fusun, Tayanc, Tunç, *Dünyada ve Türkiye'de Tarih Boyunca Kadın*. Ankara: Toplum Yayınevi, 1977.
Timur, Serim, Socio-Economic Determinants of Differential Fertility in Turkey. *Second European Population Conference*. August. Strasbourg, 1971.
Timur, Serim, *Türkiye'de Aile Yapısı*. Ankara: Hacettepe Üniversitesi Yayınları, D–15, 1972.
Uner, Sunday, Metodoloji. *Türkiye'de Nüfus Yapısı ve Nüfus Sorunları 1973 Araştırması*. Ankara: Hacettepe Üniversitesi Yayınları. D–25, 1–12, 1978.
Yener, Samira, (Berksan), Türkiye'de Evlilik Yapısı ve Bu Yapının Doğurganlık Üzerine Etkileri. *Türkiye Demografyası*. Bozkurt Güvenc ve Frederic Shorter Ankara: Hacettepe Üniversitesi Yayınları D–13. 151–169, 1969.
Yener, Samira, *1960–1970 Döneminde İllerarası Göcler ve Göc Edenlerin Nitelikleri*. T.C. Başbakanlık Devlet Planlama Teşkilatı, Yayın No: 1528 – SPD: 293, 1977.
Yurt, İbrahim; Ergil, Gül; Sevil, Hüseyin Tekin, *Türk Köyünde Modernleşme Eğilimleri. Orman Köylerinin Sosyo-Ekonomik Durumu*. Rapor III, Ankara: Devlet Planlama Teşkilatı.

Reference list of Ayşe Öncü's chapter

Abadan, Nermin, *Üniversite Öğrencilerinin Serbest Zaman Faaliyetleri*, A.Ü.S.B.F. Yayınları, 1931.
Carr-Saunders, A. M. and Wilson, P. A. *The Professions* Oxford; Reprinted by Frank Cass, 1964, 1933.
Çavdar, Tevfik; Tümay, Demet; Yurtseven, Tuna. *Yüksek Öğretime Başvuran Öğrenciler 1974–1975: Sosyo-Ekonomik Çözümleme* Ankara: DPT Tayin No. 1496, 1976.
Devlet İstatistik Enstitüsü, *Türkiye İstatistik Yıllığı*: 1977 Ankara.
Epstein, C. F. *Women's Place: Options and Limits in Professional Careers*, Berkeley; University of California Press, 1976.
Field Gary R. *Political Involvement and Political Orientations of Turkish Law Students*, Unpublished Ph.D. Thesis, 1964.
Jonhson, Terence J. *Professions and Power*, London: The MacMillan Press Ltd., 1972.
Jamous, H. and Peloille, B. "Professions or Self-Perpetuating Systems? Changes in the French University – Hospital System" in J. A. Jackson (ed.) *Professions and Professionalization*, Cambridge; Cambridge University Press, 1970.

Kâğıtçıbası, Çiğdem. *Cultural Values and Population Action Programs: Turkey*, Report Prepared for The United Nations Educational, Scientific and Cultural Organization, 1977.

Kazgan, Gülten. "Türk Ekonomisinde Kadınların İşgücüne Katılması, Meslekî Dağılımı, Eğitim Düzeyi ve Sosyo Ekonomik Statüsü", Tebliğ, *Türk Toplumunda Kadın Semineri*, 16–19 Mayıs 1978, İstanbul, 1978.

Lees, D. S. *Economic Consequences of the Professions*, Research Monograph 2, Institute of Economic Affairs, England, 1966.

Özbay, Ferhunde, "Türkiye'de Kırsal/Kentsel Kesimde Eğitimin Kadınlar Üzerinde Etkisi"Tebliğ, *Türk Toplumunda Kadın Semineri*, 16–19 Mayıs 1978, İstanbul.

Safilios-Rothschild, Constantina. "A Cross-Cultural examination of Women's Marital, Educational and Occupational Options" in, Mednick, M.T.S. et al., *Women and Achievement*, John Wiley & Sons, 1971.

Safilios-Rothschild, Constantina. *Toward a Sociology of Women*, Xerox College Publishing, 1972.

Silver, Catherine Bodard. "Salon, Foyer, Bureau: Women and the Professions in France", in Joan Huber (ed.) *Changing Women in a Changing Society*, Chicago: University of Chicago Press, 1973.

Theodore, A. (ed.) *The Professional Women* Cambridge: Schenkman Publishing Co., Inc. 1971.

Timur, S. *Türkiye'de Aile Yapısı* Ankara: Hacettepe Üniversitesi Yayınları, D-15, 1972.

Uysal, Şefik. *Lise Öğrencilerinin Meslek Seçimleri*, Ankara: Yeni Desen Matbaası, 1970.

White, James J. "Women in the Law", in C. Safilios-Rothschild (ed.) *Toward a Sociology of Women*, Xerox College Publishing, 1972.

Reference list of Deniz Kandiyotti's chapter

Abadan, N. "Turkey" *Women in the Modern World*, Ed. R. Patai, New York, Free Press, 1977.

Abadan-Unat, N. *Social Change and Turkish Women* Ankara Üniversitesi, Yayın No. 171–153, A.Ü.Basımevi, Ankara, 1973.

Abadan-Unat, N. "Implications of Migration on Emancipation and Pseudo-emancipation of Turkish Women", *International Migration Review*, Cilt. 11 No. 1, s. 31–57, 1977.

Bar-Tal, D. ve Frieze, I. "Achievement motivation and gender as determinants of attribution for success and failure". mimeo, Pittsburgh University, 1973.

Başaran, F. *Psiko-sosyal Gelişim*, A.Ü. Dil ve Tarih Coğrafya Fakültesi yayını, No. 154, Ankara, Kalite Matbaası., 1974.

Başaran, "Diyarbakır köylerinde vaziyet alışların değişmesiyle ilgili psiko-sosyal bir araştırma", *Araştırma VII*, 1969'dan ayrıbasım, A.Ü. Basımevi, 1971.

Benedict, P. "The Kabul Günü: Structured Visiting in an Anatolian Provincial Town", *Anthropological Quarterly*, Cilt 47, s. 28–47, 1974.

Bott, E. *Family and Social Network*, Tavistock Publication, Londra, 1957.

Chodorow, N. "Family Structure and Feminine Personality" *Woman, Culture and Society* kitabında, der. Rosaldo, M. ve Lamphere, L., Stanford University Press, s. 43–66, 1974.

Çitçi, O. "Kadın ve Çalışma", *Amme İdaresi Dergisi*, Cilt 7, No. 2, s. 45–76, 1974.

Deaux, K. ve Elmswiller, T. "Explanations of Successful Performance on Sex Linked Tasks: What is Skill for the Male is Luck for the Female", *Journal of Abnormal and Social Psychology*, Cilt 67, s. 684–54, 1974.

Fallers, L. ve Fallers, M. "Sex Roles in Edremit", *Mediterranean Family Structure* kitabında, der. Peristiany, J., Cambridge, Cambridge University Press, 1976.
Field, W. F. *The effects of thematic apperception on certain experimentally aroused needs*, Ph.D. thesis, unpubl. Maryland Univ., 1951.
Frieze, I. "Women's Expectations for and Causal Attributions of Success and Failure", *Women and Achievment* kitabında, der. Mednick, H.T.S., Tangri, S.S. ve Hoffman, L., New York, Halsted Press, 1975.
Garai, J. E. ve Scheinfeld, A. "Sex Differences in Mental and Behavioral Traits", *Genetic Psychology Monographs*, Cilt 77, s. 169–299, 1968.
Horner, M. "Toward an Understanding of Achievement – Related Conflicts", *Journal of Social Issues*, Cilt 28, No, 2, s, 157–175, 1972.
Horner, M. S. "Femininity and Successful Achievement: basic inconsistency", *Feminine Personality and Conflict* Ed. Bardwick, J. M., Douvan, E., Horner, M. S. ve Guttman, D., Wadsworth Publishing Co. Inc., Belmont, California, 1970.
İnan, A. *Atatürk ve Türk Kadın Haklarının Kazanılması, İstanbul*, Millî Eğitim Basımevi, 1964.
Kâğıtçıbaşı, Ç. (a) *Cultural Values and Population Action Programs: Turkey, Birleşmiş* Milletler, UNESCO, Istanbul, 1977.
Kâğıtçıbaşı, Ç. ve Kansu, A. (b) "Cinsiyet Rollerinin Sosyalleşmesi ve Aile Dinamiği: Kuşaklararası bir Karşılaştırma", *Boğaziçi Üniversitesi Dergisi*, Sosyal Bilimler Serisi, Cilt 5, s. 35–48, 1977.
Kandiyoti, D. (a) "Sex Roles and Social Change: A Comparative Appraisal of Turkey's Women", *Women and Development: The Complexities of Change* Ed. Wellesley Editorial Committee, Chicago University Press. Chicago, 1977.
Kandiyoti, D. (b) "Toplumsal Değişme ve Kadinin Yeri", *Boğaziçi Üniversitesi Dergisi*, Sosyal Bilimler Serisi, Cilt 5, s. 49–61, 1977.
Kıray, M. *Ereğli: Ağır Sanayiden Evvel bir Sahil Kasabası*, Ankara, Devlet Plânlama Teşkilâtı, 1964.
Kıray, M. (a) "Changing Roles of Mothers: Changing Intra – Family Relations in a Turkish Town", *Mediterranean Family Structure*, Ed. Peristiany, J., Cambridge. Cambridge University Press, 1976.
Kıray, M. (b) "The Family of Immigrant Worker", *Turkish Workers in Europe: 1960–1975* Ed. N. Abadan – Unat, N., Leiden, Brill, 1976.
Komarovsky, M. *Blue Collar Marriage*, Vintage Books, New York, 1967.
Mansur, F. "Bodrum: A Town in the Aegean", Leiden. Brill, 1972
McKee, J. P. ve Sheriffs, A. C. "Men's and Women's Beliefs, Ideals and Self-Concepts", *American Journal of Sociology*, Cilt 64, s. 356–63, 1959.
Olson–Prather, E. "Natality is Women Business", Washington D. C., 1976.
Papanek, H. "Purdah in Pakistan: Seclusion and Modern Occupations for Women", *Journal of Marriage and the Family*, Ağustos, s. 517–530, 1971.
Papanek, H. (a) "Men, Women and Work: Reflections on the Two-Person Career", *Changing Women in a Changing Society* kitabında, der. Huber, J., University of Chicago Press, Chicago, 1973.
Papanek, H. (b) "Purdah: Separate Worlds and Symbolic Shelter", *Comparative Studies in Society and History*, Cilt 15, No. 3, s. 289–325, 1973.
Rainwater, L., Coleman, R. P. ve Handel, G. *Workingman's Wife*, New York, McFadden Bartell, 1962.
Rainwater, L. *Family Design: Marital Sexuality, Family Size and Family Planning*, Aldine Publishing Co., Chicago, 1965.
Rosenkrantz, P. S., Vogel, S. R., Bee, H., Broverman, I. K. ve Broverman, D. M. "Sex Role Stereotypes and Self-Concepts in College Students", *Journal of Consulting and Clinical Psychology*, Cilt 32, s. 287–295, 1968.

Rotter, J. B. "Generalized expectancies for internal versus external control of reinforcement" *Psychological Monographs*, Cilt 80, No. 1, 1966.

Simmons, A. B. ve Turner, E. J. "The Socialization of Sex Roles and Fertility Ideals: A Study of Two Generations in Toronto", 1974.

Tangri, S. S. "Implied Demand Character of the Wife's Future and Role Innovation: Patterns of Achievement Orientation Among College Women", *Women and Achievement* Ed. Mednick, M., Tangri, S. ve Hoffman, L. s. 239–254, 1975.

Taşkıran, T. *Cumhuriyetin 50. Yılında Türk Kadın Hakları*, Başbakanlık Basımevi, Ankara, 1973.

Taynor, ve Deaux, K. "When Women are More Deserving Than Men: Equity, Attribution and Perceived Sex Differences", *Journal of Personality and Social Psychology*, Cilt 28, No. 3, s. 360–367, 1973.

Timur, S. *Türkiye'de Aile Yapisı*, Ankara, Hacettepe Üniversitesi yayınları, 1972.

Veroff, J. Wilcox, S. ve Atkinson, J. "The Achievement Motive in High School and College age Women", *Journal of Abnormal and Social Psychology*, Cilt 48, s. 103, 119, 1953.

Young, M. ve Willmott, P. *Family and Kingship in East London*, Londra, Routledge and Kegan Paul 1957.

INDEX OF AUTHORS

INDEX OF SUBJECTS

AUTHORS

Professor Dr. Nermin Abadan-Unat graduated in 1944 from the Istanbul Law Faculty, pursued graduate studies at Minnesota University in 1952/53 and obtained her Ph. D. from Ankara Law Faculty in 1955. N. Abadan-Unat joined the Faculty of Political Science, Ankara University in 1953 as teaching assistant, in 1958 she promoted to Associate professor and became full professor in 1966. Her field of specialization is political sociology, political behaviour, public opinion and mass communication. In 1966 N. Abadan-Unat established the chair of "Political Behaviour" and until 1978 remained its chairholder. In addition since 1963 N. Abadan-Unat has undertaken studies and research on international migration and women studies. N. Abadan-Unat was guest professor in 1969/70 at the Geschwister-Scholl Institute, University of Munich and in 1973/74 at the City University of New York. N. Abadan-Unat contributed to the creation of the School of Journalism and Mass Communication attached to the Faculty of Political Science and was twice its director. Her most important publications in Turkish are "Bureaucracy" (SBF, 1959), "Major problems of Turkish workers in Federal Germany" (DPT, 1964), "Elections of 1965" (SBF, 1966); in English she published "Turkish Workers in Europe" (Brill, Leiden, 1976), with Ruşen KELEŞ and others "Migration and Development" (Ankara, 1976) N. Abadan-Unat has published a number of articles in German, English and French. She was for a long period vice-president of the Turkish Political Science Association and is the president of the Turkish Social Science Association. N. Abadan-Unat was appointed in July 1978 as contingent member of the Senate by the President of the Republic. N. Abadan-Unat is married. She has one son and two daughters.

Dr. Füsun (Altıok) Akatlı graduated from the department of Philosophy of the Faculty of Letters, Ankara University. She obtained her Ph. D. at the department of Philosophy, Hacettepe University in 1974 with a thesis on "The Problem of Evaluating Literary Works". Her field of specialization is philosophy of art. Aside from numerous articles, she has published a book entitled "Why Dialectics" (Çagdaş Y., 1977). She is at present teaching assistant at the department of philosophy, Hacettepe University, Ankara. She has one daughter.

Professor Dr. Ayşe Baysal completed the secondary education at the Village Institute of Divriz and the Higher Teacher's College. She obtained her B. A. in 1961 and her M. A. in 1962 in the United States from the Technical University of Virginia. After completing her Ph. D. in 1965 at the University of Wisconsin, Dr. Baysal was promoted to associate professorship in 1970 and to full professorship in 1975. At present. Dr. Baysal is the head of the chair of Nutrition and Diet of the Faculty of Medicine, Hacettepe University. Her major books are "Food, Nutrition and Diet" (Sağlık Bak., Third Ed., 1976), "Nutrition" (Hacettepe University, Second Ed., 1977). Dr. Baysal is also the editor of the review entitled "Journal of Nutrition and Diet". She is married and has one daughter.

Dr. Leila Erder obtained her Ph. D. in the field of demography from Princeton University. Her specific interests are problems related to city administration of the Middle East and North Africa as well as historical and present problems of population structure. Her articles on the demographic structure of Ottoman cities has been published in scientific journals in the United States. She published in 1970 together with Dr. Ilhan Tekeli a book entitled "International Migration as a Process of Settlement Adjustment" (Hacettepe Univ. D—26). Dr. Erder was teaching until recently at the City Planning Department of the Middle East Technical University (M. E. T. U.). At present the Near East representative of the Population Council, she is stationed at Amman, Jordan. She has two daughters.

Dr. Çiğdem Kâgıtçıbaşı obtained her B. A. in the field of psychology from Wellesley College in 1961 and completed her Ph. D. in the same field at Berkeley University of California. Her special field of interest is socialisation, social change, population and sex roles. To date Dr. Kâgıtçıbaşı has written five books, two of which were published by the Turkish Social Science Association. They are: "Dimensions of Social Change" (1972) and "Man and Men—Introduction to Social Psychology" (1974). Dr. Kâgıtçıbaşı is the author of a great number of articles in English and Turkish. She is full Professor at the Social Science Department of the Bosporus University, Istanbul. Dr. Kâgıtçıbaşı is married and has one son and one daughter.

Dr. Deniz Kandiyoti graduated from the Faculty of Psychology at the University of Paris (Sorbonne) in 1966. She obtained her Ph. D. in Social Psychology from the London School of Economics in 1971. Her field of specialization is stratification, social psychological dimensions of social change in urban and rural areas and sex roles. She has published a number of articles in English and Turkish on social change and sex roles as well as on the structure of Turkish villages. She has also written a comprehensive English summary of the seminar on "Women in Turkish Society" organized in May 1978 by the Turkish Social Science Association. At present Dr. Kandiyoti is Associate Professor at the Department of Social Sciences of Bosporus University, Istanbul. Dr. Kandiyoti is married.

Professor Dr. Gülten Kazgan after graduating from the Faculty of Economics of Istanbul University, obtained her Ph. D. from the University of Chicago. Dr. Kazgan has been a full professor at the chair of Economic Theory since 1968. Her field of specialization is international economics. Her major publications are "Evolution of Economic Thought", "Agriculture and Development" and the "Common Market and Turkey". Her article on women has been published in the review "Toplum ve Bilim". She is married and has one son.

Professor Dr. Mübeccel B. Kıray obtained in 1946 from the Faculty of Letters, Ankara University in the field of sociology, and in 1950 from Northwestern University, United States in the field of anthropology Ph. D. degrees. Between 1960—1973 she taught and was the head of the Department of Social Sciences of M. E. T. U. Her most important publications are "Eregli, a Small Town before Industrialization" (DPT, 1964 together with Hinderink "Social Stratification as on Obstacle to Development" (Praeger, 1970). The Turkish Social Science Association published Kıray's study on "İzmir, a City Which Remained Unorganized— The Structure of İzmir's Business Life and Pattern of Settlement" in 1972. Dr. Kıray was guest professor in 1968/69 at the London School of Economics. At present she is the chairholder of Sociology at the Istanbul Academy of Economics and Business Administration. She also teaches graduate courses at the Istanbul Technical University. Dr. Kıray is married and has one daughter.

Dr. Ayşe Öncü obtained in 1971 her Ph. D. degree in the field of complex organizations from Yale University. Her major interest is the sociology of organization, professional organization. Dr. Öncü's book on "Sociology of Organization" was published in 1972 by the Turkish Social Science Association. Dr. Öncü is teaching at the Department of Social Sciences of Bosporus University. Dr. Öncü is married and has two sons.

Dr. Ferhunde Özbay graduated in 1960 from the Social Work Academy in Ankara. She completed her Master at the Population Studies Center of Hacettepe University and obtained in 1975 her Ph. D. degree from Princeton University with her thesis on "Individual and Ecological Factors Influencing Fertility in Rural Areas". Dr. Özbay's field of specialization is fertility patterns, education and women studies. Dr. Özbay has published a number of articles in English and Turkish. Dr. Özbay taught at the Population Study Center of Hacettepe University until 1979. At present she is teaching sociology at the Ankara Academy of Economics and Business Administration.

Dr. Tansı Şenyapılı graduated from the Department of Business Administration of M. E. T. U in 1961. She then obtained an M. A. in city planning from the same university. After having worked for some time at the Ministry of City Planning and Reconstruction, Dr. Şenyapılı obtained a second M. A. from the Department of Regional Planning at the University of Pennsylvania. After returning to Turkey, Dr. Şenyapılı completed her Ph. D. degree at the Faculty of Political Science, Ankara University. Her field of specialization are problems concerned with shanty houses, unintegrated urbanization. Her most important publication is her book on "Aspects of Non-Integrated Urban Population, a Multidimensional Approach". Dr. Şenyapılı is teaching at the City Planning Department of M. E. T. U. She is married and has one daughter.

Dr. Şirin Tekeli studied for a while at the University of Paris, than graduated in the field of political science from the University of Lausanne. Dr. Tekeli completed her graduate studies at the Istanbul Faculty of Economics and Iowa University, United States. She obtained her Ph. D. in 1973. Dr. Tekeli's field of specialisation is political theory, political sociology and comparative politics. Her major publications are "On David Easton's Political Theory" (Istanbul, 1976) and "Political Participation of Women" (to be published). Dr. Tekeli is teaching at the chair of Political Science of the Faculty of Economics, Istanbul University. Dr. Tekeli spent the academic year 79/80 in Paris at the National Scientific Center for Research (C. N. R. S.) Dr. Tekeli is married.

Dr. Sabahat Tezcan graduated from the Medical School of Hacettepe University in 1969. She completed her graduate studies in the field of epidemiology at the Faculty of Health, University of North Carolina. Dr. Tezcan was promoted to associate professor in 1976 in the field of Community Medicine. Presently she is teaching at the Faculty of Medicine, Hacettepe University, Ankara. Her most important publication is "A Comparative Study of Induced Abortion in Turkey". Dr. Tezcan is married.

Dr. Serim Timur graduated from the Faculty of Political Science in 1963. She obtained her M. A. in the United States from Cornell University with a thesis about fertility and class differentiation. Dr. Timur received her Ph. D. from Hacettepe University in 1972 in the field of

Sociology. Her area of specialisation is sociology of the family, population studies, demography, fertility pattern and migration. Her most important publication is "The Structure of the Family in Turkey" (Hacettepe University, D—15, 1972) Dr. Timur has been working since 1974 at the Division of Population at UNESCO at Paris. Dr. Timur is married and has two daughters.

Dr. Binnaz Toprak (former Sayarı) completed her B. A. in 1970 at Hunter College attached to the City University of New York and obtained from the same university her Ph. D. with her thesis on "Religion and Politics". Her field of specialisation is political culture and comparative politics as well as sociology of religion. Dr. Binnaz Toprak is teaching at present at the Department of Social Sciences of Bosporus University, Istanbul. Dr. Binnaz Toprak is married and has one daughter.